THE ART OF
ECTOPLASM

THE ART OF ECTOPLASM

Encounters with Winnipeg's Ghost Photographs

EDITED BY
Serena Keshavjee

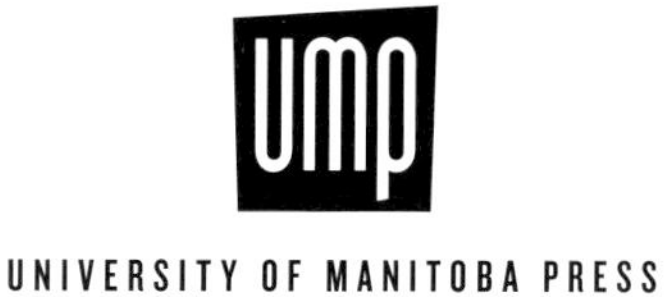

UNIVERSITY OF MANITOBA PRESS

The Art of Ectoplasm: Encounters with Winnipeg's Ghost Photographs

27 26 25 24 23 1 2 3 4 5

University of Manitoba Press
Winnipeg, Manitoba, Canada
Treaty 1 Territory
uofmpress.ca

Cataloguing data available from Library and Archives Canada
ISBN 978-1-77284-037-7 (PAPER)
ISBN 978-1-77284-039-1 (PDF)
ISBN 978-1-77284-040-7 (EPUB)
ISBN 978-1-77284-038-4 (BOUND)

Front cover photograph: T.G. Hamilton, *Hand-Shaped Teleplasm*, 1930, University of Manitoba Archives and Special Collections. Back cover art: Erika DeFreitas, *A Teleplasmic Study with Doilies, Angie no. 3a*, 2010–11. Courtesy of the artist.
Cover and interior design by Jess Koroscil

Printed in Canada

This book has been published with the help of a grant from the Federation for the Humanities and Social Sciences, through the Awards to Scholarly Publications Program, using funds provided by the Social Sciences and Humanities Research Council of Canada.

The University of Manitoba Press acknowledges the financial support for its publication program provided by the Government of Canada through the Canada Book Fund, the Canada Council for the Arts, the Manitoba Department of Sport, Culture, and Heritage, the Manitoba Arts Council, and the Manitoba Book Publishing Tax Credit.

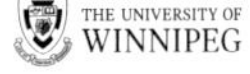

Funded by the Government of Canada | Canada SRIC

This book was researched in fits and starts between lockdowns during the COVID-19 pandemic. During those restricted periods I was sustained by family and friends who I "bubbled" with at different stages: the Keshavjees, the Botars, and my pandemic walking companions, when that was the only activity allowed, including Hazel Borys, Charlene Brown, James Hanley, Kate Ready, and Liv Valmestad.

CONTENTS

NOTE ON THE PHOTOGRAPHS

Except where otherwise identified, the photographs published here are courtesy of the University of Manitoba Archives and Special Collections (UMASC). The Hamilton Family Fonds (HFF) is catalogued as MSS 14; most of that collection's photographs are described in PC 12. Where available, the permalink number in the caption links to the photograph at https://digitalcollections.lib.umanitoba.ca. Unless otherwise stated, the Hamilton psychical research photographs are attributed to Dr. T.G. Hamilton, who is known to have set up the cameras, released the flash system, and printed the majority of them.

No 27. Hand Imitation of Jan. 5, 1930.
(Preliminary to "Lucy" form of March 10, 1930)

27

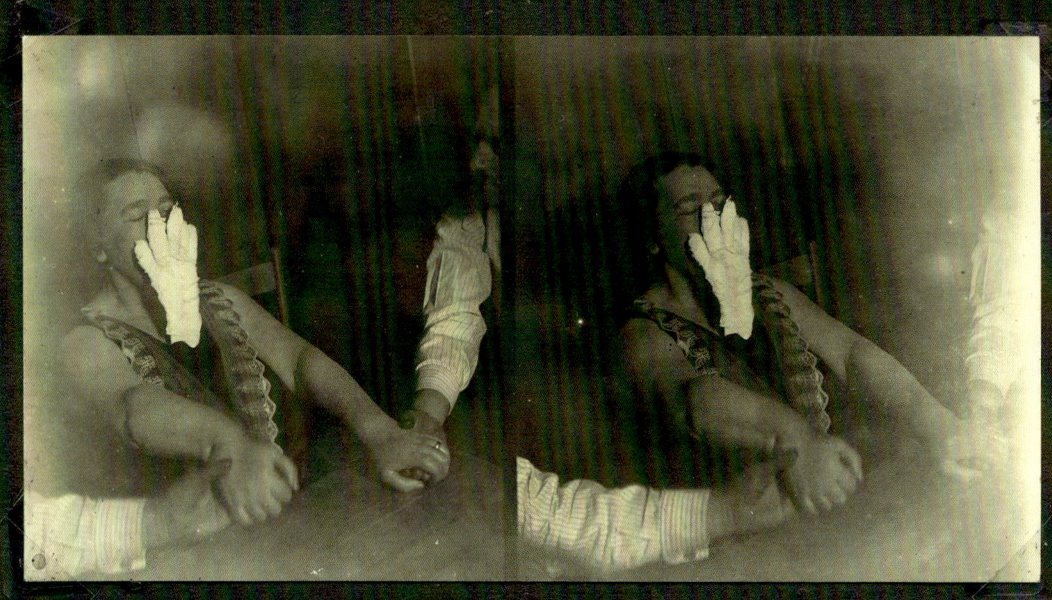

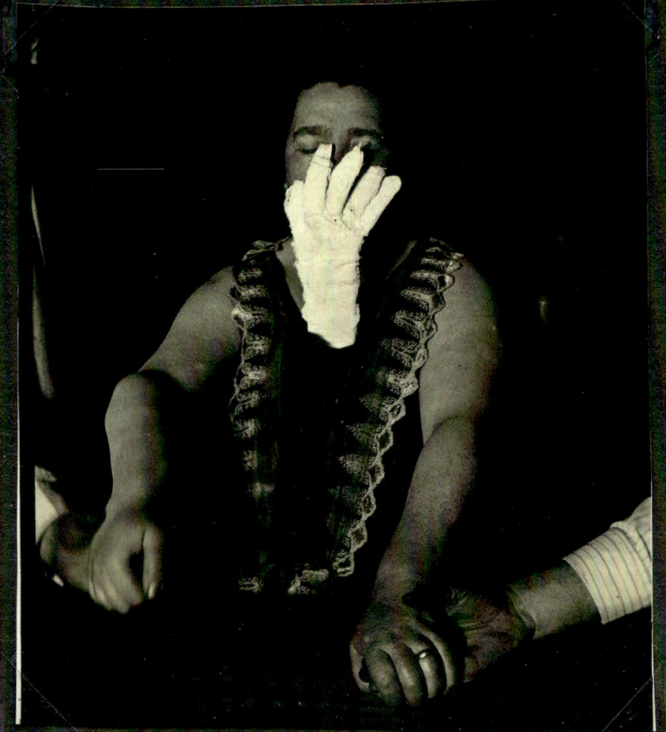

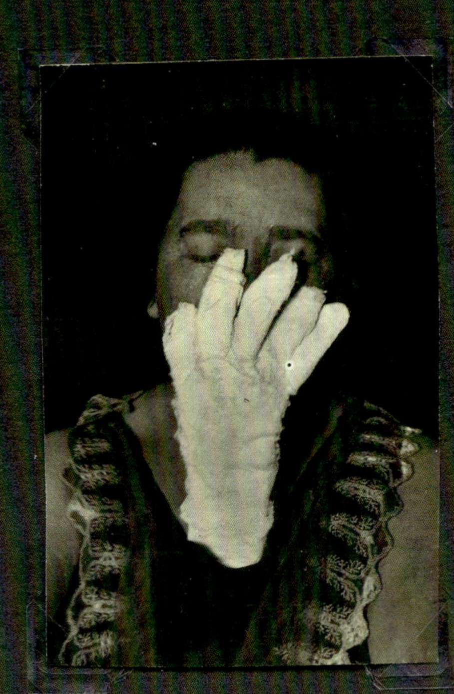

Introduction

Science and Sentiment in the Hamilton Family Fonds

Serena Keshavjee

In a public lecture held at the Fort Garry Hotel in Winnipeg in 1930, Dr. Thomas Glendenning (T.G.) Hamilton described his ectoplasmic photographs as "monstrously extraordinary," and the rough plaster-like hand hovering in front of the medium's face, reproduced on the cover of this book, is surprising in its materiality. Traditionally, images of ghosts are rendered as light or vaporous emanations, spectral in style, to indicate the characteristics of materialization and dematerialization. However, Dr. Hamilton's high contrast black-and-white photographs of shaped ectoplasmic extrusions (see Figure 0.1), and the woolly, gauze-like emanations embedded within small photographs and drawings (see Figure 2.11), focus sharply on the organic-looking ectoplasm and the medium. *The Art of Ectoplasm: Encounters with Winnipeg's Ghost Photographs* contextualizes these extraordinary photographs within the dominant science and technology of the period, as well as drawing parallels with Modernist photography and art in order to understand

Fig. 0.1. ***Annotated Photo Album, Hand Imitation***, 5 January 1930, University of Manitoba Archives and Special Collections (UMASC), PC 12, Box 8, Folder 4, Item 27, http://hdl.handle.net/10719/1411081.

how and why they received international attention during the twentieth century and continue to astonish viewers in the contemporary period. The term ectoplasm was first applied to ghostly materializations 130 years ago, and *The Art of Ectoplasm* looks at how both artists and scientists have utilized artistic formal elements to depict this mysterious substance. The Hamilton photographs were taken during a period of experimentation beginning in 1923 and continuing into the 1940s, when the family came to believe that human personalities could survive death and that, under certain circumstances, discarnate spirits could communicate with the living. Like many other families at the end of the First World War, the Hamiltons were introduced to thought transference and spirit communication through popular parlour games, in their case table tilting, which had been incorporated into family entertainment during the nineteenth century throughout Europe and North America. Beginning in 1923, medical doctor Thomas Glendenning Hamilton and his wife, Lillian Hamilton, a trained nurse, organized controlled and documented séances akin to scientific experiments a few times a week in their Winnipeg home, with the first series ending in 1935 when T.G. died and then continuing under Lillian's direction until 1944.

The family understood their séances to be scientific experiments and invited professional colleagues from their elite settler group to witness the séances in order to counter any suspicion of fraudulent behaviour.[1] Since both Lillian and T.G. Hamilton were medically trained, they applied experimental protocols to their séances, seeking hard evidence of communication with "unseen personalities" (see Figure 0.2). These experiments resulted in a large archive of over 700 black-and-white photographs, and thousands of pages of text, donated to the University of Manitoba Archives and Special Collections (UMASC) beginning in 1979 by the Hamiltons' daughter, Margaret Hamilton Bach, to form the Hamilton Family Fonds (HFF). This collection is part of a significant psychical research archive at UMASC, which includes actor Dan Aykroyd's family's foray into Spiritualism and many of

Fig. 0.2. ***Annotated Photo Album, Telekinesis – "Levitations by Psychic Force,"*** date unknown. UMASC, PC 12, Box 8, Folder 1, Item 1, http://hdl.handle.net/10719/1412050.

LEVITATIONS

BY PSYCHIC FORCE

(TELEKINESIS)

The photographs of the levitated table herein displayed were secured over a period of six years (1921-1927 inclusive), during investigation of the physical phenomena exhibited by the medium Elizabeth M.

These manifestations all occurred in the experimenter's own home, in a room set apart for the purpose of metapsychic research, and to that end especially prepared and equipped. All equipment, electrical and photographic, was prepared and installed by him or under his personal supervision. The medium was under his personal scrutiny from start to finish of each and every experiment. Special verifiers were often present. And lastly all the photographs were taken, developed and printed by him. He is therefore in a position to state that he knows the phenomena herein recorded to be the product of genuine telekinetic force.

Many hundreds of these levitations have been witnessed; some thirty have been photographed.

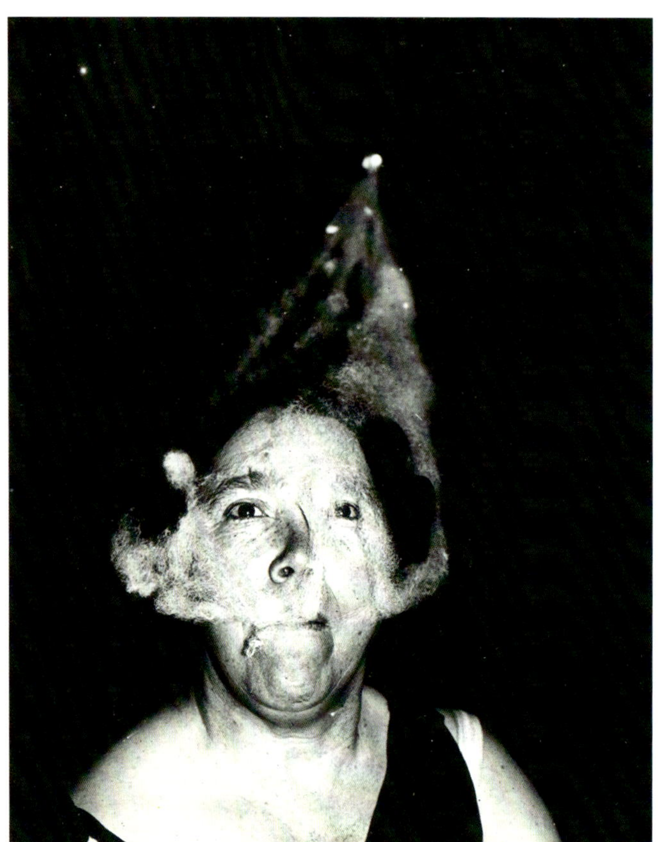

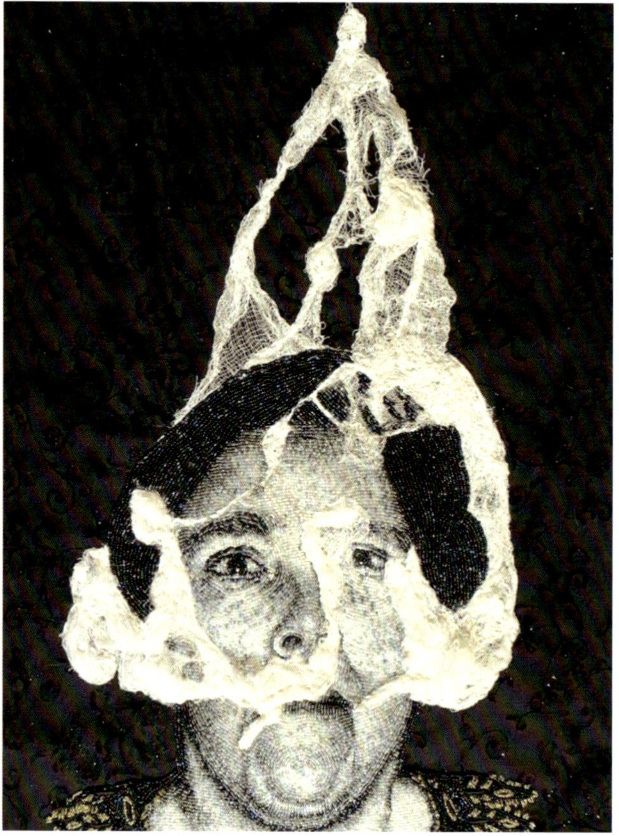

Fig. 0.3. *Left*, ***"Umbrella" Teleplasm***, excreted by medium Mary Marshall, 25 February 1934. UMASC, PC 12, Box 10, Folder 8, Item 55a, http://hdl.handle.net/10719/1409501.

Fig. 0.4. *Right*, Teresa Burrows, ***Our Lady of Ectoplasm***, Trichstar series, 2021–2022. Czech glass beads and cheesecloth stitched on fabric, 35.56 x 55.88 cm. Courtesy of the artist.

the important twentieth-century books on psychical research. Despite being the most consulted of all the private personal fonds at UMASC, many Canadians do not know about this rare collection of twentieth century "scientific" photographs.

I discovered this archive as I was finishing my PhD thesis at the University of Toronto. I was struggling to find spirit and paranormal photographs to illustrate how French Symbolist artists had participated in séances in an effort to access their creative, unconscious minds.[2] At that time, spirit photographs were not catalogued at the Bibliothèque nationale in Paris, and if something is not catalogued it might as well not exist. Despite all the textual evidence that I had gathered, high-quality original spirit photographs eluded me; they had vanished in the archive just like a ghost dematerializes in the séance chamber. At a public talk on my research at the University of Manitoba's School of Art in 1997, someone casually mentioned that there were "ghost" photographs at UMASC taken by a local family physician. That day I discovered the key texts on the phenomena of ectoplasmic materializations and a series of lantern slides that contextualized the history of the scientific study of ghosts, a topic that academics were only beginning to explore systematically.[3] Most spectacular, however, was the treasure trove of stunning pseudo-scientific photographs of ectoplasm, the white substance through which disembodied spirits apparently could manifest. The images of a woman expelling ectoplasm from her mouth, nose, and even eyes are simultaneously uncanny and compelling, silly and serious, and there I found one of the most important photographic archives in Canada (see Figure 0.3).

The Hamilton photographs were made widely accessible in 2001 when they were digitized under the direction of Dr. Shelley Sweeney. Because of her early adoption of Web technology, the photographs have been included in a number of important occulture exhibitions: *The Perfect Medium: Photography and the Occult* at the Metropolitan Museum of Modern Art in 2005, *Spiritus* in Stockholm in 2003, *My Winnipeg* at La Maison rouge in Paris in 2011, *Imponderable* at the Museum of Modern Art in 2017, *3D Double Vision* at the Los Angeles County Museum in 2018, and *Conjured Images: Spirit Photography from the Turn of the 20th Century* at the Art Gallery of Alberta in 2022. They have been reproduced in exhibition catalogues, for example in *The Spectacle of Illusion: Magic, the Paranormal and the Complicity of the Mind* (2019) and *Surnaturelles: Une histoire visuelle des femmes médiums* (2021) and most recently on the poster advertising Philippe Baudouin's and Andrea Barbe-Hulmann's exhibition, *Phénomènes: L'inexpliqué face à la science* at the Museé d'Histoire de la Médecine in Paris.[4] The photographs have been used in films, including Guy Maddin's *My Winnipeg* (2007) and *The Haunting in Connecticut* (2009), and a video art performance, *F-L-A-M-M-A-R-I-O-N*, by Susan MacWilliam, shown at the Venice Biennale in 2009.[5] The Hamiltons have formed the subject of chapters by medical and gender historians Esyllt W. Jones, Beth A. Robertson, and Claudie Massicotte.[6] They have figured in several PhD dissertations, including those by Katie Oates, Grace A. Williams, and Brian Hubner.[7] Finally, the Hamilton photographs are the source material for artwork produced by artists around the world. The earliest scientific photographs produced by Dr. Hamilton (see Figures 2.4 and 2.5) were made around 1925, and even 100 years later the photographs continue to have considerable cultural impact. This volume and the related exhibition, *The Undead Archive*, in Winnipeg from September to November 2023, will analyze the vintage photographs and the related contemporary art from an art historical point of view (see Figures 0.3 and 0.4). *The Art of Ectoplasm: Encounters with Winnipeg's Ghost Photographs* is the first edited collection about the Hamiltons' psychical research and introduces little-known aspects of Winnipeg's history by looking at the rise of popular religions, pseudo-science, and technology on the Prairies.

During the course of studying the Hamilton Family Fonds, I was repeatedly asked why I spend so much time on such a marginal topic. It is true that the documents in the fonds do not fit into any typical historical accounts of Winnipeg. The skilfully made photographs do not figure in a survey history of Canadian photography, and the "science" employed is not part of the current scientific canon. Yet I have found Dr. Hamilton's photographs in every parapsychology archive that I have visited, including Senate House Library in London, England, the University of Cambridge in the United Kingdom, the American Society for Psychical Research in New York City, the Sir Arthur Conan Doyle Collection in the Harry Ransom Centre at University of Texas at Austin, and even artist Tony Oursler's private collection. In the early twentieth century, the notion of survival after death was accepted by some professionals as a topic that could be researched using standardized scientific methodologies. The Hamiltons considered their photographs scientific illustrations constituting evidence that personalities could survive death. Today no one accepts their research as scientific in the strict sense of the term; indeed, most people regard the archive as an oddity. Sometimes, however, it is the liminal zones of scientific respectability and the realm of forgotten histories that constitute the most interesting topics for study. An exciting discovery for me is that these photographs, produced using pseudo-scientific methods based on a marginal religio-philosophy, have become a rich resource for artists, as illustrated in Chapters 6, 7, and 9. In making the decision in 1979 to accept these papers and photographs based on contested science, and to apply professional archival standards to the fonds, UMASC became one of the key centres in which to conduct scholarship on occult material, and these papers and photographs are the foundation of this book.

The Art of Ectoplasm is divided into three sections: historical context, archival exploration, and the artistic response to the visual culture of ectoplasmic pictures.

As medical professionals, the Hamiltons not only treated influenza pandemic patients but also suffered through the flu themselves, losing a child in January 1919. In the first section, in Chapter 1, historian Dr. Esyllt W. Jones notes that familial experiences of the 1918 to 1920 pandemic have been neglected by scholars, and she uses the minutes from the less formal family séance circle to fill that gap. Jones delves into the Hamiltons' little-known private séances, held regularly between 1929 and 1935, mediated by a male medium. No photographs were taken in that family circle, but séance minutes were kept. The "spirit" communications transcribed were often playful, teasing comments between the father and the deceased son, Arthur, who succumbed to influenza when he was three years old but who continued to grow up in the spirit world. These intimate conversations and the photographs of the Hamilton children at Victoria Beach in Manitoba give us an intimate account of family life and a sense of grieving practices after the devastating loses of the influenza pandemic.[8]

Similar to Jones's approach, in Chapter 3 Dr. Katie Oates looks at Lillian Hamilton's homemade family photo albums to learn more about personal reactions to the paranormal experiments. Lillian had done considerable scientific reading on the psychic force, applying this knowledge to direct her own séances into the 1940s, and Oates repositions her as a researcher in her own right.[9] Lillian Hamilton balanced her scientific and Spiritualist attitudes and resisted the scepticism characteristic of most psychical researchers. She did not shy away from expressing her conviction that discarnate personalities survived death and Lillian continued to get comfort from communicating with her son and husband after they passed away. Women did carry out psychical research in the twentieth century, but their roles have been ignored or played down. Dr. Oates's chapter is the first study of Lillian Hamilton's research.

The Hamiltons understood that their séances were experiments and considered their photographs scientific evidence that personalities could survive death. This attitude fits into a greater twentieth-century effort to re-enchant science by aligning it within orthodox religious philosophies. T.G. Hamilton was accepted in the international psychical scientific community as early as 1924 because of the quality of his skilful black-and-white photographs. In Chapter 2, I work to recuperate his place within the network of scientists researching and publishing on ectoplasm. These doctors and scientists described themselves as psychical researchers, studying the psychic force, and they differentiated their work from that of Spiritualists, who they saw as motivated by sentimentality. Although his experimental methods were compromised, as even he admitted, Hamilton was steadfast that controlled experimentation could be used to test for discarnate trancendental personalities communicating through a medium, and he released photographs out into the world as evidence.

As a field of study within mainstream science, psychic research thrived for about seventy years, from 1870 to 1940, attracting highly respected doctors and scientists who corroborated their research using ether theory and biological vitalism, suppositions still accepted as good science at the beginning of the twentieth century.[10] Like most academics researching the history of psychical science and occulture, I do not address whether the Hamiltons' psychic phenomena were real or fraudulent. Literary historian Christine Ferguson has characterized the scholarly analysis of psychical research as "subjecting scientific investigations of spiritualist phenomena to rigorous academic inquiry, paying careful attention to their scientific, religious, cultural and biological dimensions [and] . . . refusing to patronize . . . or simply debunk their subjects."[11] Academics tend to be more interested in uncovering lost histories to better understand cultural trends than in judging alternative science and marginal religious movements.

Today psychical research is rejected by the scientific orthodoxy and routinely described as "pseudo-science" or, more generously, "alternative" science. The dismissal of psychical science and ectoplasm as a mediating substance was swift after the Second World War, reminding us that scientific boundaries are fluid. In 1954, Rudolf Lambert, a member of the Society for Psychical Research (SPR), published an account of suspected fraud from the 1920s, in a scathing report suggesting that the most important psychical researchers of the early twentieth century—the scientists central to Hamilton's studies—had perpetuated "grotesque fraud" and that many of that generation could be described as suffering from "mythomania," a type of group hallucination "that may lead to a perversion of rational thought and judgement, so that those attacked by it sink back into magical ideas."[12] This type of experimental bias has been noted before in the case of French neurologist Dr. Jean-Martin Charcot's studies of the trance state and "hysteria," and Claudie Massicotte has made the comparison between the "hysterical" body and the medium's body in her PhD thesis, "Talking Nonsense: Spiritual Mediums and Female Subjectivity in Victorian and Edwardian Canada."[13] I cite this example of an SPR member rejecting the most important psychic researchers of the early twentieth century to demonstrate how scientific standards can vary over time. The reception of the Hamilton photographs is a good illustration of the shifts in orthodox science and mainstream Christian religion during the twentieth century.

The central section of this book, Chapters 4 and 5, bring in the perspectives of archivists Shelley Sweeney and Walter Meyer zu Erpen, who have worked with and promoted this collection for twenty-five years. UMASC acquired the Hamilton

Family Fonds (HFF) in 1979. It was under Dr. Sweeney's direction during the early 2000s that the archive was promoted internationally by using the then relatively new World Wide Web to post digitized photographs, and by releasing a YouTube video of the photographs set to music in the early years of that platform (2008), followed by a Herculean effort in 2013 to submit a UNESCO application for heritage status. Although unsuccessful, the complex application made it all the way to the international advisory committee, which finally deemed it too controversial to accept, nonetheless demonstrating the respect and care with which the HFF has been treated. Working closely with Sweeney, Walter Meyer zu Erpen has been active in bringing new material to the psychical research collections and in working on the biographies of the men and women within the Hamilton scientific group since 1991. T.G. Hamilton gave lectures in Toronto, New York, and London, and an impressive group of professionals sat in on his séances, including Sir Arthur Conan Doyle, Winnipeg medical scientist Dr. Bruce Chown (who with colleagues produced an Rh immune vaccine), lawyer Isaac Pitblado (one-time chair of the Board of Governors of the University of Manitoba, vice-president of the Canadian Bar Association, and prominent leader of the Citizens' Committee of One Thousand), not to mention that Prime Minister William Lyon Mackenzie King visited and corresponded with the Hamiltons about their research. Meyer zu Erpen's chapter introduces us to the elite settler class who participated with the Hamiltons in their endeavours.

Historian Efram Sera-Shriar has noted that academics tend to privilege scientific (even pseudo-scientific) views over Spiritualist or survivalist points of view.[14] With this criticism in mind, Meyer zu Erpen brings another perspective to the book, that of an archivist-researcher who accepts the survival hypothesis. After years of careful study, he concludes that the Hamiltons' experiments do support the belief in survival of discarnate personalities. He co-founded the Survival Research Institute of Canada in 1991 and continues to test the hypothesis. Meyer zu Erpen's chapter "Defending the T.G. Hamilton Family Psychical Research Legacy" is dedicated to defending the Hamiltons from mislabelling, ridicule, and sometimes artistic licence.[15]

The final section of this book looks at the cultural and artistic impacts of the Hamiltons' remarkable photographs of "unseen personalities." A century ago, after spending a few days in Winnipeg, author and famous Spiritualist Arthur Conan Doyle stated that the city should be a "psychic centre" (see Figure 6.2), setting the tone for Winnipeggers to see their city as a site of strange and creative energies, an attitude reflected in Guy Maddin's popular film *My Winnipeg* (2007) and the exhibition in Paris at La Maison rouge in 2011. Having worked with all the playwrights, filmmakers, TV producers, artists, and authors who utilized the HFF to illustrate "supernatural" or "weird" Winnipeg, archivist Dr. Brian Hubner reviews the effects of this cultural phenomenon in Chapter 6. Dr. Hamilton's photographs of ectoplasm have been used in a number of films to create an ambience of authenticity. For the doctor, these photographs constituted scientific evidence of life after death, but, as film historian Dr. Murray Leeder points out in Chapter 7, ectoplasm is used most often as a comedic tool by Hollywood (see Figure 0.5). The word *ectoplasm*, adopted in the 1890s in France to explain the substance of materialization, is well known in popular culture because of the blockbuster movie of 1984, *Ghostbusters*, outlined in Leeder's chapter. The movie was written by Dan Aykroyd, whose great-grandfather Samuel visited the community of Lily Dale during the 1920s and knew about Hamilton's research by 1928.[16]

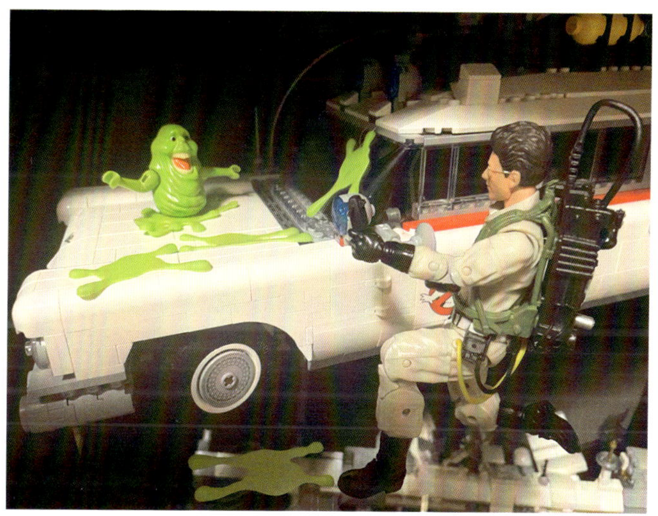

Fig. 0.5. The ***Ghostbusters'*** vehicle Ecto-1 is here covered with green ectoplasm. Courtesy of Alex Miller.

Emigrating from Scotland, the Hamilton family eventually joined a temperance colony and settled in Saskatchewan in the 1880s. T.G.'s father participated in the Canadian government's campaign against the Métis forces at the Battle of Batoche in 1885. As was common in settler séances across North America in the nineteenth and twentieth centuries, there were occasions when an Indigenous "spirit control" communicated through the medium Mary Marshall during the Hamiltons' séances, exemplifying how settlers appropriated aspects of Indigenous culture even as they tried to eradicate it. To acknowledge the Hamiltons' misuse of Indigeneity, Anishinaabe, Ininew, and British artist KC Adams introduces her research reclaiming suppressed Indigenous practices regarding death and communication with ancestors. Informed by Métis archaeologist Kevin Brownlee and the Manitoba Museum's excavation of a young Nêhiyaw woman, buried 360 years ago with her tools and wearing a simple belted dress with pointed moccasins, Adams animates the academic research with a poem and a virtual reality artwork describing the end-of-life rituals and how spirits travel through the medium of smoke to Thunderbird and into the cosmos (see Figure 8.1).[17] Her work also reminds us that many cultures accept spirits in one way or another.

The "oldest" drawing of a "ghost" has been identified on an ancient Babylonian clay tablet indicating a long artistic tradition to depict invisible spirits. The engraved Babylonian ghost is hard to see and appears only under direct light, when the figure "leaps out," representing the greatest challenge for artists and scientists trying to illustrate the characteristics of ghostly materialization and dematerialization, to capture a barely visible entity.[18] The last chapter in *The Art of Ectoplasm* outlines the formal and iconographic elements of ghostly figures created by artists and scientists from the mid-nineteenth century to the contemporary period, celebrating 150 years of representing ghosts.

The photographs by the Hamiltons, made between 1923 and 1944, are all black-and-white and exemplify a minimal aesthetic related to the artistic Modernism current at the time. In the frozen frame of the photograph, the cropped mediums are in sharp focus, and the biomorphically shaped ectoplasm signifies the vital force of

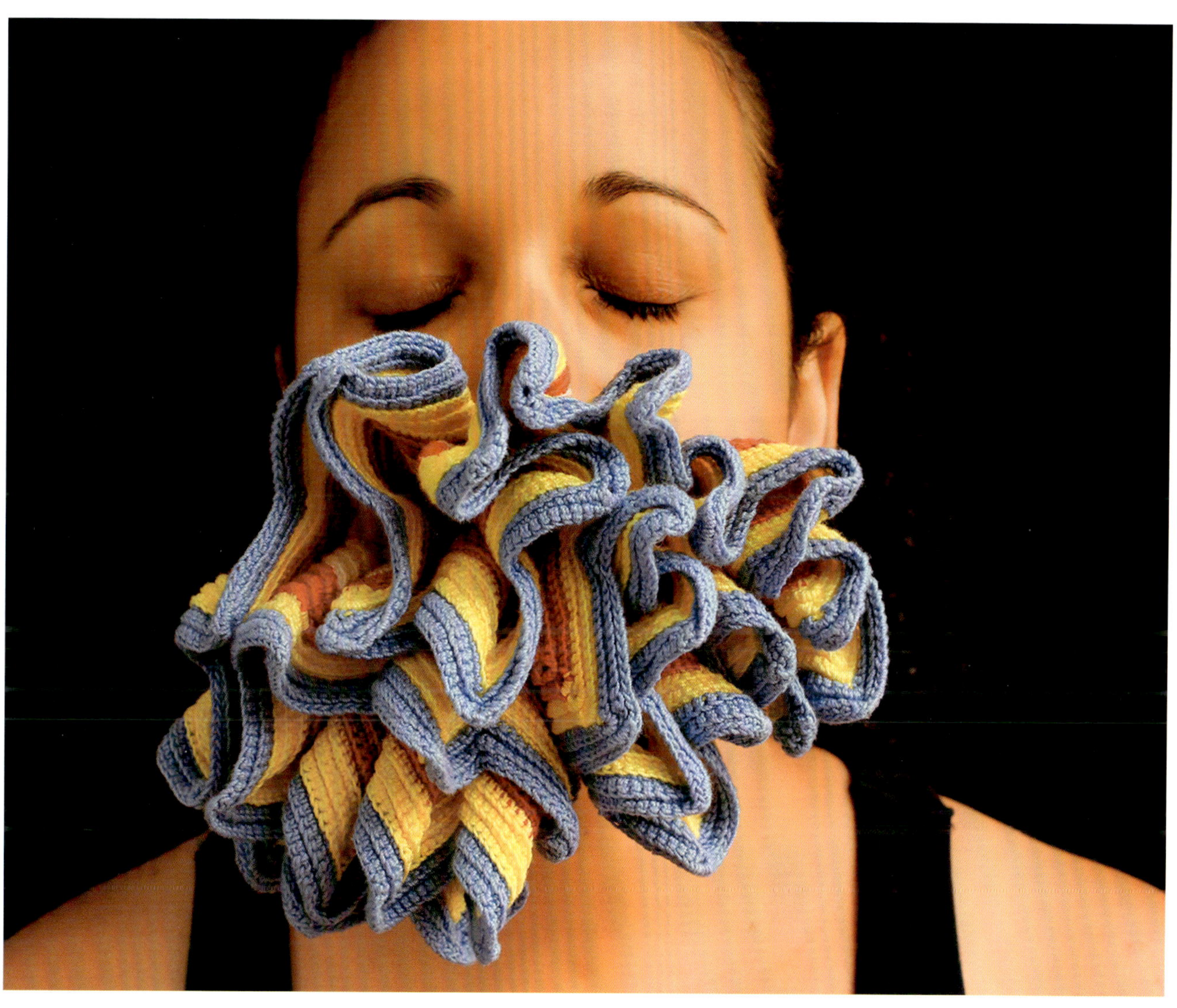

Fig. 0.6. Erika DeFreitas, ***A Teleplasmic Study with Doilies (Angie no. 3)***, 2010–2023. Archival inkjet print, 60.9 x 91.4 cm. Courtesy of the artist.

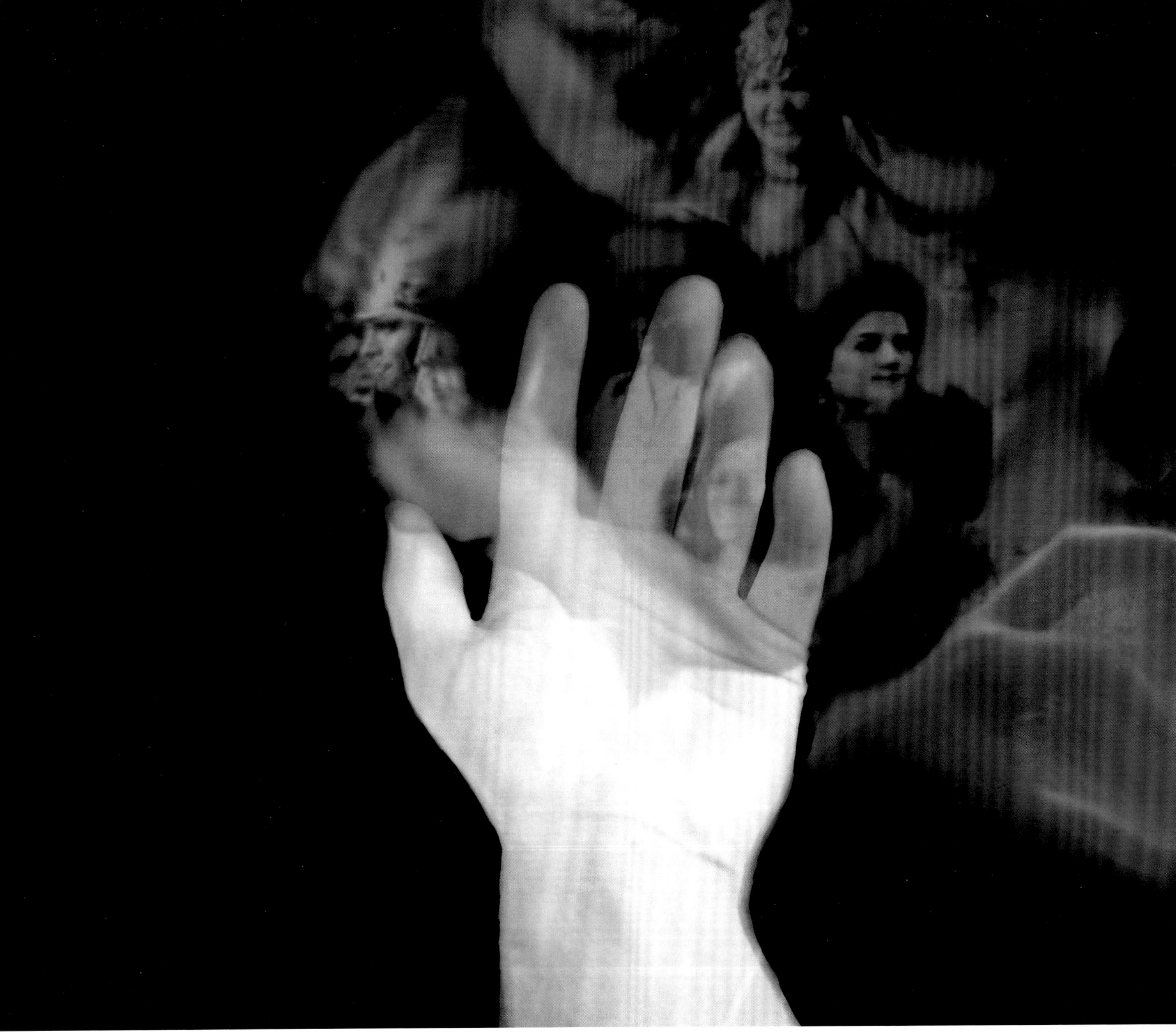

Fig. 0.7. Grace A. Williams, ***Fingertip Forgeries 2***, 2013. Fine art giclée on Hahnemühle photo rag paper, 41.9 x 29.5 cm. Courtesy of the artist.

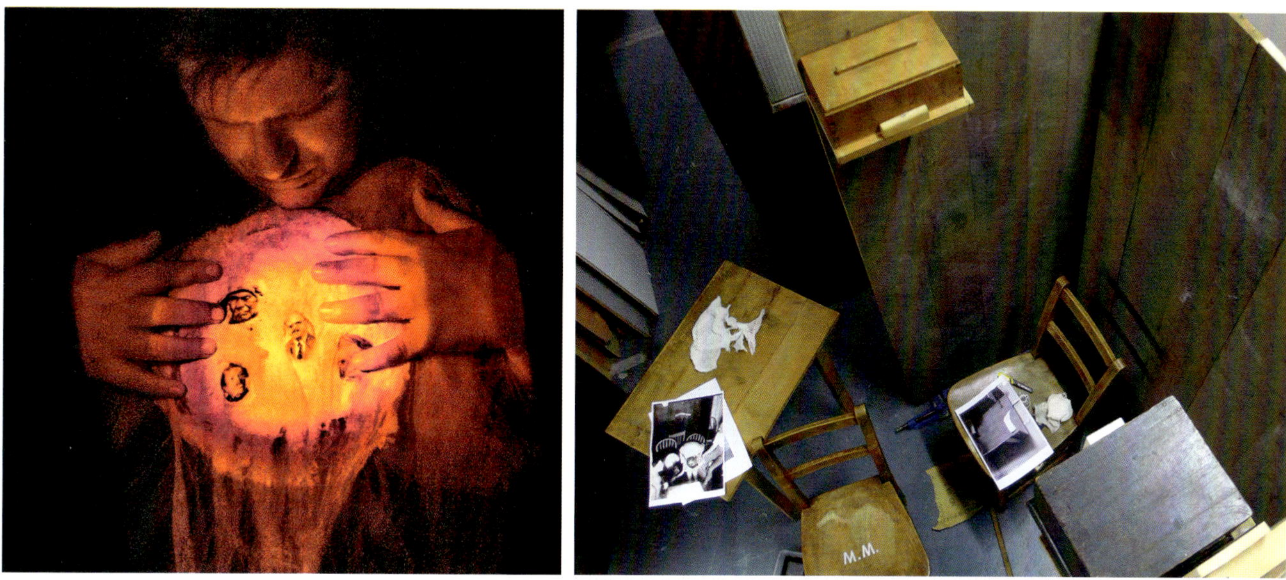

Fig. 0.8. *Left*, Shannon Taggart, ***Medium Kai Muegge displays ectoplasm filled with images of the dead***, detail, 2018. Digital print. Courtesy of the artist.

Fig.0.9. *Right*, Susan MacWilliam, ***View of the Reconstruction of T.G. Hamilton Séance Cabinet***, 2008. © Susan MacWilliam. Courtesy of the artist.

the plasm. Although ectoplasm is no longer in vogue with mediums, artists continue to work with the photographic material as laid out in Chapter 9.

Dr. Esyllt W. Jones explains that there was a historical amnesia about the "Spanish Flu" until March 2020 with the outbreak of COVID-19. Manitoba artist Teresa Burrows found Hamilton's scientific visualizations online while in lockdown, and began altering the images, making a visual link between the two pandemics (see Figures 0.4 and 9.28). Some artists identify with the dramatic performances of the mediums, posing themselves in the role of Mary Marshall, as Erika DeFreitas does, commenting on how women's bodies are regulated (see Figure 0.6). Other makers focus on ectoplasm's original definition from the 1890s as a moulding material, like pottery and clay, as Grace Williams's *Fingertip Forgeries* demonstrates so well (see Figure 0.7). Contemporary digital photographers are fascinated by the parallels between the nineteenth-century

Fig. 0.10. Chris Dorosz, ***Séance Room,*** concept sketch for forthcoming installation, 2022–23. Courtesy of the artist.

analogue photographic processes used to capture an invisible entity on film and the psychical researchers' efforts to make visible an invisible force. Shannon Taggart has worked with a contemporary medium who has revived the physical manifestation of ectoplasm and she has captured remarkable digital colour photographs and a rare stop motion film of ectoplasmic extrusions (see Figures 0.8 and 9.22).

Chris Dorosz and Susan MacWilliam have chosen to recreate parts of the séance laboratory for their research creation. For her 2009 installation, MacWilliam rebuilt Hamilton's séance cabinet, which was said to harness the psychic energy in the room. Dorosz uses occult colour theory to make visible those same "energies" in his concept sketch (see Figures 0.9 and 0.10).

Using the rich variety of visual material from the HFF, including Dr. Hamilton's photographs, his collection of rare books, and scientific visualizations by other scientists, as well as artistic responses to the Hamilton photographs, this volume illustrates, for the first time, the visual history of ectoplasm over its 150-year history.

The Art of Ectoplasm begins with the losses that Winnipeggers suffered as a result of the Great War, the pandemic and the social disruption of the General Strike. In 1923 Arthur Conan Doyle, during a stay at the Fort Garry Hotel, made two claims about the city that seem prescient. First, he described Winnipeg as a "real garden city," "a wood with occasional high buildings projecting from among the trees," perhaps sensing the economic slowdown after 1919 that halted the development of most large-scale buildings between 1926 and 1948.[19] Second, Conan Doyle dropped the "Chicago of the North" epithet and instead suggested that the city was a "psychic centre." A century later, considering the lasting effect of the Hamilton archives, and the rich artistic profile it has helped create, this seems like a fitting description.

Thanks

I thank Oliver Botar, Emma Dux, Walter Meyer zu Erpen, Shelley Sweeney, and Christina Thomson for discussing this introduction with me.

NOTES

1 The Hamiltons had two séance groups. The scientific group was the large group, which followed experimental protocols, including handwritten and typed séance minutes, registers of attendance, affidavits, and the photographing and publishing of their research internationally. The small group was mostly family members and met from 1929 to 1935; no photographs were taken in that group, but minutes were kept.

2 See Serena Keshavjee, "*L'Art inconscient*: Imaging the Unconscious in Symbolist Art for the Théâtre d'art," *RACAR: Revue d'art canadienne/Canadian Art Review* 34, no. 1 (2009): 62–76, https://doi.org/10.7202/1069501ar.

3 Some of the books and articles on psychical research that I have relied on include Sophie Lachapelle, *Investigating the Supernatural: From Spiritism and Occultism to Psychical Research and Metapsychics in France, 1853–1931* (Baltimore: Johns Hopkins University Press, 2011); Brady Brower, *Unruly Spirits: The Science of Psychic Phenomena in Modern France* (Champaign: University of Illinois Press, 2010); Richard Noakes, *Physics and Psychics: The Occult and the Sciences in Modern Britain* (Cambridge, UK: Cambridge University Press, 2019); Jeremy Stolow, "Mediumnic Lights, X[x] Rays, and the Spirit Who Photographed Herself," *Critical Inquiry* 42, no. 4 (2016): 923–51, https://doi.org/10.1086/686962; and Robert Brain, "Materialising the Medium: Ectoplasm and the Quest for Supra-Normal Biology in *Fin-de-Siècle* Science and Art," in *Vibratory Modernism*, ed. Anthony Enns and Shelley Trower (London: Palgrave Macmillan, 2013), 112–41. Also see the series by Emma Merkling for the Media of Mediumship at https://www.scienceandmediamuseum.org.uk/objects-and-stories/science-investigating-paranormal.

4 Chéroux Clément and Andreas Fischer, eds., *The Perfect Medium: Photography and the Occult* (New Haven, CT: Yale University Press, 2005); *Spiritus*, https://www.magasin3.com/en/exhibition/spiritus-2/; Paula Aisemberg et al. *My Winnipeg*, Winnipeg: Plug In Editions and La Maison rouge, 2011; Anne Wehr, ed., *Imponderable* (New York: Museum of Modern Art, 2017); Britt Salvesen, ed. *3D Double Vision* (Los Angeles: Los Angeles County Museum, 2018); Philippe Baudouin, *Surnaturelles: Une histoire visuelle des femmes mediums* (Paris: Éditions Pyramyd, 2021); Matthew L. Tompkins, *The Spectacle of Illusion: Magic, the Paranormal and the Complicity of the Mind* (London: Wellcome Collection, 2019); Philippe Baudouin and Andrea Barbe-Hulmann, *Phénomènes: L'Inexpliqué face à la science*. Exhibition Museé d' L'Histoire de la Médecine, Paris, 2023.

5 Susan MacWilliam, *F-L-A-M-M-A-R-I-O-N*, a seventeen-minute video, was part of her installation *Remote Viewing*, 53rd Venice Biennale, 2009.

6 Beth A. Robertson, *Science of the Seance: Transnational Networks and Gendered Bodies in the Study of Psychic Phenomena, 1918–40* (Vancouver: UBC Press, 2016); Esyllt W. Jones, "Spectral Influenza: T.G. and Lillian Hamilton, Interwar Spiritualism, and Pandemic Disease," in *Epidemic Encounters: New Interpretations of Pandemic Influenza in Canada, 1918–1920*, ed. Esyllt W. Jones and Magda Fahrni (Vancouver: UBC Press, 2012), 193–221.

7 Katie Oates, "Women, Spirit Photography and Psychical Research: Negotiating Gender Conventions and Loss" (PhD diss., University of Western Ontario, 2022); Grace Alexandra Williams, "The Supernatural Sex: Women, Magick, and Mediumship: Assembling a Field of Fascination in Contemporary Art" (PhD diss., Birmingham City University, 2017); Brian Edward Hubner, "'The Ghostly Shadow' in the Archives: An Archival Case Study of the Creation and Recreation of the Hamilton Family Fonds at the University of Manitoba Archives and Special Collections" (PhD diss., University of Amsterdam, 2020); Claudie Massicotte, "Talking Nonsense: Spiritual Mediums and Female

Subjectivity in Victorian and Edwardian Canada" (PhD diss., Western University, 2013), Electronic Thesis and Dissertation Repository, 1656, https://ir.lib.uwo.ca/etd/1656; Claudie Massicotte, *Trance Speakers: Femininity and Authorship in Spiritual Séances, 1850–1930* (Montreal and Kingston: McGill-Queen's University Press, 2017.

8 The small circle met weekly from 1929 to 1935. No photographs were taken in that family circle, but séance minutes were kept, and thus it was different in purpose from that of the "scientific" séances, as Jones demonstrates. The smaller and mostly family group was led by Lillian Hamilton, with T.G. and the children attending regularly over the six years. That circle worked with a male medium, John David (Jack) MacDonald, known as Jay in the séances. Jones analyzes the intimate family conversations and notes that the deceased son Arthur did come through often in the circle. I also noted that Dr. Hamilton's favourite scientist, Dr. Gustave Geley, made two appearances to defend the accusations of fraud against Schrenck-Notzing's photographs. See notes for 9 March 1933 and 24 March 1933, Jack MacDonald, UMASC, HFF, MSS 14, Box 14, Folder 17. Dr. Schrenck-Notzing and Juliette Bisson make a brief appearance on 25 August 1933 in the séance, yet Bisson was alive in 1933, only passing away in 1956. By 1924 she has been excluded from psychic research meetings, and she and Eva Carrière were no longer sought after, and perhaps Hamilton thought she was dead. Hamilton bought Schrenck-Notzing's book in 1922 and Charles Richet's book in 1925.

9 Lillian Hamilton put together photo albums to promote her husband's—and her own—experiments in materialization. All this is an accomplishment considering that women were mostly cast into the role of passive mediums or dutiful secretaries in the period. As scholars have noted, women were active in the Society for Psychical Research, especially in organizing meetings, taking notes, acting as chaperons to the mediums, and carrying out research, yet they are rarely given credit. Some of the other women who published in psychical research include the trained psychologist Helen Verrall Salter; Florence Marryat, *There Is No Death* (New York: National Book Company, 1891); and Felicia Rudolphina Scatcherd, *Ectoplasm as Associated with Survival* (London: Two Worlds Publishing, 1926). See Alex Owen, *The Darkened Room: Women, Power, and Spiritualism in Late Nineteenth Century England* (London: Virago, 1989), and Ruth Brandon, *The Spiritualists: The Passion for the Occult in the Nineteenth and Twentieth Centuries* (New York: Alfred A. Knopf, 1983), for feminist interpretations of mediumship.

10 Richard Noakes, *Physics and Psychics: The Occult and the Sciences in Modern Britain* (Cambridge, UK: Cambridge University Press, 2019); Carlos S. Alvarado, "Human Radiations: Concepts of Force in Mesmerism, Spiritualism and Psychical Research," *Journal of the Society for Psychical Research* 70.3, no. 884 (2006): 138–62. For a philosophical understanding of the way that academics discuss fraud versus science, see Stolow, "Mediumnic Lights."

11 See Christine Ferguson, "The New Prometheans: Faith, Science, and the Supernatural Mind in the *Victorian Fin de Siècle,* by Courtenay Raia," *Victorian Studies* 63, no. 4 (2021): 580–82, quotation on 580–81, https://www.muse.jhu.edu/article/842988; Courtenay Raia, *The New Prometheans: Faith, Science, and the Supernatural Mind in the Victorian Fin de Siècle* (Chicago: University of Chicago Press, 2019).

12 Rudolf Lambert, "Dr. Geley's Reports on the Medium 'Eva C,'" *Journal of the Society for Psychical Research* 37, 682 (1954): 380–86. I used the translated manuscript of the report in Senate House Library, Harry Price Collection, quotations on 6, 25, and 11–12. Lambert's long and detailed report on Geley, Bisson, and Eva Carrière, translated into three languages, is housed in all the major psychical archives, reflecting the mainstream scientific turn away from the study of ectoplasm. For a different opinion, see Michel Granger, *La Saga de l'ectoplasme, Tome 1: Enquête critique et objective sur le phénomène des matérialsations médiumniques d'hier et d'aujourd' hui* (Blengy: Le Mouvement Spirite Francophone, 1921). Meyer zu Erpen tells me that the quantitative testing of ESP grew in the 1940s, somewhat displacing the study of materializations. See Lachapelle, *Investigating the Supernatural*, 144–45, for an analysis of the report. Lambert would have been more convinced of mythomania had he known that all the "continental

researchers of standing" came to Hamilton as spirits in his séances. By the 1930s, Hamilton's scientific heroes, Geley and Schrenck-Notzing, had passed away, and the physical testing side of psychical research fell off after 1940. The quotation "continental researchers of standing" is from Hamilton, "Mary M. Teleplasms," UMASC, HFF, MSS 14, British Medical Association, Winnipeg, Box 1, Folder 12, 2.

13 Some of the most important sources on psychical studies include Henri F. Ellenberger, *The Discovery of the Unconscious: The History and Evolution of Dynamic Psychiatry* (New York: Basic Books, 1970); Massicotte, "Talking Nonsense"; Massicotte, *Trance Speakers*; Janet L. Beizer, *Ventriloquized Bodies: Narratives of Hysteria in Nineteenth-Century France* (Ithaca, NY: Cornell University Press, 1994); Beth Rae Gordon, *Darwin's Dancers: On the Construction of Hysteria and the Influence on the Arts* (Farnham, UK: Ashgate Publishing, 2009); and Robertson, *Science of the Seance*, who makes the point that the acceptance of psychical research for seventy years by some of the most respected scientists calls attention to the fact that science is constructed and constantly redefines its boundaries. Robertson presents Hamilton as performing the role of a scientist through his "scientific inscriptions," the numerous notes, photographs, and witnesses' statements that he used to legitimize his endeavours, 9.

14 Efram Sera-Shriar, "Photographic Plates and Spirit Fakes: Remembering Harry Price's Investigation of William Hope's Spirit Photography at Its Centenary," *Science Museum Group Journal* 17 (2022), https://doi.org/10.15180/221707. Sera-Shriar and Ferguson are the principal investigators of the Media of Mediumship; see https://www.sciencemuseumgroup.org.uk/project/media-of-mediumship/.

15 Meyer zu Erpen has found no evidence of fraud in the photographs in the HFF; see his introduction to Chapter 4. Analogue photographers William Eakin and Sarah Hodges-Kolisnyk examined the photographic plates, and both indicated that they were not tampered with. As part of SSHRC research creation study, Hodges-Kolisnyk recreated a number of photographs for this project (see Figure 9.33).

16 Peter H. Aykroyd, *A History of Ghosts: The True Story of Séances, Mediums, Ghosts and Ghostbusters* (Emmaus, PA: Rodale Books, 2009). An article written by Samuel Augustus Aykroyd demonstrates that he learned about and praised the Hamiltons' research. See Student of Psychic Phenomena, "Psychic Science" [T.G. Hamilton in Winnipeg], *Kingston Whig-Standard*, 20 November, 1928, 4. I thank Anton Wagner for sharing this information. Some of the Aykroyd family papers are housed at UMASC. See Dan Aykroyd's introduction to his family's history in Shannon Taggart, *Séance* (Somerset, UK: Fulgur Press, 2019), 9.

17 Kevin Brownlee and E. Leigh Syms, *Kayasochi Kikawenow: Our Mother from Long Ago* (Winnipeg: Manitoba Museum of Man and Nature, 1999).

18 Irving Finkel, *First Ghosts: Most Ancient of Legacies* (London: Hodder and Stoughton, 2021). Also see Susan Owens, *The Ghost: A Cultural History* (London: Tate Publishing, 2017).

19 Arthur Conan Doyle, *Our Second American Adventure* (London: Hodder and Stoughton, 1924) https://www.arthur-conan-doyle.com/index.php/Our_Second_American_Adventure, n.p. Chapter 12 (accessed 1 January 2022): "The whole town is more like a real garden city than any I have seen. As you look over it from the high windows of the Fort Garry Hotel, it is difficult to realize that it is really a considerable city, and not a wood with occasional high buildings projecting from among the trees."

Facing page, King Notes, Hamilton Family Fonds, MSS 14, Box 1, Folder 1 and 2.

Overleaf, More Lectures, Hamilton Family Fonds, MSS 14, Box 1, Folder 10.

PART ONE: HISTORICAL CONTEXT

More Lectures

Jan 7, 1929. King Memorial Forum: Historical background, materialisation — Eva C., M.M., E.N. slides.

Ap. 1929

A meeting of the University Women's club was held Monday evening in the Fort Garry hotel. Dr. T. Glen Hamilton gave an illustrated lecture on Experiments and Experiences in Psychic Research. The size of the audience gave evidence of a growing interest in this subject that seems such a mystery. Puzzling occurrences had been looked upon as magic or absurdities. It was Sir William Crookes who began a scientific study of these phenomena. Very mysterious seemed the experiments performed not only of table moving, but of complete levitation. Several slides showed the psychological symptoms of the trance. In these the most amazing was the evidence of the building up of ectoplasm. No one can foretell what research in this field will yet accomplish for humanity.

IN THE BUSY WOMEN'S WORLD

Ap. 1929

UNIVERSITY WOMEN'S CLUB

The University Women's club was last night addressed at the Fort Garry hotel by Dr. T. Glen Hamilton, on the "Experiments and Experiences of Psychic Research." The three phases dealt with by Dr. Hamilton were the cryptesthesia, telekinesia and ectoplasm. Eminent authorities were quoted by the lecturer, such as Sir William Brookes, and Richet. Many thorough experiments have been carried out in this subject, and to convince that there was no fraud attached to some remarkable demonstrations produced through one medium, Dr. Hamilton arranged for four Presbyterian ministers and two doctors to be present at one of the meetings. Levitation was another of the phenomena that was discussed, photographs taken by flashlight showed tables springing across the room, rising to the ceiling, and rotating in space. The terms telekinesia and cryptesia were explained as meaning in the former case manifestations of power from a distance, or not of physical contact, and cryptesia were demonstrations of a nature not yet understood. The lecture was well attended, and Dr. Hamilton invested his subj[illegible] with more of a human interest [illegible]an an adherence to technical terms and phrases, the selection of photographs which he had taken were extraordinary and fascinating.

Jan 14, 1929. Womens' [illegible] (Fort Garry Hotel). 500 pres[ent] [illegible] splendidly presented. Read intr[illegible]

Feb 11. Scientific Liming [illegible]

Feb 12. Rev. Kalenoff's Ukrainian Young People's Club.

1

Ghostly Pandemics: Speaking to the Dead in the Hamilton Family

Esyllt W. Jones

In January 1919, as the deadly fall 1918 wave of pandemic influenza was receding in Winnipeg, the Hamilton family all became infected with the virus. One of their twin three-year-old sons died. Arthur Lamont Hamilton, born in 1915, was mourned by his parents and three siblings—his surviving twin James, sister Margaret (age nine), and brother Glen (age seven). Thomas Glendenning (T.G.) Hamilton, a physician, was forty-five at the time, and his wife, Lillian, trained as a nurse, was thirty-nine. In family narratives, Arthur's death during the pandemic was linked to the development of the Hamiltons' interest in psychical phenomena and survival of bodily death. Describing her response to the work of Frederick Myers, a co-founder of the British Society for Psychical Research, Lillian wrote that "a new world had opened up—a world of belief that helped me part with Arthur without tears and with an inner joy that one of my beloveds was safely over and ready for other-world evolutionary endeavors."[1] While taking care not to overprivilege the loss of Arthur (it cannot solely explain the intensity or duration of the Hamilton circle's interest in psychical phenomena), I seek in this chapter to historicize the Hamilton family's psychical practices by placing them in the context of the flu

Scholars have situated the interwar rise in Spiritualism and psychical research in different ways. Some, such as literary historian Elizabeth Outka, have put the pandemic at the centre of their descriptions of interwar Modernism and popular cultural practices.[2] Others, such as Beth A. Robertson, have not foregrounded the impact of the pandemic on "the science of the séance."[3] As a historian of disease, I am more inclined to adopt the former approach than the latter. Speaking with the dead is perhaps an unsurprising response to the period's massive loss of life not only to world war but also to an infectious disease outbreak that killed 50 million people. Historical amnesia surrounding the impact of the influenza pandemic, however, has been widespread.[4] Jay Winter recently remarked that the family history of the flu pandemic "has hardly been written."[5] Nancy Bristow has observed that in the United States initial recognition of suffering and loss during the fall 1918 wave of the pandemic quickly gave way in 1919 to narratives stressing "progress and success."[6] If memory of the influenza pandemic has been suppressed and obscured, as scholars have suggested, then careful attention to its role in the Hamilton family's history is warranted. Acknowledging the long-term impact of the pandemic adds something to the Hamilton story, and that story enriches historical knowledge of how families mapped meanings and forged recollections of the pandemic, in a society that largely forgot its lingering significance.

The visual evidence provided in the Hamilton photographs, supplemented by a rich archival record, helps us to understand the family circle's interest in life after death as part of a broad and significant cultural and scientific moment. My focus here, however, is on the private experience of the Hamilton family, the importance of the history through which they lived, and the affective landscape of their loss (see Figures 1.1, 1.2, 1.3, and 1.4). I consider the family séances during which they shared their daily lives (trips to the beach) and moments of celebration (weddings) with a deceased son and brother. These can be interpreted not only as researches but also as practices dedicated to remembering and preserving their love for Arthur and mitigating their grief as influenza survivors.

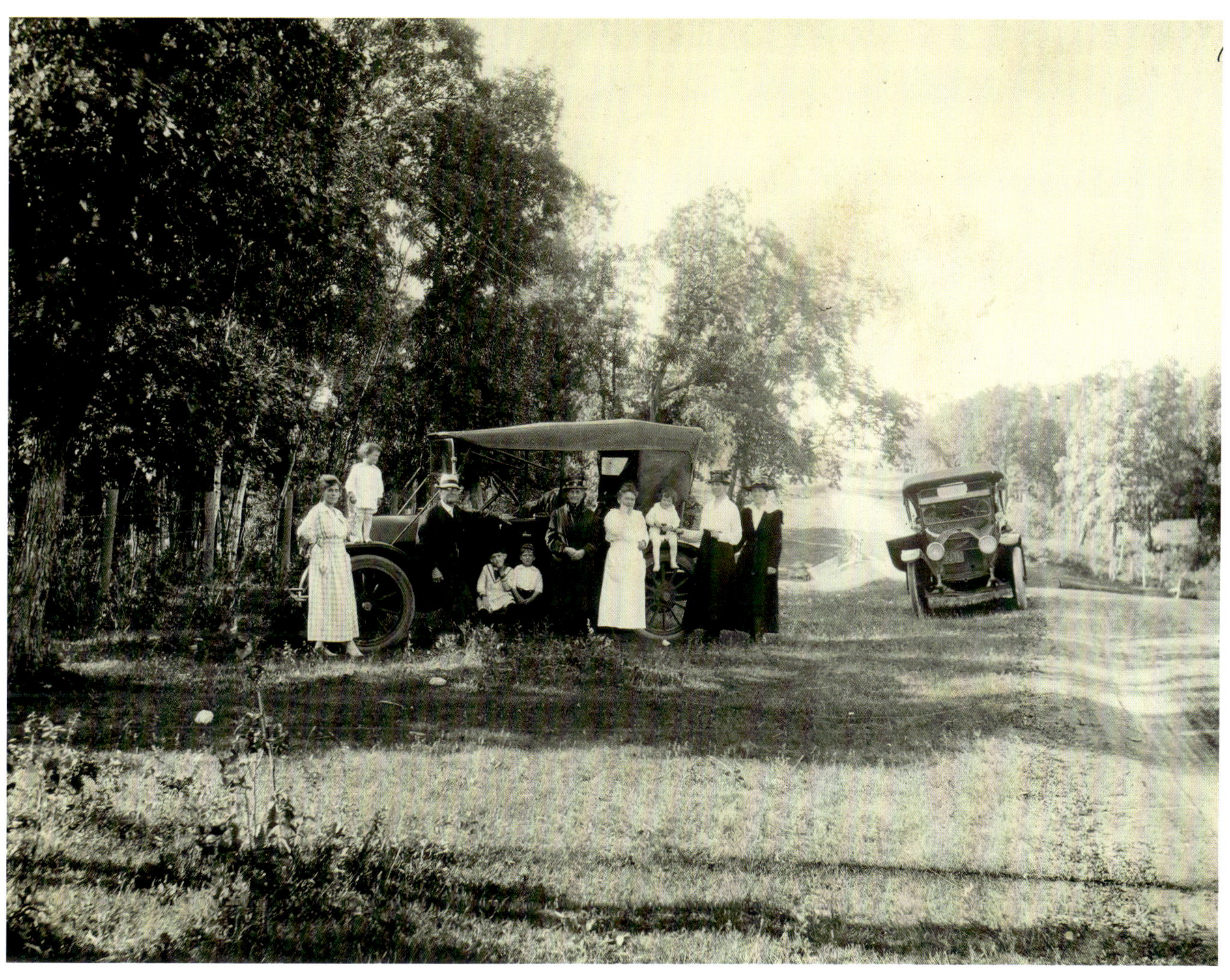

Fig. 1.1. Photographer unknown. Hamilton family photograph, pre-1919. UMASC, Janice Hamilton Fonds, MSS 323, Box 1, Folder 1, Item 1.

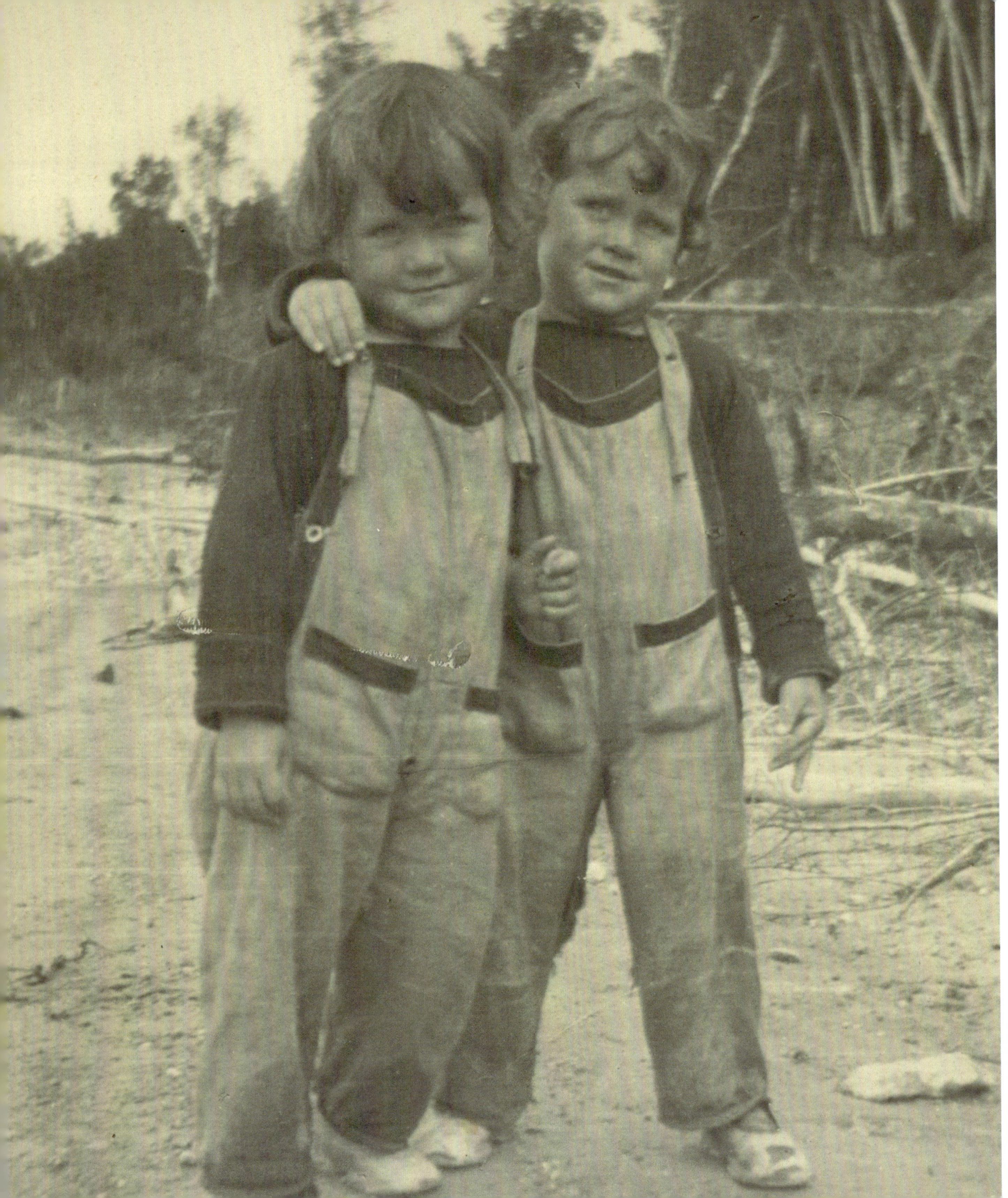

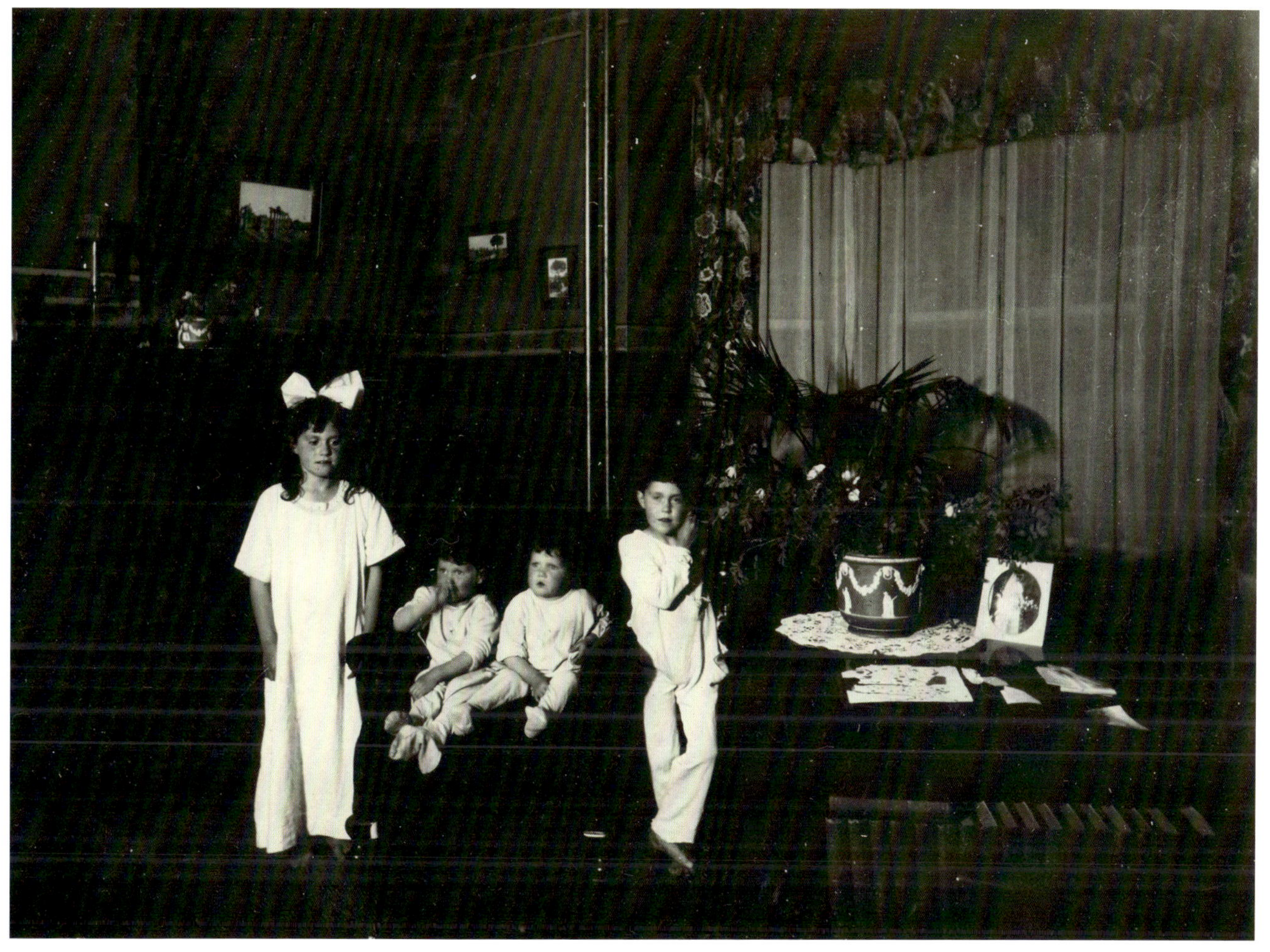

Fig. 1.2. *Left,* Photographer unknown. James (left) and Arthur (right) Hamilton, c. summer 1918. UMASC, Janice Hamilton Fonds, MSS 323, Box 1, Folder 1, Item 1.

Fig. 1.3. *Above,* Photographer unknown. Margaret, James, Arthur, and Glen Hamilton, c. 1917. UMASC, Janice Hamilton Fonds, MSS 323, Box 1, Folder 1, Item 1.

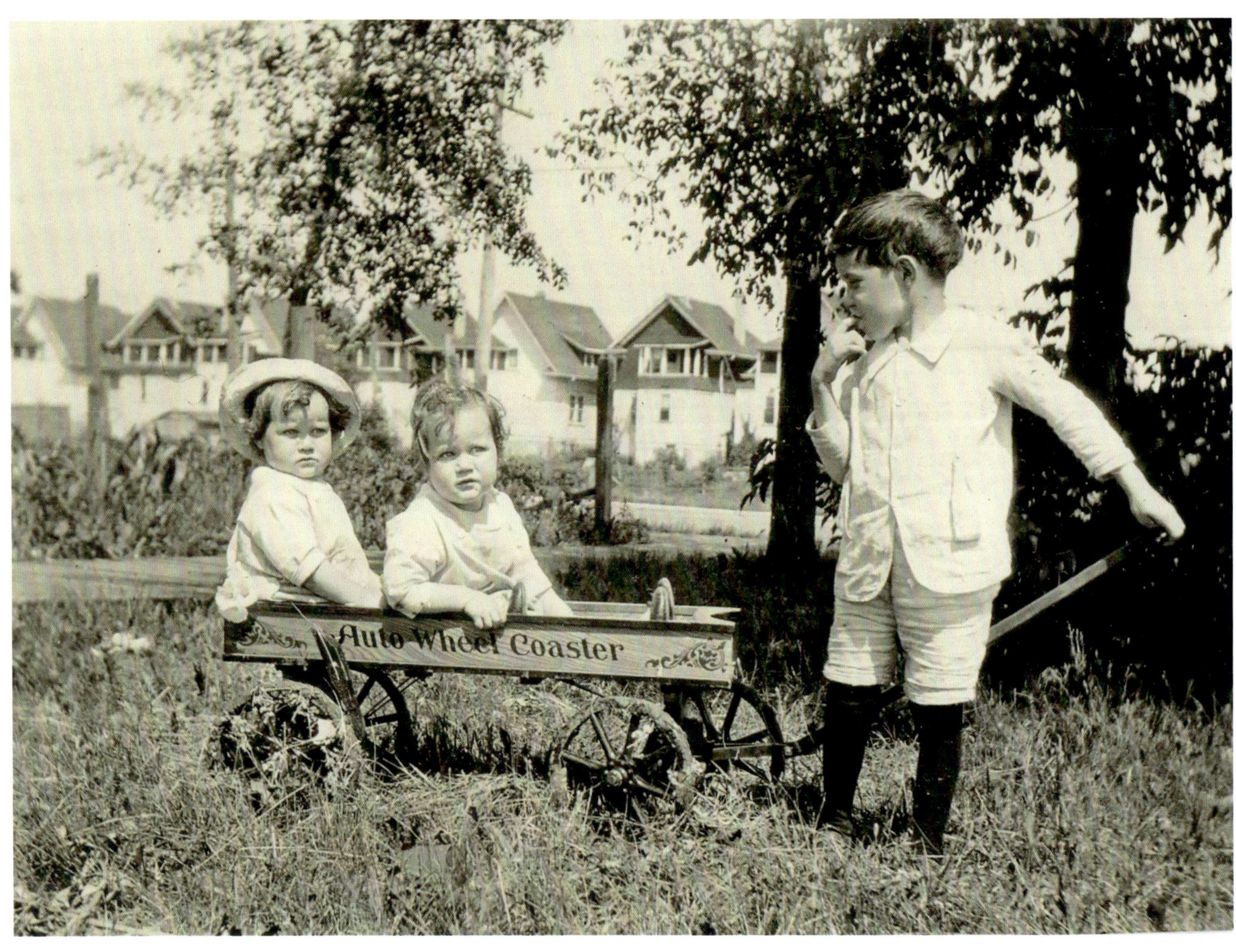

Fig. 1.4. Photographer unknown. Glen Hamilton with the twins, c. 1917. UMASC, Janice Hamilton Fonds, MSS 323, Box 1, Folder 1, Item 1.

The fall 1918 wave of the influenza pandemic arrived in Winnipeg in the closing days of September. In a city of approximately 180,000, over 1,200 lost their lives to the disease between September 1918 and March 1919. Infection rates were likely much higher, and public health data significantly underestimated case counts. In the earliest days of the outbreak in Winnipeg, most cases occurred in the wealthier south end and the centre of the city, which gave health officials some hope for optimism. By early November, however, working-class and immigrant districts, including Elmwood, where the Hamiltons lived, were the centre of the outbreak—and of public health anxieties. According to public health reports, Elmwood residents suffered crude death rates of 6.4 per 1,000 people, as high as those across the Red River in the impoverished North End (6.3 deaths per 1,000 people). In the wealthier area south of the Assiniboine River, the death rate was 4.0 per 1,000 people.[7]

The war years were difficult for many in Winnipeg, then Canada's third-largest city and its most ethnically diverse. Soldiers' wives and widows were struggling to survive on mothers' pensions. Many veterans returned from the war with physical and mental health disabilities and faced unemployment. Wages were stagnant, and the cost of living was rising; basic consumer goods such as fuel were increasingly scarce and expensive. Social tensions over military conscription and opposition to the war reached their peak in 1918. "Enemy aliens" (that is, those who had emigrated from combatant European states) were interned and monitored, and they experienced widespread discrimination. Precursors to the 1919 General Strike erupted among city workers, for example. If disease outbreaks expose the fault lines of our society, then in the fall of 1918 Winnipeg had deep inequities about to be laid bare.

As a community physician, T.G. Hamilton would have witnessed the health impacts of poverty and poor housing. Although he and Lillian came from middle-class backgrounds, they had settled in the Elmwood neighbourhood, where T.G. served the needs of his neighbours, many of whom were working class. His physician's office was located on the main floor of their home on what is now Henderson Highway. In 1918 to 1919, when physicians were in short supply because of military service, he probably cared for many influenza sufferers in his home district and across the Red River, at the Winnipeg General Hospital, where he had admitting privileges. Elmwood was a medically underserviced neighbourhood with limited health-care infrastructure. It had no hospital. Some of the area's influenza victims would have been isolated and received treatment at the nearby LaSalle Hotel, converted into an emergency hospital by public health authorities.

Various sources, including Lillian Hamilton's records and publications, the transcripts of family séances, photographs, memoirs, and interviews with the surviving siblings, help us to understand the role of the pandemic influenza in the family's history and narratives. According to a family history by Janice Hamilton, the daughter of James Hamilton, Arthur's surviving twin, James had a vivid and frightening recollection of the flu: "Dad once told me that his first childhood memory was of seeing [his sister] Margaret with blood streaming down her face from a nosebleed, a result of the influenza that hit the household in February, 1919. Jim lost his right eardrum when he had the flu and was deaf in that ear for the rest of his life. He also lost his twin brother. . . . Jim felt a strong connection to Arthur all his life and asked to be buried next to him."[8] Glen's recollection of Arthur's death tells us a bit about what the children witnessed. Arthur died in the family home, and Glen described being shown his corpse, which he described as being like a "little wax doll." Glen (who became a family physician) recalled that his brother had been treated with eucalyptus oil in a basin with boiling water to ease his breathing and that there had been an oxygen tank near his crib. The use of oxygen for treating illnesses such as pneumonia was first proposed in the 1880s, and oxygen therapy was further developed during the First World War to improve outcomes of soldiers who had inhaled poisonous gases.[9] John Scott Haldane had published his research in 1917, but oxygen was not standard treatment during the flu pandemic.[10] T.G. Hamilton had both knowledge of and access to the most current tools that medicine had to offer to treat influenza, and he used all of his capabilities to try to save his son's life.

Margaret recalled the sorrow of her father and her attempts as a child to comfort him: "Dad's grief was profound. I remember being in wonderment as I watched my father cry. . . . I can remember crawling into his bed and putting my arms around him and patting him and saying 'Well, dad, you've got the rest of us, don't cry so hard. We love you too.'"[11] Glen remembered that it was the only time that he "saw his parents embrace publicly."[12]

Margaret and Glen were interviewed in the 1980s when they were in their seventies. They recollected events that had occurred over sixty years earlier, when they were young children. As Irish historian Ida Milne has noted, oral histories with elderly influenza survivors have to be carefully interpreted and contextualized.[13] The interviews with the Hamilton children did not focus on the pandemic and were conducted by non-historians interested mainly in psychical research. At the time of the interviews, the history of the influenza pandemic in Canada had been researched only sparsely, and there was very little scholarly research available to provide a broader interpretive context. Since both Margaret and Glen have been dead for decades, it is impossible to ask new questions or to probe their memories. Nonetheless, both saw Arthur's death as central to their family's history.

T.G. and Lillian Hamilton characterized their interest in bodily survival of death in gendered ways. T.G. framed his interest in psychical research as an intellectual endeavour driven by scientific curiosity.[14] Lillian was more inclined to acknowledge the emotional impact of Arthur's death on her and how it led her to explore existence beyond the grave more deeply. She began to meet with Mrs. Elizabeth Poole (later known as "Elizabeth M."), a working-class Scottish immigrant living in the Elmwood district. In the period leading up to and through the influenza pandemic, Poole was employed in the Hamilton household. She was close to the children and continued to care for them into the 1920s. Margaret recalled that "she was our second mother, and a dearly loved friend and nurse, our nurse during influenza [in] 1919. We owe her so much."[15] Lillian Hamilton, in class- and

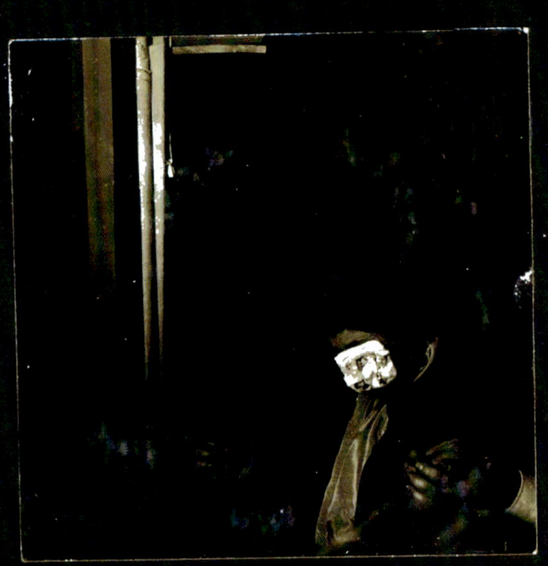

25th November 1928.

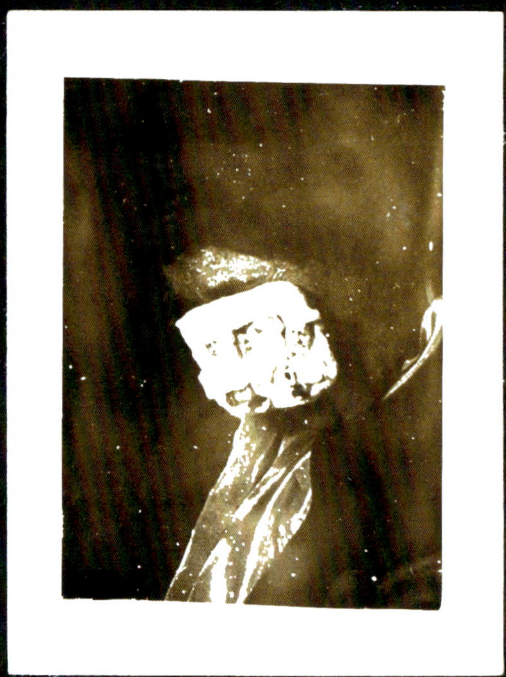

Enlargement of photograph of 25th November 1928.

Five Faces, including R.L. Stevenson and David Livingston.

Present:- Mary M., Elizabeth M., Mrs T.G. Hamilton, Dr. T.G. Hamilton, Dr. J.A. Hamilton, Miss A. Turner, Mrs. Alder, H.A. Reed, W.B. Cooper, and H.A.V. Green.

gender-bound language, described her as "uneducated, illiterate, but loved by all who knew her well, for her sunny gaiety, her warm kindliness, her loving and childlike heart."[16] As Robertson has noted, "investigators prized psychics they perceived as easily malleable to empirical pursuits—compliant, uneducated women of a lower social rank."[17] Elizabeth M. acted as the medium in nearly 400 Hamilton séances, exhibiting extensive psychical abilities, including telekinesis (table-tipping), rapping, precognition, clairvoyance, automatic writing, and deep trance vision and speech.[18]

The first archival reference to spirit communication with Arthur occurred in 1923, then another in 1927. And he appeared to Elizabeth M. in a vision on the tenth anniversary of his death on 27 January 1919.[19] But another working-class Scottish Canadian woman was a key conduit for communication with Arthur. Mary Marshall, known as "Mary M.," joined the Hamilton circle in 1928. She was the medium body through which ectoplasm flowed during the circle's meetings. Photographs of ectoplasm were presented as key evidence of the existence of life after death. That year Arthur appeared as a baby in an ectoplasm photograph during a séance at which the spirit control Walter guided the photographer (see Figures 1.5, 1.6, and 1.7).[20] The appearance of Walter was linked to the Hamiltons' close relationship with Boston psychical researchers Mina Stinson (Margery) and Le Roi Crandon, with whom they were "intimately intertwined." Walter was Margery's dead brother, and as Robertson has noted, the two families sometimes "shared" his ghost.[21]

Until T.G. Hamilton's sudden death from a heart attack in 1935, the family had weekly sessions with a larger group and a separate, smaller, more intimate group limited to family members. Like the Conan Doyle "home circle," the family sessions appear to have been "an intense, emotional, and highly motivated affair"[22] "akin to a family reunion."[23] The family sittings included (in addition to the medium) Lillian, Margaret (who recorded the sessions), and sometimes T.G. The surviving twin, James, attended sometimes at first and then more regularly by 1933. Glen

Fig. 1.5. T.G. Hamilton, ***Teleplasmic Mass with Arthur Hamilton's face***, 25 November 1928. UMASC, H.A.V. Green Fonds, MSS 439, Box 1, Folder 2, Item 1.4.

main group
engineering - them
said to be
J.W.H. Myers
Raymond Lodge
R.L.S.
W.T. Stead
Spurgeon
+ others
Myers friend of Raymond & father Sir Oliver - see communications obtained with Feda (Mrs Leonard) England. See "Raymond" & "Past years" of Lodge.

no photo of R.L.S. like this one known to exist.

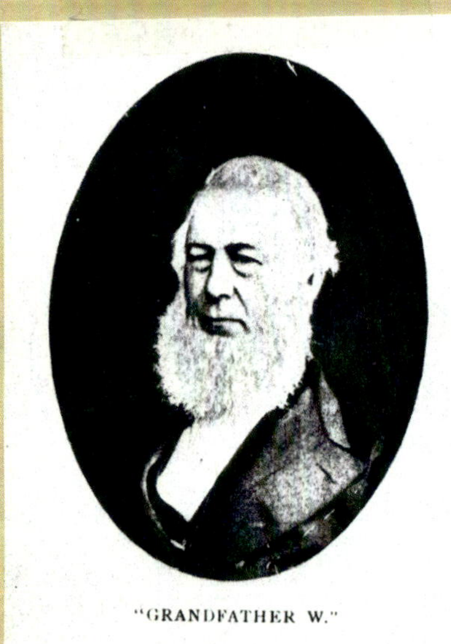

"GRANDFATHER W."

Lady Lodge's father, upper left.

(See Lodge's book "Raymond")

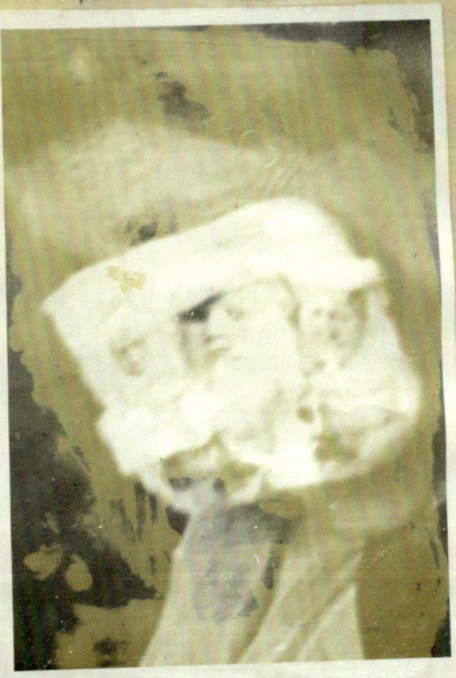

Top left - Grandfather W
Centre, Arthur Lamont Hamilton
Top right - unrecognized.
Lower left R.L.S.
Lower rught - Livingstone.

Upper left now seen to resemble Lady Lodge's father (See Raymond page 258. page 181: "broad forehead, upper lip bare, beard, etc.

Arthur upper middle
others unknown
[illegible] lower right.

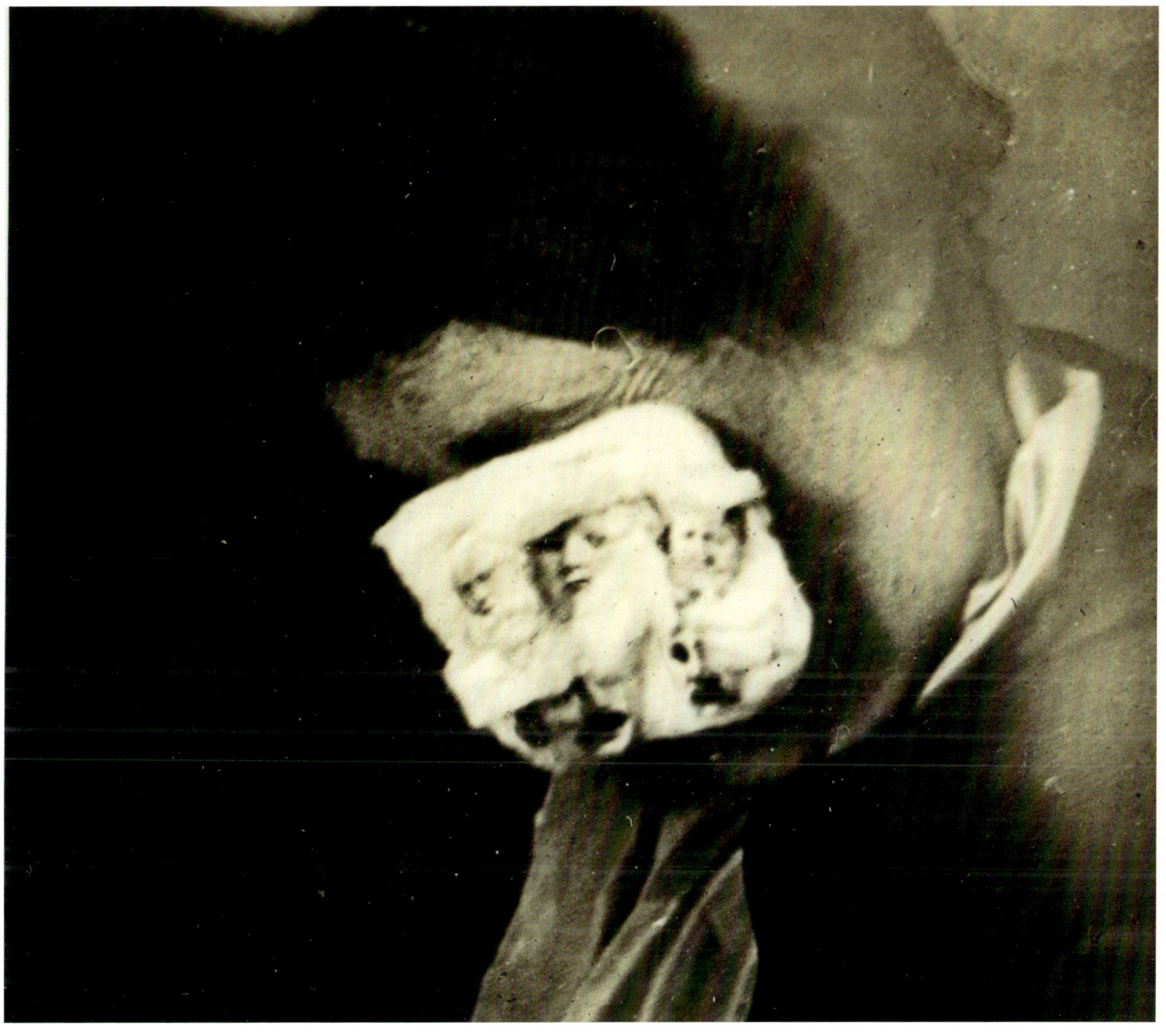

Fig. 1.6. *Left*, **Teleplasmic Mass attached to the face of the medium Mary Marshall**. Arthur Hamilton's face is in the centre, 25 November 1928. UMASC, MSS 14, Box 15, Folder 13.

Fig. 1.7. *Above*, **Five-Faces Group**. Close-up of the teleplasmic mass attached to the face of the medium Mary Marshall, with Arthur Hamilton's face in the centre, 25 November 1928. UMASC, PC 12, Box 9, Folder 4, Item 9b, http://hdl.handle.net/10719/1412173.

participated only occasionally. The mediums in the larger Hamilton group were almost all women. However, the family in its more private Spiritualism sometimes worked with a male medium, John ("Jay") MacDonald. In February 1933, Lillian, T.G., and Margaret gathered for a séance with MacDonald, Margaret recording. Through the medium, "Arthur purported to speak. He greeted the sitters, remarked that his father was present at this time and after about two or three minutes [of] conversation left."[24] Margaret's séance record in June 1933 noted that Arthur "reminisce[d] about the lake and holidays, and says he comes with us from year to year." In September, he reminded Lillian and Margaret of his impending birthday. In March 1934, Glen attended a séance, an unusual occurrence. Arthur's spirit called his father "Pop" and told "Glen that he will be used in his work as an instrument through his own motivation, but with the help of unseen friends." Later that year, just before Margaret was to be married, he teased her about preparations for the wedding, joking that, "if they [the Hamilton family] do this for the departure of a daughter, what more will they do for the return of a son? . . . Arthur seeing himself clad in armor, like King Arthur. We chat together, and Arthur leaves very quietly," Margaret recorded.[25] T.G. was absent from this gathering.

With his death at the height of the Depression, the family entered a new period of hardship. Lillian relied on young Glen, who had graduated from the University of Manitoba Medical College in 1934, to help support the family. After her husband's death, she continued his psychical research, and her belief in the afterlife again sustained her. Via Mary Marshall, Lillian received messages from her dead husband, who reassured her that he was among friends and fellow Spiritualists on "the other side."

The Hamilton oeuvre, and the transnational psychical research network through which the family flourished and achieved some fame, need not be read in its entirety through a pandemic lens. There are other elements of the interwar context, such as the social relations of gender, class, and colonialism, that "refused to be shut out from their experiments."[26] However, the private séances conducted by the Hamilton family give voice to the intimate experience of influenza survivors and the emotional quality of their loss, a loss experienced by thousands of other Canadians and millions of people around the world. The Hamilton archive is one more window into those silenced pandemic histories. The family's conversations with Arthur across the great divide pushed against scientific, cultural, and religious orthodoxies and challenged the historical amnesia that enveloped the post-pandemic era. When we listen to them, they bring influenza out of the shadows. After all, in the family's own story, and in the memories of surviving children, Arthur was not forgotten. On the contrary, the family privileged the impact of his death as a sort of origin story in their psychical journey. As a form of remembrance, Arthur's ghostly presence highlights the creativity and resilience of societies that experience mass death. As many historians have discovered, there is no singular narrative of the impact of the influenza. It weaves through the twentieth century as a ghost itself, visible to some, made invisible by others, a "shadow twin" of war, a phantom thread.

NOTES

1 Lillian Hamilton, "An Interval," UMASC, Hamilton Family Fonds (hereafter HFF), MSS 14, Box 15, Folder 6.

2 Elizabeth Outka, *Viral Modernism: The Influenza Pandemic and Interwar Literature* (New York: Columbia University Press, 2020); Elizabeth Outka, "'Wood for the Coffins Ran Out': Modernism and the Shadowed Afterlife of the Influenza Pandemic," *Modernism/Modernity* 21, no. 4 (2014): 937–60, especially 943. See also Jane Fisher, *Envisioning Disease, Gender, and War: Women's Narratives of the 1918 Influenza Pandemic* (New York: Palgrave Macmillan, 2012).

3 Beth A. Robertson, *Science of the Seance: Transnational Networks and Gendered Bodies in the Study of Psychic Phenomena, 1918–40* (Vancouver: UBC Press, 2016). Other studies of psychical research and Spiritualism in Canada include Claudie Massicotte, *Trance Speakers: Femininity and Authorship in Spiritual Séances* (Montreal and Kingston: McGill-Queen's University Press, 2017); and Stan McMullin, *Anatomy of a Seance: A History of Spirit Communication in Central Canada* (Montreal and Kingston: McGill-Queen's University Press, 2004). For interwar Britain, see Jenny Hazelgrove, *Spiritualism and British Society between the Wars* (Manchester: Manchester University Press, 2000).

4 See Esyllt W. Jones, "Open Secrets: Silence, Suppression and Memory in the History of Canada's 1918–1920 Influenza Pandemic," *Canadian Journal of Health History* 39, no. 1 (2022): 99–124.

5 Jay Winter, "History, Memory and the Flu," in *Pandemic Re-Awakenings: The Forgotten and Unforgotten "Spanish" Flu of 1918–1919*, ed. Guy Beiner (Oxford: Oxford University Press, 2022), xxvii.

6 Nancy Bristow, "The Practices of Social Forgetting: Rewriting, Obscuring and Silencing the 1918 Influenza Pandemic in the United States," in *Pandemic Re-Awakenings*, 335.

7 "14,029 Persons Are Attacked by 'Flu' in Winnipeg Between Oct. 5 and End of January," Winnipeg *Tribune*, 12 March 1919, 2. See also Esyllt W. Jones, *Influenza 1918: Disease, Death and Struggle in Winnipeg* (Toronto: University of Toronto Press, 2007), 59.

8 Janice Hamilton, *Reinventing Themselves: A History of the Hamilton and Forrester Families* (Montreal: Self-published, 2021) 293, 300.

9 Christopher Grainge, "Breath of Life: The Evolution of Oxygen Therapy," *Journal of the Royal Society of Medicine* 97, no. 10 (2004): 489–93.

10 See, for example, the recollections of Isaac Starr, a medical student in 1918, in "Influenza in 1918: Recollections of the Epidemic in Philadelphia," *Annals of Internal Medicine* 145, no. 2 (2006): 139.

11 R.E. Bennett, "Interview with Margaret Hamilton Bach," 26 November 1980, UMASC, Richard E. Bennett Fonds, TC 43 (A.80-07, A.89-04); Richard E. Bennett, "Interview with Margaret Hamilton Bach," UMASC, HFF, Box 3, Folder 9.

12 Linda Klassen, "Glen Hamilton, Family Doctor," in *Reinventing Themselves*, 279.

13 Ida Milne, "Through the Eyes of a Child: 'Spanish' Influenza Remembered by Survivors," in *Growing Pains: Childhood Illness in Ireland, 1750–1950*, ed.

Anne MacLellan and Alice Mauger (Newbridge, Ireland: Irish Academic Press, 2013), 162–63.

14 For further discussion, see Esyllt W. Jones, "Spectral Influenza: Winnipeg's Hamilton Family, Interwar Spiritualism, and Pandemic Disease," in *Epidemic Encounters: Influenza, Society, and Culture in Canada, 1918–20*, ed. Magda Fahrni and Esyllt W. Jones (Vancouver: UBC Press, 2012), 209–10.

15 Margaret Hamilton Bach, "Elizabeth Macdonald Wilson (Mrs. John Poole)," UMASC, HFF, MSS 14, Box 9, Folder 15.

16 Mrs. Glen Hamilton, "'Elizabeth M': The Wonderful Story of Dr. Glen Hamilton's First Medium," *Light*, 18 June 1936, 385.

17 Robertson, *Science of the Seance*, 49.

18 "The Various Psychic Phenomena Manifested by the Gifted Psychic Mrs. Elizabeth Poole, 1920–1927," UMASC, HFF, MSS 14, Box 9, Folder 15.

19 Group III, 6 January–27 April 1929, UMASC, HFF, MSS 14, Box 15, Folder 14.

20 "Report of Sitting Held Sunday November 25, 1928," UMASC, HFF, MSS 14, Box 15, Folder 13. For biographical information on the Hamilton circle, see McMullin, *Anatomy of a Seance*, 209–12.

21 Robertson, *Science of the Seance*, 6.

22 Ruth Brandon, *The Spiritualists: The Passion for the Occult in the Nineteenth and Twentieth Centuries* (New York: Alfred A. Knopf, 1983), 220.

23 McMullin, *Anatomy of a Seance*, xiv.

24 Jay MacDonald Scripts, February 1933, UMASC, HFF, MSS 14, Box 14, Folder 17.

25 Jay MacDonald Scripts, 24 June 1933, 22 September 1933, 30 March 1934, 22 June 1934, UMASC, HFF, MSS 14, Box 14, Folder 17.

26 Robertson, *Science of the Seance*, 49.

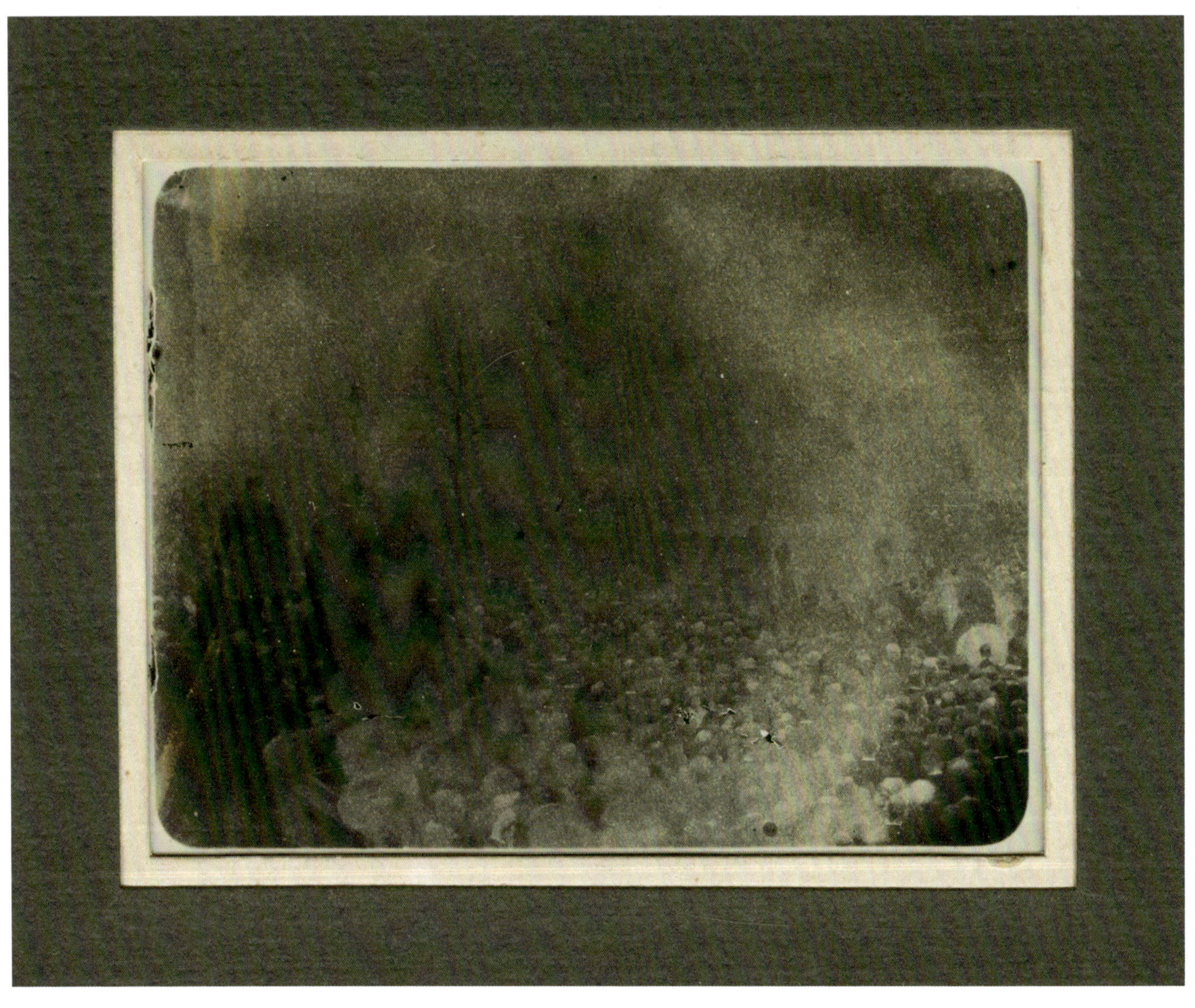

Fig. 2.1. Attributed to Ada Emma Deane, ***Spirit photograph taken at Whitehall, during the "Silence,"*** 11 November 1922. Gelatin silver print, 7.2 x 9.8 cm. Courtesy of the Harry Ransom Centre.

2

"Experiments and Experiences in Psychical Research": Scientific Séances in Winnipeg

Serena Keshavjee

I came away with the conclusion that Winnipeg stands very high among the places we have visited for its psychic possibilities.
—Arthur Conan Doyle, *Our Second American Adventure* (1924)[1]

Arthur Conan Doyle and his wife, Jean Leckie, visited Winnipeg in 1923 as part of a grand North American tour, promoting the unorthodox but popular religion of Spiritualism.[2] Conan Doyle lectured in over thirty cities on that tour, introducing a heady mix of science, religion, and celebrity to thousands of people. On 3 July, the author of the Sherlock Holmes stories inspired his audience at the Walker Theatre in Winnipeg with detailed descriptions of life after death that he had gleaned through communication with discarnate spirits in séances over a period of thirty years.[3] Conan Doyle ended his lecture, as he usually did on that four-month tour, with a set of photographs (see Figure 2.1) by the British spirit photographer Ada

Emma Deane taken on Armistice Day, 11 November 1922, during the period of silence honouring those who had died in the First World War.

In a theatrical manner, Conan Doyle projected the spirit photographs in two stages. At first, all that the Winnipeg audience saw was a "dim luminous halo" of emerging ectoplasm positioned over a cenotaph in London (see Figure 2.1).[4] Then a second photograph, taken a few minutes after the first one, revealed "shadowy, but at the same time quite plainly defined faces of young men beneath service caps, the typical British soldier." The lantern slides that night, described as "remarkable," made a "deep impression on the audience."[5]

Conan Doyle was a member of the Society for Psychical Research (SPR), an organization of scientists examining claims of psychic and paranormal phenomena, inaugurated in 1882 in England.[6] Psychic researchers studied the "psychic" force, an invisible force that was thought to manifest ectoplasmic materializations. Science historian Richard Noakes notes that by 1900 the SPR was flourishing, indicating wide interest in applying a scientific method to the supernatural.[7] Eventually, Conan Doyle became discouraged by the sceptical attitude that SPR members were encouraged to maintain. In 1916, he declared his acceptance of Spiritualism and soon became one of the main propagandists for the religious movement, disseminating evidence of life after death through public lectures:[8] "Spiritualism comes to the world with a definite message that the dead have passed on to life immortal. No longer is it a matter of faith but a matter of knowledge. The spirits are anxious to communicate with the earth and to help us and our mission is to awaken the world to a knowledge of this truth."[9]

Conan Doyle framed his Winnipeg lecture as combatting the "curse" of materialism, and he wove together elements of pseudo-science and popular religion, offering a compelling model of the scientific man of faith with a touch of showmanship.[10] In the audience that night in Winnipeg were Lillian and Dr. Thomas Glendenning (T.G.) Hamilton with their friend, lawyer Isaac Pitblado, as well as William Talbot Allison, the minister of King Memorial Church and a professor of English at Wesley College, who had introduced the Hamiltons to spirit communication in 1918.[11] Included in Conan Doyle's presentation were lantern slide photographs of ectoplasm based on a "new research science" that he spoke about "at length" and was careful to define: "It [ectoplasm] is soft, jellylike and full of life. It is drawn from the medium. Among its peculiarities is that it is very sensitive to light. That is why physical séances are held in the dark, because the ectoplasm, the base of all phenomena dissolves in the light."[12]

After the success of the movie *Ghostbusters* in the 1980s, ectoplasmic materializations are a part of common culture and often the stuff of gags (see Figures 7.4 and 9.2). In the early twentieth century, however, ectoplasm was a subject of scientific study and regarded as a version of protoplasm, the vivified material of the amoeba, the fundamental substance of all living forms on the planet. The definition of ectoplasm was based on vitalist biology and teleological evolutionary theory, reflecting a biocentric vision of a holistic interconnected universe, and it attracted scientific attention at the *fin de siècle*.[13] Conan Doyle's talk was one of the first times that the public in Winnipeg had seen ectoplasm, but it would not be the last. Between 1926 and 1934, T.G. Hamilton gave many public lectures in Winnipeg about his psychical research, and in 1930 he was invited to curate a display of 100 photographs of ectoplasmic manifestations at the Winnipeg Winter Club for participants at the joint conference of the Canadian and British Medical Associations.[14] This exhibit was possibly one of the earliest displays of scientific visualizations in Canada, and Hamilton sent a smaller version of the exhibit to the University of Bulgaria in 1933, for which we have photographic documentation (see Figure 2.2).

As a psychical scientist T.G. Hamilton distanced himself from the religion of Spiritualism, calling it a "cult," and he might have been uncomfortable with aspects of Conan Doyle's lecture that evening.[15] Yet, in terms of using science and technology to deliver a hopeful message of immortality, the two men had much in common. Hamilton joined the American Society for Psychical Research in 1923 and with Isaac Pitblado organized the Winnipeg Society for Psychical Research in 1931.[16] The scientists and medical doctors who joined these types of societies to test supernormal happenings were often moved to fight against growing materialism

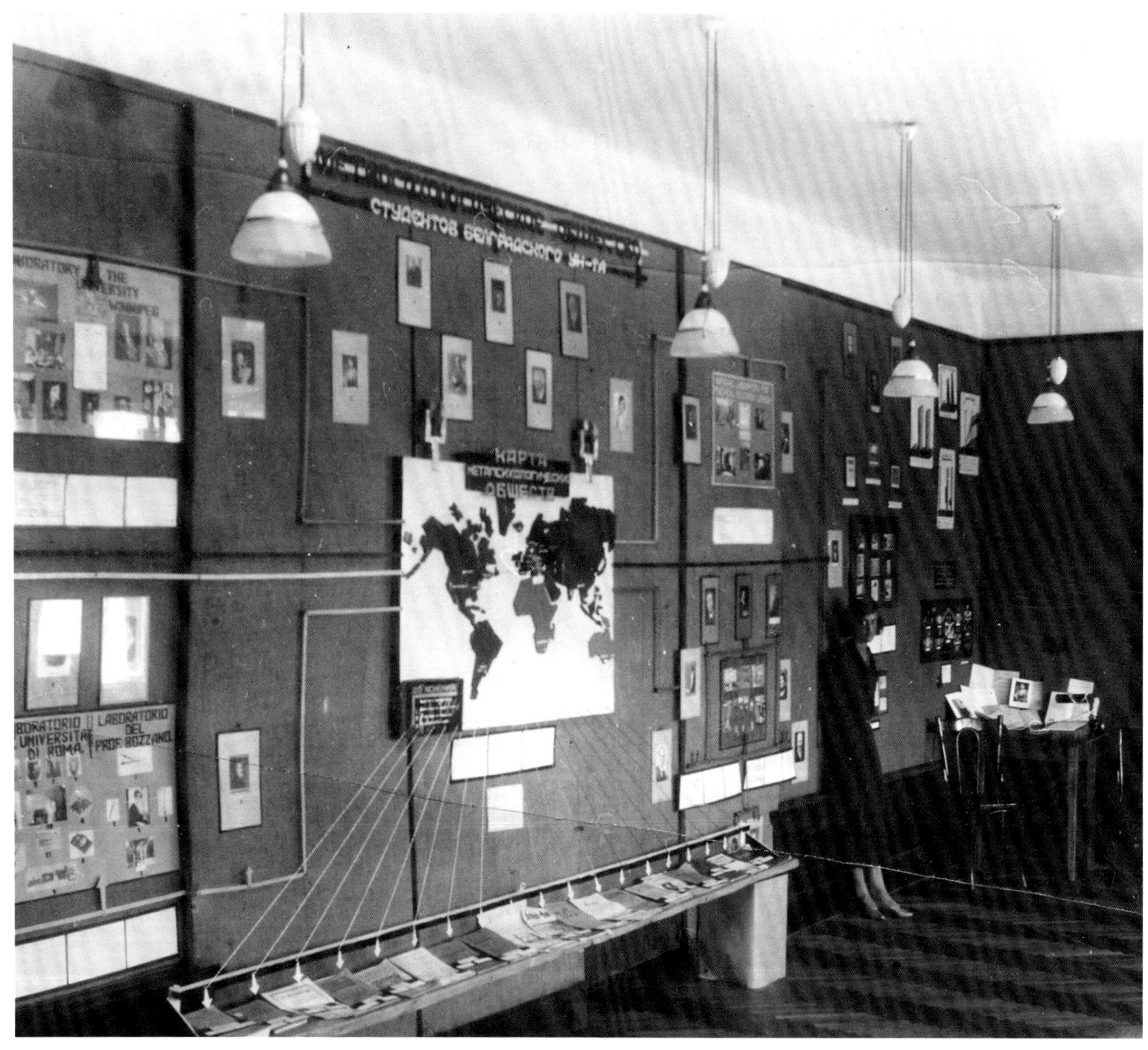

Fig. 2.2. Documentary photograph of T.G. Hamilton's Metapsychic display in Bulgaria in 1933, based on his 1930 exhibition at the Winnipeg Winter Club. UMASC, PC 12, Box 11, Folder 20, Item 2, http://hdl.handle.net/10719/1524256.

using empirical methods. As historians of science have explained, scientists were motivated to find hard evidence to bolster their Christian beliefs, and this seems to have been a part of T.G. Hamilton's motivation for his serious study of ectoplasm.[17] Hamilton believed that the Bible already described supernormal occurrences, including truth-telling dreams and visions, and these events were comparable to the extraordinary communications he witnessed in the séance room: "Religion finds it necessary to pass over in silence the many manifestations of an alleged psychic nature recorded in her sacred writings, upon which her whole structure has been founded."[18] Searching for a scientific foundation to support faith-based belief systems was not uncommon in 1900, and sometimes contested or outdated science was used in such endeavours. Today psychical research is often referred to as pseudo-science, but in the 1920s and 1930s it remained within the bounds of accepted scientific inquiry. Conan Doyle summed up the attitude to psychic science:

> Psychic Science is a very real science with enormous literature—I have 400 books around me as I write—and which has engaged the attention of the greatest group of thinkers that any simple Science or Philosophy has ever called together. Where could you get such a varied galaxy as Barrett, Hyslop, Richet, Flammarion, Lodge, Crookes, Hodgson, Stead, Geley, Rayleigh, Myers and others, who *all* endorse the phenomena, and most of whom accept the spirit explanation. Their opinion is not likely to be set aside and so it would be well to see what their extended experiments and continued thought have to say which might bear upon this matter.[19]

At the beginning of the twentieth century, various thinkers were increasingly dissatisfied with a purely mechanistic understanding of the universe, a view that eradicated the idea of a grand design; they were drawn to mediumship because of its claims of extraordinary communication and events.[20] The eminent scientists whom Conan Doyle listed above all studied the mysteries of mediumship. For example, the physicist and inventor of wireless telegraphy Sir Oliver Lodge, who visited Winnipeg in 1920 and corresponded with the Hamiltons, and the renowned chemist Sir William Crookes, both accepted that human personalities could survive death, commune through a medium, and materialize into the human realm. These men had distinguished scientific careers even as they dabbled in the core beliefs of Spiritualism and posited the survival hypothesis.[21] Others, including "continental researchers" Drs. Gustave Geley, Albert von Schrenck-Notzing, and Charles Richet, did not believe in the existence of ghosts but agreed that strange phenomena were happening in the séance room, spawning years of sanctioned scientific séances. Although T.G. Hamilton was a long way off from the psychical research centres of Paris and London, with the help of Lillian Hamilton, as laid out in Chapter 3, he set up a laboratory and produced scientific illustrations that rivalled those of the international scientists.[22] As I will outline in this chapter, T.G. Hamilton brought together seemingly contradictory views from science, the practice of séances, and even mainstream Christianity, utilizing his medical training to investigate whether personality survives death, and in doing so became a world-class psychical researcher.

Scientific Séances in the Twentieth Century

As the Hamiltons' daughter Margaret Hamilton Bach explains, Spiritualism was "rampant following the tragedy of World War 1," and "a movement of this kind is very open to fraudulent behavior," giving us insight into why T.G. Hamilton avoided the religion of Spiritualism. Nonetheless he relied on the séance as the basis of his experimental research and was described in a British newspaper as the "the doctor of one thousand séances."[23] Séances date from soon after the Modern Spiritualist movement began in 1848, and many Europeans and North Americans were intrigued by the popular religion and comforted by spirit photographs. Esyllt W. Jones demonstrates in Chapter 1 that after the First World War, and the influenza pandemic of 1918 to 1920, the religion of Spiritualism, whose rituals involved communicating with discarnate spirits in a séance setting, experienced a revival in Europe and North America as an expression of bereavement, resulting from great personal loss.[24]

Yet not everyone who went to séances was a practising Spiritualist. Parlour games such as Ouija boards, table rapping, and séances drew in audiences,[25] and served as sites of entertainment, and they have been compared with improvisational theatre employing light effects, singing, and chanting to create a charged atmosphere.[26] By the late nineteenth century séances were also a foundation for the systematic study of mediumship. In 1874, as part of his study of mediumship, Crookes took forty photographs—scientific visualizations—of the ghost of Katie King (see Figure 9.12). Both Hamilton and Conan Doyle saw Crookes as the pioneer of psychical research, and photography became foundational to psychic investigations.[27]

In the 1920s, Doyle and Leckie were the most famous Spiritualists in the world, and they were invited to sit in on séances wherever they went, including two séances in Winnipeg.[28] One was a religious séance with a medium named Mrs. Bolton. Of more interest to us is the controlled experiment organized by the Hamiltons in their house to test the mediumistic power of their children's nanny, Elizabeth Poole. Conan Doyle published his recollections in *Our Second American Adventure* (1924), describing the forceful telekinetic event that he experienced in the Hamiltons' laboratory when a wooden table moved violently into the air without anyone touching it:

> On our first night in Winnipeg we attended a circle for psychical research which has been conducted for two years by a group of scientific men who have obtained remarkable results. The medium is a small, pleasant-faced woman from the Western Highlands of Scotland. Her psychic gifts are both mental and physical. The circle, which contained ten persons, including my wife and myself, placed their hands, or one hand each, upon a small table, part of which was illuminated by phosphorus so as to give some light. It was violently agitated, and this process was described as "charging it." It was then pushed back into a small cabinet made of four hung curtains with an opening in front. Out of this the table came clattering again and again entirely on its own, with no sitter touching it. I stood by the slit in the curtain in subdued red light and I watched the table within. One moment it was quiescent. A moment later it was like a

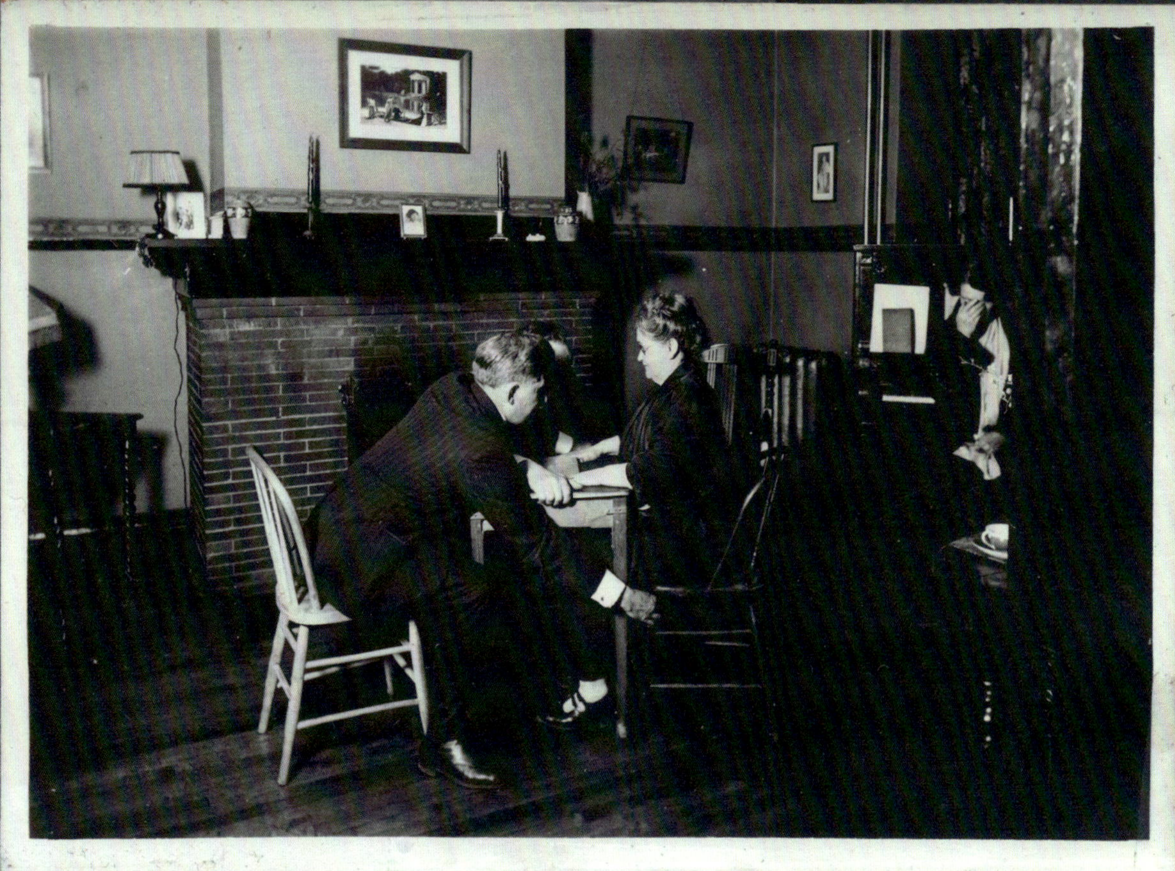

Experiment C. Here the experimenters are endeavouring to prevent movement in both the table and the chair. For a moment or two they are successful but presently, in spite of their greatest efforts to the contrary, the whole mass - medium, experimenters, table and chairs - is lurched and rotated about the floor - a truly astonishing manifestation when one considers the weight of the mass.

Following the experiment the medium showed signs of great exhaustion - perspiration, pallor, dazed mental condition. Dr.T.G.H., Mr.D.B.MacDonald, Mrs. Poole. March,1923
Living Room, 185 Kelvin St. Wpg.

> restless dog in a kennel, springing, tossing, beating up against the supports, and finally bounding out with a velocity which caused me to get quickly out of the way. It ended by rising up in the air while our finger-tips were on it and remaining up for an appreciable period.[29]

Both Conan Doyle and Hamilton agreed that the table had been propelled by an invisible energy, a psychic or vital force channelled through the medium in a trance state.[30]

The Hamiltons had briefly conducted experiments in telepathy in 1918, and Lillian Hamilton began hosting casual séances in their living room between 1920 and 1923 (see Figure 2.3).[31] In her account of the experiments, she states that it was only a few months before Conan Doyle arrived in Winnipeg in 1923 that T.G. decided that there might be "more here than meets the eye or ear. I must admit to myself at least that here is a region of fact which must be investigated along scientific lines," and he was thus "convinced for the first time of the reality of psychic force." [32] The power of the communication is captured in this description: "We held an impromptu sitting for a friend who was our guest, and to our surprise raps again appeared and out in the shadows of our living room, letter by letter 'Go on with your work. More ahead. W.T. Stead.' Never before had I seen my husband so impressed. All had been simple, four people alone in the room while the fire light played over our hands, and yet out . . . there was a mind communicating who belonged to an invisible state.[33]

In the spring of 1923, T.G. Hamilton took over his wife's séances, turning the informal circle into a scientific séance by applying systematic methods with "rigorous control of experimental details, [and] repeated observations." Between 1924 and 1926 he began to incorporate photography into his setup, with the intention of getting an "accurate record," of the telekinetic activity.[34] He moved the séances to a "laboratory" in July 1923, the very month that Doyle and Leckie joined the Hamiltons.[35]

Fig. 2.3. ***Living Room Séance***, 26 March 1923 (posed photograph). UMASC, PC 12, Box 8, Folder 1, Item 1c, http://hdl.handle.net/10719/1410501.

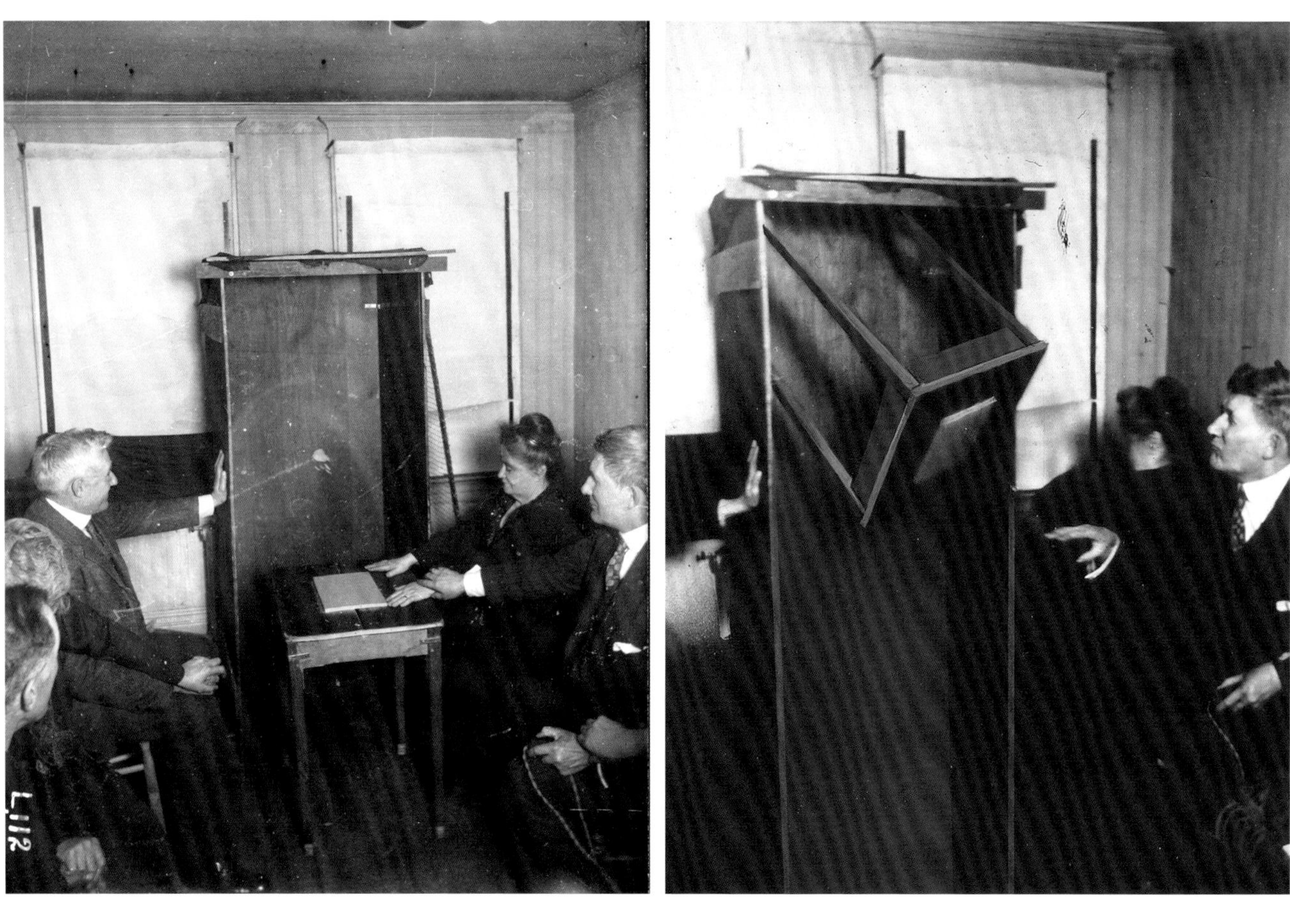

Fig. 2.4. *Left*, ***Telekinesis #7, Elizabeth Poole "charging the table,"*** 1925. UMASC, PC 12, Box 9, Folder 1, Item 7, http://hdl.handle.net/10719/1412189.

Fig. 2.5. *Right*, ***Telekinesis #22, Table Levitation and Inversion***, 11 February 1926. UMASC, PC 12, Box 1, Folder 3, Item 22, http://hdl.handle.net/10719/1410750.

From that point on, in line with the standard twentieth-century protocols of experimental science, the photographs taken in that room can be considered scientific illustrations (see Figures 2.4 and 2.5). Conan Doyle moved seamlessly back and forth between the religion of Spiritualism and psychical science; Hamilton, however, insisted that his work should be understood only as hard science. His scientific inscriptions, and his high-quality, documentary-style photographs, now housed in the Hamilton Family Fonds (HFF), contributed to his acceptance as one of the most respected psychical scientists of the twentieth century.

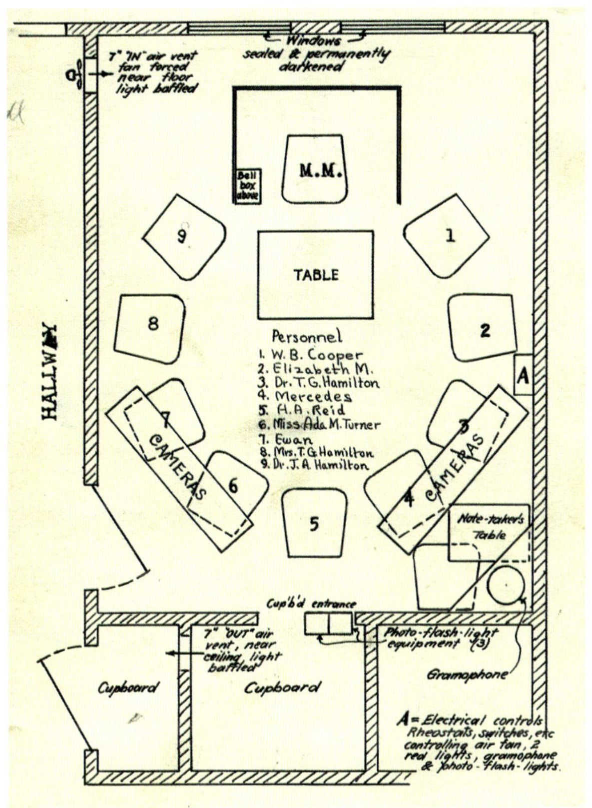

Fig. 2.6. ***Diagram of the Seance Room***, c. 1929–30. UMASC, PC 12, Box 9, Folder 1, Item 6, http://hdl.handle.net/10719/1411515.

Margaret Hamilton Bach states that "everything was under his control." T.G. Hamilton "set up a séance room on the second floor—in essence it became a *scientific laboratory*. Cameras were set up, the room was equipped with chairs, a table, and a red ceiling light. . . . Fortunately my father had a great deal of mechanical skill, he was an excellent amateur photographer, with his own dark room, where he did all his own developing, enlarging and printing." Figures 2.4 and 2.5 of tables telekinetically moving are examples of some of the earliest photographs taken by Hamilton after he moved into the "old and funny junk room," turning it from a catch-all space, into a controlled experimental space (see Figure 2.6).[36]

VIEW OF THE SEANCE ROOM
AS SEEN FROM THE CABINET

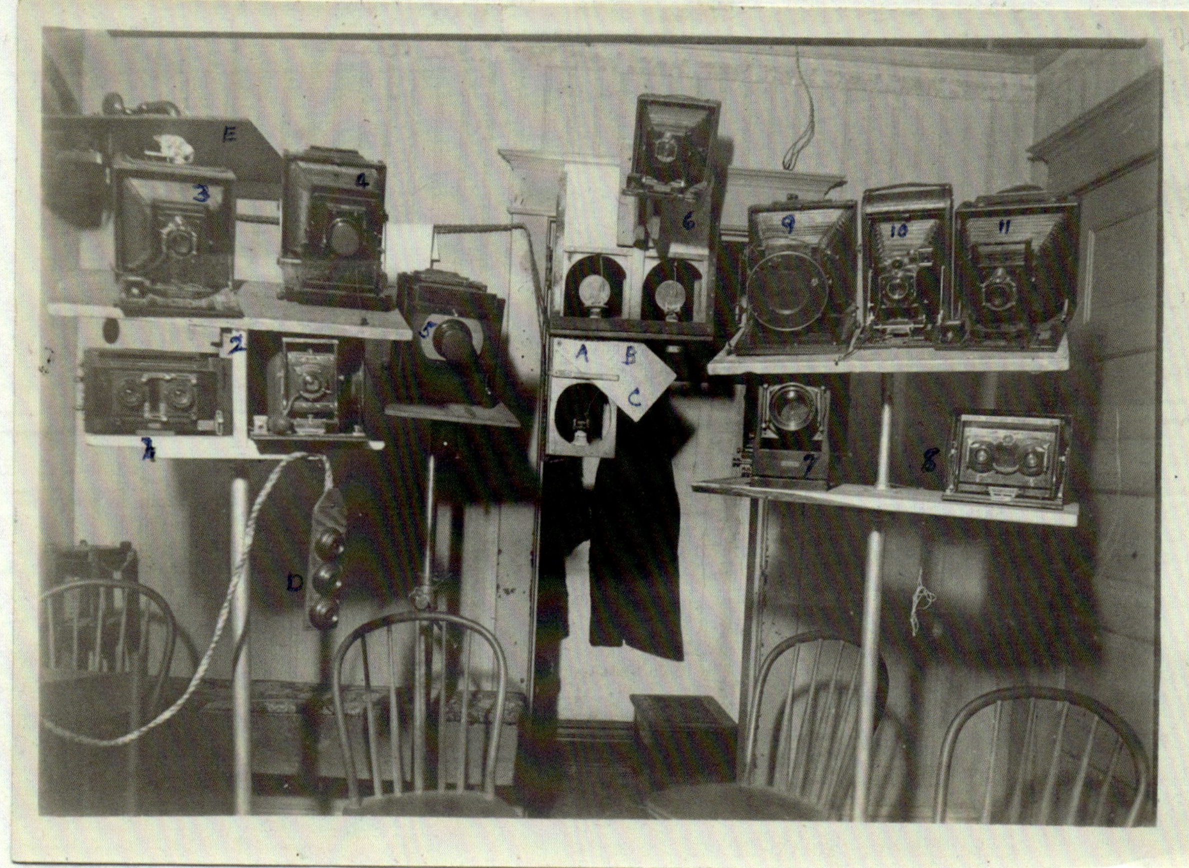

A, B, C, are flash light devices, always loaded with flash powder ready for action.

D. Three push buttons, which, when pressed, will explodes three flashes in sequence.

E. A deck holding a phonograph, operated by a motor-driven mechanism, which is controlled by a switch attached to Dr. Hamilton's chair.

CAMERA EQUIPMENT:

1. Goerz Stereoscopic, using plates or films.
2. 5 x 7 rapid Rectilinear camera.
3. 5 x 7 rapid Rectilinear camera.
4. $4\frac{1}{2}$ x $6\frac{1}{2}$ Thornton Picard Portrait camera.
5. 5 x 7 Quartz lens camera.
6. 5 x 7 Wide Angle lens camera.
7. 5 x 7 Seneca Portrait camera.
8. Woollensak Stereoscopic camera.
9. 5 x 7 Doppel Anastigmat camera.
10. 5 x 7 Zeiss Anastigmat roll film or plate camera.
11. 5 x 7 rapid Rectilinear camera.

Artist Susan MacWilliam recreated Hamilton's wooden cabinet for the installation *F-L-A-M-M-A-R-I-O-N*, shown at the Venice Biennale in 2009, giving us a sense of the ordered conditions in the small séance room (see Figure 0.9). Hamilton staged the space to control as many aspects as possible by blocking out the windows to make the room completely dark, adding a red lightbulb with a dimmer switch, and designing and building a special cabinet of pine wood to harness the medium's powers and restrict her movements, as laid out in his diagram in Figure 2.6.[37]

Over the next few years, T.G. Hamilton borrowed and bought a series of cameras from the Kodak Supply House in Winnipeg, including two stereoscopic cameras, several large-plate models, and wide-angle, anastigmat, portrait, and quartz lenses, with the intention of capturing images of the controlled phenomena in his séance room.[38] The cameras were set up on two stands with two levels each and positioned facing the cabinet to capture the medium and the physical phenomena that she produced from several different angles. To the best of our knowledge, he set up the plates, released the flash, took and printed almost every photograph in the HFF, with only a few exceptions (see Figure 2.7).

The Hamiltons organized about two séances a week for twelve years using state-of-the-art technology, including up to eleven cameras and a remote-controlled apparatus to release the hand-packed magnesium flashes instantaneously. Detailed minutes were taken at each séance, and witnesses and scrutineers were used to guard against accusations of fraudulent behaviour. T.G. controlled the space, but Lillian organized the meetings, wrote to experts, managed the minutes and registers, and supervised the cross-referencing of the supernormal messages received during the séances.[39] She sometimes chaperoned the mediums, choosing the clothing that they wore and monitoring the washing and physical examining of their bodies before séances at which physical phenomena were anticipated.[40] The mediums were costumed in black shift dresses or a silk house coat with bloomers, contributing to the minimalist

Fig. 2.7. ***View of Séance Room with Cameras from Cabinet***, c. 1929–30. UMASC, PC 12, Box 8, Folder 1, Item 1, http://hdl.handle.net/10719/1411030.

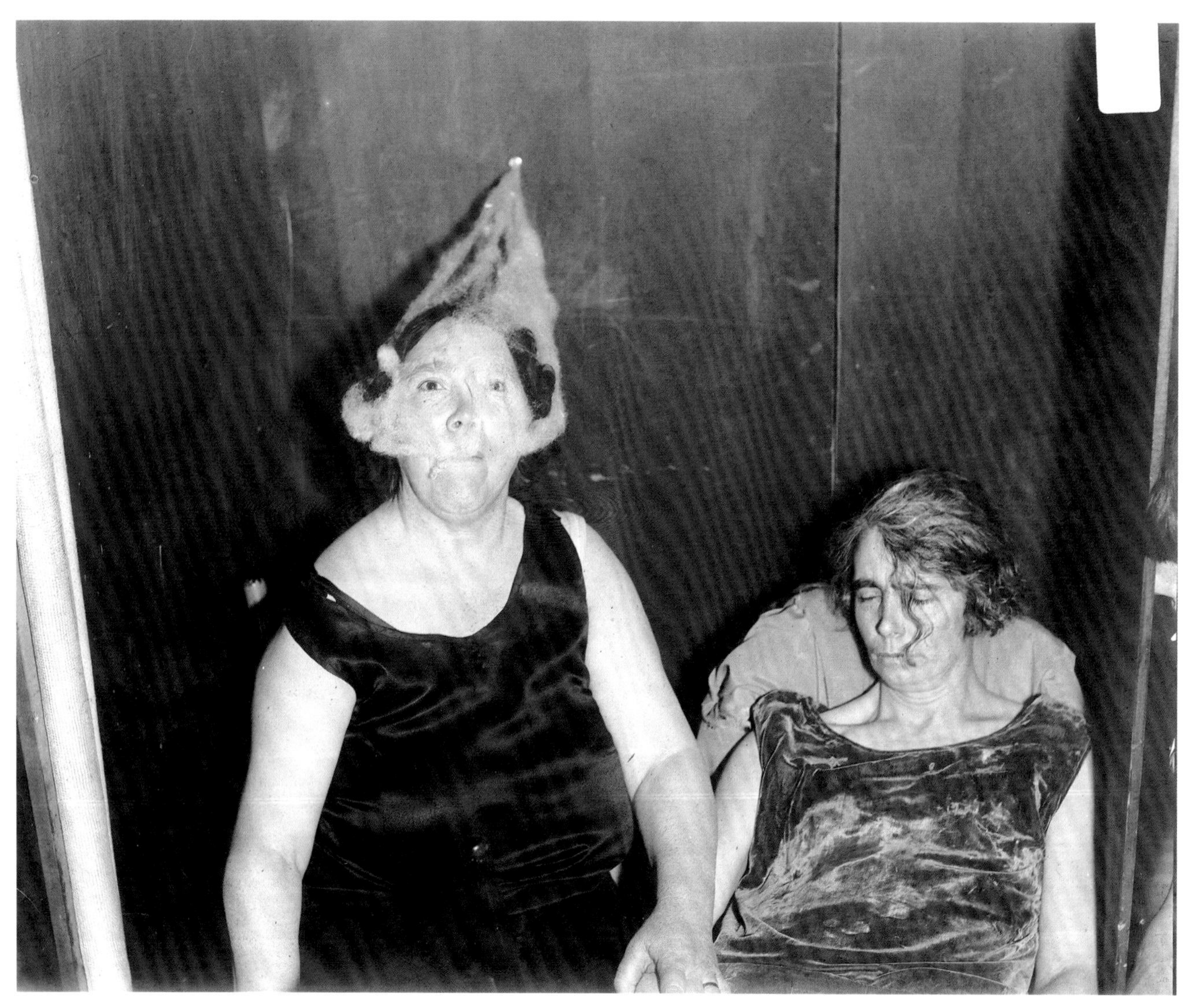

Fig. 2.8. ***"Umbrella" Teleplasm,*** 25 February 1934. UMASC, PC 12, Box 15, Folder 20, Item 55, http://hdl.handle.net/10719/1524229.

aesthetic of the photographs, as seen in Figure 2.8 and following the style of the photographs of the French medium Eva Carrière (see Figure 9.19). After T.G. died in 1935, Lillian Hamilton continued the sittings with two co-experimenters until 1940, and she solicited automatic writing from Mary Marshall until 1944.

In 1928, ectoplasmic manifestations or, as T.G. Hamilton preferred, teleplasmic masses became the focus of the group's research over table turning exercises (see Figure 2.8). By 1930, Hamilton was considered one of the premier photographers of ectoplasm worldwide. The high-quality paper, careful compositions, and Modernist aesthetics of his photographs, also dominant in fine art and other scientific visualizations by the 1930s, contributed, I believe, to the positive reception of his research in international psychical circles.[41] The psychic research that the Hamiltons undertook was marginal to orthodox science, or "official science," as T.G. called it, but it was not totally rejected. Mediums were thought to induce a trance state in order to communicate with the "other world," and because of their medical training T.G. and Lillian, a registered nurse, felt comfortable monitoring the heart rate and respiration of Elizabeth Poole to measure the depth of her trance and ensure her safety during the experiments (see Figure 2.10). This was expensive and time-consuming research. T.G. kept up his full-time medical practice, but his family noted that it became increasingly challenging for him, especially as he was invited to lecture around North America on his experiments and scientific photographs.[42]

The Hamiltons' dedication to psychical research and the high-quality photographs must have impressed Conan Doyle, who kept abreast of the Winnipeg experiments. In his 1929 tour of South Africa and Kenya, he projected the Hamilton photographs of the teleplasms believed to include a miniature face form of deceased Reverend Charles Haddon Spurgeon, a celebrated preacher in London (see Figure 2.9), alongside scientific photographs by some of the most respected psychical researchers in the world at that time: Dr. Gustave Geley, Dr. Albert von Schrenck-Notzing, and Juliette Bisson.[43] Hamilton owned books by these scientists, whom he regarded, along with Dr. Charles Richet, as key to discovering the truth about the ectoplasmic masses.[44] This group of researchers, who had worked in Paris before and after the First World War, influenced

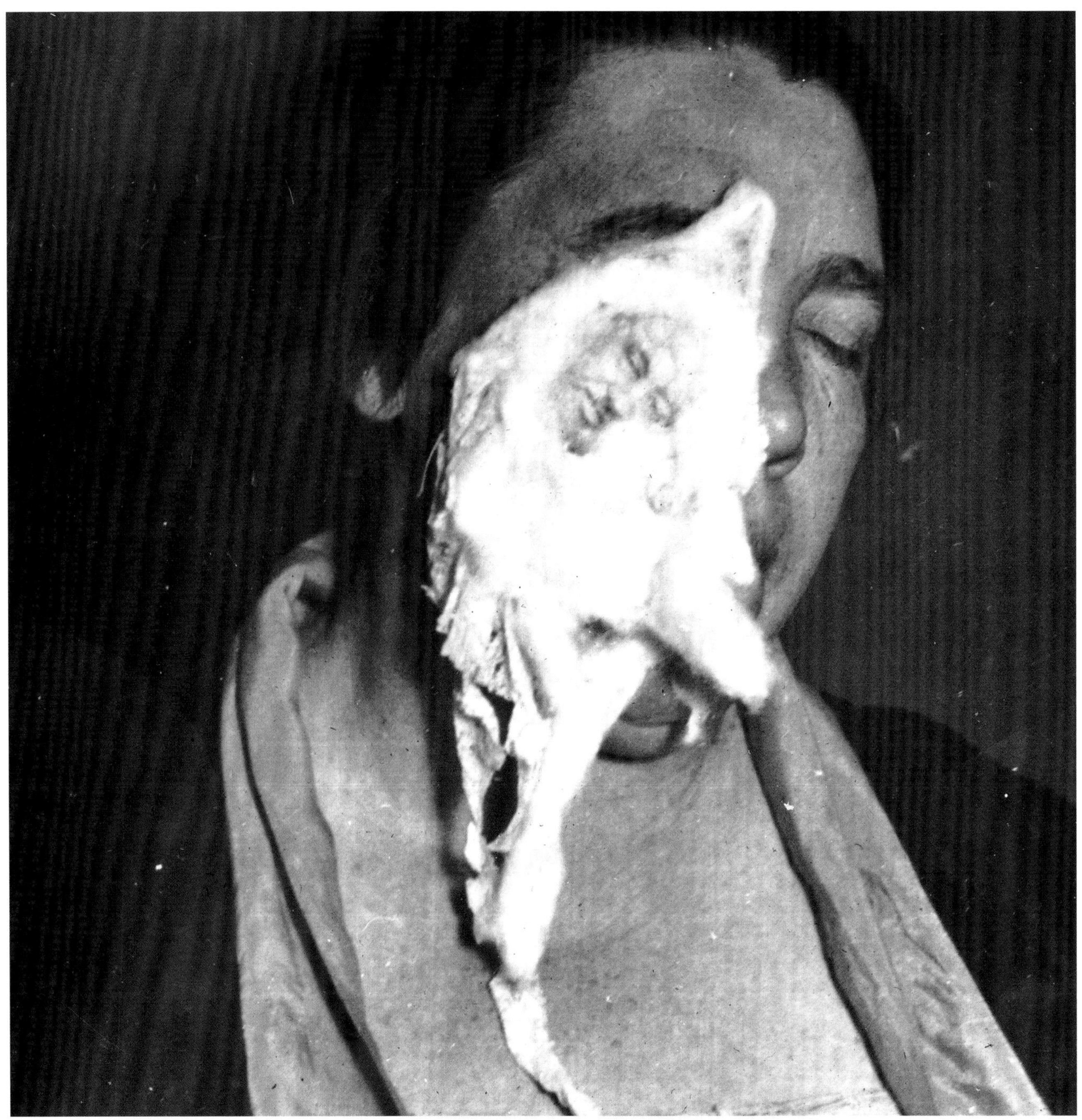

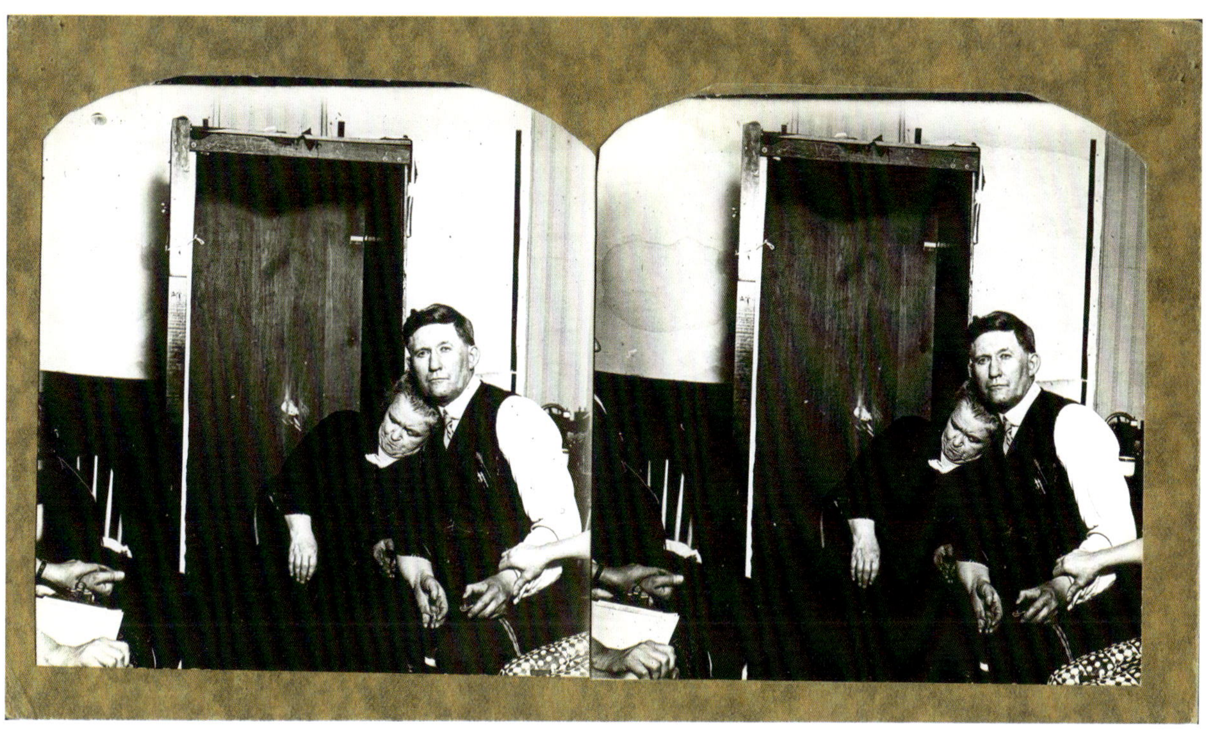

Fig. 2.9. *Left*, ***The Fourth Spurgeon Teleplasm (Reverend Charles Haddon Spurgeon)***, 1 May 1929. UMASC, PC 12, Box 9, Folder 6, Item 18e, http://hdl.handle.net/10719/1412414.

Fig. 2.10. *Above*, ***Elizabeth Poole in a Trance State of Complete Relaxation***, c. 1924–26. Stereo photographic print. UMASC, PC 12, Box 6, Folder "Trance," Item 28.

Hamilton's formal construction of his scientific visualizations. That his photographs were shown on Conan Doyle's popular international tours demonstrates how well his research was received in elite psychical circles (see Figure 2.9). Even Samuel Aykroyd, Dan Aykroyd's great-grandfather, had high praise: "Dr. Hamilton is doing for Canada what Dr. Crandon is doing for the States, Sir Oliver Lodge for England and Dr. Geley for France." All of this acclaim justifies Hamilton's boast that "I am aware the research we are doing—photographing ectoplasm—is unique in its results in the world today. The

First flash of May 1, 1932.

{sitting no 311}
{Fil no 44.}

No materializing substance is visible.

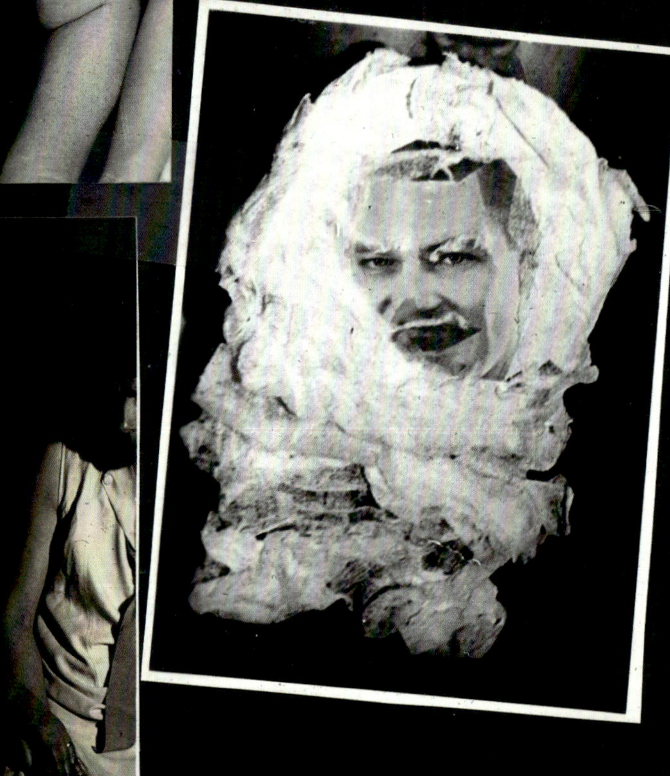

2nd flash of May 1. 1932.
The first Conan Doyle miniature appears
Right hand of Mary M held by

substance quite evidently undergoes marvelous morphological changes in the course of a few minutes."[45]

Conan Doyle was to provide another boost to Hamilton's career. In life, the author had always promised to return as a "spirit extra" after he died—to prove his thesis of immortality. In 1932, two years after he passed away, Conan Doyle's face turned up twice in the Hamilton photographs, embedded in woolly-looking ectoplasm. I have found copies of these photographs in every psychical research archive that I have researched in North America and Europe (see Figures 2.11 and 2.13).

The Phenomena of Materializations

Beginning in the 1870s with photographs taken by the British chemist William Crookes of a materialization calling herself Katie King (see Figure 9.12), scientists in Britain, Europe, and the United States noted that mediums were communicating alleged messages from spirits, speaking in languages that they did not know, demonstrating thought transference, directing long-distance movement, and displaying other extraordinary phenomena that warranted further study.[46]

One of the books that Hamilton cited frequently was *Thirty Years of Psychical Research*: *A Treatise on Metapsychics* (1923), by renowned physiologist, psychical researcher, and Nobel Prize winner Dr. Charles Richet. This 600-page treatise contextualized scientific interest in mediumship by explaining that many new discoveries and inventions, such as "electricity, the telephone, x-rays, bacteria, and the airplane," were challenging scientific orthodoxy about the physical world and opening up areas of study into "metapsychics," or as it was commonly called, psychical research.[47] Historian Carlos Alvarado explains that it was not unusual for the "vital force," a popular concept beginning in 1900, to be conflated with the psychic force and to be conceptualized as the mechanism of the unconscious mind. By the end of the nineteenth century, a range of

Fig. 2.11. ***First Sir Arthur Conan Doyle Face***, 1 May 1932. UMASC, PC 12, Box 8, Folder 6, Item 44, http://hdl.handle.net/10719/1411482.

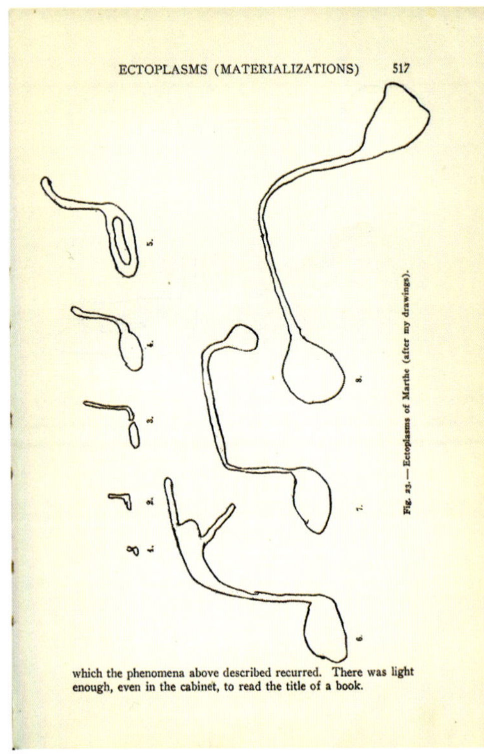

ECTOPLASMS (MATERIALIZATIONS) 517

Fig. 23.—Ectoplasms of Marthe (after my drawings).

which the phenomena above described recurred. There was light enough, even in the cabinet, to read the title of a book.

Fig. 2.12. Charles Richet, ***Ectoplasms of Marthe Béraud (Eva C).*** Reproduced in ***Thirty Years of Psychical Research*** (New York City: Macmillan Company, 1923), 517. Courtesy of University of Manitoba Archives and Special Collections.

"new" energies, variously called "animal magnetism, neo-magnetism, nervous force, neuric force, Od, psychic fluid, psychic force, vital energy and vital force," were compared to discoveries in electricity, light, and heat.[48]

To explain the physical happenings inside the séance room, especially telekinesis and extrusion of ectoplasmic (teleplasmic) materializations, psychic investigators theorized that the vital or psychic force could be projected outside the body, sometimes like a lever.[49] Richet proposed that the vital force could manifest as a mechanical force and exteriorize as "rigid rods," for which he drew a crude rendering (see Figure 2.12): "The substance that produces these telekinetic movements is a kind of lever, cantilever or rod which emerges from the body of the medium and is reabsorbed into it."[50]

T.G. Hamilton took up the physiological terminology, describing the "nervous energy" or the "vital electricity" of his mediums as the power that generates the unseen lever, which moved the table in the séance with Doyle and Leckie He understood the projection itself was biological in nature.[51] Although this vitalistic biological science is rejected today, it was received by many as legitimate in the 1920s. The reputation of the scientists involved, as well as their detailed methodologies, supported this pseudo-science. Hamilton adopted the concept of "supernormal" biology promoted

Fig. 2.13. T.G. Hamilton, ***Second Sir Arthur Conan Doyle Face***, 27 June 1932. UMASC, H.A.V. Green Fonds, MSS 439, Box 1, Folder 2, Item 1.27.

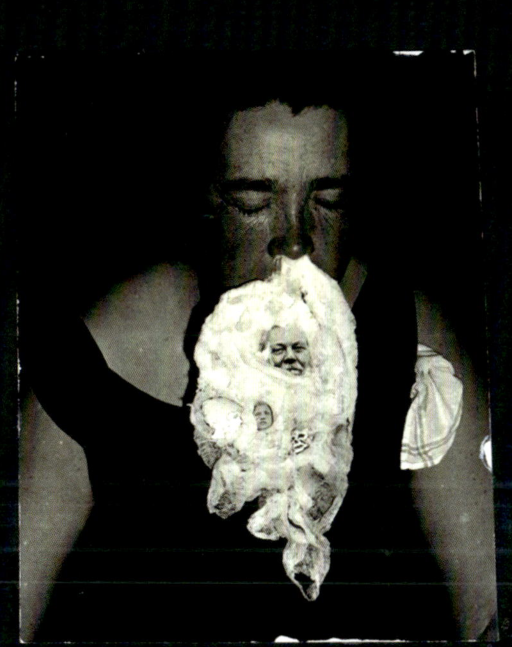

27th June 1932.
Sir Arthur Conan Doyle.
C. H. Spurgeon as a youth.
"Walter's" drawing.
& skull.

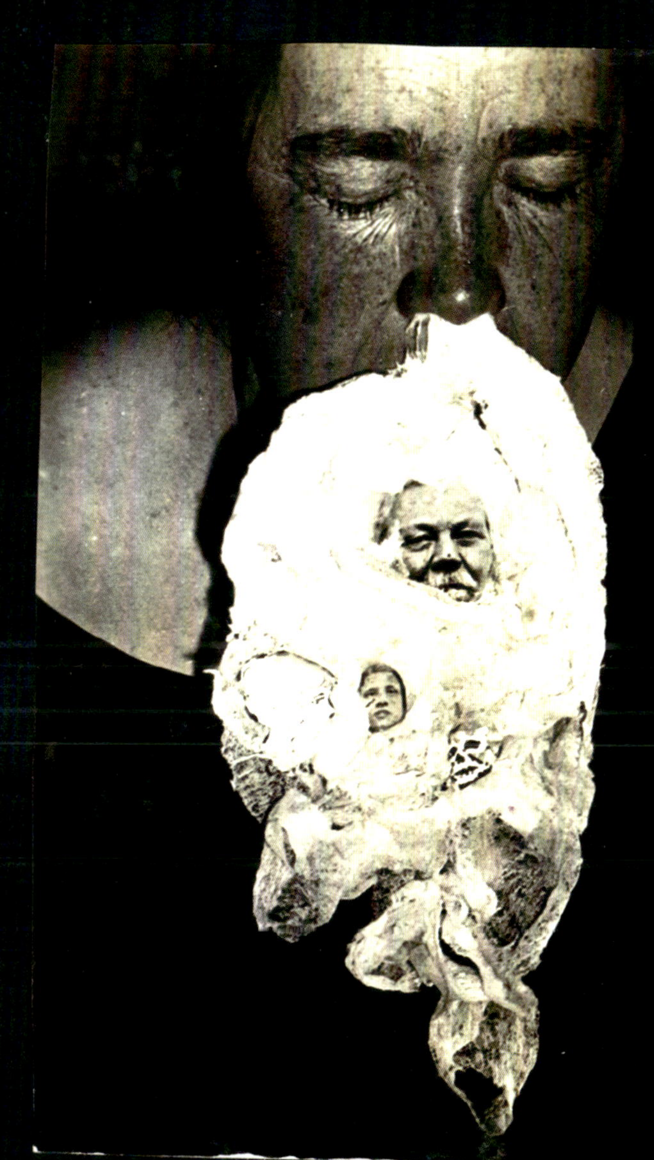

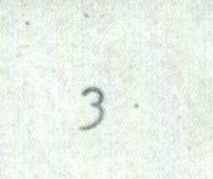

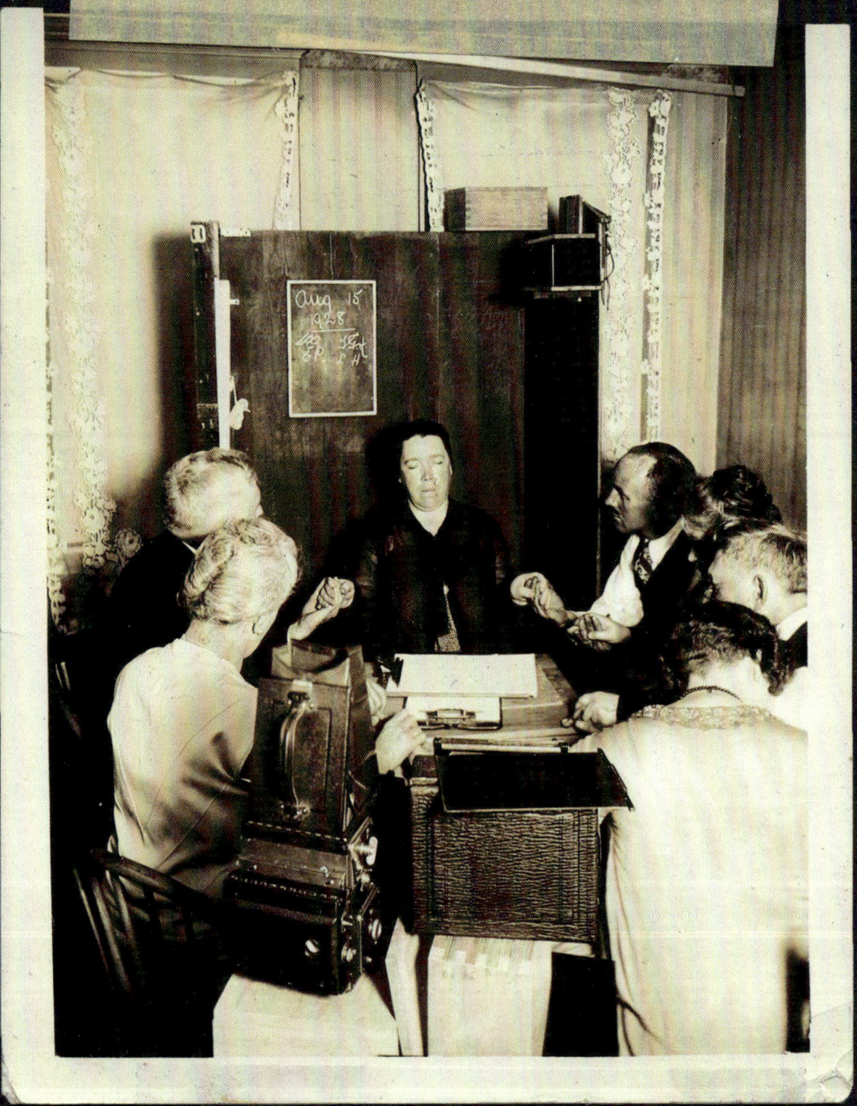

Knotted teleplasm of Aug 15, 1928.
Sitters: W.B.C, Elizabeth, Dr H, Mrs J.B. McMillan, L.H, Dr J.A.H.
Hands of M. held throughout by J.A.H & W.B.C.
Exp. sitting no 41.

(3)

by Richet and the director of the Institut Métapsychique International of Paris, Dr. Gustave Geley.[52] It was the medium's vital force or energy that projected or "emptied" out the plasma from her cells into the room, building a hardly visible lever or rod that moved the table.[53] Hamilton reckoned that the plasm could transform from a vaporous state into a thicker "paste" and that it was extruded from the medium's eyes, nose, mouth, and sometimes fingertips (see Figure 2.14).[54]

The plasmic foundation of all cells is linked etymologically to words such as *plaster* and *plastic* as the building material of biological forms, indicating its ability to create forms such as the hand-shaped ectoplasm reproduced on the cover of this volume, and in Figures 0.1 and 9.5. Doctors Geley, Richet, and Schrenck-Notzing turned to processes observable in the natural world, including amoeboid mobility, chrysalis formation, embryology, and childbirth, to explain the simulacra of shapes, such as human limbs that emanated out of the mediums, which they saw in photographs.[55] By current standards, this is pseudo-science, but scientific theories constantly change and develop. Around 1900, when so many forces were being discovered, as Richet noted above, a psychic-vital force seemed to be in the realm of possibility. Scientific research on ectoplasm propelled by the vital force utilized a popular, biocentric combination of biology and evolutionary theory.[56] Historian Sebastien Normandin explains that by 1900 vitalist biological theories boosted the emerging sciences of Lamarckian evolutionary theory, embryology, dynamic psychology of the unconscious mind, and, I would add, psychical studies.[57] Science historian Robert Brain has demonstrated that Richet, Geley, Bisson, and Schrenck-Notzing, Hamilton's key resources, accepted philosopher Henri Bergson's popular concept that the vital force was aesthetically oriented and teleological in its creation of forms and that biological forms, including ectoplasm, progressed from the simple to the complex and were directed by a built-in "intelligence."[58] I will explore how these ideas developed visually in Chapter 9 of this book.

Fig. 2.14. ***Knotted Teleplasm***, 15 August 1928. UMASC, PC 12, Box 8, Folder 3, Item 3, http://hdl.handle.net/10719/1412924.

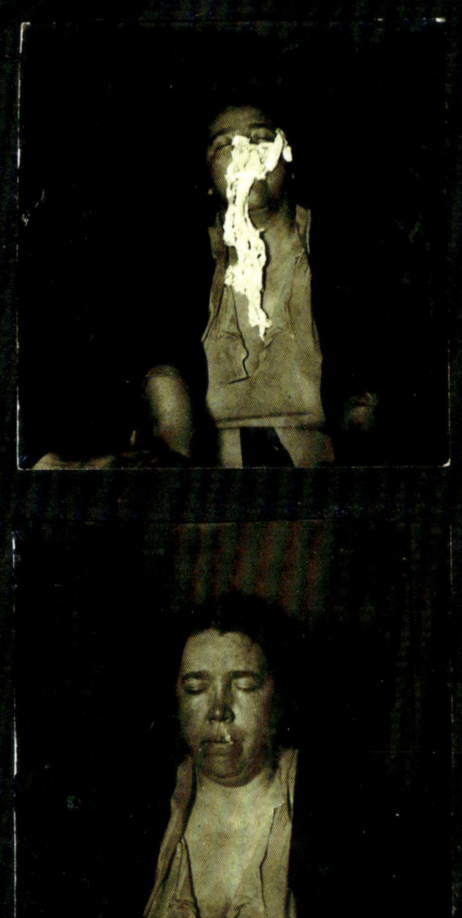

24th March 1929.

Above. Amorphous teleplasmic mass.
Below. Residue of above mass photographed two minutes later.

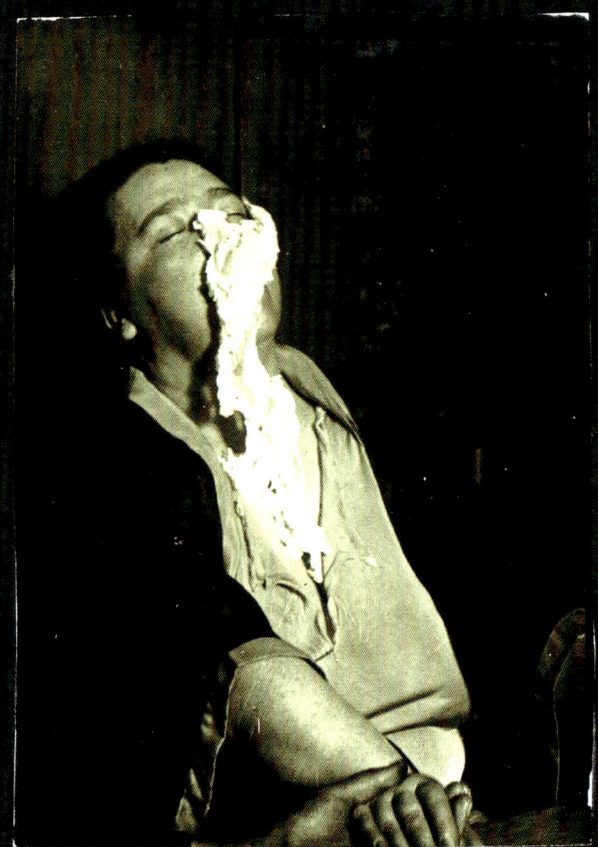

Enlargement of another view of first photograph of 24th March 1929.

Present:- In circle, Mary M., W.B. Cooper, Elizabeth M., Dr. T.G. Hamilton, Mrs Alder, Miss A. Turner, W.E. Hobbs, Mrs. T.G. Hamilton, H.A.V. Green, Dr. J.A. Hamilton. Outside circle, A.C. Whittaker, Jim Hamilton and D.B. McDonald, note-taker.

Richet took credit for coining the term "ectoplasm" in the 1923 edition of *Thirty Years of Psychical Research*: "The word 'ectoplasm,' which I invented for the experiments with Eusapia, seems entirely justified. The ectoplasm is a kind of gelatinous protoplasm, formless at first, that exudes from the body of the medium and takes form later. This embryo-genesis of materializations shows clearly on nearly all the photographs. In the early stages there are always white veils and milky patches and the faces, fingers and drawings are formed little by little in the midst of this kind of gelatinous paste that resembles moist and sticky muslin."[59] Hamilton's group witnessed "pale green ribbons of ectoplasm" when Dr. Le Roi Crandon and Mina Crandon visited Winnipeg in December 1926, and experienced their own ectoplasmic masses in 1928, a few months after the medium Mary Marshall joined the group on a regular basis (see Figure 2.14).

Over the next seven years, T.G. Hamilton photographed seventy-two separate ectoplasmic masses with Mary Marshall and her sister-in-law Susan Marshall. Hamilton used his many cameras to photograph those ectoplasms on fifty evenings, from multiple angles, resulting in 300 aesthetically stunning photographs.[60] He wrote that "observations show this ectoplasm (teleplasm) is an amorphous substance which may be either solid or vaporous. Then, usually very soon, the formless substance becomes organic, it condenses, and forms appear which, when the process is complete, have all the anatomical and physiological characteristics of biological life. The ectoplasm has become a living being, or a fractional part of a living being, but is always closely connected to the body of the medium into which it is absorbed at the end of the experiment."[61] Hamilton preferred the term "teleplasm" (based upon the ancient Greek *tele*, meaning long distance, and *plasm*, meaning moulding or shaping) because he thought that it was more accurate than the term "ectoplasm." But both terms ground the substance in biological cell structure and thus designate it as a natural substance (see Figure 2.15).[62]

Fig. 2.15. T.G. Hamilton, ***Amorphous Mass***, 24 March 1929. UMASC, H.A.V. Green Fonds, MSS 439, Box 1, Folder 2, Item 1.10.

In the homemade, traditional, "Victorian-style" family photo albums in the Hamilton Family Fonds, Marshall's ectoplasms appear to "fall naturally" into the biological conventions developed by Geley in *From the Unconscious to the Conscious* (see Figure 2.15).[63]

Teleplasm moved independently, was very sensitive to light, and showed an "instinct analogous to that of the invertebrate animals." Hamilton went further in animating the substance, suggesting that it acts like a "defenceless animal"; in other words, the substance had an instinct or even intelligence to protect itself from harsh light. It was important to his theory that the substance was vivified, and showed behaviour of sorts, which he attributed to the "trance personality," that survived death and demonstrated "human-like directing intelligences."[64] Hamilton also believed that "the individual makes the transition without changes in memory, personality, and character," using the cellular material of the medium extruded through her skin to materialize and communicate with the human world.[65]

T.G. Hamilton became well known for his "miniature face forms," photographs of the faces of dead people that appeared in the ectoplasm, such as the photograph of the preacher Charles Haddon Spurgeon (see Figure 2.9) and the "face bearing teleplasm" of Conan Doyle in Figures 2.11 and 2.13.[66] Hamilton's group members sometimes glimpsed the ectoplasmic masses on or near the medium during the brief blinding, bright flash release, but the full extent of the substance became visible to Hamilton only on the photographic plates as he developed them.[67] For him, the simplest explanation of the faces poking through the "paste" was that they were manifestations of personalities "independent" of the medium. He rejected the popular term "ghost" and never used the term "spirit," instead preferring terminology from the disciplines of biology, physiology, and psychology.[68] As outlined in Chapter 9, Richet and Geley can be credited with contributing to the early-twentieth-century prominence of ectoplasm as a subject of study among psychical researchers as well as encouraging the minimalist style of scientific visualization epitomized by Hamilton.[69]

Science Supporting Faith in the Twentieth Century

By the 1930s, T.G. Hamilton was at the top of his game. His laboratory and photographs rivalled those of the most respected scientists studying materializations.[70] He "lobbied" to bring the British Medical Association's joint conference with the Canadian Medical Association to Winnipeg, in part I suggest so that he could publicize his research on teleplasm to a more international audience.[71] The organizing committee invited Hamilton to curate a "metapsychic exhibit" of his research photographs and to give a public lecture to explain them. His exhibition of about 100 photographs was one of the earliest displays of scientific photographs in Canada (see Figure 2.2).[72] At the Fort Garry Hotel in August 1930, 500 people paid $1.50 each for lunch and a lecture on the "Mary M. Teleplasms." Later that year, Hamilton developed the talk as "Milestones in Psychical Research," moving into the history of science.[73] In the lectures, Hamilton described himself as a "pioneer" researcher, going against "official" scientific paradigms to redefine both scientific and religious knowledge: "Those of us who stand at the threshold of a new undertaking must travel alone. The only thing to do, is to go straight on, observing, recording, classifying, and comparing all worthwhile and firmly established phenomena, until, by the very strength of our facts, our purpose and our numbers, religion and science shall come to us for such knowledge as we have gained."[74] When he died in 1935 he was praised for advancing knowledge about immortality by many, including Prime Minister William Lyon Mackenzie King, and members of his church.

Psychic science was tolerated as a field of study for about seventy years, and Hamilton participated in the last stage. The death of his generation of researchers between 1930 and 1945—Schrenck-Notzing in 1929, Conan Doyle in 1930, and Richet in 1935[75]—and then the events of the Second World War sounded the death knell for ectoplasm as a topic of credible scientific study and even as a practice in séances. Joining the discipline as its impact was declining, Hamilton was not immune to the increasing questioning of the validity of psychical research. Before his first public lecture in 1926 to the Winnipeg Medical Association, he wondered whether he would have a "shred of professional prestige left when I was through."[76] Given the apparent need for a completely dark space because of the sensitivity of ectoplasm to light, and his own capitulation during his experiments to a "spirit control," he was well aware of compromises in his methodology. Margaret Hamilton Bach lists twenty procedures "demanded by Walter," a trance personality from the beyond who barked out orders in the séances, all of which indicate that Hamilton's laboratory was not an unbiased space.[77] "Winnipeg Walter's" instructions included technological advice about the equipment, the type of clothing that the medium should wear, and that they should be washed and examined physically before the séances.[78]

Hamilton also took exception to the fact that his research fell between the disciplines of science and religion. Some scientists, he suggested, were not interested in the spiritual world and deemed it a matter for religion. At the same time, Christian theologians also ignored psychic research, as he complained in his lectures in 1930:

> Official science, fearing to besmirch her robes of learning, what she hold[s] to be dead and buried superstition, will have none of this new inquiry. To her—a seeker after readily demonstrable facts, there are no such things as spirits of the dead, a spiritual world, or directing intelligences of any kind. Science has relegated such matters entirely to religion, the realm of authority and faith. But religion too looks askance at us. For some years influenced by the scientific point of view, religion has found it the better part of wisdom to ignore many beliefs now held to be based on superstition and the ignorance of an unenlightened age. In other words, religion finds it necessary to pass over in silence the many manifestations of an alleged psychic nature recorded in her sacred writings.[79]

One of Hamilton's first public declarations that the messages received in the séance room and the miniature face forms were directed from outside the medium—by an intelligent trance personality—came in his lecture in 1930 to the British Medical Association.[80] By 1932, he was no longer holding back on his belief that "unseen intelligences" were behind the messages. Furthermore, his experiments were directed by these "unseen collaborators": "Five years, from 1928 to 1933, we gave to this study. Through all these stages, *unseen intelligences* led us, directed us, co-operated with us, and did their best to maintain rigorous conditions of séance-technique-intelligences claiming to be the dead. Reluctant at first, as are most investigators in the beginning, to face these most astounding agencies and their equally astounding claims, we were forced—if worthwhile phenomena were to be secured and made available for examination—to *capitulate* and walk humbly before their greater knowledge in these matters."[81] Having a discarnate personality (ghost) direct your experiments is unorthodox to say the least and violates the objectivity of the scientific method. Hamilton understood this and accepted the consequences.

As a respected family doctor, a former member of the Manitoba Legislative Assembly, and a part of elite Winnipeg settler society, Hamilton enjoyed a status that went a long way toward reassuring his peers that his controls, witnesses, and affidavits were good science and ensuring that his reputation was not tarnished.[82] As his correspondence details, by the 1930s, his photographs were getting high praise, and Hamilton was receiving invitations from Germany, France, Britain, and the United States to take his lectures on the road.[83] He lectured over 100 times in twelve years. Despite the liminality of his research topic for orthodox scientists, Margaret Hamilton Bach mentions that all of his public lectures were received respectfully.[84] His obituaries in 1935 were laudatory, and he was consistently described as a productive citizen who made major contributions to medicine, teaching, Manitoba governance, and his church.[85] William Lyon Mackenzie King, the prime minister of Canada, summed up Hamilton's work this way: "I felt close attachment to him, and was profoundly interested in his work of psychical research. I have looked at him as one of the great pioneers in that field of thought and discovery. I now feel that not only our country, but science, and even civilization itself, has lost one of its greatest servants. . . . His work will go on with even greater effect, though it may take time to disclose this fact."[86]

In her recollections, Lillian Hamilton noted that her husband was sometimes anxious about his field of study. She emphasized, as did Margaret Hamilton Bach, that T.G. Hamilton was sceptical of the idea of spirits surviving death in the first years of his inquiry:[87] "We were to watch little by little the coming of proof that led us step by step to believe that the dead lived and as discarnates did indeed play a large part in the production of so called psychical phenomena."[88] Yet there are hints that he was open from early on to the possibilities of trance personalities communicating after death. Lillian disclosed an event in 1918 that she described as a "prophecy," when T.G. inadvertently became a medium.[89] One day a disembodied voice speaking through him stated "that a great revelation of life after death would come to light . . . and that I, his wife, was blessed among women because the share of this work would fall on my shoulders."[90] T.G. was so rattled by this takeover of his mind and body that he stayed in bed for three days while Lillian administered sedatives. Margaret Hamilton Bach recounted that T.G. had heard a prophetic voice when he was a teenager, and communicated in 1921 with his deceased sister Margaret.[91] In correspondence with Dr. William Franklin Prince in 1924, eight months after Conan Doyle's visit, T.G. admitted that "other intelligences" were directing the experiments.[92] In this volume, historian Esyllt W. Jones asserts the Hamiltons' private séances between 1929 and 1935 were efforts to reach out to their son Arthur, who had died in 1919 during the influenza pandemic. These private séances were in line with popular Spiritualist beliefs and bereavement practices. In the notes for the family séances, Hamilton engaged in warm and sweet conversations with his son Arthur. He also communicated in that setting with the French physician and psychical researcher Gustave Geley, who had died in 1924 and whose book *From the Unconscious to the Conscious* Hamilton relied on, providing a supernatural support system to help him sort out the accusation of fraud against Schrenck-Notzing, a scientist whose work was foundational for him, as will be elaborated on in Chapter 9.

Among the several hundred scientific photographs in the Hamilton Family Fonds are spirit photographs (see Figures 2.16 and 2.17) from 1932 by mediumistic photographers Ada Deane and William Hope, taken during the Hamiltons' visit to

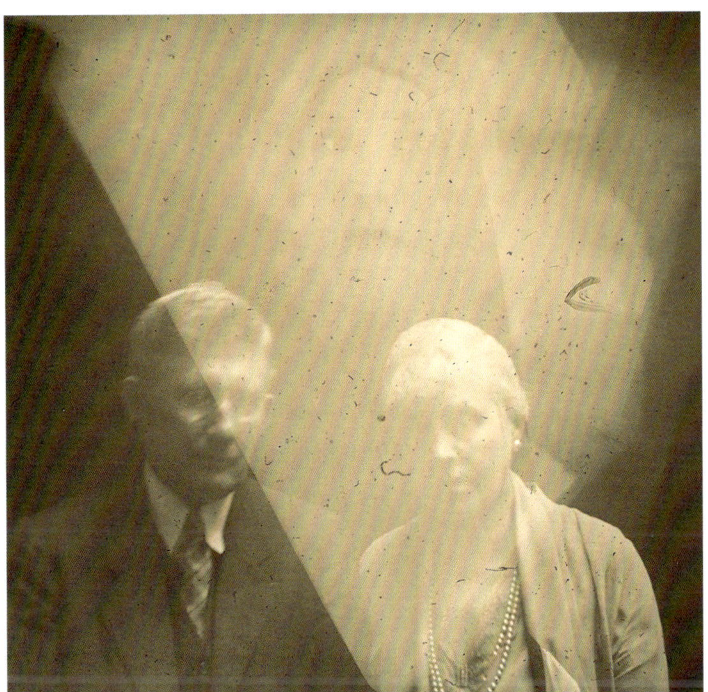

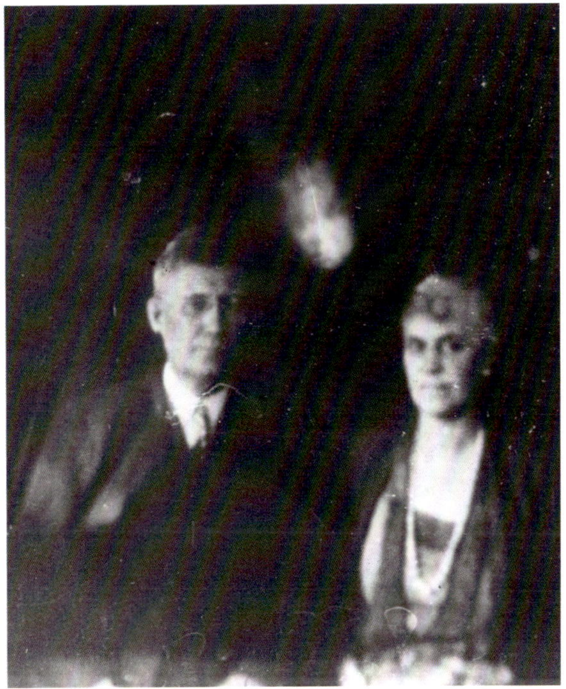

Fig. 2.16. *Left*, Ada Emma Deane, ***T.G. and Lillian Hamilton with a Spirit Extra***, August 1932. UMASC, MSS 14, Box 16, Folder 9, Item 13.3, http://hdl.handle.net/10719/1412659.

Fig. 2.17. *Right*, William Hope, ***T.G. and Lillian Hamilton with Spirit Extras identified as Lillian's Paternal Grandparents***, August 1932. UMASC, Linda Klassen Collection, MSS 480, Box 1, Folder 1.

London, England. Hamilton was said to have accepted the spirit extra in the Deane photograph as his dead sister.[93] Lynn Sharp describes the popularity of Spiritualism, and its variations such as Spiritism, as reformist and decentralized religious philosophies. However, psychic researchers who also accepted "unseen collaborators" were often put off by the "sentimental," consolatory attitude of Spiritualism, believing that it undermined their research and their status.[94] Although T.G. Hamilton accepted that personalities and memories could survive death and even commune with the living early on in his experimentation, and he used séances to conduct his experiments, he never became a Spiritualist, and was dismissive of Spiritualism. As Hamilton put it, "I regard spiritualism as a religion, as a dismal mistake, which ought not to be confused with the research which has for many years, consistently based its findings solely on the proven scientific experimental method." Through his daughter we learn that he felt that those attracted to Spiritualism, while in a state of mourning, might be easy prey for fraudsters. He explained, a new religion was unnecessary because Christianity already contained the fundamentals of the theory of survival: "Let me make it plain that I am not a spiritualist in the commonly accepted or popular sense of the word. Spiritualism as a cult to me is unnecessary since we have already in the essentials of our Christian religion, all and more than is to be found in the higher type of spiritualism."[95] Beth A. Robertson, a historian of gender, science, and technology, argues persuasively that the expression of grief associated with Spiritualism was considered a feminine trait, and Hamilton felt compelled to reject this sentimental response to questions of immortality.[96] In an unpublished manuscript entitled "The Mysteries of Teleplasm," he elevated his research beyond a ritual for bereavment into a philosophical inquiry: "Metapsychics is not a religion but a patient, persistent and on the whole, scientific inquiry into the actuality, nature and implications of these obscure phenomena which appear to have roots in the psyche of the human being."[97] Dr. Hamilton offered his psychic research not simply as chatting with the dead, or as a new religion, but as a hopeful message for all world religions about life after death.

Hamilton successfully negotiated theories from science and Spiritualism while remaining a devout Presbyterian. As Walter Meyer zu Erpen notes in Chapter 4, Hamilton was introduced to supernatural studies through Elmwood Presbyterian, later renamed King Memorial with the establishment of the United Church. Daniel Norman McLachlan, the pastor of King Memorial Church (1904–20), conducted simple experiments with thought transference in 1918 with Hamilton and Reverend Dr. William Talbot Allison, one of Hamilton's closest friends, a professor at Wesley College (now the University of Winnipeg), a Doctor of Divinity, and the minister of King Memorial Church in 1919–20. Both McLachlan and Allison were important in getting the Hamiltons interested in spirit communication in 1918, and it seems, at least in this church, dabbling with popular religions was tolerated, if not encouraged. One telling comparative tale is that in 1899 the Parkdale Methodist Church in Toronto charged Reverend B.F. Austin with heresy for his belief in clairvoyance and Spiritualism. The Methodist Church might have been strict about allowing its members to commune with the dead, but no such pressure seems to have been levied at King Memorial.[98]

Psychic researchers were uncomfortable with some characteristics of Spiritualism, but at the same time they also cherry-picked scientific theories from biology, evolutionary theory, and the pre-Einsteinian model of a universe filled with "ether" to explain the messages and materializations that they were receiving. In this passage from 1934, T.G. Hamilton applies Oliver Lodge's outdated theories of the etheric universe to situate the animate teleplasm through which unseen, "transcendental intelligences" were communicating with him. Teleplasm is a "bridge substance" revealing "other world energy": "I regard teleplasm as a highly sensitive substance responsive to other-world energies, and at the same time visible to us in the physical. It therefore constitutes an intervening substance by means of which transcendental intelligences are enabled, by ideoplastic or other unknown processes, to transmit their conception of certain energy-forms."[99]

In his 2019 book *Physics and Psychics*, Richard Noakes suggests the term "alternative science" to better understand this contested research, explaining how these scientists were able to justify using old-fashioned theories of vitalism and the ether.[100] In 1900, the boundaries of orthodox science were still fluid, and scientists had the freedom to think about unknown realities and parallel worlds.[101] At the same time, the rise of materialism was undermining the Christian church, and psychical research was part of a much deeper societal desire to re-enchant the universe through science, as explained by historian Egil Asprem in *The Problem of Disenchantment: Scientific Naturalism and Esoteric Discourse, 1900–1939*.[102] Immersed in countering the disenchantment that some scientists experienced at the turn of the century, and feeling like they had meaningful information to share, Hamilton, Conan Doyle, and Oliver Lodge pushed through the contradictions and anxieties faced by psychic scientists to disseminate their knowledge to the public. Unsatisfied with the mechanistic concept of the universe, Conan Doyle left behind the cautionary voice of the SPR to spread the optimistic comforting message of immortality: "We believe materialism is the great curse of the world, and it will destroy the world if it is not checked. The old religions have failed to check it. It increases continually. It is clear then that if we are not to despair some new force is needed. It is a force which we believe we can supply."[103] Hamilton could not shed his scientific training and cloaked his views of immortality in scientific language.

By the 1930s psychic science was a conflicted field of study and T.G. Hamilton lived with these paradoxes. He was dedicated to scientific experimental methodology, but he knew that his experiments failed in objectivity; he was an elected elder for his congregation and committed to Presbyterian doctrines, yet he communed with spirits alongside members of his congregation.[104] He took several hundred scientific photographs of teleplasm, but he might also have found consolation in the spirit photograph of his sister's ghost by the one of the best known spirit photographers Ada Deane (see Figure 2.16) and the miniature face form of his deceased son Arthur buried in his archive (see Figures 1.5, 1.6, and 1.7).[105] T.G. clearly enjoyed the private family séances in which he chatted amicably with his son, but he never mentioned those conversations in his publications or research. Publicly, he felt the pressure to position his research within natural laws and scientific inquiry, playing down any of the comfort he may have received from communing with spirits: "If there should be those who deem my findings too incredible for belief or too unusual or bizarre for their liking, may I remind them, in all courtesy, that these are *not my facts but Nature's*, and as Nature's they can accept or reject them. Mother of us all, who can question her integrity?"[106] Before his death, he restated that natural laws governed his work: "Nature guards her secrets well. But it does not require the permission nor the effort of official science, to discover nor to pronounce. Such secrets are free to all to explore. But we must check carefully what we think we may have found."[107] Historian Efram Sera-Shriar notes the strong bias among academics against marginal religious beliefs, privileging even pseudo-scientific psychical research over Spiritualism, and this attitude might have encouraged Hamilton to perform the role of the heroic scientist.

T.G. Hamilton began his search with a curiosity to discover what was going on in the parlour of his house during séances that his wife, Lillian Hamilton, had organized. After twelve years of intense investigations, he had incorporated elements from Spiritualism, science, and mainstream religion, in order to ground Christian theology in what he considered its greatest revelation—the promise of immortality.

Thanks

I thank Oliver Botar, Emma Dux, Walter Meyer zu Erpen, Tim Pearson, Shelley Sweeney, and Christina Thomson for reading and discussing this chapter with me. A special thanks to Walter Meyer zu Erpen for fact checking.

NOTES

1 Arthur Conan Doyle, *Our Second American Adventure* (London: Hodder and Stoughton, 1924), 231. Doyle is the proper family name, but we use Conan Doyle as it is in common usage. The title of this chapter comes from T.G. Hamilton's lecture of 21 May 1926 to the Manitoba Medical Association. He mentioned the title "Experiments and Experiences in Psychical Research" to Dr. L.R.G. Crandon in his letter of 13 May 1926, UMASC, HFF, MSS 14, T.G.H. Correspondence Outgoing 1924–30, Box 4, Folder 5. He reused the title on 11 February 1927 in a lecture to the Winnipeg Women's University Club, as noted in "Clubs," *Winnipeg Evening Tribune*, 12 April 1927, 12, and "Clubdom," *Manitoba Free Press*, 12 April 1927, 11. "Experiencing" the séance is a good title because like all séance rooms, Dr. Hamilton's was also an interactive theatrical space.

2 On Conan Doyle's lecture in Winnipeg, see Michael W. Homer, "Arthur Conan Doyle's Adventures in Winnipeg," *Manitoba History* 25 (1993), http://www.mhs.mb.ca/docs/mb_history/25/doyleinwinnipeg.shtml; Michael W. Homer, "Sir Arthur Conan Doyle: Spiritualism and 'New Religions,'" *Dialogue: A Journal of Mormon Thought* 23, no. 4 (1990): 97–121, http://www.jstor.org/stable/45225937; James B. Nickels, "Psychic Research in a Winnipeg Family: The Recollections and Views of Dr. Glen F. Hamilton," *Manitoba History* 55 (2007), http://www.mhs.mb.ca/docs/mb_history/55/psychicresearch.shtm; "Conan Doyle Lectures on Spirit Phenomena," *Winnipeg Evening Tribune*, 4 July 1923, 8, "Doyle spoke at length on the substance called ectoplasm"; Alvin E. Rodin, Audrey M. Kerr, and Jack D. Key, "Kindred Souls: The Meeting of Drs. Arthur Conan Doyle and Thomas Hamilton," *Canadian Medical Association Journal* 135 (1986): 1216–17; and A.E. Rodin, A. Kerr, and J.D. Key, "Thomas Glen Hamilton MD FACS—Winnipeg Physician Politician and Spiritualist," *Manitoba Medicine* 60, no. 3 (1990): 121–24.

3 Regarding the Winnipeg visit, see Walter Meyer zu Erpen, "Sir Arthur Conan Doyle," 1998; I thank the author for sharing his unpublished draft with me. On audience reaction, see "Conan Doyle Lectures on Spirit Phenomena."

4 "Conan Doyle Lectures on Spirit Phenomena." Conan Doyle described Deane's photographs as the "greatest spirit photograph" ever taken, and during the 1923 tour people wept openly on seeing them. See Kyle Falcon, "The Ghost Story of the Great War: Spiritualism, Psychical Research and the British War Experience, 1914–1939" (PhD diss., Wilfrid Laurier University, 2019), 250 ff. https://scholars.wlu.ca/etd/2125).

5 "Conan Doyle Lectures on Spirit Phenomena": "The spirit photographs shown by Sir Arthur were most remarkable and made a deep impression on the audience." Winnipeg residents were exposed to psychic phenomena through lectures by Arthur Conan Doyle in 1923, and L.R.G. Crandon in 1926, and perhaps by Oliver Lodge in1920 and B.F. Austin in 1921. On the Crandons' visit, see T.G. Hamilton to J. Malcolm Bird, 18 January 1927, UMASC, HFF, MSS 14, T.G.H. Correspondence Outgoing, 1924–30, Box 4, Folder 5. It is notable that Crandon also became more engaged in psychical research after corresponding with Conan Doyle, who had great influence during the 1920s in terms of introducing psychical and Spiritualist points of view, according to David Jaher, *The Witch of Lime Street: Séance, Seduction, and Houdini in the Spirit World* (New York: Crown, 2015), 139. See

also Thomas Tietze, *Margery: An Entertaining and Intriguing Story of One of the Most Controversial Psychics of the Century* (New York: Harper and Row, 1973), 10. I thank Emma Merkling for sharing these sources. Sir Oliver Lodge spoke about Spiritualism on 27–28 April,1920 in Winnipeg at the Board of Trade Hall. He accepted that Christianity included the survival hypothesis.

6 Homer, "Spiritualism and 'New Religions,'" 107.

7 Richard Noakes, *Physics and Psychics: The Occult and the Modern Sciences in Modern Britain* (Cambridge, UK: Cambridge University Press, 2019), 5.

8 Conan Doyle attended his first Spiritualist lecture as early as 1881 and joined the SPR in 1893. Roger Straughan, "Sir Arthur Conan Doyle: 'The St. Paul of Spiritualism,'" in *The Spiritualist Movement: Speaking with the Dead in America and around the World*, vol. 1, ed. Christopher M. Moreman (Santa Barbara: Praeger, 2013), 116. Thanks to Walter Meyer zu Erpen for the information.

9 "Conan Doyle Lectures on Spirit Phenomena." Also see Homer, "Sir Arthur Conan Doyle," 108, in regard to Conan Doyle as a proselyte for Spiritualism after 1916; Homer, "Arthur Conan Doyle's Adventures in Winnipeg"; Rodin, Kerr, and Key, "Thomas Glen Hamilton MD FACS," 8; and Rodin, Kerr, and Key, "Kindred Souls," 1216–17.

10 Regarding the "curse" of materialism, see Conan Doyle: "We spiritualists are all waging the war against materialism. This is the most terrible enemy; it is the cause of all the evils of humanity. It will destroy the world if we do not succeed in strangling it, in overthrowing it. It presents itself as a many headed monster, the materialism of a society thirsting after pleasure and material riches, the materialism of science, materialism of morals, materialism of Churches, temples, mosques and synagogues, formalist, dogmatic, and trivial, forgetful of that which is true living communion with the Higher World. The different religions, belated in their worn-out conceptions and their rigid formulas, have forgotten the very meaning of these words 'Communion with the Higher World.'" Arthur Conan Doyle, "First Lecture (Sunday 6 September 1925)," https://www.arthur-conan-doyle.com/index.php=Lectures_at_the_International_Spiritualist_Congress_of_Paris_1925.

11 The Hamiltons likely attended Conan Doyle's talk; see Walter Meyer zu Erpen, "The Quest for Immortality: Psychical Research in Winnipeg and the Role of Medical Doctors, Lawyers, Clergymen, and Other Community Leaders between 1918 and 1935," compiled 1992–2018, 17, https://survivalresearch.ca/Quest_for_Immortality_1992-2018_compilation.pdf. Given that Isaac Pitblado spent the day with Doyle and Leckie (see Homer, "Arthur Conan Doyle's Adventures in Winnipeg," n. p.), and because Reverend Allison, the minister of King Memorial in 1919 and 1920 took them to the Hamiltons' house (according to Margaret Hamilton Bach), I think it probable that all these men attended the lecture. See Margaret Hamilton Bach, UMASC, MSS 14, HFF, Telekinesis 1922–27, Box 15, Folder 8. Meyer zu Erpen, "The Quest for Immortality," 2 ff., states that Hamilton, Allison, and McLachlan conducted experiments in thought transference in 1918. One register in the HFF suggests that there were twenty-eight sittings between 1920 and 1921; see UMASC, HFF, MSS 14, Box 15, Folder 6. Also see Margaret Hamilton Bach, UMASC, HFF, MSS 14, Notes 1921–85, Box 17, Folder 10, 5.

12 "Metapsychical" science began in 1905, Hamilton stated, quoting Richet; see "Milestones in Psychical Research," UMASC, HFF, MSS 14, British Medical Association, Winnipeg, 1930, Box 1, Folder 12, 4. "Sir Arthur spoke at length on the substance called ectoplasm which he said emanated from the medium and which spirits used for materialization. It was the forms so materialized which had been photographed"; "Conan Doyle Lectures on Spirit Phenomena."

Homer, "Arthur Conan Doyle's Adventures in Winnipeg," 113, states that Conan Doyle repeated his lecture throughout the North America 1923 tour and that he showed both spirit photographs and ectoplasmic photographs. This definition of ectoplasm comes from Arthur Conan Doyle, "Lectures at the International Spiritualist Congress of Paris 1925," *The Arthur Conan Doyle Encyclopedia*, n.p. https://www.arthur-conan-doyle.com/index.php?title=Lectures_at_the_International_Spiritualist_Congress_of_Paris_1925 (accessed 9 January 2023). Also see his slide lecture where he included "examples of ectoplasm taken from different mediums in different parts of the world." Sir Arthur Conan Doyle Collection, Works, 2.9, Notes for Lantern Slide Lectures, 57, Harry Ransom Centre. For academic analyses of ectoplasm, see Karen Beckman, *Vanishing Women: Magic, Film, and Feminism* (Durham, NC: Duke University Press, 2003); Marina Warner, *Phantasmagoria* (Oxford: Oxford University Press, 2006); Marina Warner, "Ethereal Body: The Quest for Ectoplasm," *Cabinet* 12 (2003), https://www.cabinetmagazine.org/issues/12/warner.php; Neil Matheson, "Ectoplasm and Photography: Mediumistic Performances for Camera," in *The Machine and the Ghost: Technology and Spiritualism in Nineteenth to Twenty-First-Century Art and Culture*, ed. Neil Matheson and Sas Mays (Manchester: Manchester University Press, 2013), 78–102; L. Anne Delgado, "Bawdy Technologies and the Birth of Ectoplasm," 1 September 2011, Genders 1998–2013: College of Arts and Sciences, University of Colorado Boulder, https://www.colorado.edu/gendersarchive1998-2013/2011/09/01/bawdy-technologies-and-birth-ectoplasm; Andreas Fischer, "The Reciprocal Adaptation of Optics and Phenomena: The Photographic Recoding of Materializations," in *The Perfect Medium: Photography and the Occult*, ed. Chéroux Clément and Andreas Fischer (New Haven, CT: Yale University Press, 2005), 171–216; and M. Brady Bower, *Unruly Spirits: The Science of Psychic Phenomena in Modern France* (Urbana: University of Illinois Press, 2010).

13 My understanding of ectoplasm is based upon Robert Brain, "Materialising the Medium: Ectoplasm and the Quest for Supra-Normal Biology in *Fin-de-Siècle* Science and Art," in *Vibratory Modernism*, ed. Anthony Enns and Shelley Trower (London: Palgrave Macmillan, 2013), 112–41, specifically 128–29.

14 Thanks to Anton Wagner and Walter Meyer zu Erpen for alerting me to the lecture by Reverend B.F. Austin in which he planned to display over 100 "spirit photos and psychic pictures" in Winnipeg on 3 October 1921. Oliver Lodge was in Winnipeg speaking about Spiritualism in 1920. There were four press reviews of Hamilton's "Metapsychic Exhibit"; see "Pictures of Teleplasm Shown to Delegates," *Winnipeg Free Press*, 28 August 1930; The Winnipeg Meeting of the British Medical Association, 26–29 August 1930 reprint from a report of lecture as published in a Winnipeg paper, "Psychic Expert Shows Pictures of Experiments," *Winnipeg Tribune*, 28 August 1930; H.A.V. Green, "Report of the BMA Convention in Winnipeg 27 August 1930," quoted in part in *British Psychic Review*, 30 October 1930; and C.B. Pyper, "Psychic Research," publication unknown, 29 August 1930, all articles found in UMASC, HFF, MSS 14, British Medical Association, Winnipeg, 1930, Box 1, Folder 12. According to Margaret Hamilton Bach, T.G. Hamilton "lobbied" to have the BMA conference of 1930 in Winnipeg, with steep competition from Toronto and Montreal. See UMASC, HFF, MSS 14, Index of T.G.H.'s Professional Life 1903-1935, Box 1, Folder 6, comments on the life and interests of T.G.H., 8. He was offered a space to exhibit his psychical research photographs. The exhibition was large, consisting of 100 photographs and charts, and he was then invited to speak at the BMA conference in a lunch slot to explain the photographs. See T.G. Hamilton to Dr. J.C. Grant, 6 May 1930, in which Hamilton says, "I beg to apply for space in

your exhibit" for ten frames (twenty-four by thirty inches with ten photos each), plus stereoscopic views and equipment, in UMASC, HFF, MSS 14, T.G.H. Correspondence Outgoing 1924–30, Box 4, Folder 5. Hamilton lectured in New York City at Carnegie Hall and Dartmouth in December 1930, "Milestones in Psychical Research." See UMASC, HFF, MSS 14, Index of T.G.H.'s Professional Life 1903–35, Box 1, Folder 6, 7, and UMASC, HFF, MSS 14, British Medical Association, Box 1, Folder 12.

15 T.G. Hamilton to Rev Allen Hubband, February 8, 1928, UMASC, HFF, MSS 14, T.G.H. Correspondence Outgoing, 1924-1930, Box 4, Folder 5. Hamilton, "Milestones in Psychical Research," op. cit., 9. Margaret Hamilton Bach described Conan Doyle as gullible, perhaps reflecting the attitude of her father. She thought the bereavement aspect of Spiritualism left participants vulnerable to fraud. UMASC, HFF, MSS 14, Richard E. Bennett, "Interview with Margaret Hamilton Bach," 26 November 1980, Box 3, Folder 9, 10.

16 Conan Doyle was a long-standing member of the Society for Psychical Research in the United Kingdom and the vice-president of the short-lived Society for the Study of Supernormal Pictures. Hamilton joined the American Society for Psychical Research in 1923 and started the Winnipeg Society for Psychical Research in 1931. See UMASC, HFF, MSS 14, Index of T.G.H. Profile 1903–35, Box 1, Folder 6, 4. See Meyer zu Erpen, "The Quest for Immortality," n 35.

17 Noakes, "Introduction" in *Physics and Psychics*, 1–20, especially 18; Peter J. Bowler, *Reconciling Science and Religion: The Debate in Early-Twentieth-Century Britain* (Chicago: University of Chicago Press, 2001); Efram Sera-Shriar, "Photographic Plates and Spirit Fakes: Remembering Harry Price's Investigation of William Hope's Spirit Photography at Its Centenary," *Science Museum Group Journal* 17 (2002), http://dx.doi.org/10.15180/221707, (accessed 9 September 2022).

18 Hamilton, "Milestones in Psychical Research," UMASC, HFF, MSS 14, British Medical Association, Winnipeg, Box 1, Folder 12, 7. Noakes, *Physics and Psychics*, 4–5.

19 Arthur Conan Doyle to an unidentified person, 5 May 1929, 3, 8, Letters, 1835-1964, Sir Arthur Conan Doyle Collection, Harry Ransom Center. As he hints, Richet, Geley, and Flammarion did not accept the notion of discarnate personalities, but they did accept the phenomenon of materialization. Harry Price also had a library of hundreds of books about psychical phenomena by the late 1920s that Conan Doyle would have known. Hamilton built up a significant research library. I follow Noakes' terminology of psychical research and psychical science as the common term for the study of psychic phenomena especially in the 1920s, *Physics and Psychics*, 2, n 5.

20 For the development of psychical research in France at the *fin de siècle*, see Sofie Lachapelle, *Investigating the Supernatural: From Spiritism and Occultism to Psychical Research and Metapsychics in France, 1853–1931* (Baltimore: Johns Hopkins University Press, 2011); John Monroe, *Laboratories of Faith: Mesmerism, Spiritism, and Occultism in Modern France* (Ithaca: Cornell University Press, 2008); Bower, *Unruly Spirits*; and Jeremy Stolow, "Mediumnic Lights, X^x Rays, and the Spirit Who Photographed Herself," *Critical Inquiry* 42, no. 4 (2016): 923–51, https://doi.org/10.1086/686962 (accessed 9 September 2022). A key text for Hamilton was Gustave Geley, *From the Unconscious to the Conscious*, trans. Stanley de Brath (London: William Collins, Sons and Company, 1920), 66–67. He bought a hardcopy of the book, housed in the Janice Hamilton fonds UMASC, MSS 323, A10-01, PC 272. Geley stated that "the purely mechanical concept of nature is insufficient," arguing that the concept of a directed "dynamo-psychicism," that

is the vital force, was challenging materialism. Hamilton's copy of the book is underlined, especially where de Brath explains Bergson's vitalism in the introduction.

21 Noakes, *Physics and Psychics*, 2; Egil Asprem, *The Problem of Disenchantment: Scientific Naturalism and Esoteric Discourse, 1900–1939* (Boston: Brill, 2014). According to Arthur Conan Doyle, *History of Spiritualism*, (1926, reprinted, New York: Arno Press, 1975) vol. 2, 248, "it [spiritualism] founds our belief in life after death and in the existence of invisible worlds, not upon ancient tradition or upon vague intuitions, but upon proven facts, so that a science of religion may be built up."

22 Heather Wolffram, "In the Laboratory of the Ghost-Baron: Parapsychology in Germany in the Early 20th Century," *Endeavour* 33, no. 4 (2009): 152–57.

23 Quotation from Bennett, "Interview with Margaret Hamilton Bach," 10; "doctor of one thousand séances" quoted from "First Archival Symposium," University of Manitoba, 23 November 1979, 7, UMASC, HFF, MSS 14, "Interview with Margaret Hamilton Bach," 1979–1981, Box 3, Fonds 9.

24 Esyllt W. Jones, "Spectral Influenza: T.G. and Lillian Hamilton, Interwar Spiritualism, and Pandemic Disease," in *Epidemic Encounters: New Interpretations of Pandemic Influenza in Canada, 1918–1920*, ed. Esyllt W. Jones and Magda Fahrni (Vancouver: UBC Press, 2012), 193–221.

25 On the popularity of the reformist religion of Spiritism and Spiritualism, see Lynn L. Sharp, *Secular Spirituality: Reincarnation and Spiritism in Nineteenth-Century France* (Lanham, MD: Lexington Books, 2006). Lillian Hamilton recalled how the parlour game of table turning got her interested in séances in 1920. Lillian Hamilton Recollections, UMASC, HFF, MSS 14, "The Story of the Hamilton Experiments/Process," Box 15, Folder 6. See also Nickels, "Psychic Research in a Winnipeg Family."

26 Simone Natale, "The Medium on the Stage: Trance and Performance in Nineteenth-Century Spiritualism," *Early Popular Visual Culture* 9, no. 3 (2011): 239–55.

27 T.G. Hamilton, "The Mysteries of Teleplasm," annotated c. 1926 (Meyer zu Erpen dates it c. 1928–30), UMASC, HFF, MSS14, "The Story of the Hamilton Experiments/Process," Box 15, Folder 6. On Crookes, see Noakes, *Physics and Psychics*, especially Chapter 2.

28 Margaret Hamilton Bach stated in a *Morningside* interview on 8 April 1981, UMASC, HFF, MSS 14, Box 3, Folder 9, that Conan Doyle wrote to the Hamiltons asking to attend a séance, but I have not located that letter in the HFF; see also UMASC, HFF, MSS 14, Telekinesis 1922–27, Box 15, Folder 8, 10. Conan Doyle sent the Hamiltons a dedicated copy of *Our American Adventure*, 1923, and a thank you note written on 5 July where he mentions "Winnipeg should be a psychic centre." I thank Dorothy Bach, and Walter Meyer zu Erpen for sharing this discovery with me.

29 Conan Doyle, *Our Second American Adventure*, 226–27; Nickels, "Psychic Research in a Winnipeg Family." The séances between 1921 and 1922 were not photographed and were conducted in the family living room, and thus I am not considering them "science" experiments. Conan Doyle accepted that the experiment had been going on for two years, though he credited T.G. and not Lillian. It should be noted that Lillian Hamilton began the inquiry with the mediums in 1920–21, and Conan Doyle, as stated in this quote, accepted the early séances as scientific. Lillian Hamilton, "Records of a Canadian Circle; A Study of Psychic Messages and Physical Phenomena," *Light* 10 June, 1922, 632–3. For a description of the luminous painted legs and the 8 by 10 inch square on the table, see letter to William

Prince in 24 January, 1923, UMASC, HFF, MSS 14, T.G.H. Outgoing Correspondence, Box 4, Folder 5.

30 Hamilton did not use the term "spirit" or "ghost," and he tended to use terms from psychical research such as "psychic force." See Lillian Hamilton, "T.G.'s First Public Lecture," UMASC, HFF, MSS 14, "The Story of the Hamilton Experiments," Box 15, Folder 6, 14, and Hamilton's responses to Agnew Harvey, 21 March 1931, UMASC, HFF, MSS 14, T.G.H. Correspondence Incoming, 1931-32, Box 4, Folder 3; he described teleplasm as an unstable combination of matter plus energy. See "Nervous Energy of the Medium or Vital Electricity," "Psychic Expert Shows Pictures of Experiments," *Winnipeg Tribune*, 28 August 1930, UMASC, HFF, MSS 14, British Medical Association, Winnipeg, 1930, Box 1, Folder 12. Meyer zu Erpen, "The Quest for Immortality," 1, explains Hamilton's trance personalities as "human mind, consciousness, or personality survives bodily death."

31 Some scholars attribute Lillian Hamilton's sustained interest in trance personalities to the loss of their young son in 1919 to influenza. In "The Story of the Hamilton Experiments/Process," UMASC, HFF, MSS 14, Box 15, Folder 6, Lillian described joining table-turning "parlour games," for the entertainment value, with family friends (Ernest Court) and Elizabeth Poole in which messages were spelled out; in particular the 20 October 1920 séance really impressed her. There are lists and notes throughout the HFF suggesting regular séances were organized by Lillian between 1920 and 1923. See UMASC, HFF, MSS 14, Notes, 1921–1985, Box 17, Folder 10, UMASC, HFF, MSS 14, "The Story of the Hamilton Experiments/Process," Box 15, Folder 6, and UMASC, HFF, MSS 14, Telekinesis 1922 -1927, Box 15, Folder 8. We can conclude that Lillian was interested in table turning before T.G. and that she read some of the key books, including those by F.W.H. Myers and W. J. Crawford, early on and promoted their research. In UMASC, MSS 14, HFF, "The Story of the Hamilton Experiments/Process," Box 15, Folder 6, she mentions how she laboured with T.G. to set the right tone for his talk in 1926 to the Manitoba Medical Association. See also in the same file "T.G.'s First Public Lecture," 14.

32 T.G. Hamilton began to take the séances more seriously in winter/spring 1923. Lillian Hamilton, UMASC, HFF, MSS 14, "The Story of the Hamilton Experiments/Process," Box 15, Folder 6. As she states, "we were to watch little by little the coming of proof that led us step by step to believe that the dead lived and as discarnates did indeed play a large part in the production of so called psychical phenomena." T.G. Hamilton determined at one point that table turning was beyond involuntary muscle spasms; Margaret Hamilton Bach's account of T.G. becoming interested in Lillian's séances in UMASC, HFF, MSS 14, Telekinesis 1922–27, Box 15, Folder 8. See brief notes on the first few years in Hamilton Bach, UMASC, HFF, MSS 14, "The Story of the Hamilton Experiments in Psychic Experiments/Process," Box 15, Folder 6; Nickels, "Psychic Research in a Winnipeg Family"; and Meyer zu Erpen, "The Quest for Immortality."

33 Lillian Hamilton states that he had become serious about testing mediumship after this message was delivered from W.T. Stead in 1923, UMASC, HFF, MSS 14; "The Story of the Hamilton Experiments/Process," Box 15, Folder 6, 9. Before July 1923, the Hamilton séances were mostly set up in their parlour with the fireplace as a light source, seen in Figure 2.3, a "posed" photograph from March 1923. Lillian described the séance by firelight in UMASC, HFF, MSS 14, "The Story of the Hamilton Experiments/Process," Box 15, Folder 6.

34 The date of January 1923 comes from Lillian Hamilton in UMASC, HFF, MSS 14, "The Story of the Hamilton Experiments/Process," Box 15, Folder 6. The quotation about the scientific method comes from "Psychic Expert Shows Pictures of

Experiments," *Winnipeg Tribune*, 28 August 1930, 6; Hamilton's "scientific method, rigorous control of experimental details, repeated observations, and experiments . . . with photography wherever possible, had been followed from the first." The Hamiltons also conducted a family circle from 1929 to 1935 led by Lillian Hamilton with a male medium.

35 UMASC, HFF, MSS 14, Richard Bennett, "Interview with Margaret Hamilton Bach," 26 November 1980, Box 3, Folder 9, 11, 13.

36 Quotations from UMASC, HFF, MSS 14, Bennett, "Interview with Margaret Hamilton Bach," Box 3, Folder 9, 11. Emphasis mine. There is a photograph of the new laboratory dated July 1923, but it is a "posed" photograph re-enacting elements of the Conan Doyle visit with the illuminated table, UMASC, HFF, PC 12, Box 8, Box 1. Margaret Hamilton Bach states that there are three posed photographs in the HFF; UMASC, HFF, MSS 14, Bennett, "Interview with Margaret Hamilton Bach," Box 3, Folder 9, 11–13. One way to date photos is by the badminton net attached to the wood cabinet in 1926, although according to Dr Hamilton to William Prince there was a mosquito net in place in 1924. UMASC, HFF, MSS 14, T.G.H. Outgoing Correspondence, Box 4, Folder 5. There are a few photographs of telekinetic events dated between 1924 and 1925, but these dates are uncertain, and sometimes there are contradictory dates inscribed on them. Hamilton also used photography to illustrate his medical publications by 1924, but it seems successful, systematic photography in the séance room probably began between 1925 and 1926. Hamilton used the terms "psychic photography" and "laboratory" for this room and described using flashbulbs by 1931; see T.G. Hamilton to Dr. Mees, Kodak Laboratory, 17 October 1931, UMASC, HFF, MSS 14, Outgoing Correspondence, 1931 -1935, Box 5, Folder 1. The Doyle séance was in the newly set-up laboratory, and Conan Doyle described a curtain, so we know the wooden cabinet had not yet been constructed. The "junk room" was converted into the laboratory, and note the sewing machine in the corner; see UMASC, HFF, MSS 14, "The Story of the Hamilton Experiments/Process," Box 15, Folder 6. Margaret Hamilton Bach, "Taken from Tape," UMASC, HFF, MSS 14, Notes 1921–85, Box 17, Folder 10, and Telekinetic Phenomena 1921-1927 details the laboratory, UMASC, HFF, MSS 14, Telekinesis 1922-1927, Box 15, Folder 8.

37 Glen Hamilton describes his dad building the cabinet in Nickels, "Psychic Research in a Winnipeg Family," 5. T.G. Hamilton described the séance cabinet he built in March 1923 in a letter to William Prince on 24 January 1923; see UMASC, HFF, MSS 14, T.G.H. Outgoing Correspondence, Box 4, Folder 5. For details on cabinet construction, the best wood to use, and low light levels, see T.G. Hamilton to Chester Doty, 6 April 1931, UMASC, HFF, MSS 14, T.G.H. Outgoing Correspondence, Box 5, Folder 1.

38 These details come from Hamilton's correspondence in the late 1920s; see UMASC, HFF, MSS 14, Box 4, Folder 5. Also see T.G. Hamilton, "Mary M. Teleplasms," UMASC, HFF, MSS 14, British Medical Association, Winnipeg, 1930, Box 1, Folder 12, 4. Margaret Hamilton Bach stated that Hamilton was an amateur photographer with a darkroom and was friends with studio photographers William Metcalfe and A.C. Whittaker from Imperial Optical. UMASC, HFF, MSS 14, Bennett, "Interview with Margaret Hamilton Bach," Box 3, Folder 9, 23. It should be noted that photographs were enlarged, cropped, and copied, especially for publication.

39 Lillian Hamilton described herself as the "custodian" of the experiments, but "collaborator" is a better term; see Lillian Hamilton, UMASC, HFF, MSS 14, Experiments—Notes, January–June 1936, Box 17, Folder 5, 7, and UMASC, HFF, MSS 14, Bennett, "Interview with Margaret Hamilton Bach," Box 3, Folder 9, 18. Lillian was an active reader and researcher of psychical phenomena.

She led the early experiments between 1920 and 1922 (see UMASC, HFF, MSS 14, "The Story of the Hamilton Experiments/Process," Box 15, Folder 6), and the family circle (1929–35, once a week), and then directed her own experiments after T.G. died. Lillian helped T.G. with his first public speech, outlined his research in photo albums, and sometimes wrote to scientists on his behalf. She also looked after the mediums. T.G. oversaw the lab and equipment. See Margaret Hamilton Bach in her taped discussion, "Taken from Tape," UMASC, HFF, MSS 14, Notes 1921–85, Box 17, Folder 10, and UMASC, HFF, MSS 14, Telekinesis 1922-27, Box 15, Folder 8.

40 Margaret Hamilton Bach laid out the protocols in "Taken from Tape," UMASC, HFF, MSS 14, Notes 1921–85, Box 17, Folder 10, 4, and UMASC, HFF, MSS 14, "The Story of the Hamilton Experiments/Process," Box 15, Folder 6, page marked 3-III. T.G. Hamilton explained the costume and set-up in a letter to L.R.G. Crandon, 21 March 1930, UMASC, HFF, PC 12, Annotated Photo Album, Group IV–VIII, Box 8, Folder 4. Mediums were often women, and the position afforded certain privileges, but also subjected mediums to invasive and highly unethical treatment by investigators, including regular vaginal exams and forced regurgitations, as Schrenck-Notzing outlines in *Phenomenon of Materialisation*, trans. E. E. Fournier d'Albe (London: Kegan Paul, Trench, Trubner; New York: E. P. Dutton, 1923) 149 ff. The mediums in the Hamilton experiments were undressed, washed, and searched. See UMSAC, HFF, MSS 14, Historical Summary, Notes 1921-85, Box 17, Folder 10.

41 Conan Doyle, in the quotation on page 43, noted that there was a growing scientific literature on mediumship, and the Hamiltons also collected books and articles and pasted together albums of hand-transcribed quotations from key scientists, building the best paranormal library in Canada. I believe that Hamilton's photographs were better received than those of Dr. Le Roi Crandon because they are Modernist in style. Crandon's photographs go past the uncanny into the uncomfortable.

42 Margaret Hamilton Bach mentioned the high costs to carry out and disseminate this research, UMASC, HFF, MSS 14, Notes 1921–85, Box 17, Folder 10, page marked 99.

43 The Sir Conan Doyle archive at the Harry Ransom Center holds two Hamilton photographs of ectoplasmic materialization from the 1920s showing the development of ectoplasm; one is the Spurgeon photograph of 1 May 1929. Perhaps Pitblado sent the photograph to Conan Doyle; Homer, "Arthur Conan Doyle's Adventures in Winnipeg," n.p., states that they knew each other. Pitblado attended only four séances with the Hamiltons but was there for the December 1928 Spurgeon mass. Also see John Harvey, *Photography and Spirit* (London: Reaktion, 2007), 55, on Spurgeon as a spirit extra.

44 Hamilton, "Milestones in Psychical Research," UMASC, HFF, MSS 14, British Medical Association, Winnipeg, 1930, Box 1, Folder 12, 3 Also important for Hamilton were researchers Dr. William Jackson Crawford and Dr. L.R.G. and Margery Crandon from Boston. The Crandons travelled up to Winnipeg in December 1926 and organized three sittings. Margaret Hamilton Bach states that they saw "ribbons of green ectoplasm"; UMASC, HFF, MSS 14, Index of T.G.H.'s Professional Life 1903–35, Box 1, Folder 6. Hamilton spent four days with the Crandons in Boston; see letter to Clive McAlister October 23, 1928, UMASC, HFF, MSS 14, T.G.H. Correspondence Outgoing 1924-1930, Box 4, Folder 5. Not only did Hamilton buy the translated works of Schrenck-Notzing and Geley, but he also communicated with Geley in 1933, as a discarnate personality, in the private family circle. Geley's elaborate explanation of ideoplasm in the Eva Carrière photos demonstrates how the séance communications were targeted to meet the needs

of the sitters and that by the 1930s Hamilton knew that Geley, Schrenck-Notzing, Bisson, and Carrière were suspect in psychical research circles.

45 Samuel Aykroyd quotation, Student of Psychic Phenomena (Samuel Aykroyd), "Psychic Science," *The Kingston Whig-Standard*, 20 Nov 1928, 4. T.G. Hamilton to Dr. Mees, 17 October 1931, UMASC, HFF, MSS 14, T.G.H. Correspondence, Outgoing, Box 5, Folder 1. I make this observation based on the profuse praise that he received in letters. Crandon compared Hamilton to Schrenck-Notzing; see L.R.G. Crandon to T.G. Hamilton, 12 November 1930. "You have Geley and Schrenck-Notzing and Walter all knocked out of the park"; L.R.G. Crandon to T.G. Hamilton, 8 March 1931 UMASC, HFF, MSS 14, T.G.H. Correspondence Incoming 1931-32, Box 4, Folder 3. Hamilton compared his own photographs with those of Schrenck-Notzing: "Dr. Schrenck-Notzing's work is particularly interesting to us since our photos of people *are so like them*" (emphasis mine); T.G. Hamilton to J.E. Hett, 22 April 1931, UMASC, HFF, MSS 14, T.G.H. Correspondence Outgoing 1931–34, Box 5, Folder 1. Also see T.G. Hamilton to L.R.G. Crandon, 21 March 1930, UMASC, HFF, PC 12, Annotated Photo Album, Group IV–VIII, Box 8, Folder 4: "The materialized mass very closely resembles some teleplasmic makeup in Schrenck-Notzing's and in your own experiences." He also pasted his own photo into his copy of Schrenck-Notzing's book. Lillian Hamilton worried that Crandon's comments were too strong. See Lillian Hamilton to Dr. Malcolm Bird, 14 March 1929, UMASC, HFF, MSS 14, Lillian Hamilton Correspondence Outgoing, 1931-1956, Box 5, Folder 9.

46 See Hamilton, "Milestones in Psychical Research," 1–2 op cit.; T.G. Hamilton, *Intention and Survival: Psychical Research Studies and the Bearing of Intentional Actions by Trance Personalities on the Problem of Human Survival*, ed. J.D. Hamilton (Toronto: Macmillan, 1942); and Margaret Hamilton Bach's interesting writings on psychical history in the 1970s and 1980s in the HFF.

47 Charles Richet, *Thirty Years of Psychical Research: Being a Treatise on Metapsychics*, trans. Stanley de Brath (London: William Collins Sons, 1923), 9–10. On lucidity, see Chapter 1. On French psychical research, see Lachapelle, *Investigating the Supernatural*, and John Monroe, *Laboratories of Faith*.

48 See Carlos S. Alvarado, "Human Radiations: Concepts of Force in Mesmerism, Spiritualism and Psychical Research," *Journal of the Society for Psychical Research* 70, no. 3 (2006): 138–62, quotation at 138; and Bowler, *Reconciling Science and Religion*, 135–36.

49 Hamilton, "Mary M. Teleplasms," 3.

50 Richet, *Thirty Years of Psychical Research*, 442. Richet calls them rigid rays, based upon Ochorowicz's observations, 440. On Ochorowicz, see Stolow, "Mediumnic Lights."

51 "'Nervous energy of the medium or vital electricity'"; quoting Hamilton, "Psychic Expert Shows Pictures of Experiments," *Winnipeg Tribune*, 28 August 1930, 6.

52 Geley created a category called "supernormal" biology and physiology that Hamilton adopted. Geley, *From the Unconscious to the Conscious*, 163–64. In the translator's note, Stanley de Brath states that Geley was updating Bergson's *élan vital* with a "concrete energy," defining "energy as an influence forming all the varieties of cellular tissue out of one primordial substance and molding those tissues into organic form under the impulsion of a Directing Idea" (vii). Hamilton underlined vitalist quotations in his copy of Geley's book, *Intention and Survival*. Hamilton personifies nature as a woman, 226; he also uses the term "directing intelligences," 11, 50. Margaret Hamilton Bach, UMASC, HFF, MSS 14, Index of T.G.H.'s Professional Life,

1903-35, Box 1, Folder 6, 8. On how Lamarckian evolutionary theory was widely accepted in Europe and North America at the turn of the century, see Peter J. Bowler, *The Non-Darwinian Revolution: Reinterpreting a Historical Myth* (Baltimore: Johns Hopkins University Press, 1988). On the context of biological interpretation, see Brain, "Materialising the Medium."

53 Hamilton took this understanding from Richet. As Richet put it, "the medium *empties herself*, so to speak, in order to constitute the new being which emanates from her"; Charles Richet, "Concerning the Phenomenon Called Materialisation," *Annals of Psychical Science* 2 (Nov. 1905), part 1, 207–210, and part 2, 269–289, 288. During the summer of 1894, Richet invited respected scientists to join in séances with Italian medium Eusapia Palladino. This group included sexologist and medical doctor Schrenck-Notzing, who had trained in therapeutic hypnotism in France; Dr. Frederic W.H. Myers, engineer and Spiritualist Gabriel Delanne, Professor of Psychology and photographer Julien Ochorowicz, and respected British physicist Oliver J. Lodge. These scientists popularized the term "ectoplasm."

54 Hamilton, "Mary M. Teleplasms," 3.

55 Geley, *From the Unconscious to the Conscious*, Part 2.

56 Robert J. Richards, *The Romantic Conception of Life: Science and Philosophy in the Age of Goethe* (Chicago: University of Chicago Press, 2002).

57 Sebastien Normandin, "Visions of Vitalism: Medicine, Philosophy and the Soul in Nineteenth-Century France" (PhD diss., McGill University, 2003), 22, discusses the differences between Neo-Lamarckian and Darwinian versions of evolutionary theory; he also identifies how vitalism thrived within transformist France (208–09).

58 Brain, "Materialising the Medium," has thoroughly explained how and why Richet's ectoplasmic theory came to underwrite psychical research for scientists, philosophers, and artists by the early twentieth century. As he outlines, Lodge and Richet promoted biological "amoeboid theories of neuronal mobility" to describe how medium Eva C.'s cellular "substance," exteriorized from her body while in a trance state, entailed shape-shifting pseudopodial extensions (see, especially, 113–14, 122–24; on the significance of vitalistic biology, see 125 ff.). Geley used vitalist philosophies to challenge the purely mechanical concept of nature as insufficient, arguing that the scientific concept of a directed "dynamo-psychicism" was challenging materialism. See Serena Keshavjee, "Visualizations of the Vital-Psychic Force," in *Vitalist Modernism: Art, Science, Energy and Creative Evolution*, ed. Fae Brauer (Oxfordshire: Routledge, 2023), 81–104.

59 Richet, *Thirty Years of Psychical Research*, 515. The term "ectoplasm" came to dominate, though Schrenck-Notzing preferred "teleplasm," and Bisson used "substance"; for more on this term, see Michel Granger, "D'où vient le mot 'ectoplasme' dans son acception spirite et métapsychique," *Revue spirit* 157, no. 2 (2014): 15–17. Hamilton explained that "the discoverer of teleplasm Madame Bisson is casting about for a name for this quasi material [and] used the term substance. Teleplasm is matter plus energy." T.G. Hamilton to Harvey Agnew, 21 March 1931, UMASC, HFF, MSS 14, T.G.H. Correspondence Incoming 1931-32, Box 4, Folder 3. On ectoplasmic photographs, see Fischer, "The Reciprocal Adaptation of Optics and Phenomena"; and Matheson, "Ectoplasm and Photography." On seeing "pale green" ectoplasm, see "Comments on the life and interests of T.G.H.," UMASC, HFF, MSS 14, Index of T.G.H.'s Professional life 1903-1935, Box 1, Folder 6, 5.

60 Statistics are from Meyer zu Erpen, "The Quest for Immortality," 3, and UMASC, MSS 14, HFF, Summary of Experiments, Box 17, Folder 3.

61 Hamilton, "Mary M. Teleplasms," 3. Hamilton owned a copy of Geley's *From the Unconscious to the*

Conscious and often paraphrased and underlined sections from the book (located in UMASC, Janice Hamilton Fonds, MSS 323, A10-01, PC 272, Box 1/1). He also had a typed document titled "Excerpts from the Unconscious to the Conscious by Dr. Gustave Geley" in UMASC, HFF, MSS 14, Scrapbook of Psychics 1869–1930, Box 18, Folder 1. "Ectoplasm is sensitive even to rays of light. A bright and unexpected light perturbs the medium. The magnesium flash causes the medium to start violently but the substance can stand it. This allows an instant photo." Quote from Hamilton, "Mary M. Teleplasms," UMSAC, HFF, MSS 14, British Medical Association, Winnipeg, 1930, Box 1, Folder 12, 3. Margaret Hamilton Bach quotes her father from 1934 on teleplasms characteristics in her taped discussion in "Hamilton on the Nature of Teleplasm," UMASC, HFF, MSS 14, Notes 1921-1985, Box 17, Folder 10.

62 Definitions from Margaret Hamilton Bach, UMASC, HFF, MSS 14, Notes 1921–85, Box 17, Folder 10, 2. *Ektos* means outside and *tele* means at a distance. See comparisons to biological processes in Geley, *From the Unconscious to the Conscious*, 5; and similarly see Hamilton, "Mary M. Teleplasms," 3–5; and "Like the seed in the ground it, or the chick within the egg, [ectoplasm] appears to require darkness for its initial development" quotation Hamilton, "The Mysteries of Teleplasm," misdated 1926, more likely 1932 or later. UMASC, MSS 14, HFF, "The Story of the Hamilton Experiments/ Process," Box 15, Folder 6, n. p.

63 I take this comment from the Annotated Photo Album most likely compiled by Lillian Hamilton, with her handwriting and typed notes from T.G. Hamilton's lectures UMASC, HFF, PC 12, Annotated Photo Telekinesis, Box 8, Folder 1. In this album and in the lecture, "Mary M. Teleplasms," UMSAC, HFF, MSS 14, British Medical Association, Winnipeg, 1930, Box 1, Folder 12, Hamilton follows Geley's theories closely in *Intention and Survival*, see introduction.

64 "Seems to show a kind of instinct analogous to that of the invertebrate animals. It seems to have the same kind of distrust as a defenceless animal, and projects itself by retreat into the body from which it has issued." Hamilton, "Mary M. Teleplasms," UMSAC, HFF, MSS 14, British Medical Association, Winnipeg, 1930, Box 1, Folder 12, 3–4. "Trance personalities" is from T.G. Hamilton to J.W. Melson, 6 May 1931, UMASC, HFF, MSS 14, T.G.H. Outgoing Correspondence, Box 5, Folder 1. "Human-like directing intelligences" is from Hamilton, "Milestones in Psychical Research," 6. Margaret explains that the behaviour showed intelligence. UMASC, HFF, MSS 14, Bennett, "Interview with Margaret Hamilton Bach," Box 3, Folder 9, 15.

65 For the quotation about retaining personality and memory after death, see T.G. Hamilton to J.W. Melson, 6 May 1931, UMASC, HFF, MSS 14, T.G.H. Outgoing Correspondence, Box 5, Folder 1. On being extruded through the skin, see UMASC, HFF, MSS 14, Hamilton, "Mary M. Teleplasms," 5, 1930, British Medical Association, Winnipeg, 1930 Box 1, Folder 12.

66 Quote "Mary M. Teleplasms," 7. UMASC, HFF, MSS 14, British Medical Association, Winnipeg, 1930, Box 1, Folder 12, and "face bearing," UMASC, HFF, MSS 14, "The Story of the Hamilton Experiments/Process," Box 15, Folder 6.

67 Hamilton's letter to Dr. Mees, Kodak Laboratory, 17 October 1931, UMASC, HFF, MSS 14, T.G.H. Outgoing Correspondence, 1931-1935, Box 5, Folder 1. Margaret Hamilton Bach states the séances were in complete darkness, and the red light only turned on at the end of the séances "to let group members leave the room. UMASC, HFF, MSS 14, Bennett, "Interview with Margaret Hamilton Bach," Box 3, Folder 9, 15.

68 Lillian Hamilton described them working on his first public lecture of 1926 to the Winnipeg Medical

Association, "Experiments and Experiences in Psychical Research," and that the word *survival* was not mentioned, "no ghosts, no spirits in it but a factual recital of telekinesis." UMASC, HFF, MSS 14, Lillian Hamilton, "The Story of the Hamilton Experiments/Process," Box 15, Folder 6. Also see Bruce Chown, "Obituaries," *Canadian Medical Association Journal* 32 (1935): 710–11; Hamilton mentioned "no ghost, nor spirit, nor personality."

69 Hamilton, *Intention and Survival*, 12–14, directly quotes Geley, who used the term "creative energy."

70 Crandon wrote to Hamilton that "your last pictures are marvelous beyond words! A critic would say they are either the grossest fraud, or they represent spirit pictures better than any others yet produced." UMASC, HFF, MSS 14, L.R.G. Crandon to T.G. Hamilton, 27 December 1928, T.G.H. Correspondence Incoming, 1929-30, Box 4, Folder 2. Lillian Hamilton worried that Crandon's comments were too complimentary; see Lillian Hamilton to Malcolm Bird, 14 March 1929, UMASC, HFF, MSS 14, Lillian Hamilton Correspondence Outgoing, 1931-1956, Box 5, Folder 9.

71 According to Margaret Hamilton Bach, this involved energetic "lobbying." See UMASC, MSS14, HFF, Index of T.G.H.'s Professional Life 1903-1935, Box 1, File 6, comments on the life and interests of Hamilton, 8.

72 See details of his "Metapsychic Exhibit" in T.G. Hamilton to Dr. J.C.B. Grant, 6 May 1930, UMASC, HFF, MSS 14, T.G.H. Correspondence Outgoing 1924–30, Box 4, Folder 5. Also see the description by H.A.V. Green, "Report of the British Medical Association Convention in Winnipeg." UMASC, HHF, MSS 14, British Medical Association, Winnipeg, 1930, Box 1, Folder 12 and UMASC, HFF, MSS 14, Lecture Circuit Index, Box 1, Folder 10.

73 Hamilton, "Milestones in Psychical Research" and "Mary M. Teleplasms" in UMASC, HHF, MSS 14, British Medical Association, Winnipeg, 1930, Box 1, Folder 12.

74 Hamilton, "Milestones in Psychical Research," UMASC, HHF, MSS 14, British Medical Association, Winnipeg, 1930, Box 1, Folder 12, 8.

75 Noakes, *Physics and Psychics*, 2, n 5. Shannon Taggart, *Séance* (Somerset, UK: Fulgur Press, 2019). In a personal discussion Taggart explained that extrusion of ectoplasm was performed infrequently after the 1950s. Lillian Hamilton and Sylvia Barber continued the studies into 1940s and 1950, respectively (see Chapter 3 in this book). Meyer zu Erpen has examples of the physical phenomenon continuing in Canada into the 1950s and 1960s, including Jack Webber infrared photographs from 1938–39, and Minnie Harrison photographs from c. 1940s–50s. Geley died in a plane crash in 1924.

76 T.G. Hamilton to William Prince, 24 January 1924, UMASC, HFF, MSS 14, T.G.H. Correspondence Outgoing 1924–30, Box 4, Folder 5; Hamilton, *Intention and Survival*, chapter 15.

77 See explanations of and excuses for methodological breaches in Hamilton, *Intention and Survival*, 291–2. See the list of twenty stipulations or "procedures outlined and demanded by Walter," the spirit control, in Margaret Hamilton Bach, UMASC, HFF, MSS 14, Notes 1921–85, Box 17, Folder 10. On the need for low light levels, see T.G. Hamilton to Chester Doty, 6 April 1931, UMASC, HFF, MSS 14, T.G.H. Correspondence Outgoing 1931–34, Box 5, Folder 1.

78 Walter suggested clothing for the medium, a black silk robe; see Margaret Hamilton Bach, "Taken from Tape," UMASC, HFF, MSS 14, Notes 1921–1985, Box 17, Folder 10, 4. Mediums were undressed and searched before the séance; see UMASC, HFF, MSS 14, "Historical Summary" in Notes, 1921–1985, Box 17, Folder 10. Also see Hamilton,

"Milestones in Psychical Research," UMASC, HHF, MSS 14, British Medical Association, Winnipeg, 1930, Box 1, Folder 12, 6–7. Applying experimental methodologies to the question of immortality was a quandary that many scientists faced. On the tension between science and religion at the start of the twentieth century, see Bowler, *Reconciling Science and Religion*; and Noakes, *Physics and Psychics*.

79 Hamilton, "Milestones in Psychical Research," UMASC, HHF, MSS 14, British Medical Association, Winnipeg, 1930, Box 1, Folder 12, 6–7. Quotation continues, "The phenomenon of Moses, the truth telling dreams and visions of prophets. . . . Logically (modern) religion cannot give attention to the phenomena of the séance room, even though such phenomena *undoubtedly parallel* many happenings of the dim and distant times when religion's sacred writings came into being."

80 Hamilton, "Mary M. Teleplasms," 6: all of her teleplasms were "supernormal." Also see Hamilton, "Milestones in Psychical Research," UMASC, HHF, MSS 14, British Medical Association, Winnipeg, 1930, Box 1, Folder 12, 6.

81 T.G. Hamilton *Intention and Survival* 1942, 291. http://www.survivalafterdeath.info/library/hamilton/contents.htm (accessed 14 January 2023). Emphasis mine. He continues in this quote: "I make no apology for this state of affairs; I cannot, for it was not of our doing; they came and that was the end of the matter. Either we worked with them or backed away, afraid of the issue, and we chose the former course."

82 See Meyer zu Erpen's biography in this volume. See in the HFF letters from Britain, Germany, and France during the 1930s. The Hamiltons received William Lyon Mackenzie King in 1933 and were invited to lunch with Jean (Leckie) Conan Doyle at her country estate when they visited London in 1932.

83 Hamilton, "Milestones in Psychical Research," delivered in New York City, Dartmouth, and Boston in 1930. The lecture notes and lantern slides are housed in the UMASC, HHF, MSS 14, British Medical Association, Winnipeg, 1930, Box 1, Folder 12. See Margaret Hamilton Bach, UMASC, HFF, MSS 14, Index of T.G.H.'s Professional Life 1903–35, Box 1, Folder 6, Folder 12.

84 UMASC, HFF, MSS 14, Bennett, "Interview with Margaret Hamilton Bach," Box 3, Folder 9, 12.

85 See the obituary in *Elmwood Herald*, 11 April 1935, l: Hamilton was regarded as "one of Winnipeg's leading citizens." See also Horace Leaf, "Obituary," *Light*, 13 June 1935, 373; and "City Mourns as Pioneer Doctor Is Laid to Rest: Many Prominent in Public Life Attend Services for Dr. T. Hamilton," *Winnipeg Tribune,* 9 April 1935, 3, and from *Winnipeg Free Press*, April 8 1935, "worthy citizen," from an excerpt in UMASC, HFF, MSS 14, Notes 1921–85, Box 17, Folder 10, n.p.

86 "Private Letters," UMASC, HFF, MSS 14, Notes 1921–85, Box 17, Folder 10. In outlining Prime Minister William Lyon Mackenzie King's interest in their séances, Lillian Hamilton explained that both King and her husband took a scientific view of the supernatural, and her words go a long way to explain how the Hamiltons saw their research. She emphasized that the prime minister was interested in the experiments over any emotional consolation that spirit communication might bring. Echoing the manner in which T.G. distanced himself from Spiritualism, Lillian explains that King "was not a spiritualist in the popular sense," but "a scientific investigator and through his experience had come to believe in survival after death. He took the same attitude as my husband insisting that facts as they presented themselves through research be kept on the strictest scientific basis." Hamilton and King were interested in the implications of their research for Christianity: See Meyer zu Erpen, "The Quest for Immortality," 11; the original quotation is from Lillian Hamilton in "Helped Research," *Winnipeg Tribune*, 14 December 1951, 8.

87 Lillian Hamilton, UMASC, HFF, MSS 14, "The Story of the Hamilton Experiments /Process," Box 15, Folder 6.

88 Lillian Hamilton, 'Steps in the Hamilton Inquiry," UMASC, HFF, MSS 14, "The Story of the Hamilton Experiments/Process," Box 15, Folder 6, n.p.

89 Lillian Hamilton, "A Strange Prophecy Now Fulfilled." UMASC, HFF, MSS 14, "The Story of the Hamilton Experiments/Process," Box 15, Folder 6; UMASC, HFF, MSS 14, Bennett, "Interview with Margaret Hamilton Bach," Box 3, Folder 9, 5.

90 Lillian Hamilton, UMASC, HFF, MSS 14, "The Story of the Hamilton Experiments/Process," Box 15, Folder 6.

91 UMASC, HFF, MSS 14, Bennett, "Interview with Margaret Hamilton Bach," Box 3, Folder 9, on Hamilton's sister, 3, the prophetic voice, 4, and thought transference, 5.

92 "At no time could it be said a line of action was definitely dictated by us, but frequently our requests or plans would seem to have been met by *other intelligences* and in a reciprocal way we endeavored to anticipate their plans and to co-operate with them." Emphasis mine. T.G. Hamilton to William Prince, 24 January 1924, UMASC, HFF, MSS 14, T.G.H. Correspondence Outgoing, 1924–1930, Box 4, Folder 5.

93 This information comes from a typed sheet and photograph in UMASC, HFF, MSS 14, PC 12, Box 11, Folder 13, Item 1.

94 Hamilton, "Milestones in Psychical Research," 7.

95 Quotations, Hamilton "Milestones in Psychical Research," 9; T.G. Hamilton to Rev Allen Hubband, February 8, 1928, UMASC, HFF, MSS 14, T.G.H. Correspondence Outgoing, Box 4, Folder 5. Also letter to Mrs. J. M. Robinson 18 April 1932, where he says he has kept wide of Spiritualism. T.G.H. Outgoing Correspondence, Box 5, Folder 1. In *Intention and Survival*, published posthumously by Lillian and their son James, the latter writes that T.G. accepted the survival hypothesis by 1927. James Hamilton uses the term "spiritistic," defined as an acceptance that trance personalities in the séance room can demonstrate intelligence beyond that of the medium, and thus they have to be considered to come from beyond her control: "If the understanding which the trance personalities had of teleplasm exceeds that of any known living intelligence, then it follows that the trance intelligence could not have arisen from a living agency. It is therefore necessary to postulate a non-living intelligence. This is the spiritistic hypothesis." T.G. Hamilton and James D. Hamilton, *Intention and Survival: Psychical Research Studies and the Bearing of Intentional Actions by Trance Personalities on the Problem of Human Survival* (Toronto: Macmillian,1942), 226, http://www.survivalafterdeath.info/library/hamilton/chapter1.htm (accessed 1 December 2023). These tensions continue in contemporary literature, with some researchers describing the Hamiltons as Spiritualists and Walter Meyer zu Erpen adamantly stating that they were not Spiritualists. Hamilton rejected Spiritualism but philosophically it is hard to see the difference. To my knowledge, Hamilton used the term "spiritistic" for the first time in 1930 in "Milestones in Psychical Research," 6–7, and in a lecture in 1935 reproduced in *Intention and Survival*, Chapter 1. Margaret Hamilton Bach says that he used the term in 1934; UMASC, HFF, MSS 14, T.G.H.'s Professional Life, Box 1, Folder 6, 8. For the spiritistic hypothesis, see Hamilton, *Intention and Survival*, Chapter 11. The difference between Spiritualism and Spiritistic is not explained in the volume.

96 Hamilton, "Milestones in Psychical Research," 9. Beth A. Robertson, *Science of the Seance: Transnational Networks and Gendered Bodies in the Study of Psychic Phenomena, 1918–1940*

(Vancouver: UBC Press, 2016). Also see the analysis of gendered roles and the marginalization of Lillian, Claudie Massicotte, *Trance Speakers: Femininity and Authorship in Spiritual Séances, 1850–1930* (Montreal and Kingston: McGill-Queen's University Press, 2017), 158 ff.

97 T.G. Hamilton, "The Mysteries of Teleplasm," c. 1926–1930, UMASC, HFF, MSS 14, "The Story of the Hamilton Experiments/Process," Box 15, Folder 6. The quotation continues thus: "It will be seen also that in no sense is psychical research a religion." Also see Hamilton on the nature of teleplasm expert from an article in *Psychic Science,* Jan. 1934: "I regard teleplasm… as a highly sensitive substance responsive to other-world energies, and at the same time visible to us in the physical. It therefore constitutes an intervening substance by means of which transcendental intelligences are enabled, by ideoplastic or other processes, to transmit their conception of certain energy-forms . . . ." He also uses the phrase "Continental savants" in this text. Excerpt in UMASC, HFF, MSS 14, Notes 1921–85, Box 17, Folder 10.

98 Margaret Hamilton Bach also explains that T.G. Hamilton was introduced to the notion of spirits by the Reverends Allison and McLachlan at his church. UMASC, HFF, MSS 14, Bennett, "Interview with Margaret Hamilton Bach," Box 3, Folder 9, 5 and 8–9. Interesting to compare that B.F. Austin was charged with heresy at the Parkdale Methodist Church in Toronto on January 8, 1899 for his Spiritualist beliefs (clairvoyance). See also "A Case of Heresy" and "The Heresy Sermon," *Winnipeg Free Press Home Journal*, 25 May 1899, 6, and 1 June 1899, 7. B.F. Austin planned to display over 100 "spirit photos and psychic pictures" in Winnipeg's Scott Memorial Hall on 3 October 1921. I thank Anton Wagner and Walter Meyer zu Erpen for sharing this information with me. For more on Allison and the Patience Worth spirit, see Meyer zu Erpen, "The Quest for Immortality."

99 T.G. Hamilton "On the Nature of Teleplasm," excerpt from *Psychic Science,* Jan. 1934, UMASC, MSS 14, HFF, Notes 1921-85, Box 17, Folder 10. UMASC, HFF, MSS 14, Bennett, "Interview with Margaret Hamilton Bach," Box 3, Folder 9, 21.

100 Noakes, *Physics and Psychics*, 4–5; "alternative science," 8–9. Hamilton learned by the 1930s that the Schrenck-Notzing and Bisson photos were being pilloried by the press. His conversations with Geley's ghost in the private family séances about the scandal are evidence that he was grappling with this issue. By 1935, Hamilton was moving away from biological, supernormal, physiological explanations of ectoplasm and toward the older scientific theory of the etheric universe promoted by Lodge.

101 Noakes, *Physics and Psychics*, 8.

102 Asprem, *The Problem of Disenchantment*.

103 Conan Doyle, Second Lecture, Friday, 11 September 1925. https://www.arthur-conan-doyle.com/index.php?title=Lectures_at_the_International_Spiritualist_Congress_of_Paris_1925 (accessed 1 September 2023).

104 Walter Meyer zu Erpen, Chapter 3, this volume.

105 There are three spirit photographs in the HFF. One photograph is attributed on the back to Ada Deane. See UMASC, HFF, MSS 14, PC 12, Box 11, Folder 13, Items 1 and 2. The second photograph Lillian Hamilton attributed to William Hope, another well-respected spirit photographer who worked closely with Conan Doyle during the early 1920s. See UMASC, A10-83, Linda Hamilton Klassen Collection, Hamilton Experiments, 1/1. Both photographs are dated 1932, and likely the Hamiltons were introduced to these photographers by Jean Conan Doyle, at the Spiritualist Alliance office in London. Lillian stated that the photograph by Hope was of her paternal grandfather. According to Margaret Hamilton Bach, T.G. accepted that the figure floating behind the Hamiltons in Figure

2.16 was his dead sister Margaret, who had died of typhoid fever in 1886. See UMASC, HFF, MSS 14, Index of T.G.H.'s Professional life 1903–35, Box 1, Folder 6, 7. Efram Sera-Shriar confirms the identification of the Ada Deane photograph but is puzzled by the attribution of the Hope photograph. The photograph fits stylistically into Hope's 1920s period, but Hope was not active by the 1930s, having fallen from favour after the attacks by Harry Price. I thank Sera-Shriar for this information. On Hope and his fall from grace, see Efram Sera-Shriar, "Photographic Plates and Spirit Fakes."

106 Hamilton, *Intention and Survival*, 292; emphasis mine.

107 Margaret Hamilton Bach, UMASC, HFF, MSS 14, Index of T.G.H.'s Professional Life, 1903-35, Box 1, Folder 6, 8.

Stereo. findings one side only — due to light getting in & destroying that part of negative

Miss L.C. — a friend of T.G.H.'s in his youth — who predeceased him. Saw the same girl

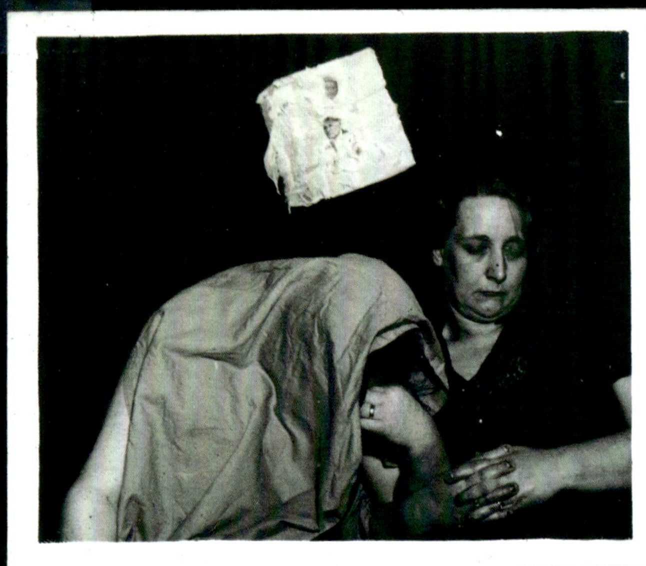

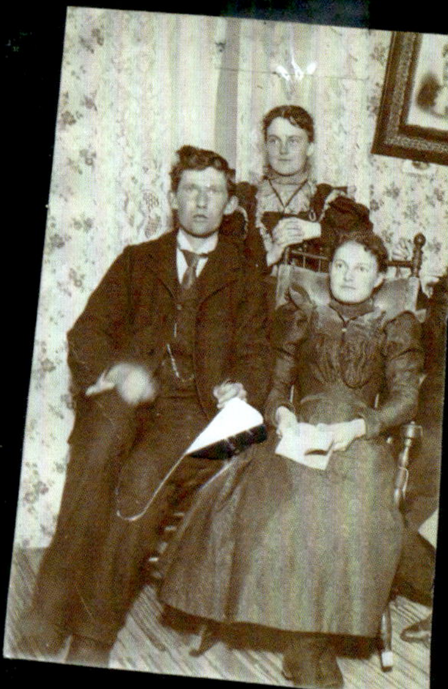

Stereo enlarged.

Note fine "screen" on which teleplasm is formed. This "screen" seen by the writer some days before, by clairvoyant vision. nothing like this ever photographed before. L.H.

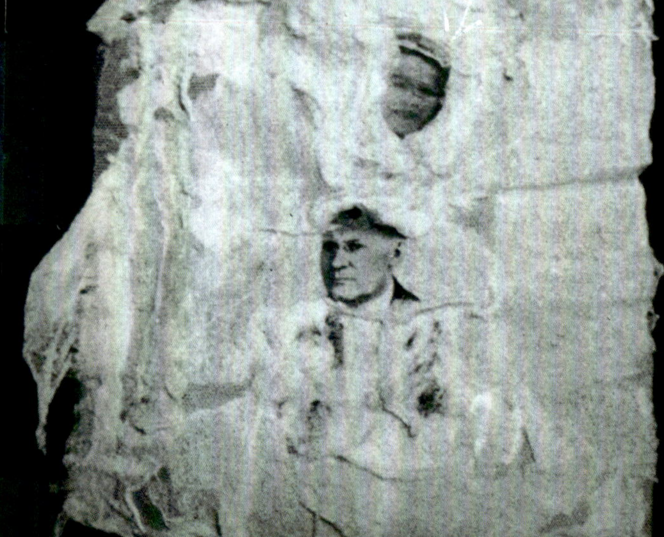

3

Seeing and Feeling, Science and Religion: Negotiating Binaries in Lillian Hamilton's Photographic Albums

Katie Oates

Lillian May Hamilton, née Forrester (1880–1956), approached psychical research from a spiritual and scientific perspective. Her experiments in séance were grounded in methods of science, with her deeply rooted emotions propelling her work, particularly after the death of her young son. Her investigations were vested in the nature of life after death and founded upon empirical evidence to verify the psychical phenomena that materialized in séance. The vast amount of work that she produced, and how it contributes to Winnipeg's cultural heritage, however, have yet to be recognized in the field of psychical research or in Canadian and photographic histories.

Fig. 3.1. Lillian Hamilton, ***Lucy Cleland and Thomas Glendenning Hamilton***, 22 May 1939. UMASC, PC 12, Box 8, Folder 7, Item 66, http://hdl.handle.net/10719/1409714.

Lillian Hamilton was the impetus behind the investigations of her husband, Dr. Thomas Glendenning (T.G.), in Winnipeg as his motivational and supportive collaborator. She experimented in psychics with their neighbour, Elizabeth Poole, before collaborating with her husband, and she continued to do so after his death in 1935. Lillian led formal séances in the Hamilton family home until April 1940, after which she continued to conduct informal experiments until 1944, primarily through correspondence with medium Mary Marshall.[1] Lillian was highly knowledgeable about psychics, studying topics within the field as early as 1915, according to her daughter, Margaret Hamilton Bach, who recalls that her mother had read Frederic William Henry Myers's *Human Personality and Its Survival of Bodily Death*, which belonged in the Hamilton home.[2] Lillian continued to study these topics, including historical and emerging phenomena, until her health began to fail in 1955. She also indexed the Hamilton records, catalogued her husband's talks, scientific papers, letters, and lecture notes, along with newspaper reviews about his work. Most significant for this chapter, she organized their corresponding documentation into annotated albums for her three surviving children. They feature photographs and the types of cameras used, typed fragments of transcripts and handwritten captions, psychic journal articles, programs, and correspondence that illustrate her spiritual and intellectual process.[3] Her albums also include degrees and documents related to the Hamilton family, as well as those about T.G.'s medical training and career in medicine and politics. These albums are an integral part of the Hamilton Family Fonds (HFF) for providing a visual and textual picture of séance activities. Since few women have been credited as investigators within the field of psychical research, this chapter reconsiders Lillian as a psychical researcher who incorporated Spiritualist elements into her practice.

Images of the albums draw viewers into the séance experience with their captivating detail. In one such image, three photographs are adhered to the page as evidence of teleplasm that appeared on 22 May 1939 (see Figure 3.1). Lillian Hamilton also wrote brief descriptions around them to identify the subjects and the dates of the phenomena. More significantly, her ardour and resolute belief in the authenticity of her investigations are conveyed through her annotations. She created these albums as records of psychical evidence, intended to be viewed by close friends and family members. Yet filled with snippets of photographs, typed and handwritten captions, they encapsulate and elicit the feelings of séance.

Lillian Hamilton worked alongside T.G. Hamilton from 1920 to 1935. Her contributions to psychical research, however, have been overshadowed by his accolades as a highly regarded member of Winnipeg's medical community and international psychical networks, even though both of them had scientific training and were accomplished medical practitioners—he was a doctor, and she was a nurse.[4] And, while research on the Hamilton collection is abundant, Lillian is typically mentioned in passing as T.G.'s wife, assistant, and collaborator. She appears more as a cultural footnote than as a psychical investigator, researcher, and album creator in her own right. Her work has therefore received little attention in scholarship, and her albums have yet to be studied in a scholarly context. Most discussions focus on the period when Lillian worked with T.G. Archival documents between 1935 and 1944, however, present a fuller picture of the ways in which her spirituality intersected with her psychical work.

Although this study is not comprehensive, it explores a previously unstudied area of Canadian and women's histories, both nationally and regionally. This chapter builds upon literature by Esyllt W. Jones, Claudie Massicotte, and Beth A. Robertson that addresses the role of women mediums in Canada to further assess their involvement in psychical and spiritual investigations.[5] Their texts provide rich analyses of how women's bodies were regarded in experiments and represented in séances photographically and how mediumship epitomized expressions of selfhood and agency. Following from these discussions, I analyze Lillian Hamilton's albums from a feminist social history perspective to show how they both adhere to and challenge ideas about femininity, and about family and personal photography. Her work challenged gender binaries, particularly in relation to scientific and psychical communities' conceptions of the status of men and women. Her effort to provide evidence of her belief in the afterlife reveals her multi-faceted approach to psychical research, which sheds light on the ways in which Lillian approached her practice from an intellectual and spiritual perspective. Her work thereby challenged the rational/irrational, thinking/emotional binaries that saturated the field of psychics and persist in mainstream culture. This chapter shows how she used her practice, and her compilation of albums, to reconcile her feelings of grief after the physical loss of her husband.

The ways in which Lillian Hamilton's albums can be viewed through the lens of family and personal photography is highlighted with literature by Patricia Holland, Marianne Hirsch, Jo Spence, and Patrizia di Bello.[6] Their discussions are framed around ideas about women's culture and domesticity, family and women's histories, and notions of memory to consider the social uses of personal photography and to argue that family photographs should be apprehended on their own terms. Adopting such theories, I argue that, through her album creations, Lillian gained agency by (re) scripting the Hamilton narrative from her perspective; that the album pages provided a space in which she could communicate her experiences of séance. In this way, my study shows how women were able to uphold their autonomy even as they were subjected to nineteenth-century patriarchal structures. It further illustrates the multi-faceted contributions that women made to various facets of psychical photography in Canada, with the aim to illuminate Lillian's practice in her own right.

Lillian's Investigations in the Hamilton Home

Lillian Hamilton conducted and recorded psychical experiments with the support of family members and colleagues. Several members of her and T.G. Hamilton's group, comprised of approximately twelve close friends and relatives who regularly sat for the experiments, remained active in her investigations.[7] Lillian collaborated with Hugh A. Reed, Dr. Bruce Chown and his wife, Gladys, and Winnipeg photographer H.J. Metcalfe, particularly for photographing and developing the plates, yet she was highly educated and well equipped to lead séances.[8] With her youngest son, James Drummond Hamilton, Lillian edited and posthumously published her husband's book *Intention and Survival* in 1942; and with Margaret Hamilton Bach, she wrote, compiled, and published *Is Survival a Fact?* in 1969.[9] As Marina Warner notes, "throughout the decades after 1870 till the Second World War, advanced, intelligent women were active in psychic research and related experiments," even though their recognition remains minimal across disciplines.[10] Lillian's investigations were supported by her female colleagues—namely mediums Mary Marshall, Elizabeth Poole, and Jeannie Wither, who appear in the images discussed here—yet her contributions to the psychical field nonetheless elucidate Warner's observation.

Gender Dynamics in Psychical Research

Like the earlier generation of Victorian practitioners, the Hamiltons established routine investigations of psychical phenomena after they experienced a profound loss in the family. Following the death of their son Arthur in January 1919 during the influenza pandemic, the Hamiltons began to explore the realm of the spiritual. Wondering where his son's soul had gone after physical death, and longing for answers and solace after the First World War, seem to have inspired the doctor to engage with questions of life after death.[11]

T.G. and Lillian Hamilton contributed equally to their experiments, undertaking different yet gendered tasks. T.G. oversaw their psychical experiments, constructed the séance room, set up each of his eleven cameras, developed plates in the darkroom, publicized their findings, and gave lectures on his theory of survival. He also had a team of male colleagues who assisted him in these processes.[12] Lillian undertook the invisible yet supportive labour and remained her husband's closest colleague. In preparing for séances, at times she conducted physical examinations of the mediums' bodies before entering the room dedicated to investigations. Lillian connected with colleagues in the field via correspondence to share and receive experimental developments and methods, she transcribed séance notes during and after the experiments, and she filed and cross-indexed all records and photographic plates and negatives. After T.G.'s death, she indexed the Hamilton records; catalogued all of his talks, scientific papers, letters, and lecture notes and newspaper reviews of their work; and compiled annotated photographic albums. Her valuable contributions therefore reflect Steven Shapin's notion of invisible technicians; those who "have arguably been invisible as relevant actors to those persons in control of the workplaces in which scientific knowledge is produced."[13] Yet Lillian is remarkable for being the impetus behind the Hamiltons' investigations and for bringing their experiments into the public sphere.

She appears to have been a motivational force for her and her husband's research. Their granddaughter Janice Hamilton explains that, "although it was T.G. Hamilton who achieved the recognition, she [Lillian] had pushed his investigations from the very beginning. Even after little Arthur died, Margaret Hamilton Bach recalled that Lillian Hamilton had been stronger than T.G. and he turned to her for strength."[14] While her husband's interest in telepathy and telekinesis experiments waxed and waned between 1918 and 1921, Lillian recognized Elizabeth Poole's psychical potential and maintained faith and praxis in paranormal research. Determined to find its value, she continued to hold sittings with Poole for several months after T.G. initially gave it up. He required further proof that spirits were communing with them to dispel his concern for his medical reputation.[15] He dismissed the women's experiments as resulting from "unconscious muscular activity," rather than mediumistic skills.[16] T.G. was unconvinced about "the reality of psychic force," only deeming it "potentially valuable" once he experienced it himself firsthand.[17] He then believed psychical study worthy of his investment. Robertson's discussion of how the "scientific self envisioned as explicitly male became the standard of a credible investigator" can be related to T.G.'s dismissal of the women's independent investigations.[18] Lillian also brought their investigations to the attention of the public by writing to *Light* magazine and having information about their experiments with developing Poole's mediumistic powers published in June 1922.[19] Their work was widely publicized in subsequent years, though Lillian merits credit for this seminal article. The Hamiltons' gender dynamic was consistent with notions of the rational male scientist as necessary for credible investigations, while showing how women's perspectives were considered less valuable than men's.

Lillian Hamilton achieved positive séance results in the earliest years of experimentation, and after T.G. Hamilton's death, even though—unlike her husband—she engaged with spirituality and emotionality. She expressed that her spiritual beliefs "went hand in hand with evidence of a scientific nature,"[20] whereas he maintained that women's psychology predisposed them to be "innately trusting, emotional, uncritical," and thus "more disposed to accept with less demand for fundamental detail."[21] Yet her table-tilting experiments with Elizabeth Poole proved to be successful when the table tipped up onto two legs and remained stagnant for several minutes.[22] Stan McMullin and Beth A. Robertson similarly observe that Lillian embraced the link between women and spirituality, which was different from T.G.'s focus.[23] She did not view the scientific and the spiritual as binaries, much like many Spiritualists, who "denied basic categorial binaries: the distinctions between men and women, science and magic, life and afterlife, the past and the present," as Molly McGarry writes.[24] Lillian maintained the scientific outlook that her husband upheld and that Margaret Hamilton Bach notes in the early years of her parents' research: "The type of research my father engaged in was purely scientific. He was extremely skeptical, cautious, and conservative."[25] T.G. reiterates this point in *Intention and Survival* to establish the historical lineage of scientific methods in the field of psychics and metaphysics. He references the work of Sir William Crookes from 1870 to state that "in no case does the work instituted by the main pioneers of this new research appear to have been instituted or carried out in other than the true spirit and outlook of science."[26] It is clear that the Hamiltons were resolute about clarifying the scientific nature of their work. And since Lillian's experiments post-1935 can be viewed as extensions of her collaborations with her husband, her work can similarly be viewed through the lens of scientific research. The only difference is that Lillian did not deny or reject emotional, spiritual elements; rather, she researched psychical phenomena from an intellectual perspective that incorporated spirituality.

Dissolving Binaries: Infusing Spirituality in Psychical Research

The twentieth-century séance was founded upon empirical ideals, and the gendered dynamics in science infiltrated psychical studies. Evelyn Fox Keller explains how the discipline of science as a masculine domain derived from seventeenth-century Europe to create "dichotomies between mind and nature, reason and feeling, masculine and feminine."[27] Such understandings subsequently left women alienated from leading scientifically informed studies because they were conceived of as passive, weak subjects for the scrutiny of the male scientists' gaze.[28]

The associations between passivity and femininity and intellect and masculinity further reinforced the hierarchy between thinking and feeling and between men and women within the twentieth-century séance. Yet the characteristics of passivity, compliance, and subjectivity were perceived as necessary qualities for mediumship and credible spirit communication.[29] Many scholars note that these traits were presented as inherently feminine, whereas intellect and reason were presented as inherently masculine.[30] Viewed as "beneath" the faculties of thought and reason, feminist theorist Sara Ahmed maintains that emotions have historically been associated with women, "who are represented as 'closer' to nature, ruled by appetite, and less able to transcend the body through thought, will, and judgement."[31] She articulates the ways in which feminist philosophers have acknowledged the problems with this framework, whereby the subordination of emotions becomes the subordination of the feminine and the body.[32] As the séance became popular in the nineteenth century, Robertson states that women mediums were the "norm," rather than men.[33] She continues that mediums were not always as passive as previously presumed but often proved to be dynamic forces.[34] Robertson thus contends that mediums played the parts assigned to them at one moment, then subverted the known scripts of behaviour at another moment.[35] Warner further argues that, by the end of the nineteenth century, women mediums and photographers remained at the centre of the spirit circle in a reorientation of gender roles.[36]

In the twentieth century, women mediums maintained agency as the point of contact between supernormal forces and the scientists who investigated them. They exerted power in ways that only the séance could facilitate, for their association with stereotypical feminine qualities—malleability, passivity—made them the primary instruments through which spirits could communicate.[37] It was still uncommon, however, for women to hold leadership roles within the male-dominated field of psychical research.

The Feminine Subject Under Masculine Objectives in Scientific Endeavours

Fraudulent spirit and psychical photographs continued to be produced in the twentieth century, even as photography remained a critical component in validating supernormal phenomena. The Hamiltons therefore recognized the necessity to distinguish their work from darkroom trickery, even though the "credibility of the Spiritualist doctrine had been boosted . . . by a number of high-profile scientists and literati who publicly endorsed its tenets" by the end of the nineteenth century, as Serena Keshavjee explains.[38] Researchers had dedicated spaces for conducting experiments, which were typically in the home, though confined to a secure room used solely for that purpose. The séance room became a masculine, scientific space that mimicked the controlled conditions of a laboratory.[39] This gave investigators greater control over the variables of their experiments, while effectively increasing their rigour.

T.G. Hamilton accordingly moved their provisional séance room to a dedicated space, which was locked while not in use, and where conditions could be controlled. Midway through 1923, the Hamilton photographs show how the setting of the experiments moved from the main floor parlour, in which family photos are hung above a brick fireplace and polished mantel, to the austere laboratory that T.G. constructed in the family home (see Figure 3.2). Margaret Hamilton Bach outlines how the laboratory-like séance room was set up as one of the "precautions imposed by [her] father in ensuring that no conscious or unconscious fraudulent behaviour would occur which would damage the validity of the phenomena: The séances were held in a room on the second

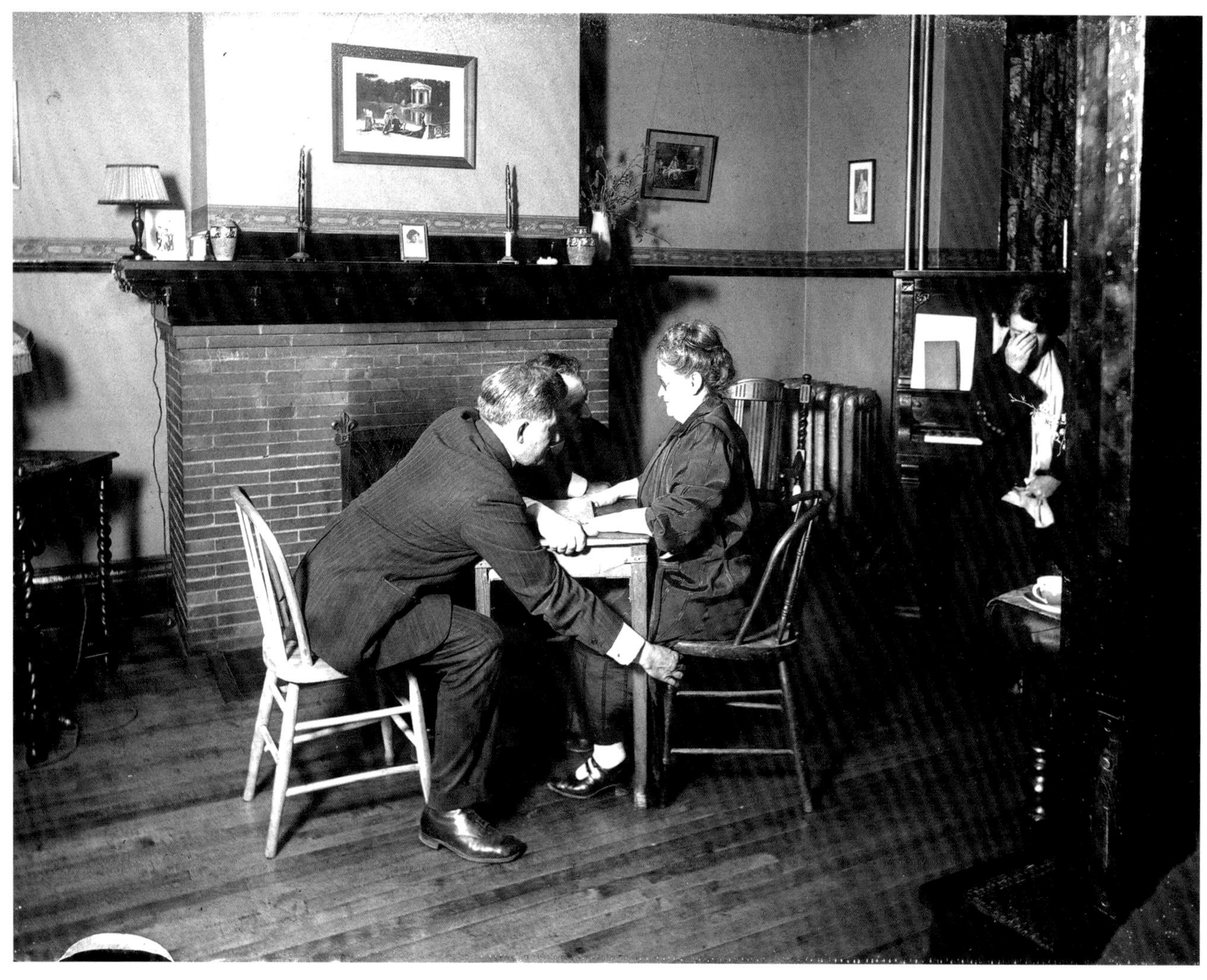

Fig. 3.2. ***Restraining Table and Chair***, T.G. Hamilton and D.B. MacDonald with medium Elizabeth Poole, 1923. UMASC, PC 12, Box 12, Folder 1, Item 3, http://hdl.handle.net/10719/1524073.

floor of our home. It had one door, opening off the hall. Its two windows were boarded over, and were about 15 feet above ground level. The floor was bare. Plain wooden chairs and a plain unvarnished wooden table, plus a[n] open three-sided cabinet, standing against the east wall, and bolted to the floor, a ruby-red ceiling light, were the simple furnishings."[40] The séance room adhered to scientific standards, making it easier to monitor mediums' behaviour without obstructions in the room. The Hamiltons, like most twentieth-century psychical researchers, rid the séance of stereotypical feminine markings—artwork, plush furniture, familial memorabilia—that adorned the parlour, yet they still relied on the feminine qualities of the body to support their scientific empiricism.[41] More significantly, the regulation of the space also meant the regulation of the bodies within it.

The female body was liable as an object of control under the scrutiny of the rational male observer. To capture photographic evidence of supernatural phenomena, psychical investigations relied on the medium's body as obedient, passive, and subjective. Robertson elucidates how women's bodies—rather than their minds—operated as sites where meaning was generated.[42] Although it appears that T.G. Hamilton did not cede to women's capacity for critical thinking, he did admit that the "men in the group are not as essential as the women."[43] Their assumed passivity created powerful séance conditions upon relinquishing control of their bodies in the séance room. Yet McMullin notes that the "major weakness in the use of trance mediums working in séance was the inability to exercise strict control over the medium."[44] To mitigate this, a set of procedures was implemented to maintain as much control as possible. Before entering the room, mediums were often stripped, inspected, bathed, and redressed. And throughout the séance, their limbs could be held or tied to avoid misconduct and accusations of fraud.[45]

Women's position in psychical work can be read through Ahmed's politics of emotion, which argues against feminist action as pre-emptively assuming the thinking/feeling binary. Ahmed explains that, though "thought and reason are identified with the masculine and the Western subject, emotions and bodies are associated with femininity and racial others."[46] Accordingly, if the feminine subject is deemed emotional, and thus unable to deploy rationality to the same extent as the masculine subject, then the feminine body in the séance room falls within this hierarchy. That is, the objective male investigator conducts empirical research over and through the feminized subject.

More specifically, Lillian Hamilton's (invisible) work in support of T.G. Hamilton, and her minimal recognition post-1935, can be understood in light of Ahmed's theory that the role of emotions implies the politicization of subjects. As Robertson contends, Lillian was irrevocably tied to qualities of womanhood and, by extension, qualities of impressionability, irrationality, and emotionality as they have traditionally been associated with the feminine and the domestic. This is in opposition to the rational, the logical, and the precise associated with the masculine. Such ideological correlations impeded Lillian and other women from gaining credibility as investigators in their own right, thwarted from transcending their positions as researchers, recorders, and witnesses.[47] Ahmed discusses how the projection of emotion onto the bodies of others can effectively exclude them from the realms of thought and rationality, while concealing the emotional and embodied aspects of thought and reason.[48] She therefore argues against binary structures of thought and emotion, because understanding emotion as "the unthought" simultaneously assumes the unemotionality of rational thought.[49] Robertson observes that Lillian "adhered to scientific empiricism much like her husband, but she did not equate her dedication to empiricism with an inability to express grief and hope."[50] She did not privilege thought over emotion; rather, she allowed the emotional aspects of séance to coincide with the empirical. Her spiritual and scientific approach thus challenged the male-normative approaches to psychical research. She instilled her albums with emotion and intellect, while maintaining the rigour of her male contemporaries.

For example, Figure 3.3 shows two photographs of the same teleplasm. Lillian Hamilton identified it as the residual screen of the T.G. Hamilton teleplasm that had

Fig. 3.3. Lillian Hamilton, ***Residue of "Screen" and Teleplasm***, 28 May 1939. UMASC, PC 12, Box 8, Folder 6, Item 65, http://hdl.handle.net/10719/1410641.

Residue of screen and teleplasm photographed May 28, 1939.

65

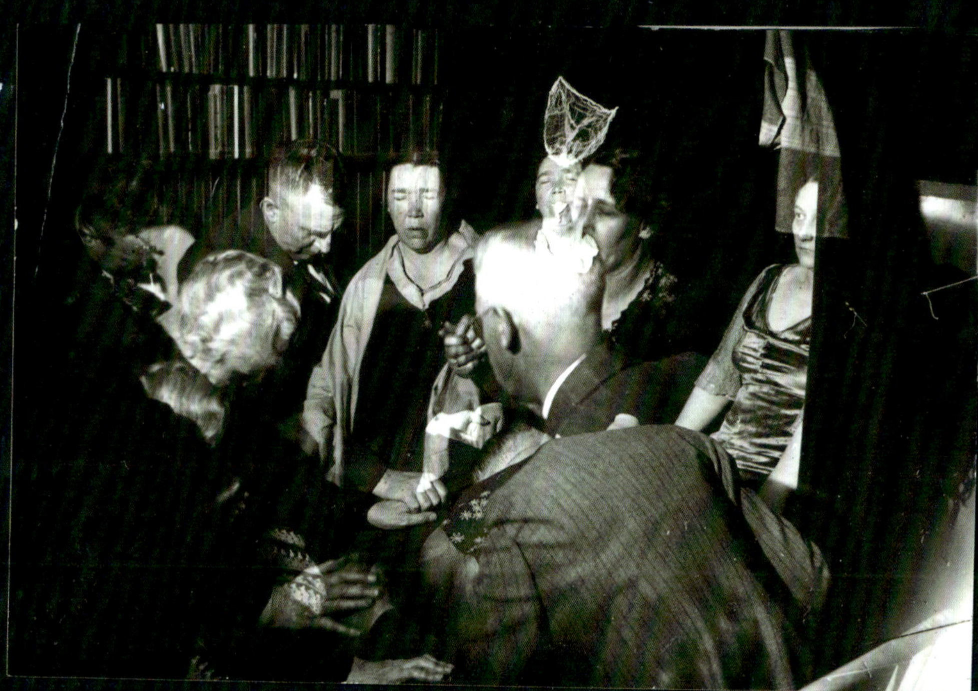

Note: the teleplasm coming on mouth was photographed during sitting of May 20 – two days before J. S. H. tel. came into view.

Note: Dawn under strict manual control throughout.
Fraud utterly impossible.

L. H.

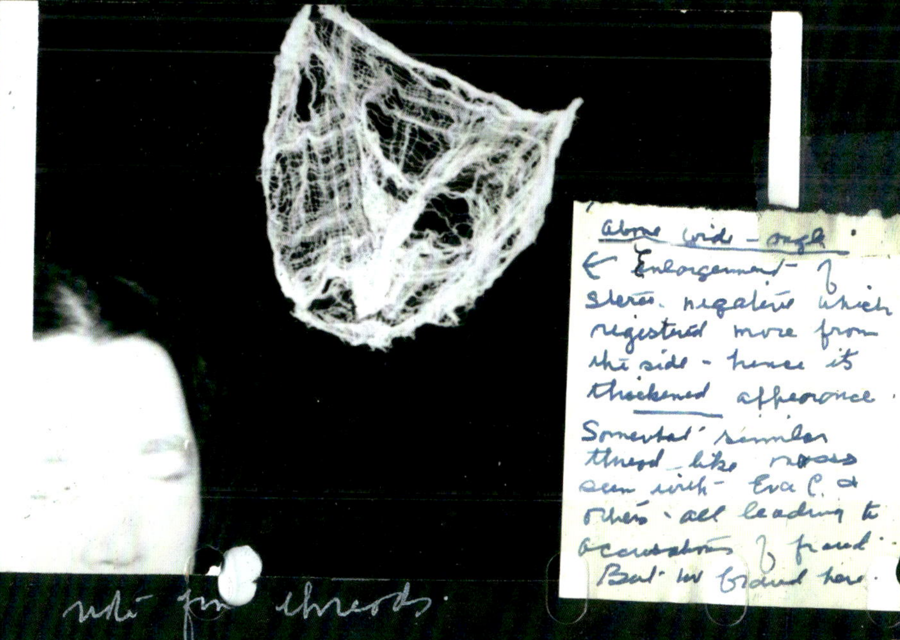

Above side-angle.
← Enlargement of stereo negative which registered more from the side – hence its thickened appearance.
Somewhat similar thread-like masses seen with Eva C. & others – all leading to accusations of fraud.
But no fraud here.

note fine threads.

manifested on 22 May 1939. Her albums report objective details of her experiments, such as names of the sitters, dates, types of camera used, and photograph formats, in the way that professional researchers had done. But they also include her emotional responses to, and thus her convictions about, the phenomena captured—"nothing like this ever photographed before," "fraud impossible," and "fraud utterly impossible," twice underlined for greater emphasis. Lillian's annotations defy the privileging of thinking over feeling, infused with observations that demonstrate her ability to advance rational thought without assuming the "unemotionality" of it.

Negotiating Negativity and Masculinity: Psychic Albums and Family Photography

Preserving memories in the form of photographic albums was a domestic activity associated with women and enmeshed in notions of femininity.[51] Writing about family photography, Holland remarks that "looking inwards towards the domestic and creating an exclusive record of your family became an increasingly important message, directed largely at the women of the middle classes."[52] Within the Victorian home, albums reasserted familial bonds and pastimes to create a sense of unity and belonging among family members. Family albums became an integral part of the modern family and even extended the notion of family beyond the domestic by including leisure activities and images of the outside world. Lillian Hamilton's albums align with Holland's and di Bello's concepts of family photography for transcending the domestic to include images associated with the masculinized terrains of psychics and science.

Emerging from nineteenth-century ideals, the home became a site of leisure. Albums also functioned as a form of entertainment, for they typically contained images of the outside world—including masculine enterprises. Leisure activities, as well as military and entrepreneurial endeavours, were preserved in family albums, expanding the notion of family beyond the home.[53] As Holland notes, the home was used for both "scientific experimentation and the creation of works of art."[54]

And although Lillian Hamilton's albums were intended more as records than as art, they remain at the intersection of these practices.

Holland further notes that family albums may act as a self-expressive "emotional centre" in which the past is confirmed and carried into the present.[55] Lillian Hamilton created her albums with care and intention in the way one would in constructing a family album. She used expressive captions to infuse the pages with the emotions enlivened in séance. In viewing the albums, those in the Hamiltons' circle would have engaged in a particular act of recognition that Holland describes as a reconstruction of private histories that establishes personal narratives against public accounts.[56] Hundreds of unique photographs are held in the collection, yet we can presume that Lillian selected the photographs that she deemed successful to include in her albums to help narrate her perspective of séance, including multiple angles and close-ups of particularly fascinating teleplasms. She then purposefully arranged and juxtaposed them onto the page. Lillian often incorporated other types of images, such as portraits, to show their resemblance to a teleplasmic materialization of a face, for instance. She also transcribed her emotional reactions alongside the photographs, which relay her perceptions of the sittings, thereby combining her thoughts and emotions, facts and reactions.

For instance, Figure 3.4 contains a single photograph of séance participants sitting in a circle holding hands, with Lillian Hamilton's handwritten notations below it. The room is cast in darkness except for the bright light of the flash, which accentuates the white teleplasm forming the focal point of the image. Members are seated close with heads down and eyes closed, grasping each other's hands beneath the floating square mass. Mary Marshall leans into and rests her head on Jeannie Wither's shoulder, and both of them appear tucked behind Hugh Reed in the foreground, though the image does not permit a view of anyone's face. We do not see Lillian in the photograph, just the traces of her thoughts in handwriting. Her caption details how she knelt before Dawn (Mary Marshall) to control her hands until the teleplasm formed, after which "Dawn and Mrs. W. embraced." She narrates the scene through album annotations and séance notes, which intimate the

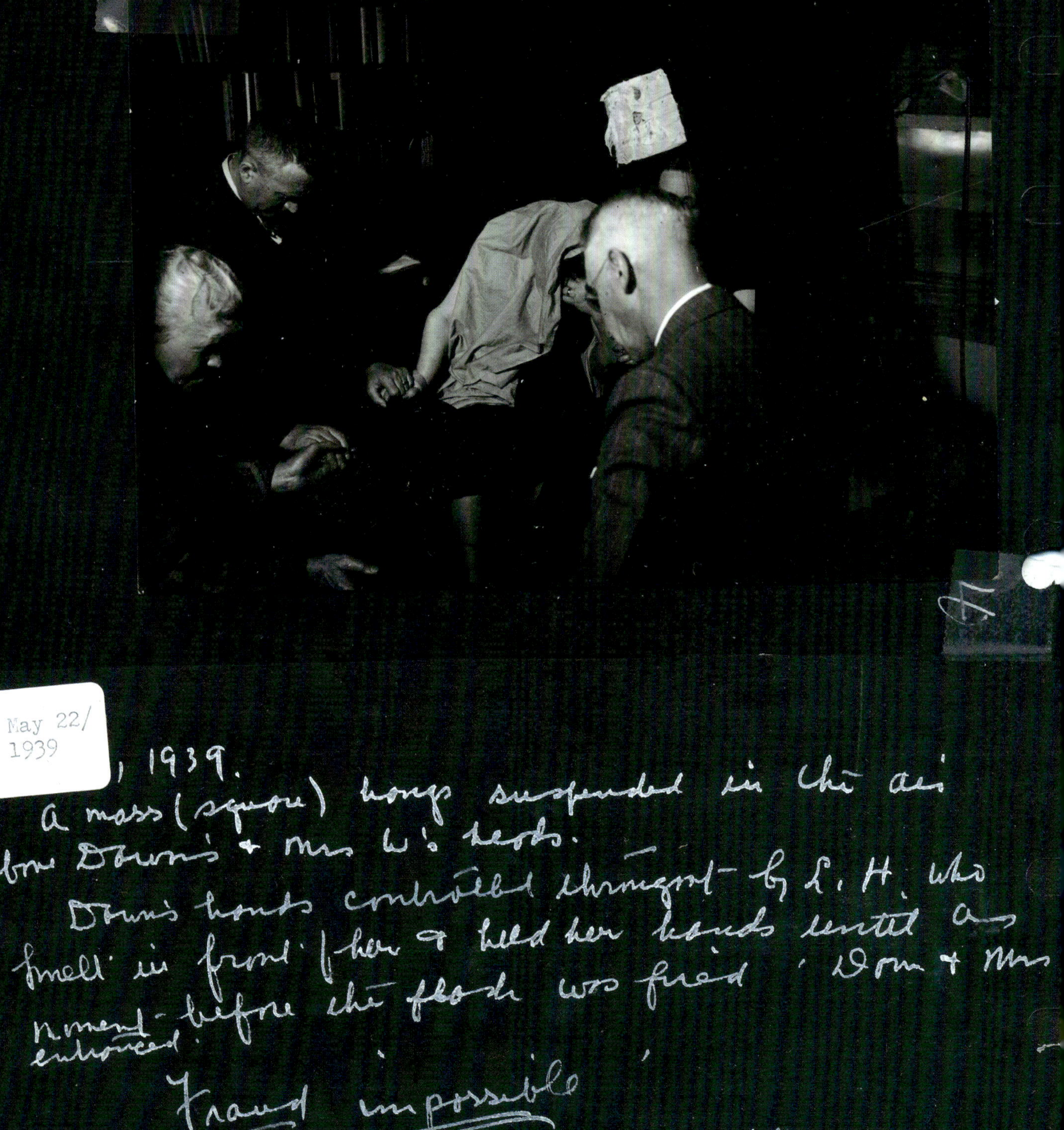
May 22/ 1939
, 1939.
A mass (square) hangs suspended in the air
above Downs's & Mrs W's heads.
Downs's hands controlled throughout by L. H. who
knelt in front of her & held her hands until a
moment before the flash was fired. Downs & Mrs
entranced.
Fraud impossible
L. H.

emotional experience at the moment "the flash was fired" (see Figure 3.4). Lillian ends the caption with her conviction "fraud impossible," authenticated with her initials beneath. Her emphatic writing seems to presume the unbelievability of what appear alongside the text: black-and-white photographs made so brilliant by the flashbulb that they look nearly overexposed, bright floating objects with a likeness to cheesecloth or a newspaper page presenting two faces, and seemingly unaware participants seated together in the dark. These pages speak to a sense of wonder and fascination that anticipates correlative reactions from viewers. Lillian's album pages function like family albums by providing the contexts for viewers to understand them, particularly since the images could be misread and their meanings lost in their bewildering appearance. The photographs and notations work together to construct a frame of reference in which meaning can be made and that simultaneously infuses the albums with the emotionality of the events captured.

In this way, the album compositions enabled Lillian Hamilton to enact authority in her collaborations with T.G. Hamilton by (re)scripting the narratives of séance from her perspective. She established a sense of agency over how the experiments were documented and perhaps a sense of independence as the creator of these albums. This is particularly relevant considering T.G.'s omission of women in reports and publications on his work. Robertson describes how this was not a singular mistake; that the women in his circle are mentioned only in passing, presented as secondary to the success of the experiments and to the reporting of his predominantly male colleagues.[57]

The merging of past and present, memory and image, in Lillian Hamilton's albums can be understood through Holland's theory of how family albums operate. Holland explains that such albums function at the "disjuncture between image and remembered experience, the uncertain borderline between fantasy and memory."[58] In Lillian's séance photographs, the past becomes mixed with the present, while

Fig. 3.4. Lillian Hamilton, ***Suspended Square Mass***, Lucy Cleland and T.G. Hamilton teleplasm, 22 May 1939. UMASC, PC 12, Box 8, Folder 6, Item 66, http://hdl.handle.net/10719/1410658.

memories of deceased loved ones are conjured, and their personal bonds with the living are enlivened. Holland also explains how family albums provide "the opportunity to relive or re-enact the past," "recapture personal history, and make sense of individual lives."[59] Lillian was reassured of her husband's continued life in the spirit world from his teleplasmic materialization, and from his communication with her through Mary Marshall's trance writing. Janice Hamilton describes how, "on several occasions throughout 1943 and 1944, Marshall sat down in her home for half an hour and, supplied with pencil, paper, envelopes and stamps by Lillian, she went into a light trance and her hand wrote letters that began, 'Hello, Lillian.' They described what T.G. Hamilton was learning and experiencing, and they were signed 'T.G.' Mary Marshall would immediately put each letter into the mail for delivery the next day to Lillian."[60] These letters reaffirmed his spiritual existence and, much like Holland articulates, could function to help Lillian make sense of his life after physical death. In this way, T.G. and Lillian could recapture and relive their personal history together through Marshall's mediumship. I accordingly consider her albums, including their photographs, séance notes, and letters, as existing on this borderline between image and memory.

This instantaneous merging of the past into a single moment frames the nature of psychical photography. It makes permanent moments of communication that can then be used to "sustain complex relationships."[61] For Lillian Hamilton, Mary Marshall's mediumship allowed her to retain her connection to her husband after his death and preserve it in the albums. We can further understand her album making as bestowing meaning on their psychical work and for those involved—herself and séance participants, as well as family members and friends, for whom they were created. The albums also function as reassurance of T.G. Hamilton's spiritual survival. And, much like Holland contends about personal photography, I suggest that the séance "derives its power from its role as a social practice, embedded in its context."[62] Routinely gathering in the dark each week to join hands and beckon discarnate beings into the material world became a ritual that fortified the séance as a social practice.

Conclusion

Lillian Hamilton led psychical investigations for ten years after the death of her husband, Dr. T.G. Hamilton. Her approach to psychics aligned with Spiritualists' belief in denying categorical binaries, and her album compilations illuminate her spiritual and scientific method. The gendered nature of séance is evident in her contributions to psychical experiments, which Lillian simultaneously adhered to and challenged. Her album making allowed her to narrate the experiences and events of séance from her perspective, even though the ways in which women's positions have been represented in psychical investigators' textual and visual reports illustrate an unstable and dynamic picture of gender binaries. In this way, she was granted agency in (re)scripting the Hamilton investigations.

Lillian Hamilton's albums show familial bonds between embodied and disembodied sitters, while enlivening the relationship between viewers and subjects. They challenge traditional viewing practices with their mystifying appearance, prompting viewers to suspend their disbelief in the contemplative moment of wonder. The social practice of séance further reinforces its use as confirmation of spiritual life, while sustaining the relationships between the living and the dead.

Although the twentieth-century field of psychics was male dominated, Lillian Hamilton was able to establish her agency over how the psychical experiments were permanently documented and a sense of independence as the creator of these albums. I have suggested that she used her practice, and her assiduous composition of albums, to reconcile her feelings of grief after the physical loss of her husband with the reassurance of his continued life in the spirit world. Her albums continue to offer a unique viewing experience that opens them up to new interpretations with each viewing, for they have made permanent the emotions elicited in séance, while retaining their capacity to evoke varying emotions in viewers.

This chapter has ultimately argued that, if indeed the spiritual is linked to the emotional and by extension to femininity and women, then Lillian Hamilton's practice, as approached from an intellectual and spiritual perspective, challenged gender binaries.

In doing so, this chapter has illuminated women's multi-faceted approaches to practising photography and the varied contributions that women have made to its histories. It has more specifically highlighted Lillian as the motivational force behind the Hamiltons' psychical experiments, and her contributions to this world-renowned collection.

NOTES

1 Between 1940 and 1944, Lillian Hamilton conducted informal psychical experiments with Mary Marshall via automatic scripts that she conducted in her home and then mailed to Lillian. One of her primary co-experimenters, Hugh Reed, died in January 1942, and her other circle members, the Withers, moved to British Columbia in 1944, when Lillian also brought her research with Marshall to a close.

2 Walter Meyer zu Erpen, "The Quest for Immortality: Psychical Research in Winnipeg and the Role of Medical Doctors, Lawyers, Clergymen, and Other Community Leaders between 1918 and 1935," compiled 1992–2018, 16, https://survivalresearch.ca/Quest_for_Immortality_1992-2018_compilation.pdf (accessed 22 March 2022). Frederic William Henry Myers was a significant figure as a co-founder of the British Society for Psychical Research.

3 Such journals include *Light*, *Journal of the American Society for Psychical Research*, *Direct Voice*, and *Survival*.

4 Lillian Hamilton graduated from the Winnipeg General Hospital School of Nursing in 1905, receiving the top award for "Highest General Proficiency," and she was president of the Medical Faculty Women's Club at the University of Manitoba. Thomas Glendenning Hamilton, *Intention and Survival: Psychical Research Studies and the Bearing of Intentional Actions by Trance Personalities on the Problem of Human Survival*, ed. James D. Hamilton (Toronto: Macmillan, 1942), 3. Such international psychical networks included the American Society for Psychical Research. T.G. was a doctor and respected member of Winnipeg's medical, religious, educational, and political communities. He was a member of the Winnipeg School Board from 1905 to 1915 and the chairman from 1912 to 1913; he was an elder of Elmwood Presbyterian Church (now King Memorial United Church) from 1907 to 1935; he was elected as a Member of the Legislative Assembly for Elmwood between 1915 and 1920, helping with the introduction of the mother's allowance, the women's vote, and the Workmen's Compensation Board into legislation; in the early 1920s, he was founding editor of *Manitoba Medical Bulletin* and president of the Manitoba Medical Association; and, from 1922 to 1923, he was president of the Canadian Medical Association.

5 See Chapter 1 of this volume; Esyllt W. Jones, "Spectral Influenza: Winnipeg's Hamilton Family, Interwar Spiritualism, and Pandemic Disease," in *Epidemic Encounters: Influenza, Society, and Culture in Canada, 1918–1920*, ed. Magda Fahrni and Esyllt W. Jones (Vancouver: UBC Press, 2012), 193–221; and Beth A. Robertson, *Science of the Seance: Transnational Networks and Gendered Bodies in the Study of Psychic Phenomena, 1918–1940* (Vancouver: UBC Press, 2016). In her study, Robertson follows the work of such feminist scholars as Mary Jacobus, Evelyn Fox Keller, and Sally Shuttleworth to argue that female investigators were denied the same recognition as their male colleagues.

6 Patricia Holland, "'Sweet it is to Scan . . .': Personal Photographs and Popular Photography," in *Photography: A Critical Introduction*, ed. Liz Wells, 5th ed. (London: Routledge, 2015), 133–88; Marianne Hirsch, *Family Frames: Photography, Narrative, and Postmemory* (Cambridge, MA: Harvard University Press, 1997); Marianne Hirsch and Leo Spitzer, "School Photos and Their Afterlives," in *Feeling Photography*, ed. Elspeth H. Brown and Thy Phu (Durham, NC: Duke

University Press, 2014), 252–72; Jo Spence and Patricia Holland, eds., *Family Snaps: The Meaning of Domestic Photography* (London: Virago, 1991); Patrizia di Bello, *Women's Albums and Photography in Victorian England: Ladies, Mothers and Flirts* (London: Routledge, 2007).

7 The regular sitters in Lillian Hamilton's experiments included mediums Mary Marshall, née Speirs (1880–1963), Elizabeth Poole, née Wilson (c. 1868–70–1935), and Jeannie Wither (1894–1970), as well as legal professionals to attest to T.G.'s darkroom process and a notary public to witness each participant's signing of a typed affidavit and to authenticate the photographed supernatural phenomena.

8 Lillian worked with Bruce and Gladys Chown from 1935 to 1936 and with Hugh Reed from 1939 to 1940.

9 Thomas Glendenning Hamilton, *Intention and Survival: Psychical Research Studies and the Bearing of Intentional Actions by Trance Personalities on the Problem of Human Survival*, ed. James D. Hamilton (Toronto: Macmillan, 1942); Margaret Lillian Hamilton, *Is Survival a Fact? Studies of Deep-Trance Automatic Scripts and the Bearing of Intentional Actions by the Trance Personalities on the Question of Human Survival* (London: Psychic Press, 1969).

10 Marina Warner, *Phantasmagoria: Spirit Visions, Metaphors, and Media into the Twenty-First Century* (New York: Oxford University Press, 2006), 234.

11 James Nickels discusses this in an interview with T.G. and Lillian's son Dr. Glen Hamilton: "One may surmise that T.G.'s experiences during these investigations played a major part in his eventually coming to terms with Arthur's death through the belief that Arthur's life was ongoing in another world." James B. Nickels, "Psychic Research in a Winnipeg Family: Reminiscences of Dr. Glen F. Hamilton," *Manitoba History* 55 (2007), http://www.mhs.mb.ca/docs/mb_history/55/psychicresearch.shtml (accessed 16 December 2022).

12 His brother Dr. James Archibald Hamilton, engineer Harold Shand, lawyer Henry A.V. (Harry) Green, businessman W.B. Cooper, telephone engineer Hugh A. Reed, who assisted with some of the photography and who was responsible for the cameras on 22 May 1939, and medical scientist Dr. Bruce Chown, T.G.'s primary co-experimenter from 1931 to 1935.

13 Shapin further argues that they have traditionally been "invisible to historians and sociologists of science. Until quite recently, there was no single piece of work in the literature systematically dealing with technicians, their work, and their role in making scientific knowledge." They have largely been excluded from scientific practitioners' documentary records, and subsequently made anonymous, which "plausibly proceeds from their employers' sense that what they did was not important, or even from their employers not noticing what it was they did." Steven Shapin, *Social History of Truth: Civility and Science in Seventeenth-Century England* (Chicago: University of Chicago Press, 1994), 360.

14 Janice Hamilton, "'Bring on Your Ghosts!,'" *Paranormal Review* 77 (2016): 10.

15 More specifically, in relation to the table raps heard during séance, Margaret Hamilton Bach writes that, "while [Glen] he admitted that such raps might be paranormal in origin, he positively refused to admit at this time to himself or to any of his associates that 'Myers' and 'Stead' might actually be communicating. He went so far as to admit that such a possibility might exist, but he demanded much more in way of proof. This was as far as he wanted to go. Because he felt that the widespread prejudice which then prevailed against this type of investigation would in the end destroy his reputation as a medical man, and because he also believed Mrs. Poole's psychic powers to have become exhausted, he now put a stop to the sittings and firmly shut the door on any further inquiry. To put it bluntly, he had had enough." Hamilton, *Is Survival a Fact?*, 19.

16 Robertson, *Science of the Seance*, 34. On 24 July 1921, Lillian recorded a séance that she and Poole had with a short statement: "Mrs. Poole and Lillian H. present. They place their hands on the table. In a few moments the 'power' is exceedingly strong—the table tilts on two legs. . . . L.H. tried to depress it back to the floor but found the table seemed to be resting on a sort of 'air cushion.'" Quoted in T.G. Hamilton, "Second Period of Development," UMASC, HFF, MSS 14, A.79-41, Box 9, Folder 15.

17 Robertson, *Science of the Seance*, 35; Lillian Hamilton, "Steps in the Hamilton Inquiry," c. 1945, UMASC, HFF, MSS 14, A.79-41, Box 15, Folder 6.

18 Robertson, *Science of the Seance*, 34.

19 Based upon correspondence received from Lillian, "Records of a Canadian Circle: A Study of Psychic Messages and Physical Phenomena," *Light* 2, no. 2161 (1922): 362–63. This is the earliest published record of the Hamilton research.

20 Hamilton, "Steps in the Hamilton Inquiry," cited in Robertson, *Science of the Seance*, 35.

21 T.G. Hamilton to Isabel M. Stewart, 29 April 1931, UMASC, HFF, MSS 14, A.79-41, Box 5, Folder 1.

22 Margaret Hamilton Bach elaborates on the table-tilting experiments that her mother and Elizabeth Poole conducted for several months: "Nothing unusual happened, and my mother was about to give up her idea, when one evening, in mid-July 1921, the table suddenly tilted up on two legs and remained so for several minutes, in spite of a strong downward pressure from my mother. She called my father to see this for himself, and again the same thing happened." Hamilton, *Is Survival a Fact?*, 28.

23 Robertson, *Science of the Seance*, 35; Stan McMullin, *Anatomy of a Seance: A History of Spirit Communication in Central Canada* (Montreal and Kingston: McGill-Queen's University Press, 2004), 206.

24 Molly McGarry, *Ghosts of Futures Past: Spiritualism and the Cultural Politics of Nineteenth-Century America* (Berkeley: University of California Press, 2008), 19.

25 Margaret Hamilton Bach, "Notes 1921–1985," UMASC, HFF, MSS Notes, 1921–85, Box 17, Folder 10.

26 Hamilton, *Intention and Survival*, 1.

27 Evelyn Fox Keller, *Reflections on Gender and Science* (New Haven, CT: Yale University Press, 1985), 44.

28 Londa L. Schiebinger, *The Mind Has No Sex? Women in the Origins of Modern Science* (Cambridge, MA: Harvard University Press, 1989), 191.

29 Alex Owen, *The Darkened Room: Women, Power, and Spiritualism in Late Nineteenth Century England* (Camden Town, London: Virago, 1989).

30 Tom Gunning, "Phantom Images and Modern Manifestations: Spirit Photography, Magic Theatre, Trick Films, and Photography's Uncanny," in *Cinematic Ghost: Haunting and Spectrality from Silent Cinema to the Digital Era*, ed.Murray Leeder (New York: Bloomsbury Academic, 2015), 17–38; Robertson, *Science of the Seance*; Warner, *Phantasmagoria*.

31 Sara Ahmed, *The Cultural Politics of Emotion* (Edinburgh: Edinburgh University Press, 2014), 3.

32 For this, Ahmed, ibid., cites Elizabeth Spelman, "Anger and Insubordination," in *Women, Knowledge, and Reality: Explorations in Feminist Philosophy*, ed. Ann Garry and Marilyn Pearsall (New York: Routledge, 1989), 263–74; and Alison Jaggar, "Love and Knowledge: Emotion in Feminist Epistemology," in *Women, Knowledge, and Reality: Explorations in Feminist Philosophy*, ed. A. Garry and M. Pearsall (New York: Routledge, 1996), 166–90.

33 Robertson, *Science of the Seance*, 12; Owen, *The Darkened Room*, 6–12.

34 Robertson, *Science of the Seance*, 12.

35 Ibid.

36 Warner, *Phantasmagoria*, 225.

37 Ibid.

38 Serena Keshavjee, "The Scientization of Spirituality," in *Seductive Surfaces: The Art of Tissot*, vol. 6 of *Studies in British Art*, ed. Katherine Lochnan (New Haven, CT: Yale University Press, 1999), 213–44, quotation at 216.

39 The Victorian séance was an activity among the upper class. According to Keshavjee, ibid., by 1885 "mediumship and séances were well integrated into the drawing rooms of the best society." See also ibid., 216–17. This changed with the scientization of psychical research and the decline of the Spiritualist movement.

40 Margaret Hamilton Bach, "Telekinesis 1922–1927," UMASC, HFF, MSS 14, Box 15, Folder 8.

41 Robertson, *Science of the Seance,* 44.

42 Ibid., 39.

43 Séance notes, 5 August 1928, UMASC, HFF, MSS 14, Box 15, Folder 12.

44 McMullin, *Anatomy of a Seance*, 183.

45 The Hamilton Family Fonds contains a photograph that illustrates this, described as "a glass lantern slide of the head, hand, and foot controls used to control the mediumship of Margery during séances with her husband, Dr. Crandon." UMASC, HFF, A.79-41, PC 12.

46 Ahmed, *The Cultural Politics of Emotion*, 170.

47 Robertson, *Science of the Seance*, 36.

48 Ibid.

49 Ahmed, *The Cultural Politics of Emotion*, 170.

50 Robertson, *Science of the Seance*, 36.

51 Di Bello, *Women's Albums*.

52 Holland, "'Sweet it is to Scan . . . ,'" 160.

53 Ibid., 140.

54 Ibid., 150.

55 Ibid., 173–74.

56 Ibid. For this, Holland cites Valerie Walkerdine, "Behind the Painted Smile," in *Family Snaps: The Meaning of Domestic Photography*, ed. Jo Spence and Patricia Holland (London: Virago, 1991), 35–45; Simon Watney, "Ordinary Boys," in *Family Snaps: The Meaning of Domestic Photography*, ed. Jo Spence and Patricia Holland (London: Virago, 1991), 26–34; and Annette Kuhn, *Family Secrets: Acts of Memory and Imagination* (London: Verso, 2002).

57 Robertson, *Science of the Seance*, 25–26. T.G. writes that his group is composed of "good men and true" in "Teleplasmic Phenomenon in Winnipeg," *Psychic Science: Quarterly Transactions of the British College* 8, no. 3 (1929): 179. Omitting women's roles applies to early-twentieth-century history generally.

58 Holland, "'Sweet it is to Scan . . . ,'" 174.

59 Ibid.

60 Hamilton, "'Bring on Your Ghosts!,'" 11.

61 Holland, "'Sweet it is to Scan . . . ,'" 179.

62 Ibid.

Facing page, Research Notes, Hamilton Family Fonds, MSS 14, Box 15, Folder 9.

Overleaf, Lecture cards, Hamilton Family Fonds, MSS 14, Box 1, Folder 10.

PART TWO: ARCHIVAL EXPLORATION

Statement

Re "Bat" Teleplasm (No 40) will appear on Mary M's face with wings outspread

B. mass [illegible] 3 more sittings

Re First "Cone" [illegible] (No 44)

a. Doyle [illegible] will "put his picture through" by means [illegible] work – (that is teleplasm).

Re Second Doyle face (48)

a. Predicts coming of Second Doyle face

Re First "Cone" + face (47)

a. mass cone-shaped will appear + reveal a face-form.

D.
193
April
[illegible]
April
June
May

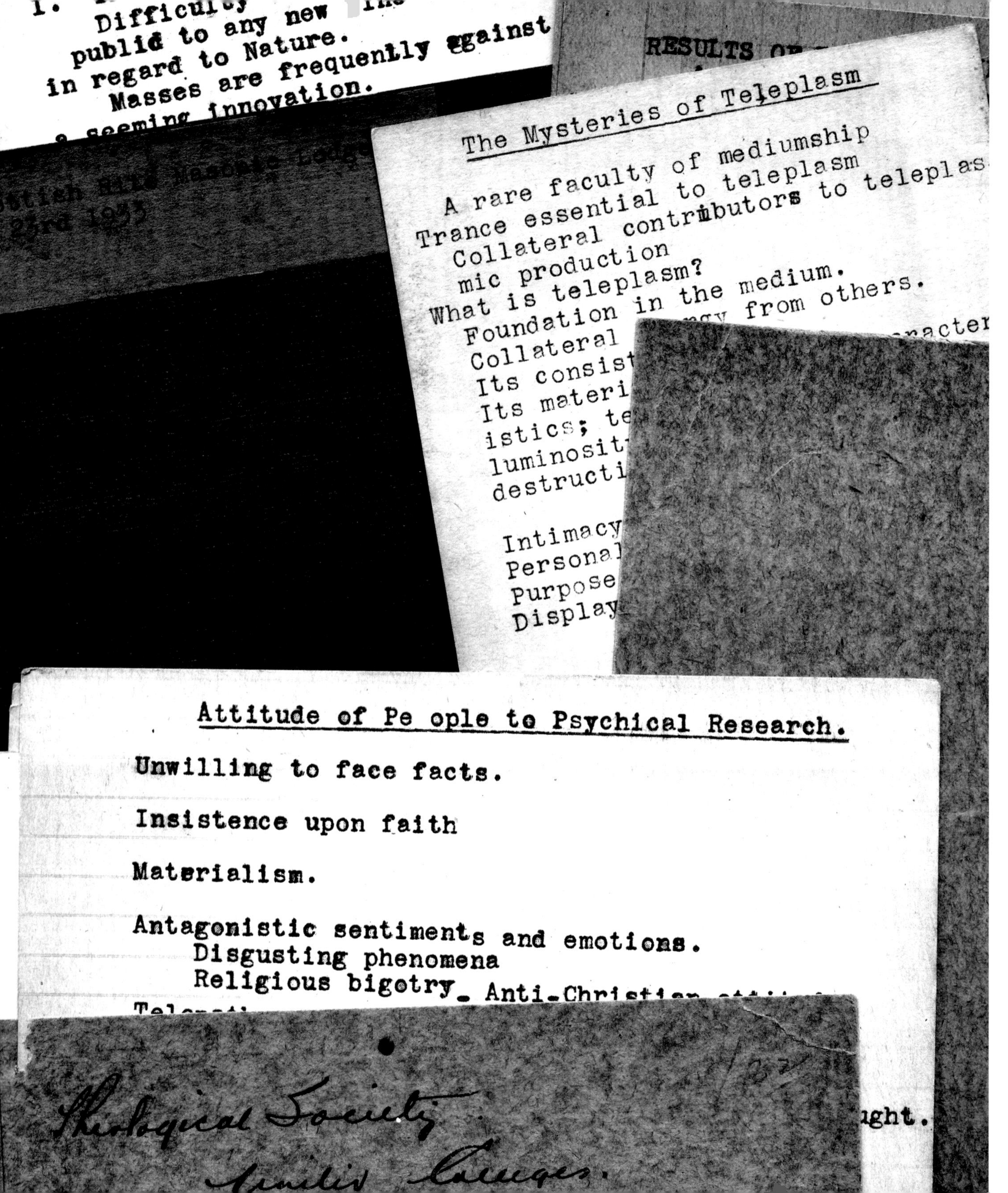

Difficulty
public to any new
in regard to Nature.
Masses are frequently against
a seeming innovation.

RESULTS OF

Scottish Masonic Lodge
23rd 1933

The Mysteries of Teleplasm

A rare faculty of mediumship
Trance essential to teleplasm
Collateral contributors to teleplasmic production
What is teleplasm?
Foundation in the medium.
Collateral energy from others.
Its consist
Its materi
istics; te
luminosit
destructi

Intimacy
Personal
Purpose
Display

Attitude of People to Psychical Research.

Unwilling to face facts.

Insistence upon faith

Materialism.

Antagonistic sentiments and emotions.
Disgusting phenomena
Religious bigotry. Anti-Christian atti

ught.

Theological Society
Annales Colleges.

4

Defending the T.G. Hamilton Family Psychical Research Legacy

Walter Meyer zu Erpen

Between 1918 and 1935, Winnipeg medical doctor Thomas Glendenning (T.G.) Hamilton and his wife, Lillian May Hamilton, conducted scientific experiments in their home into telepathy, telekinesis, teleplasm, mediumship during trance states,[1] and other psychic phenomena. Prominent community leaders, including lawyers, clergymen, engineers, schoolteachers, and medical doctors, were among the credible witnesses of the physical psychic phenomena photographed. The group's careful, systematic approach gained T.G. an international reputation. Ultimately, the Hamiltons concluded that the only theory capable of explaining all the phenomena observed was survival of human personality beyond bodily death.

Had the Hamilton children not safeguarded the photographs of the table levitations and teleplasmic manifestations, together with the séance minutes, attendance records, and correspondence, the family's experiments would be as poorly documented as those of most psychical research sitter groups. The authenticity of the records is demonstrated through the unbroken custodial chain, the organization and complexity of the records, the many cross-references, and the signs of heavy use to compile and publish two books.

My interest in the possibility of spirit communication through mediumship dates from 1972, when my maternal grandfather died. My study of the Hamilton psychical research experiments began in 1990. Financial assistance from the T. Glen Hamilton Research Grant Program in 1991 allowed me to spend two weeks at the University of Manitoba, studying the Hamilton Family Fonds (HFF), the focus of colleague Shelley Sweeney in Chapter 5.

The 2021 Bigelow Institute for Consciousness Studies essay contest caused me to evaluate many claimed approaches to obtaining evidence of life after death.[2] The study of psychic phenomena requires an open-minded yet cautious approach. Alternative explanations must be considered before attributing phenomena to surviving spirits. It was in that tradition of psychical research to understand human experience better that the Hamiltons started their investigation of mental telepathy and telekinetic table movements. They quickly discovered that, when trickery and false observation were ruled out, there remained genuine phenomena, both cognitive and physical, that could not be explained by existing scientific theory. The Hamiltons knew that not all genuine paranormal phenomena support the survival hypothesis—"the conjecture that some aspect of a person survives death."[3] To make sense of the paranormal, researchers need to distinguish between fraudulent behaviour and inexplicable psychic phenomena, to recognize that religious belief colours the lens through which phenomena are interpreted, and to acknowledge that the will to believe is as dangerous as the rejection of anything that cannot be measured by science.

My Hamilton Study

My Winnipeg research visits in 1991–92 proved to me the authenticity of the Hamiltons' documentation of their research. At that time, I was fortunate to meet James B. Nickels (1931–2021); Phyllis Hamilton, the widow of Glen F. Hamilton, whom Jim Nickels interviewed in 1987;[4] and T.G.'s medical secretary, Eileen

(McTavish) Sykes (1907–2002), among others. Dozens of individuals, including children of the séance participants, were happy to assist when contacted.

In 1988, a member of our Victoria Spiritualist study group had donated the Hamiltons' *Is Survival a Fact?* (1969) and *Intention and Survival* (2nd ed., 1977), among other books intended to start a library. Influenced by the Hamiltons' experimental work and book subtitles that claimed intentional activity by discarnate trance personalities and by the work of the Florida-based Survival Research Foundation, I co-founded in 1991 the Survival Research Institute of Canada (SRIC) with a small group of friends.[5]

Ever the sceptic, looking at the published half-tone photographs, I questioned how such bizarre manifestations could be genuine. If faked, then how was fraud sustained over so many years in a stable research group under careful observation? The level of trickery required would have involved several mediums. If there was collusion among the mediums and sitters, had they all gone to their graves without someone divulging their secrets?

I spent hours at the pay phones on street corners and in the old Taché Hall residence at Fort Garry. When the widowed Isobel Wither (1923–2007), daughter-in-law of Bill and Jean Wither, hung up on me, I called right back. A delightful meeting ensued together with her sister-in-law Lorna (Wither) Fraser (1921–2002), who gifted her parents' Hamilton photographs to SRIC.[6] I travelled about Winnipeg by bus to look at the homes where the mediums had lived and the cemeteries in which participants were buried in order to construct family trees. Years later, as part of one of the Hamilton-based documentaries, I visited their séance room.

By 1995, I had contacted hundreds of individuals and had drafted notes on the Hamiltons, their mediums, and the regular participants, including many of T.G. Hamilton's medical colleagues and some occasional witnesses. More than 100 biographical sketches, extending to over 700 pages, are destined for the University of Manitoba Archives and Special Collections (UMASC) together with my research files. Leaving no stone unturned in the early years of my study convinced me of the integrity of the Hamilton family and their associates.

My inquiries revealed nothing to suggest that they had been tricked. Rather, if the whole case was fraudulent, which I do not believe, then it would be the most successfully staged and sustained in the history of psychical research. Had I discovered any hint of trickery, I would have walked away, not spent thirty-two years studying and writing about the case. Hamilton descendants have patiently answered questions over decades; four granddaughters have contributed photograph collections or spare copies of the books. I count grandchildren of the Hamiltons and their mediums among my friends.

Participants in the Hamilton Psychical Research

My primary goal in this chapter is to share aspects of the biographies of the Hamiltons, the main mediums, and the special scrutineers to offer glimpses of the personal lives of just a handful of the Winnipeg residents who participated in the experiments. Those group members met week after week and attested to the authenticity of what they observed. Most of the written testimony is from middle-aged white men of Scottish Presbyterian background, many of whom became officers of the Winnipeg Society for Psychical Research (SPR) in 1931. Apart from the substantial contributions of Lillian Hamilton and Margaret Hamilton Bach in documenting and promoting the experiments, the women participants left few records.

The photographed phenomena have been my main interest, which aligns with Serena Keshavjee's contextualization of those images in Chapter 2. Communications from the trance personalities and other discarnates, through trance speech or writing, demonstrated intention as predictions made and fulfilled. The Hamiltons' books document the intentional actions of trance personalities, which for the family tipped the scale in favour of the survival hypothesis. I agree with their conclusion.

T.G. Hamilton and Lillian May Forrester Family Background

Thomas Glendenning Hamilton (1873–1935) was born in Agincourt, Ontario, the second-youngest son of James Hamilton and Isabella Glendenning. T.G. had four brothers and one sister. In 1882–83, the family moved to a homestead near Saskatoon as part of a temperance colony. Following the Northwest Rebellion, tragedy struck the family, with father James dying in 1885 and daughter Margaret the year following. By 1891, the family had moved to Winnipeg, which afforded better educational and professional opportunities for the five brothers.

T.G. pursued college studies and graduated with an MD from Manitoba Medical College in 1903. He specialized in internal medicine and obstetrics and was soon practising as a general practitioner in what is now Elmwood, Winnipeg. His biography is established in his *Dictionary of Canadian Biography* entry, including his career as a doctor and medical lecturer, his leadership in provincial and national medical associations, his role as a Presbyterian and later United Church elder, and his community and political engagement.[7]

Lillian May Forrester (1880–1956) was born near Belleville, Ontario, the eldest daughter of John MacFarlane Forrester and Mathilda (Mattie) Rixon. Lillian's twin brother was stillborn. The family soon moved to Emerson, Manitoba, where four younger brothers and two sisters were born. Possibly anxious to escape rural farm life, Lillian also pursued studies in Winnipeg, graduating from the Winnipeg General Hospital School of Nursing in 1905 with the top award for highest general proficiency. Historians have largely ignored the role of women leaders in psychical research. In Chapter 3, Katie Oates begins to redress that gap by focusing on Lillian's experiments after T.G.'s death.

T.G. and Lillian were married in 1906 by the minister of Elmwood Presbyterian Church in the home of the bride's uncle. They had four children: Margaret Lillian, Glen Forrester, and twins Arthur Lamont and James Drummond. Their granddaughter Janice Hamilton (1948–) is the Hamilton and Forrester family historian. Her 2021 book[8] and introductory article in the T.G. Hamilton *Paranormal*

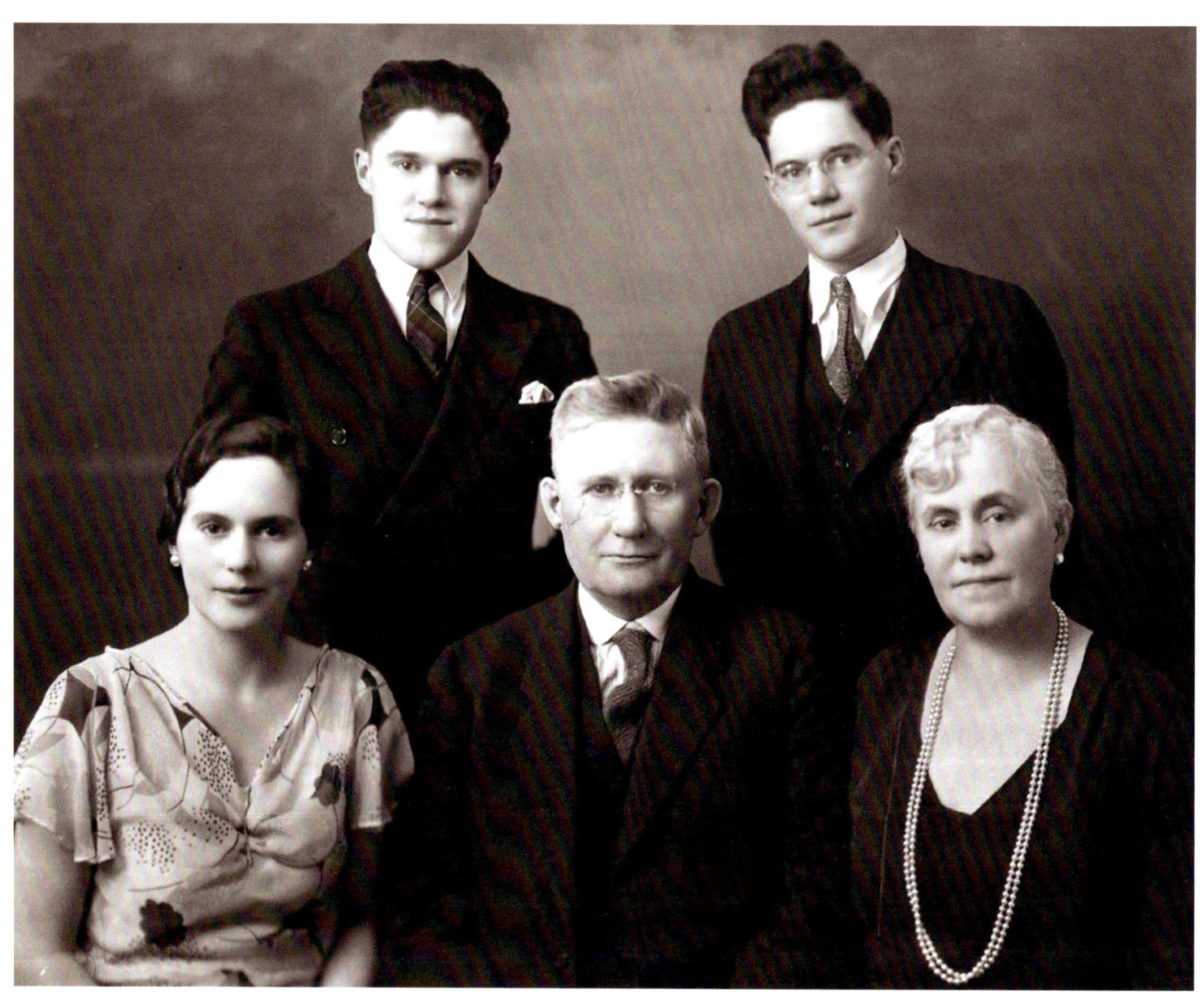

Fig. 4.1. Front row (left to right): Margaret L. Hamilton, T.G. Hamilton, Lillian Hamilton; back row: Glen F. Hamilton, James D. Hamilton, 1932. Photographer unknown. Courtesy of Janice Hamilton.

Review special issue[9] are the best sources for the family's history. In Chapter 1 of this volume, Esyllt W. Jones's discussion of the impacts of the 1918–20 influenza pandemic includes early family photographs. In 1932, the Hamilton family sat for a family portrait (see Figure 4.1).

From 1906 to 1920, T.G. was active in school board and local and provincial politics. His defeat in seeking re-election in the 1920 provincial election concluded his political activism and opened the possibility for other engagement.

Defenders of the Hamilton Psychical Research Legacy

I turn now to defenders of the Hamilton psychical research legacy involved in the experiments between 1918 and 1935, beginning with members of the immediate Hamilton family.

Throughout the experiments, Lillian was T.G.'s closest collaborator. She initiated the informal table-tilting sessions with friends and encouraged T.G. to participate in them. Responsible for coordinating the weekly meetings, Lillian had to convince T.G. and the mediums on several occasions to continue their investigations. Without her efforts, the Hamiltons' psychical research experiments would not have been possible. When the trance personalities predicted that a special phenomenon was imminent, Lillian hosted the group twice a week, and sometimes two parallel groups met to explore different aspects of psychic capacity. For instance, between March 1929 and January 1935, when T.G.'s health began to fail, the "small group" (introduced in Chapter 1) met weekly and continued through September 1935.

T.G.'s brother James (Jim) Archibald Hamilton (1870–1934) regularly participated in the séances. Graduating from Manitoba Medical College in 1904, Jim became a general practitioner. From at least 1919 to 1934, the brothers shared medical offices in the Somerset Block at 294 Portage Avenue. The attendance registers indicate that the doctors Hamilton were occasionally called out of a séance to provide emergency care.

As adults, the Hamilton children had no doubt about the authenticity of their parents' research and were the first line of defence of their legacy. The task of compiling and editing T.G.'s papers fell to his widow, Lillian, and their youngest son, James (Jim) Drummond Hamilton (1915–1980), who had three degrees and conducted medical research before obtaining his MD in 1957. After months of discussing a suitable title and obtaining financing from mining engineer Julian Gifford Cross (1888–1971), Macmillan Company of Canada published T.G.Hamilton's *Intention and Survival: Psychical Research Studies and the Bearing of Intentional Actions by Trance Personalities on the Problem of Human Survival* (1942), which recorded the family's psychical research experiments during T.G.'s lifetime. In 1946, J.D. Hamilton married Joan Murray Smith (1918–1994) and did not further pursue psychical research. Their daughter Janice is the family historian.

Margaret Lillian Hamilton (1909–1986) graduated from the University of Manitoba (BA, 1930) and enjoyed a successful career as a music teacher and adjudicator (piano and voice); she was an associate of the Royal Conservatory of Music of Toronto. Before her marriage in 1934 to James Reynolds (Jimmy) Bach (1909–1984), she attended the séances and sometimes acted as note taker. In 1956, the Bachs separated, and Margaret Hamilton Bach, as she then chose to be known, returned to Winnipeg with her two teenaged daughters.

Over the next three decades, she took on the role of archivist and historian in promotion of her parents' research. In 1969, she published, as Margaret Hamilton and based upon the manuscript begun by her mother, *Is Survival a Fact?*,[10] which focused on the deep-trance automatic scripts. It also told the story of the teleplasmic screen that bore an unmistakable likeness of T.G.'s face, photographed on 22 May 1939 with three cameras. Not mentioned is the photograph of the residue of that screen discovered as a double exposure of another meeting. The first image convinced the family of T.G.'s survival (see Figures 3.1 and 3.4). The second image supported the authenticity of the manifestations by capturing the teleplasm in the process of disintegration (see Figure 3.3).

Glen Forrester Hamilton (1911–1988) followed most directly in his father's footsteps, graduating from the University of Manitoba Medical College in 1934. During the Second World War, he served in England as a volunteer medical officer.

In 1938, he married Phyllis Farina Ellis (1911–1997); the couple had one son and three daughters. The most reticent about the psychical research, Glen revealed during his interview in 1987 with Jim Nickels that as a child he had been teased about living in the ghost house, but he also stated his belief in personal survival after death.

Religious Background of the Researchers

The Hamiltons and their associates, including the mediums, were devout Christians, mostly Presbyterian. After the amalgamation in 1925 of Canadian Protestant denominations, most of them attended United Church of Canada services. Their pursuit of psychical research through scientific experiments arose from a convergence of factors. The Hamiltons had Spiritualist friends, including prominent visitors. Since the deaths of the Hamilton children Margaret (1986) and Glen (1988), scholars have attempted to recast the Hamiltons and their research as "Spiritualist."[11] In my opinion, these attempts have been based upon superficial contextual knowledge or as an attempt to dismiss their psychical research.

The modern Spiritualist movement dates from the telekinetic raps, now better understood as poltergeist activity, that the Methodist Fox family experienced in 1848 in their home at Hydesville, near Rochester, New York.[12] The youngest daughters, Margaretta (Maggie) Fox (1833–1893) and Catherine (Kate) Fox (1837–1892), evolved a system of communication with the raps that convinced many people drawn to Hydesville that the girls were communicating with an unseen spirit world. The Fox sisters became well-known mediums, but died in poverty, having been enticed to renounce the movement they had helped found.

Initially a loose movement of mediums and small investigating bodies, the concept of Spiritualism as a religion predates 1856 when Thomas Lake Harris (1823–1906) became the pastor of a Christian Spiritualist Church in New York. That "new" church resulted from a schism within an existing congregation that continued to hold regular Sunday services at Dodworth's Hall on Broadway.[13] Preliminary research in the Newspapers.com database points to the first significant wave of

Spiritualist churches having been established during the 1880s, primarily in the United States. By the early 1890s, organizations were evolving that would attempt to unite and regulate the churches and their mediums. The Spiritualists' National Union, founded in 1901 in England, is among the oldest church governing bodies.

Parallel to the evolution of the Spiritualist church movement were investigating committees that claimed science, not religion, as their authority. In 1882, a group of Cambridge scholars in the U.K. had established the Society for Psychical Research (SPR) to determine whether the psychic phenomena claimed by Spiritualists were genuine. A secondary consideration for psychical researchers was whether such phenomena offer evidence of life after death. The American Society for Psychical Research was founded in 1884. It is in the British and American tradition of psychical research that the Hamiltons approached their séance-room experiments.

Although T.G. and Lillian never mentioned the death of Arthur (1915–1919) as a motivating factor in their psychical research, scholars have claimed his death in January 1919 from influenza as the motivation for sixteen years of research. They cite the memories of siblings Margaret and Glen, aged nine and seven when their brother died. Sixty years later they were drawn into speculation about the role of his death in their parents' research. Arthur's facial likeness was recognized in the 25 November 1928 five-faces teleplasm (see Figures 1.5, 1.6, and 1.7), and Esyllt W. Jones has discussed the role of the smaller group as a forum for communication of a personal nature, among living and deceased family members. In the Hamiltons' publications, the focus was the trance personalities who demonstrated intentionality, including historical figures such as Stevenson, Stead, Conan Doyle, explorer David Livingstone, preacher Charles Haddon Spurgeon, and characters such as the pirate John King and his alleged daughter Katie King.

When my study began, I too considered the role of "bereavement coping strategy" but abandoned that narrow approach because it fails to recognize the broader influences of the First World War, the influenza pandemic, and the lectures in Winnipeg by Oliver Lodge (1920) and Arthur Conan Doyle (1923). Lodge and Conan Doyle each in his own way presented the evidence for survival. No single death propelled the Hamilton psychical research experiments, which started in 1918, before Arthur's death. Multiple later inputs made their continuation possible. Also, death was ever present in the lives of the group members.

Experiments in Telepathy

T.G. read about psychical research while at Manitoba College, and Lillian read F.W.H. Myers's *Human Personality and Its Survival of Bodily Death* (1903). The Hamiltons' first experiments date from 1918, when Reverend William Talbot Allison (1875–1941), a professor of English at Wesley College and the minister of King Memorial Church from 1919 to 1920, piqued their curiosity. Allison had spent a week in St. Louis, Missouri, to investigate "Patience Worth," the trance control who claimed to be a seventeenth-century woman and had begun to dictate literary works through medium Pearl Lenore (Pollard) Curran (1883–1937). In his *Manitoba Free Press* "literary chat" column, Allison reported on the case's literary aspects during September and October 1918.[14]

The same year T.G., Allison, and Reverend Daniel Norman McLachlan (1875–1943), the pastor of King Memorial Church for most of 1904–20, conducted simple experiments into thought transference that convinced the three men "that telepathy was possible and did work."[15] Lillian detailed those experiments in 1951, including that McLachlan had been the telepathic recipient.[16] That fact could have caused embarrassment while McLachlan was the United Church of Canada secretary of the Board of Evangelism and Social Service (1925–38). The telepathy experiments showed that the researchers did not attribute all inexplicable phenomena to surviving spirits and that their active investigation of psychic phenomena predated Arthur's death.

The Hamiltons' First Medium, Elizabeth Poole

In 1920, in their home with several friends, T.G. and Lillian Hamilton attempted table-tilting, a popular parlour game as a means of spirit communication. The alphabet would be called out, and the table movement would stop at the intended letter. The Hamilton children's nanny, Elizabeth Poole, was among that initial group of friends. Born Elizabeth Wilson (1868/69–1935) near Glasgow, Scotland, she married John Allan Poole (c. 1872–1928) in the Church of Scotland in 1894.[17] The couple had three children before emigrating to Canada in 1904. The Pooles settled in Elmwood in 1906, living in a modest home at 270 Johnson Avenue West, East Kildonan, and attending King Memorial Church. City directories list John Poole as a stableman at Eaton's and later as an apartment block janitor.

In addition to being a second mother to the Hamilton children, Elizabeth worked for T.G. as a practical nurse. In séances, mediums were often given a *nom de séance*, in part to protect their privacy and in part not to disrupt their trance state when addressed. Poole was called Ellen but sometimes recorded in séance notes as E.M.[18] She stopped attending the Hamilton séances about 1933 when her health began to decline. She died suddenly on 4 July 1935 in the old folks' home at Middlechurch; Reverend W.T. Allison officiated at her funeral.

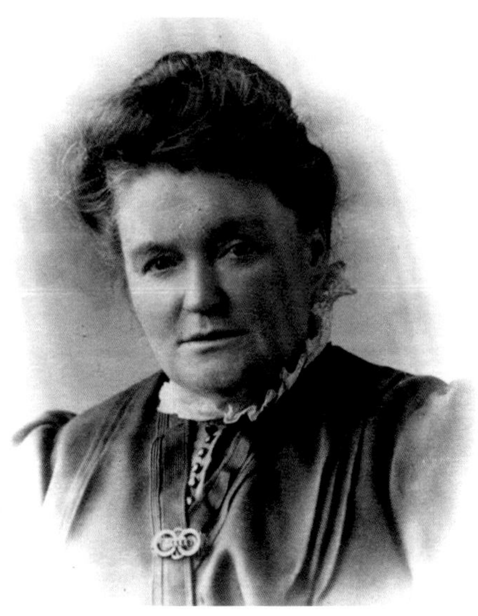

Fig. 4.2. Portrait of Elizabeth Poole, c. 1910s. Photographer unknown. UMASC, PC 12, Box 10, Folder 10, Item 69b, http://hdl.handle.net/10719/1410148.

The Pooles' eldest daughter, Elizabeth (Bessie) Shand (1895–1963), participated occasionally, often with her husband, Harold Shand (1891–1960), a civil engineer associated with the aqueduct that brought water from Shoal Lake to Winnipeg. Tragically, Bessie Shand died in Vancouver after being hit by a motorcycle. Interested in family history and his great-grandmother's psychic abilities, Richard Shand (1947–) inherited his grandmother Bessie's photographs, which he donated to UMASC.[19]

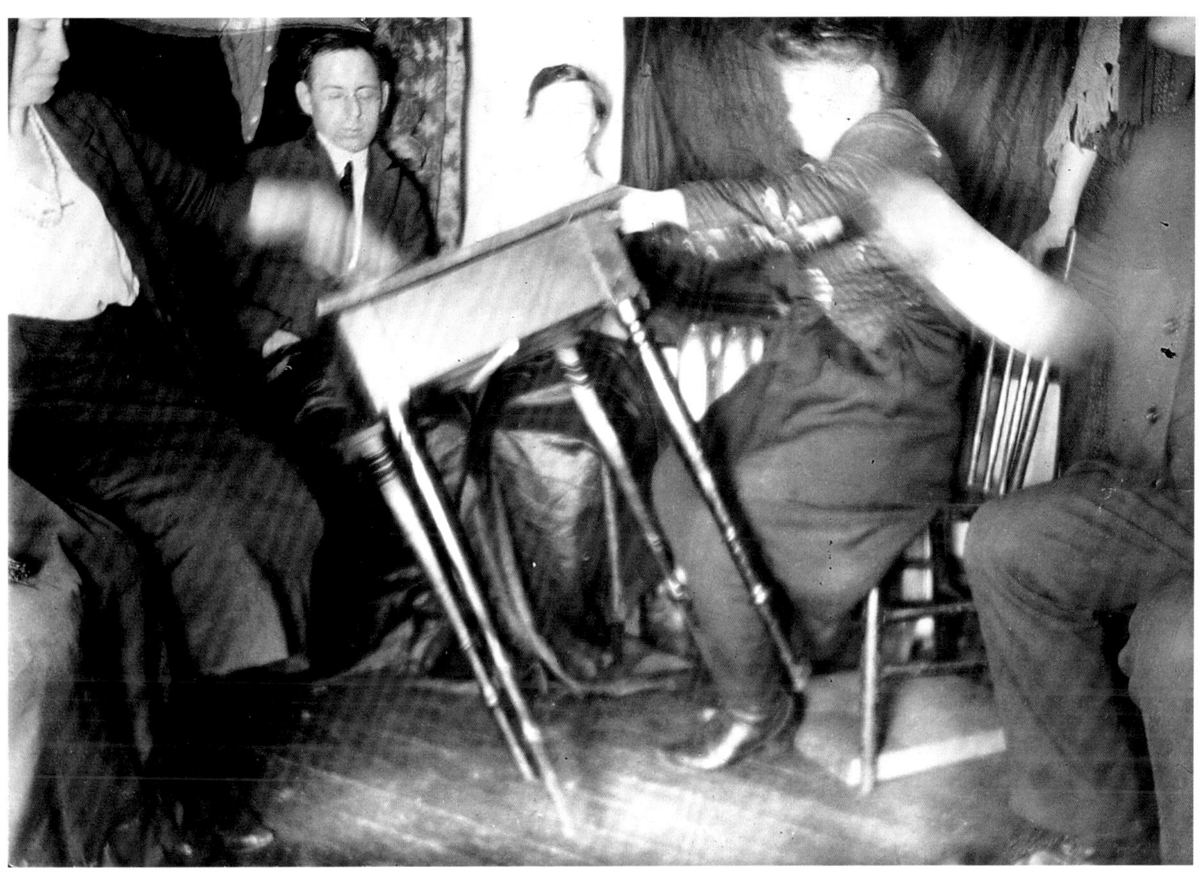

Fig 4.3. Lillian Hamilton (at left) has one hand on the tilting table, with Elizabeth Poole opposite her, and Harold and Bessie Shand behind the table, c. 1921. Photograph attributed to T.G. Hamilton. UMASC, Elizabeth (Poole) Shand Fonds, A16-024, Box 1, Folder 4.

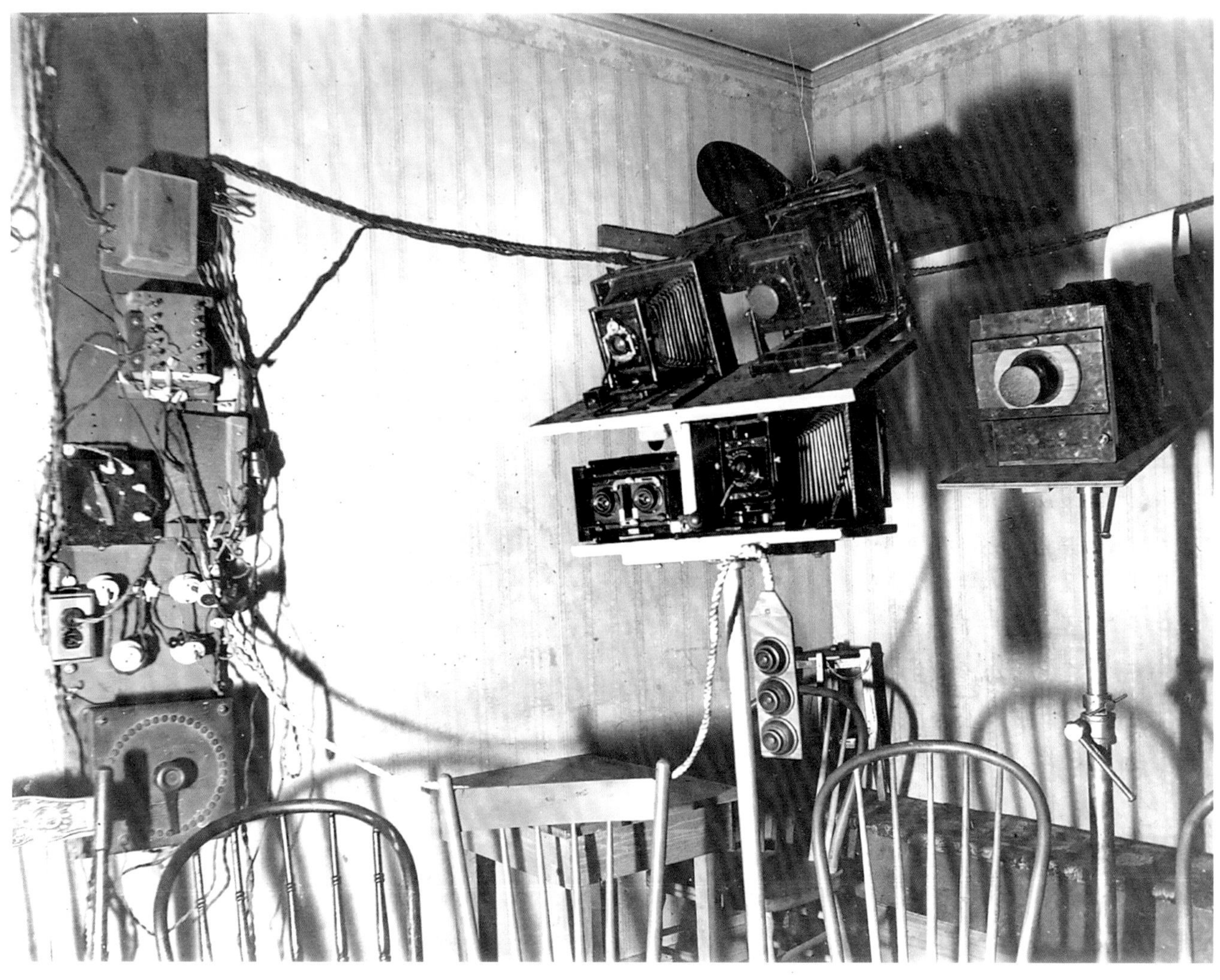

Fig. 4.4. The wiring that controlled the flash boxes and system of pressurized air that T.G. Hamilton used to open and close camera shutters, c. 1929–30. Photograph attributed to T.G. Hamilton. UMASC, Elizabeth (Poole) Shand Fonds, A16-024, Box 1, Folder 7.

Experiments with "Psychic Force," 1921–27

From 1921 to 1927, the Hamiltons turned their attention to the study of "psychic force," also referred to as telekinesis in the Hamilton records but now known as psychokinesis (PK). Lillian Hamilton had discovered that Elizabeth Poole's participation was essential in table-tilting sessions as the source of a strong telekinetic force. From August 1921, at Lillian's instigation, T.G. became increasingly involved in psychical research (see Figure 3.2). Found only in the Elizabeth (Poole) Shand Fonds, Figure 4.3 is the earliest known photograph of a table-tilting session in the Hamiltons' parlour.

The second-floor experimental laboratory, as discussed by Serena Keshavjee in Chapter 2, was established in 1923. Figure 2.6 shows the séance room layout, and Figure 2.7 shows T.G. Hamilton's photograph setup. By 1929, there were eleven cameras, three flash boxes, and a handheld remote control to ignite the flashes. A system of pressurized air installed in the basement could be accessed to open and close the camera shutters (see Figure 4.4).[20] During the teleplasmic experiments, visitors sometimes brought their own cameras, including Rae (Bruening) Cannon, whose still photograph from a movie camera using infrared film introduces Murray Leeder's chapter (see Figure 7.1).[21]

In March 1926, James Malcolm (Malcolm) Bird (1886–1964) visited Winnipeg to scrutinize the phenomena in his capacity as research officer for the American SPR. Figure 4.5 was obtained of the table suspended in the air, and Bird later "voiced his approval of the control conditions and the validity of the experiments."[22] Photographs document at least sixteen full table levitations.[23] In some, the table is suspended, motionless, in the wooden cabinet, with the surprised observers watching the table in full flight. In several, there is no bodily contact with or near the suspended table (see, e.g., Figure 4.6).

Experiments with Psychic Force Revealed

Initially, T.G. Hamilton was cautious about sharing his findings beyond a small circle of friends. One can imagine his concern about ruining his professional

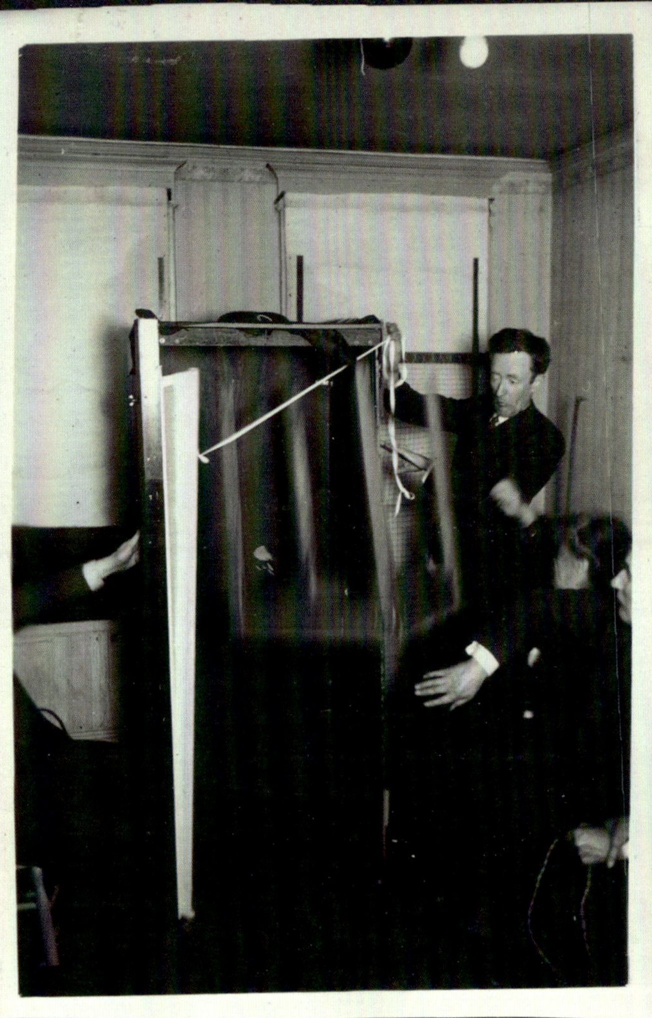

March 1, 1926 Observer - J. Malcolm Bird, then Research Officer for the A.S.P.R. Prior to the seance, he searched the room, and passed the table through a loop of rope to ascertain that there were no strings or wires attached to its legs. Under Dr. TGH's manual control Mrs. Poole first placed her hands on the table surface to activate it, then both she and Dr. TGH removed their hands. The table moved with astonishing speed and inverted. Mr. Bird exclaimed that he was amazed at the speed and the power of the levitation.

"...Quite often the table continues to rise even after the experimenters have ceased to touch it. This is movement without contact.

This phenomenon of levitation is, to me, absolutely proved."

Camille Flammarion 1907.

reputation through association with the study of paranormal phenomena. Even today affirming the reality of psychokinesis, belief in the possibility of ectoplasm, or objective evidence of life after death can be a career stopper in academia, though belief based upon religious faith is not questioned.

Encouraged by the reactions of visitors, as well as local clergymen and medical colleagues who observed the table in flight, T.G. presented his first public lecture on telekinesis in the spring of 1926 before 125 members of the Winnipeg Medical Society. Bruce Chown was present and, in his post-mortem tribute, described the effect of T.G. on his audience. Before the meeting, the crowd called out "Come on Glen! Bring on your ghosts!" Unruffled, T.G. "mentioned no ghost, nor spirit, nor personality, but he talked about a table, a table that moved at request, that rushed across the room, that leapt in the air, that defied the efforts of strong men to hold it. And as he talked he showed photographs of these actions."[24]

Beginning in 1926, T.G. published and lectured widely, gaining an international reputation for his careful experiments. New research shows that he presented over 100 lectures in Canada, the United States, and England.[25] Given the number of times that he was away from Winnipeg, his medical practice suffered, and after his death Lillian faced difficult financial circumstances.

King Memorial Church Pastors and Psychical Research

Between 1904 and 1929, the Presbyterian and later United Church congregation of King Memorial Church in Elmwood was served by three ministers, D.N. McLachlan, W.T. Allison, and E.G.D. Freeman. T.G. Hamilton was good friends with each of them; the four men somehow reconciled their Christian beliefs with their investigations of the nature of psychic phenomena. The arrival of Edwin Gardner Dunn

Fig. 4.5. ***Telekinesis #20 – J. Malcolm Bird and Levitating Table***. Inverted and levitated table that Malcolm Bird (in corner) failed to contain with the mesh screen and attached cord, 1 March 1926. Medium Elizabeth Poole is between Bird and T.G. Hamilton, who holds the remote control apparatus in his left hand. UMASC, PC 12 , Box 9, Folder 1, Item 20, http://hdl.handle.net/10719/1411137.

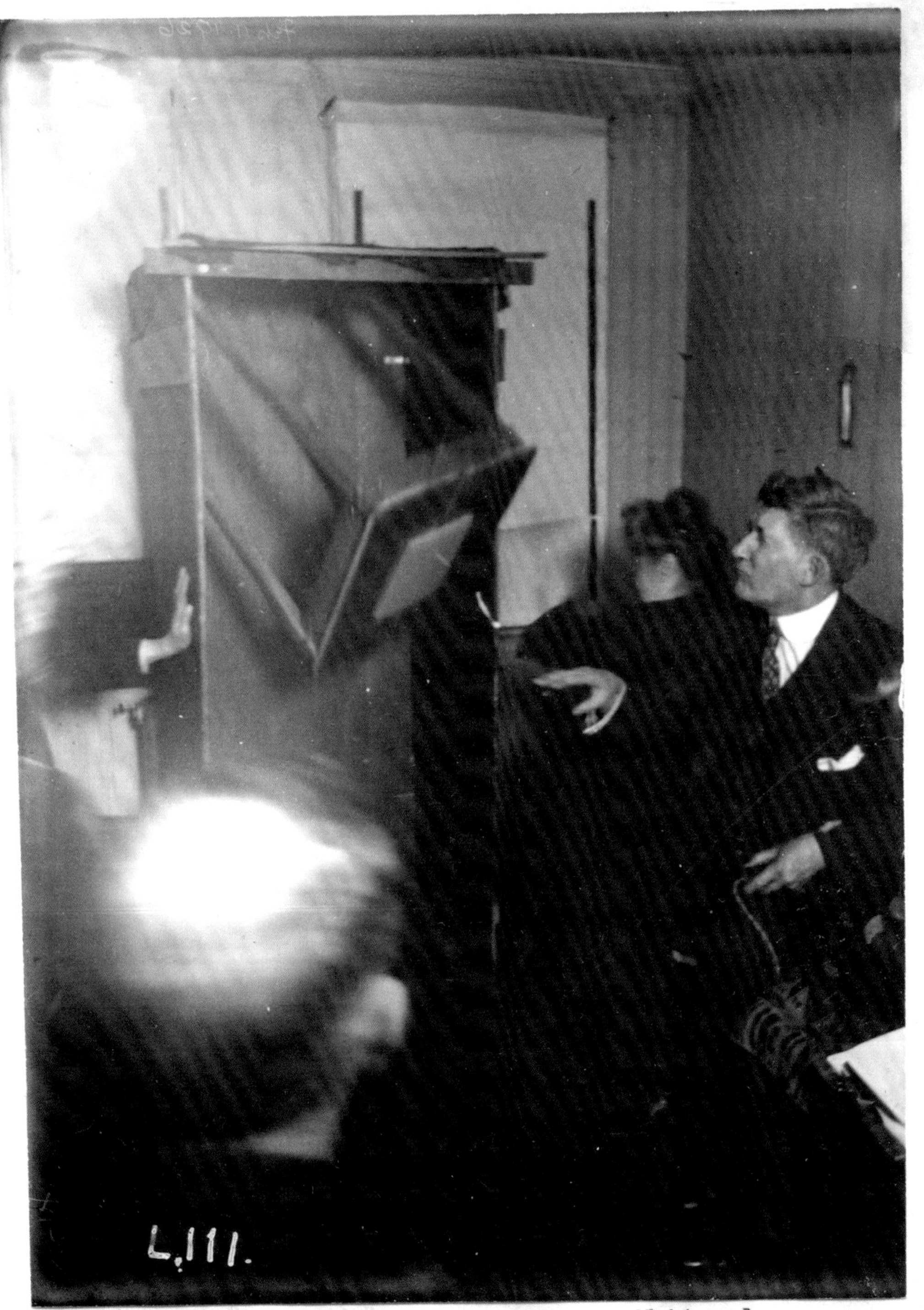

Seances were conducted in darkness. White plaque was painted with luminous paint, so that table movements would be visible to sitters.

(Gardner) Freeman (1890–1973) and his participation in the Hamilton research resulted in a valuable, additional defence of T.G.and the group's experiments.

Between 1924 and 1929, Freeman attended twenty-seven séances. On 11 February 1926, he witnessed an inverted table floating motionless with its legs inside the top of the wooden cabinet (see Figure 4.6). His balding head was identified by one of his daughters. That image, retouched to remove Freeman from the foreground, was used in early newspaper articles and more recently in the promotion of my illustrated Hamilton presentations.

From 1929 to 1938, Freeman ministered in Port Arthur but returned to Winnipeg in 1938 to an appointment as a professor of systematic theology, pastoral theology, and Christian ethics at United College.[26] Receiving an honorary Doctor of Divinity (Victoria University, Toronto, 1943), he became the dean of theology in 1946. The youngest Freeman child, Reverend Lois M. Wilson (1927–), was one of his students and recalled that her father "felt enough confidence to always include an account of the experiments in his practical theology lectures. . . . He presented it affirmatively in such a way as to raise questions for us about the findings of psychic research & stimulate our interest in continuing the research."[27]

In a memoir for his children written in retirement, Freeman included the study of psychic phenomena, noting that T.G. Hamilton was

> one of the best men I had at King Memorial, one of my elders, regular in his Church attendance, Chairman of the Committee responsible for completing the Church edifice, a skillful surgeon and a close personal friend. He had a keenly critical mind and was well informed in the natural and biological sciences, and felt that psychic phenomena ought to be studied both critically and objectively—but that they ought to be STUDIED, not just dismissed as trickery

Fig. 4.6. ***Annotated Photo Album, Telekinesis - Levitation and Inversion.*** Reverend E.G.D. Freeman observing non-contact table levitation, with medium Elizabeth Poole turned toward the corner and T.G. Hamilton holding the remote control apparatus in his left hand, 11 February 1926. UMASC, PC 12, Box 8, Folder 1, Item 8.2, http://hdl.handle.net/10719/1410276.

> or fraud. He would indignantly deny that he was a devout "Spiritualist" or a "Spiritualist" of any kind. He was a researcher.[28]

William Creighton Attests to Spirit Fingertips Dipped in Molten Wax

The wax fingertips in the Hamilton experiments have not been widely reported, possibly because of the controversy in the early 1930s about the thumbprints in the case of the Boston medium Mina Marguerite (Stinson) Crandon (1889–1941), known as Margery. For its bizarre nature, the phenomenon of materialized spirit hands dipping their fingertips in molten wax rivals the later teleplasmic manifestations. Both have contributed, as Brian Hubner argues in Chapter 6, to Winnipeg's reputation as a centre for weird happenings.

William Creighton (1885–1972) was born in Alexander, Manitoba, and after graduating from Manitoba Medical College in 1908 became a general practitioner. In 1911, he married Florence Melita Graham (1889–1982); the couple had three sons. Many of T.G. Hamilton's medical colleagues served overseas in medical capacities during the First World War. Creighton served in the 12th Field Ambulance Division of the Royal Canadian Army Medical Corps. The Creightons' first child, William Graham Creighton (1916–1924), was born in London, where Florence had joined her husband. In 1917, Creighton was awarded the Military Cross for eleven months of medical service in France, during which he contracted pulmonary tuberculosis. At the end of the war, he was emaciated and underweight, and a radiograph of his chest showed tubercles of the lung. Moving with his family to Vancouver for the more moderate climate, Creighton practised medicine there but returned to Winnipeg in 1921.

William and Florence first participated in the Hamilton experiments in 1924, including séances in which the trance personalities would materialize a teleplasmic finger or toe and dip it in a container of molten wax and then a bucket of cold water. The Creightons were invited scrutineers on 16 November 1924, and William wrote a report about that evening's sitting, during which a wax mould of a fingertip was secured.

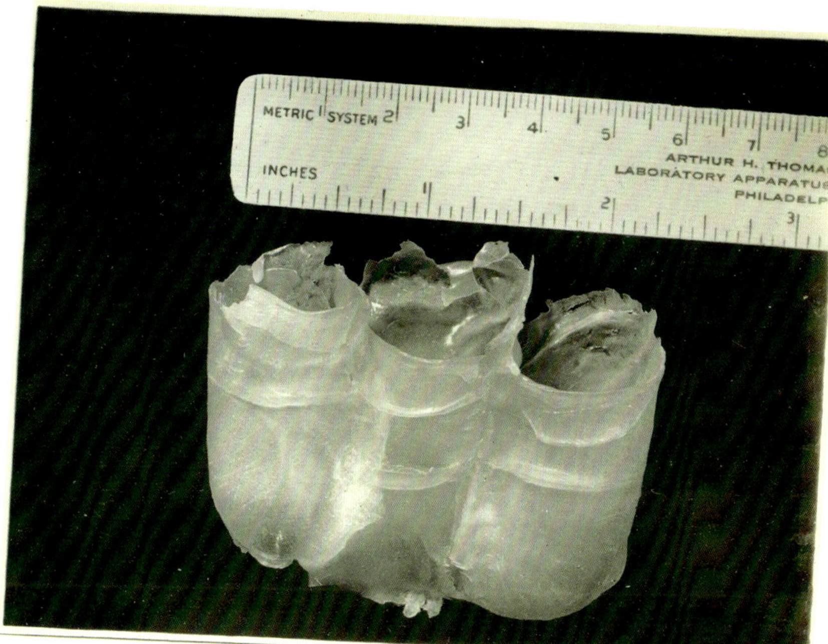

November, 1924. ("Stead" fingers.)

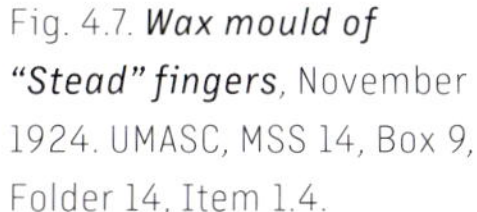

Fig. 4.7. ***Wax mould of "Stead" fingers***, November 1924. UMASC, MSS 14, Box 9, Folder 14, Item 1.4.

Fig. 4.8. ***Wax moulds of "R.L.S." fingers***, 1924. UMASC, MSS 14, Box 9, Folder 14, Item 1.3.

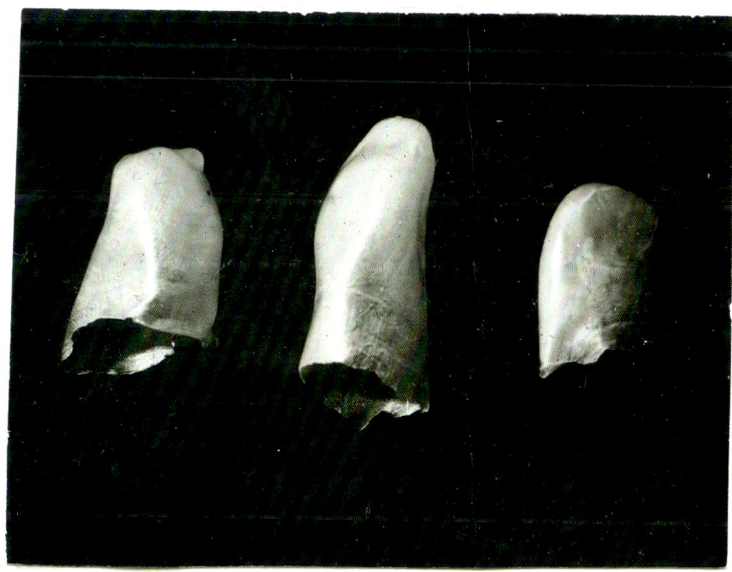

B, Jan 30/24 C. Feb 3/24 A. Jan. 27/24

"R.L.S." fingers.

With the séance room door locked on the inside, the finger form did not "correspond with that of any finger of any of those present." Creighton's report was signed by the nine sitters.[29] Photographs of the wax moulds survive in both the Hamilton Family Fonds and the Shand Fonds. Although accepted as genuine psychic phenomena, there is no way to prove that these strange creations were the fingertips of journalist William Thomas Stead (see Figure 4.7) and novelist Robert Louis Stevenson (see Figure 4.8). Equally, they could have been ideoplastic creations, as can be argued about the teleplasms. Stead and Stevenson were among the trance personalities who communicated through the Hamiltons' mediums over the next two decades.

The wax fingertips obtained in the Hamilton group postdate the European experiments with the Polish medium Franek Kluski (1873–1943) but predate the Margery wax fingerprints. Freeman was an important additional witness of the wax moulds:

> We placed two pans side by side on a table. One pan was filled with cold water. The other was filled with wax kept steady at the liquefying point by thermostatic control. Then we asked the "Control" to make an ectoplasmic mould of some sort, dip it in the melted wax, and then before de-materialization to put it into the cold water. We hoped by this means to secure a wax mould of what had been an ectoplasmic materialization. THE RESULT—wax moulds of fingers, thumbs and toes! We tried to produce some by dipping a finger into the wax, and then into the water, and then when the wax on our fingers was dry to slip it off. Our moulds were hard to pull off and none of them could match the ectoplasmic moulds in delicacy of finish.

Freeman concluded that ectoplasm is "a form of energy capable of materializing and of de-materializing" that can be "worked into all sorts of forms by the 'Control.'"[30]

Canada's First Teleplasm Photographed by a Medical Man

T.G. Hamilton credited William Creighton with having been the first medical man in Canada to photograph a teleplasmic mass. On 20 March 1927, using three cameras and in the presence of six witnesses, Creighton photographed "a strange mass falling from the mouth of the entranced medium" (see Figure 4.9).[31]

What little is known about Creighton's investigation of ectoplasm with the Scottish-born medium Elizabeth (Gibson) Young (1878–1929) is documented in the T.G. Hamilton special issue of *Paranormal Review*.[32] In 2005, I located the Creightons' youngest son, Robert James Creighton (1924–2021). He remembered the photograph and recalled that his father had likened the teleplasm to an umbilical cord, an allusion to the biology-based interpretation of some European researchers.[33] When we met at his home in Ontario in 2014, Robert and his daughter showed me the homemade séance table that his parents had brought with them from Winnipeg in 1963 and which the Creighton grandchildren have since donated to UMASC.

The Marshall Mediums and Photographed Teleplasms

Beginning in 1928, the focus of the experiments shifted to "teleplasm," the Hamiltons' preferred term, now more commonly known as "ectoplasm."[34] Without the Marshall sisters-in-law, Mary and Susan, T.G. Hamilton would not have photographed the teleplasms that manifested over five and a half years. In Scotland, Mary Ann Speirs married William (Bill) Marshall, and Susan McLements married Bill's brother Sandy.

Mary Marshall's ability as a physical medium developed quickly. Between the first teleplasm on 5 August 1928 and March 1934, seventy-two separate teleplasms were photographed in fifty photographic experiments, involving sixty flashlight exposures, over the course of 426 sittings.[35] Some 300 photographic images exist, taken from different angles.

The Hamiltons learned of Mary Marshall's gift of near-future precognition after the sudden death from acute heart disease of T.G.'s younger brother, lawyer

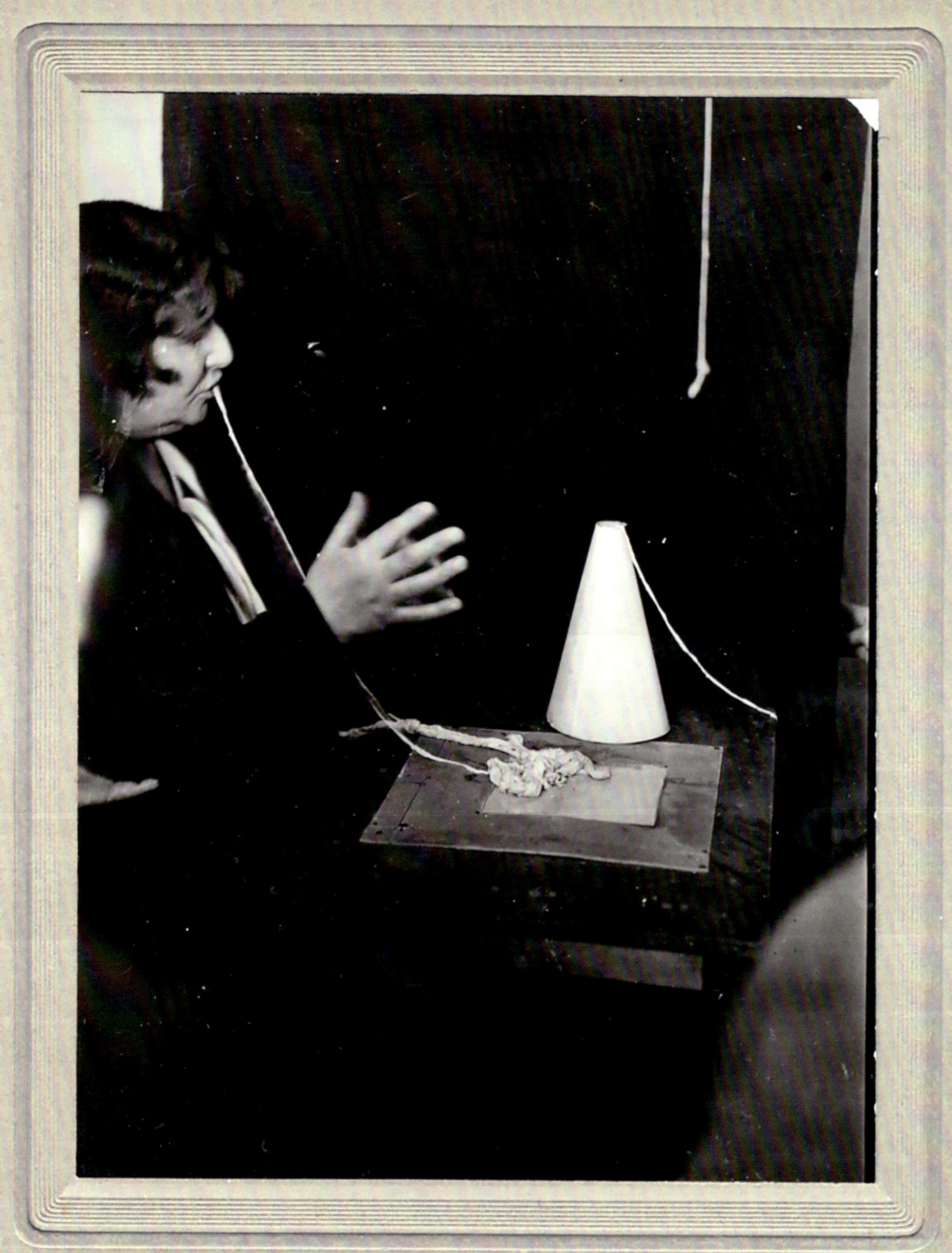

William Oliver Hamilton (1875–1924). The evening before his death, a crystal gazer had visited the home of Eva M. Broad, sister of Lloyd Broad, W.O. Hamilton's law partner. Identified as Mary Marshall, she had predicted and described the sudden death of a man named Oliver.[36] Mary had read cards in Scotland, and Daisy (Herdis Peterson) Marshall (1903–1992) recalled that her mother-in-law was arrested for card reading without a licence only two weeks after arriving in Canada.[37]

Mary Marshall first attended a Hamilton séance in December 1925, then a dozen times in 1926–27, and she participated regularly beginning in January 1928. Susan first attended séances in April 1929, after which she became one of the auxiliary mediums and the main medium for several teleplasms.

During the Hamilton séances, Mary Marshall was referred to as Mary M. (or M.M.) and later as Dawn, meaning "the dawn of a new day, of revelation of life to come."[38] Susan Marshall was named Mercedes. The Hamiltons claimed that Dawn's mediumship was largely developed within their experimental group. The experiments in 1924 with Elizabeth Poole involving materialized hands dipped in molten wax had provided the group's first exposure to teleplasm. The manifestations photographed with Mary suggest that she might have allowed the vaporous teleplasmic substance to be drawn from her body more abundantly. None of the Hamilton mediums received any financial remuneration for their services.

Mary and Bill Marshall and Family

Mary Ann Speirs (1880–1963) was born on leap year day in Govan, near Glasgow, of Irish-born parents, John Speirs, a shipyard labourer, and Ann. As told in a letter written at Lillian Hamilton's request in 1945, Mary's mother died when Mary was three years old, her early years were unhappy ones, her family was poor, and she

Fig. 4.9. Medium Elizabeth Young with the first teleplasm photographed in Canada by a medical man, whose shoulder can be seen in the bottom right foreground, 20 March 1927. Photograph by William Creighton. UMASC, H.A.V. Green Fonds, MSS 439, Box 1, Folder 3.

received only limited education. She admitted to things done in her youth of which she was ashamed, for having been naughty and run away.

Mary Speirs and Bill Marshall (1880–1947) had known one another as children in Govan and married in 1900. Her adult life was in stark contrast to her youth. In July 1945, Mary Marshall expressed her happiness in marriage and that "if I had to start married life over again I would marry the same man."[39] Bill and Mary Marshall raised three children. After their marriage, they lived in Ireland for a time. William (Bill) Edmund Johnson Marshall (1901–1978) was born in Belfast and might have been their biological son. The younger children, George Mervyn Foster Marshall (1909–1959) and Christine (Chrissie) Marshall (1910–1987), were biological brother and sister, born in Edinburgh and adopted when young. The Marshalls emigrated to Winnipeg in 1920.

Mary Marshall's role as a trance and physical medium in the Hamilton research was just one aspect of her life. With her family, Mary was very involved in St. Paul's United Church. A blacksmith by trade, Bill spent his last twenty working years (1924–44) as the church's caretaker. Together the Marshall family worked hard to keep the church clean and in working order. Everitt McKelvie (1908–1998), a friend of George Marshall, reported having witnessed Mary's telekinetic abilities in T.G. Hamilton's downtown office and at the Marshall cottage at Gimli, each time in good light.[40]After retirement, the Marshalls' eldest grandchild, George Edmund Marshall (1929–2018), the son of Bill and Daisy, was a Winnipeg municipal councillor and school trustee, representing Transcona. Although he was a child at the time, his grandmother's psychic abilities were not a secret. Her strong personality was not always appreciated, but Mary Marshall was never challenged. George believed that she was not fraudulent in either her beliefs or her actions. He never had the impression of any fakery.[41]

Fig. 4.10. ***Annotated Photo Album, Walter Eyes Mass,*** including a photograph of Walter Stuart Stinson, c. 1904–11. Photographer unknown. UMASC, PC 12, Box 8, Folder 5, Item 39, http://hdl.handle.net/10719/1411043.

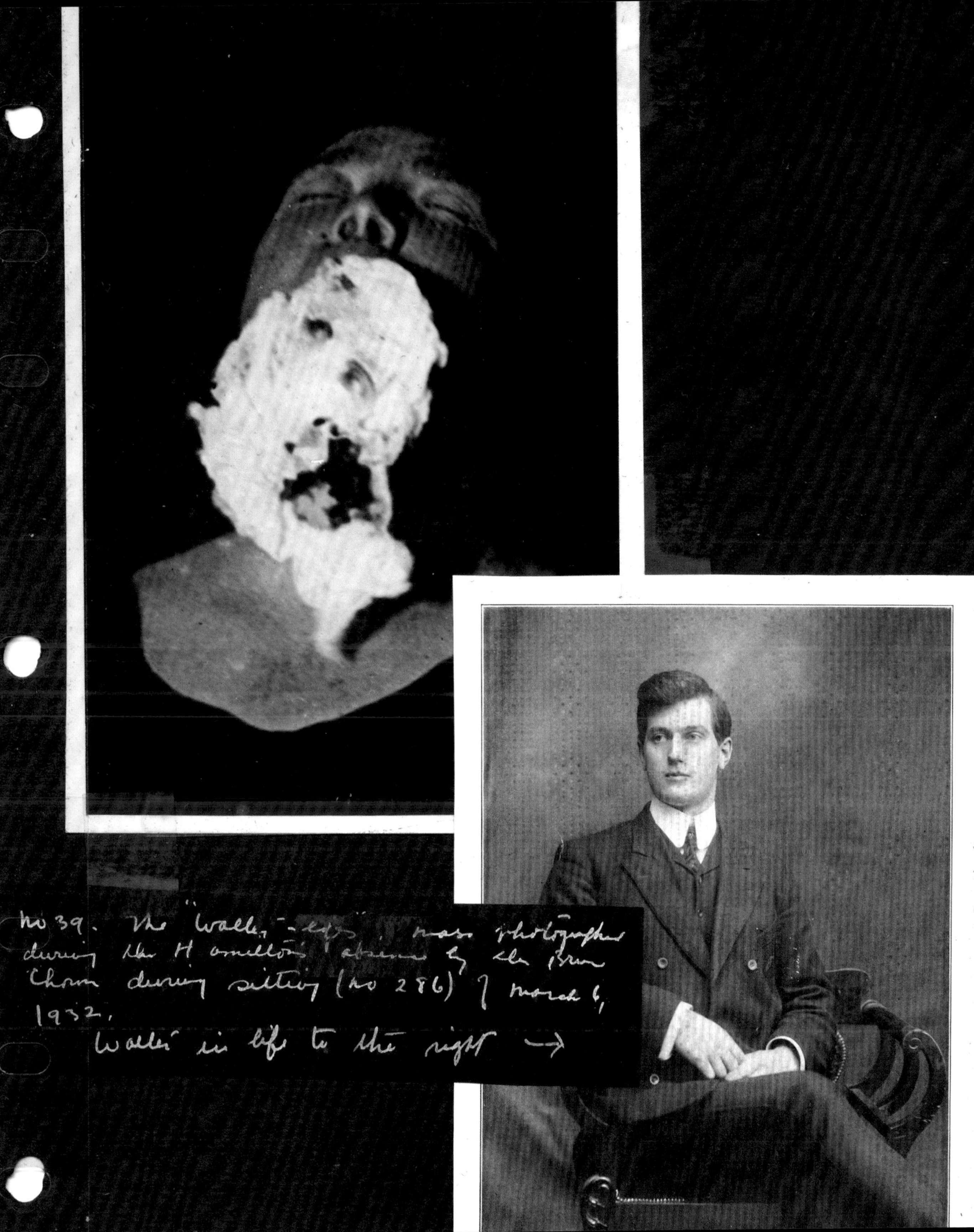

No 39. The "Walter"-"lips" mass photographed during the Hamiltons' absence by the Brown Camera during sitting (No 286) of March 6, 1932.
Walter in life to the right →

Susan and Sandy Marshall and Family

Although not as involved in the Hamilton research as her sister-in-law, Susan Marshall was the medium primarily associated with several of the Katie King teleplasms (see, e.g., Figure 5.4) and the trance personality "Lucy," whose teleplasmic image was obtained in 1930 (see Figure 4.13).

Susan McLements (1887–1942) was born in Govan; Alexander Campbell (Sandy) Marshall (1888–1953), a finishing carpenter by training, was born in Glasgow. Susan and Sandy married in 1916 in Govan, where their first three children were born. During 1922–23, with two surviving sons, the Marshalls emigrated to Winnipeg, where Alexander Campbell (Cam) Marshall (1924–2002) was born.

Cam and Orpha Marshall shared memories of his mother, and their daughter Arla has attended Hamilton lectures and participated in Winnipeg sitter groups to understand better her grandmother's role in the experiments. Susan Marshall was also a teacup reader, including at Cooperative Commonwealth Federation fundraisers that featured whist drives and teacup readings. Sandy did not believe in psychic abilities. In 1939, Susan Marshall was hospitalized following a severe stroke while attending a church bazaar.[42] Artist Susan MacWilliam (see Figure 5.5) interviewed Arla Marshall for her film about the F-L-A-M-M-A-R-I-O-N teleplasm photographed at the 1931 séance in which Susan Marshall participated (see Figure 5.6).

Walter Stuart Stinson, Trance Personality

In early 1928, a discarnate control presented himself through Mary Marshall's trance consciousness. By April, the FYM (Fair Young Man) had revealed himself to be the Ontario-born Walter Stuart Stinson (1884–1911), the discarnate brother and trance control in Margery Crandon's mediumship in Boston. In Winnipeg, Walter became the coordinator of the production of the teleplasmic manifestations. He shared many personality characteristics with the Boston Walter, including how he expressed himself. In Winnipeg, he demonstrated that he could work through more than one medium, sometimes in quick succession (see Figure 4.10). In addition to Mary Marshall, he could control H.A.V. Green (Ewan) and Susan Marshall (Mercedes), an interesting facet of the group mediumship that evolved.[43]

The Hamiltons were aware that the trance personalities could be secondary personalities of the medium,[44] but beginning in 1928 T.G. recognized the need to work hand in hand with Walter and other personalities to obtain good results. It is impossible to prove that the Winnipeg and Boston Walters were the same personality. MacWilliam has likened Walter to the director of the cast of actors in a film.[45] But twice he also attempted a guest appearance through the mediumship of Mary Marshall, such as in the March 1932 teleplasmic manifestation of his eyes (see Figure 4.12) and in the April 1950 teleplasmic manifestation of his face (see Figure 4.15) photographed by Sylvia Barber.

Lawyer Harry Green

Lawyer Henry (Harry) Archibald Vaughan Green (1888–1979) first attended a Hamilton séance on 9 May 1926; later that month he attended one again with his wife, Katharine.[46] Between March 1928 and June 1936, he was a regular participant in the séances.

Green was active in the Winnipeg theatre community, including as a co-founder of the Community Players of Winnipeg in 1921, and his experience as a playwright and stage manager, combined with his understanding of acting,[47] might have facilitated his development of trance mediumship. For years, his involvement in the Hamilton group mediumship was a secret, disguised through his séance name Ewan.

Green was the Hamilton group's first member to publicize his belief in the survival hypothesis. Three months after the first photographed teleplasmic mass, he responded to a local newspaper letter that "the energy which produces and animates the ectoplasm of the physicist . . . is directed by the continuing personalities of those whom the materialist is accustomed to think of as dead."[48] Beginning in 1931, Green was a Winnipeg SPR council member and, following T.G. Hamilton's death, its president.

During the teleplasmic experiments, Green created an album of Hamilton prints and labelled each one with the names of the sitters and circumstances. In 1989, his daughter Nancy Sirett (1918–2008) donated the album to the Vancouver Psychic Society. Ten years later SRIC acquired it from the society's last president and donated it to UMASC in 2012. The album provides invaluable corroborating evidence of the experiments. For instance, Green's compilation corroborates T.G. Hamilton's time-lapse photography of the Charles Haddon Spurgeon miniature face on 1 May 1929. It was that photograph—Spurgeon's fourth attempt to convey his facial likeness (see Figure 2.9)—that convinced me of the authenticity of the teleplasmic manifestations. Figure 4.11 shows both the first exposure and the second exposure in which the teleplasm is seen being reingested into Mary Marshall's body via her mouth.

Born in Lancashire, England, Green began his study of law at the University of Edinburgh. Engaged to Katharine Mary Frances Blackman (1889–1955), he left for Canada in 1913. Katharine followed him in 1914; upon her arrival in Winnipeg, they were married in All Saints Anglican Church. Green entered the legal department of Canadian Pacific Railway. He was called to the Manitoba Bar in 1915 and appointed King's Counsel in 1936. Green's obituary in 1979 mentioned his association "with Dr. Glen Hamilton in psychic research."[49] Among the Manitoba Historical Society's Memorable Manitobans, Green is one of the few for whom participation in psychical research is identified.

He was not the only male sitter who developed mediumistic ability within the group. Although the main mediums were women, insurance salesman William Bernard (Barney) Cooper (1891–1968), schoolteacher David Harold (Harold) Turner (1912–1987), and businessman John David (Jack) MacDonald (1906–1984) (see Chapter 1) participated as auxiliary mediums in the group, as did some of the female sitters.

Co-Experimenter Pediatrician Bruce Chown

Henry Bruce Chown (1893–1986) and Gladys Evelyn (Webb) Chown (1897–1948) joined the Hamilton group in 1931, adding their names to the list of witnesses who had more to lose than gain through association with psychical research and séances. Chown quickly became T.G. Hamilton's primary co-experimenter. On 6 March 1932, when T.G. was in eastern Canada on medical business, the teleplasmic mass revealing the Walter Stinson eyes (see Figure 4.12) was photographed under Chown's observation. In April 1935, just seventeen days after T.G.'s death, the Chowns continued the research with Lillian Hamilton for forty-one séances, concluding that series in June 1936.

Bruce Chown was born in Winnipeg, the younger son of Henry (Harry) Havelock Chown (1859–1944) and Kate (Farrell) Chown (1860–1916). His older brother, Charles (Charlie) Gray Chown (1892–1928), died in Tucson, Arizona, of pulmonary tuberculosis. H.H. Chown was associated with Manitoba Medical College from 1883 to 1918 as a teacher of anatomy, a professor of surgery, and the third dean of the college (1900–17). Under his guidance, the college became the Faculty of Medicine of the University of Manitoba in 1917; the Chown Building is named after him.

Following schooling in Winnipeg, Chown studied in Montreal and graduated from McGill University (BA, 1914). His university studies were interrupted by the First World War. As a medical student in Winnipeg, he enlisted for military service in the Canadian Overseas Expeditionary Force. From 1915 to 1919, he was an officer in the Canadian Field Artillery. He was awarded the Military Cross in 1917 for "conspicuous gallantry and devotion to duty."[50] Chown was the only officer of the 38th Battery of the Canadian Field Artillery not killed in action in France.

In 1922, while still a medical student, Bruce Chown married Gladys Webb who, born in Toronto, had come to Winnipeg as a child. The Chowns had four children. Gladys suffered a stroke in 1947 and died the following May. In 1949, Bruce Chown married Allison Grant (1909–2007), a schoolteacher who had been a good friend of Gladys; the couple had one son.

Chown was superintendent of the Winnipeg Children's Hospital (c.1940–45). In 1944, he established the Winnipeg Rh Laboratory at the University of Manitoba with Marion Jean Lewis (1925–) and later was chairman of the Department of Pediatrics in the Faculty of Medicine (1949–54). Chown was

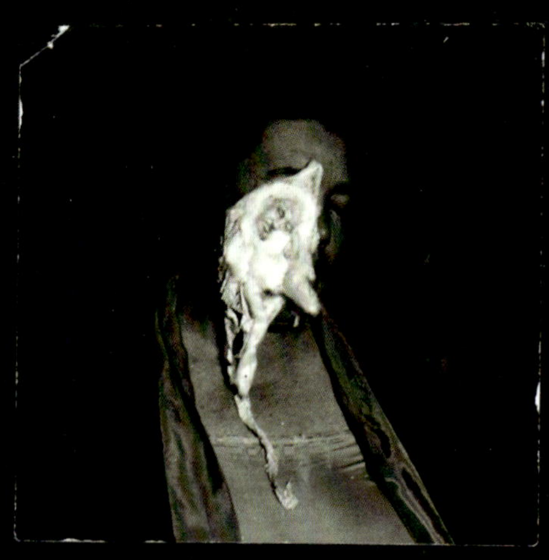

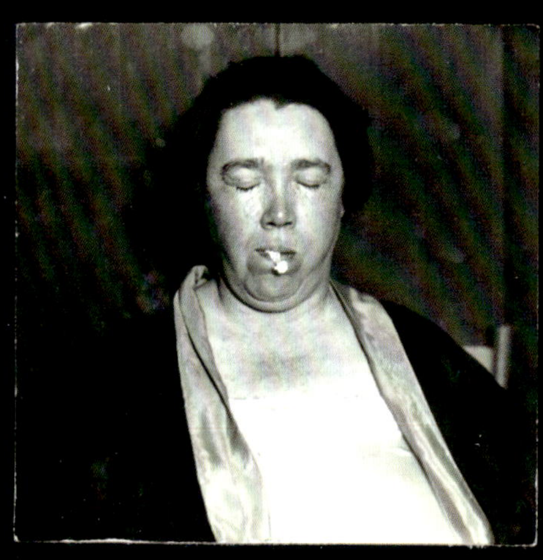

1st May 1929.

Above. Fourth photograph of C.H. Spurgeon.

Below. Residue of teleplasm in top photograph, - Second photograph taken one and a half minutes after the first.

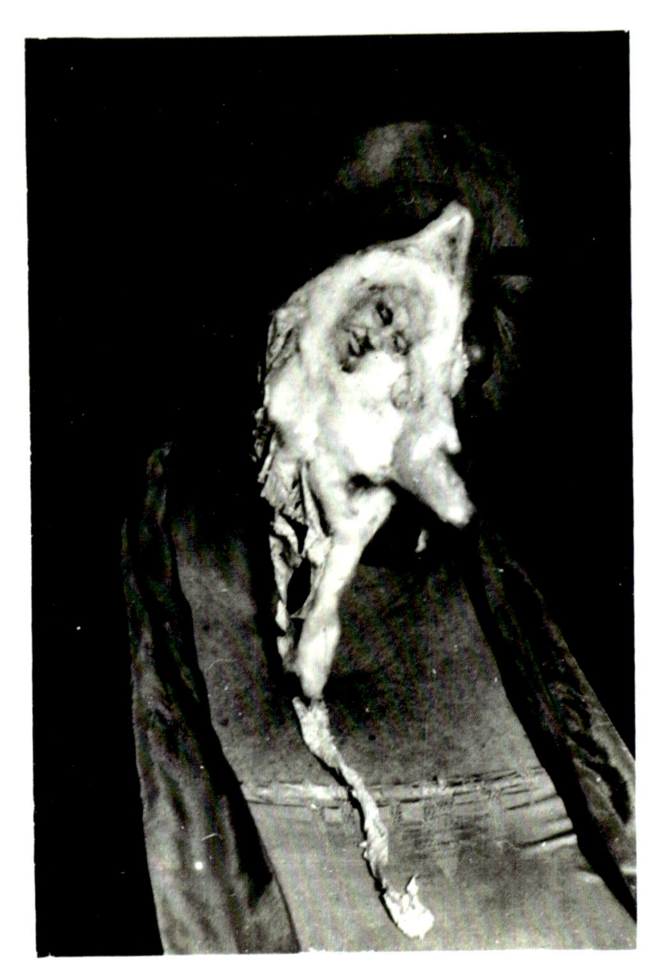

Enlargement of first photograph of 1st May 1929.

Present:- Mary M., W.B. Cooper, Elizabeth M., Dr. T.G. Hamilton, Miss Ada Turner, H.A.V. Green, Mrs. T.G. Hamilton, Dr. J.A. Hamilton, John McDonald, W.E. Hobbs, A.C. Whittaker and H.A. Reed.

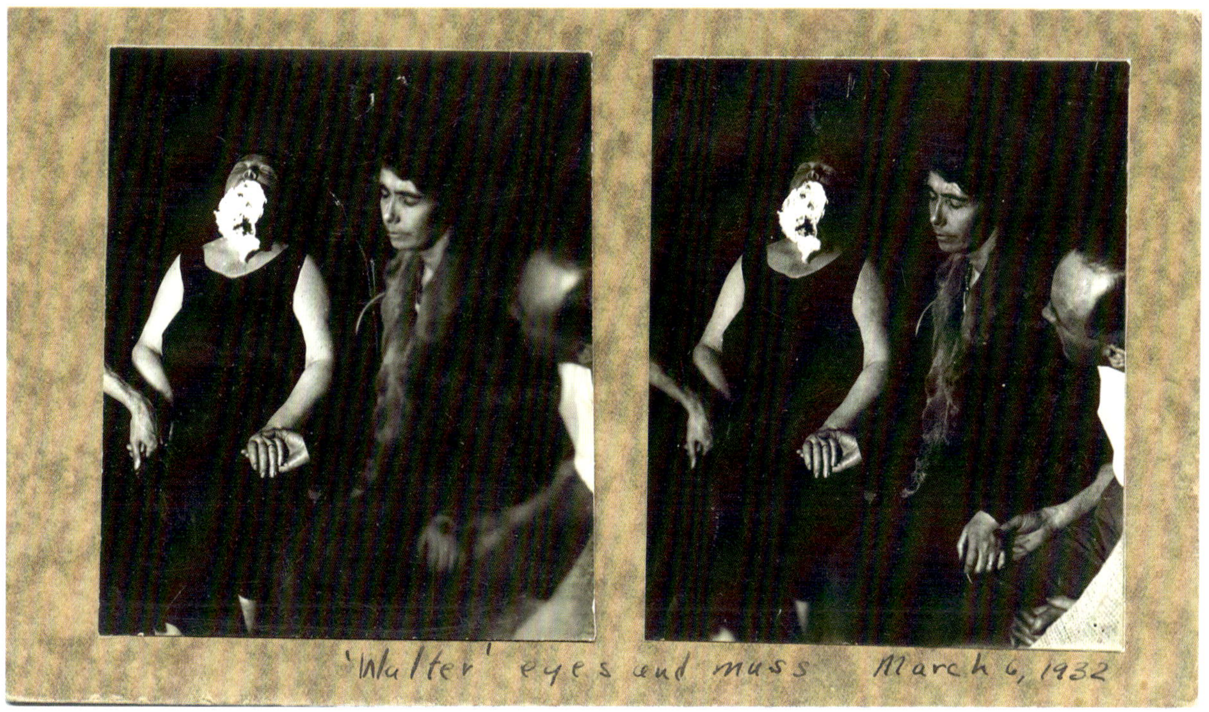

Fig. 4.11. *Left*, The fourth Charles Haddon Spurgeon miniature face in teleplasm with medium Mary Marshall, 1 May 1929, first and second exposures. Photograph by T.G. Hamilton. UMASC, H.A.V. Green Fonds, MSS 439, Box 1, Folder 2, Item 1.8.

Fig. 4.12. *Above*, Walter Stinson's eyes peeking from a teleplasmic mass on medium Mary Marshall, with Susan Marshall and Barney Cooper beside her, 6 March 1932. Photograph by H. Bruce Chown. UMASC, PC 12, Box 7, Folder 4, Item 39, http://hdl.handle.net/10719/1412284.

foremost a medical researcher. In recognition of his scientific contributions with Marion Lewis and Hiroko Kaita on the nature of blood, especially the fight to control the Rh condition in newborns, Chown received honorary degrees, awards, and memberships, including the Order of Canada.

When Victor Sifton (1897–1961), owner and publisher of the *Winnipeg Free Press*, asked Margaret Hamilton Bach in 1957 to write a series of articles dealing with the Hamiltons' deep-trance scripts, she "submitted the manuscript to Dr. Chown for his criticism, prior to publication."[51] In "Psychical Research Worthwhile Study," printed as part of the lead article, Chown wrote that

> what is termed psychical research is often derided by scientists. But that derision itself often bespeaks a lack of awareness of the nature of science in the broadest sense. Science as we commonly think of it, and which has brought immense new knowledge to man, has seemed to be dependent basically upon two things, upon the experimental method, that is to say the controlled experiment, and upon measurement; if these methods are not used the observed facts are doubted. But that these are the only roads to knowledge, the only way in which experience can be placed upon a rational, co-ordinated basis is not necessarily true, and science is the rational co-ordination of experience, any experience, all experience.[52]

Chown was a practical, down-to-earth person who would have had no patience had he suspected that fraud was involved in the Hamilton research.[53] Allison Chown shared that her husband used to talk about the medium in the Hamilton séances and thought that she was legitimate. "Dr. Chown was very sceptical about most things," so it was significant that he should attend the séances.[54]

In 1935, he stated in his tribute to T.G. Hamilton in the *Canadian Medical Association Journal* that the table rappings, the apparent animation of dead things, the trance speech and writing, and the masses extruded from the bodies of mediums and moulded into the likenesses of known dead people were all genuine.[55] Beyond the Methodist upbringing of his youth, Chown did not share the Christian beliefs of the Hamilton group. In later life, he was an agnostic. In Chapter 2, Serena Keshavjee discusses, among other European researchers, the impact on T.G. Hamilton's thinking of Charles Richet (1850–1935) and Albert Freiherr von Schrenck-Notzing (1862–1929) that ectoplasm (in France) or teleplasm (in Germany) was biological in origin but not evidence of surviving spirits. Richet declared that ectoplasm was absurd but true. Likewise, Chown did not adopt the survival hypothesis to account for the strange phenomena that he declared were genuine.

Precautions to Preclude Fraud

From the beginning, the Hamiltons took measures to preclude the possibility of fraud. Additional precautions were taken at séances at which trance controls predicted that a teleplasm would be photographed. The séance room was locked and sealed at the end of the previous sitting; the keys to the locks were given to several different sitters who did not reside in the Hamilton home. The medium was examined prior to the sitting, and all sitters and the medium held hands so that, ostensibly, no one had free use of his or her hands to produce fraudulently the effects photographed. Sittings were held in the darkness.[56] One or more note takers recorded the verbal proceedings by shorthand and/or longhand, and photographs were taken. A special scrutineer was invited to observe the proceedings, and guards were stationed outside the entrance to the séance room. On four occasions, an affidavit was typed for each participant and signed in the presence of a notary public.[57]

Lawyer Isaac Pitblado as Special Scrutineer

In 1930, lawyer Isaac Pitblado (1867–1964) was the group's best-known participant. Born in Nova Scotia, the son of a Presbyterian minister, he graduated from Manitoba College with three degrees between 1886 and 1893.

Called to the Manitoba Bar as an attorney-at-law and solicitor in 1890, Pitblado was involved in railway freight rate and other important cases over the course of his long career. He was appointed a king's counsel in 1909. During the Winnipeg General Strike of 1919, reflective of his conservative role in Winnipeg, Pitblado was a member of the Citizens' Committee of One Thousand that opposed the strike; he also helped to prosecute the strike leaders. At eighty, Pitblado successfully represented the railways in their $80 million freight rates increase case before

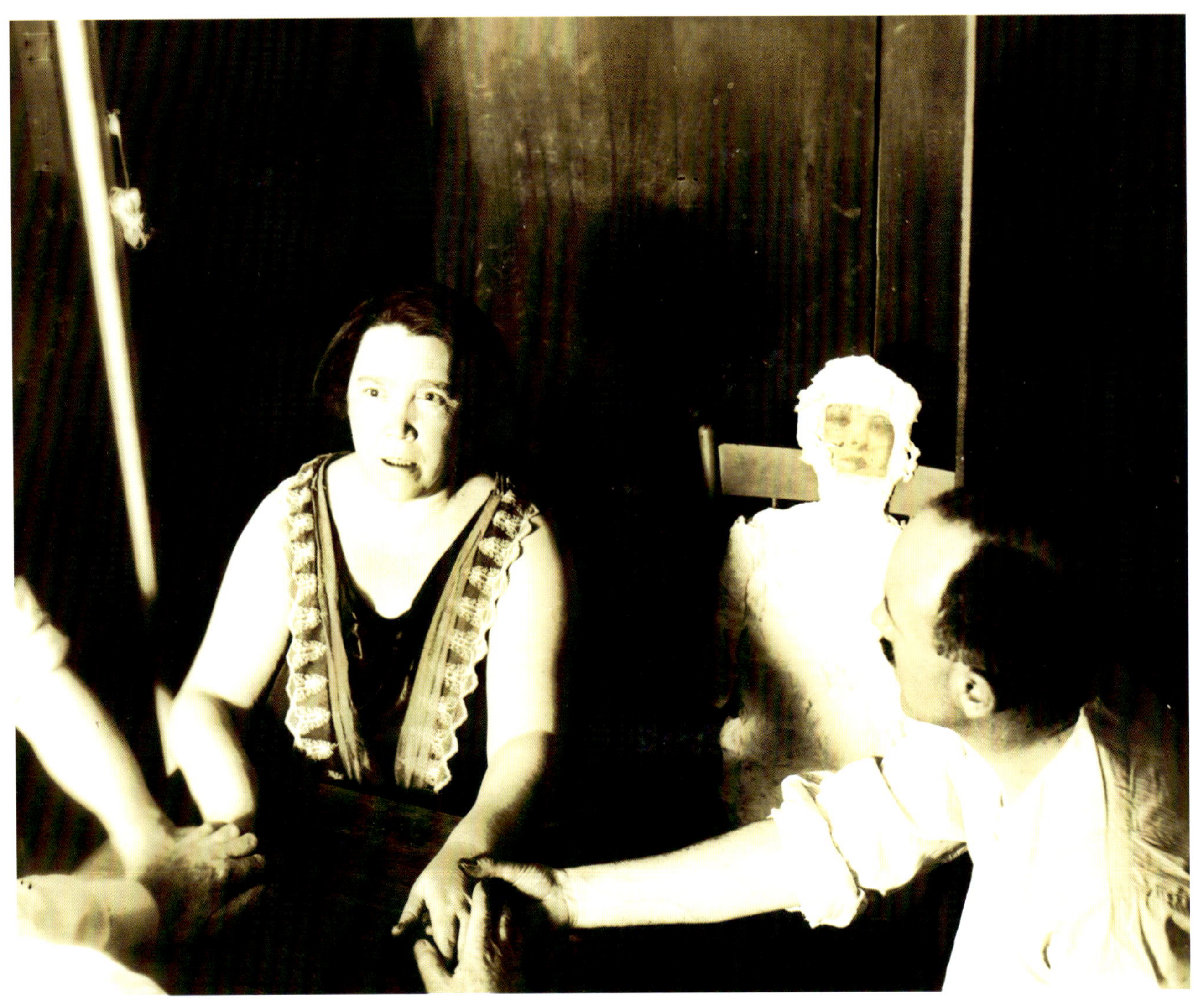

Fig. 4.13. Lawyer Isaac Pitblado's hands provide double control of medium Mary Marshall's hands on small table as well as those of adjacent sitters. The Lucy teleplasm is on chair between Marshall and W.B. (Barney) Cooper, 10 March 1930. Photograph attributed to T.G. Hamilton. UMASC, H.A.V. Green Fonds, MSS 439, Box 1, Folder 2, Item 1.17.

the Board of Transport Commissioners. In 1960, he celebrated his seventieth year at the Manitoba Bar. He continued to practise law almost until his death.

The Pitblados were infrequent participants in the Hamilton experiments. When the Ontario-born Mina Stinson and her husband, Le Roi Goddard Crandon (1873–1939), a Harvard University medical doctor and surgeon, visited Winnipeg in December 1926, Isaac and his second wife, May Edith Pitblado (1869–1950), witnessed the Margery mediumship, both in the Hamilton home and at a third séance in their home.

Invited as one of the official scrutineers of the séance on 10 March 1930 at which the Lucy teleplasm was photographed, Pitblado sat across the wooden séance table from medium Mary Marshall. In Figure 4.13, his large hands can be seen providing double control of her hands as well as those of the sitters to either side of her. W.B. (Barney) Cooper controlled the medium's left hand and is seen looking in the direction of the teleplasmic manifestation visible during the blinding flash. T.G. Hamilton's brother Jim was the "medical observer and chief controller of Mary M.'s right hand during the teleplasmic experiments."[58]

Two days later Pitblado signed an eleven-page handwritten statement about the precautionary procedures in place to preclude the possibility of fraud, including the search of the séance room, mediums, and male sitters and the examination and development of the photographic plates. Regarding the Lucy teleplasm, he concluded that "I am convinced that the phenomenon of the figure seated on the chair to the left of the medium was genuinely produced without the aid of any known physical or material means, process or apparatus, and that there was no possibility of any 'fake' or trickery."[59]

Fifteen months later, in 1931, Pitblado became a member of the council of the Winnipeg SPR.[60] In acknowledging Lillian Hamilton's condolences on his wife May's death in 1950, Pitblado wrote of his happy memories of the occasions when he was privileged to attend the Hamilton séances: "It is a great comfort to believe in personal immortality as you & I do."[61]

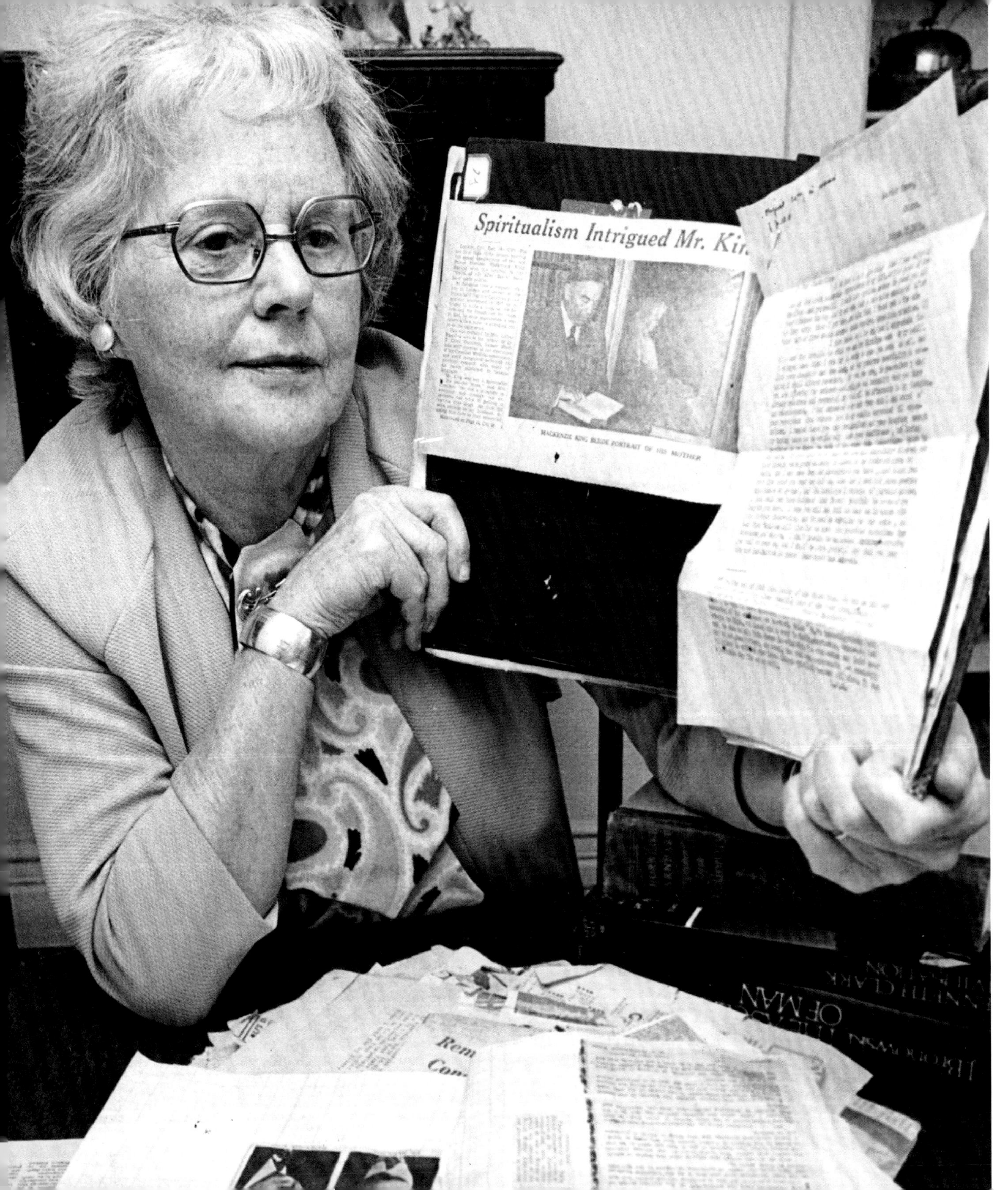
Spiritualism Intrigued Mr.
MACKENZIE KING BESIDE PORTRAIT OF HIS MOTHER

Sylvia Barber's Bequest in Support of Psychic Science

Margaret Hamilton Bach not only coordinated the deposit of her family's records at UMASC but also established the T.G. Hamilton Research Grant Program to assist scholars. She could not have done so without a sizeable bequest received in 1979. Sylvia Barber (1892–1979) deserves acknowledgement not only for her work as a female psychical research photographer (1947–1950) but also as an unsung promoter of the Hamilton legacy.

Convinced of the reality of her psychic experiences, in her 1966 will Barber left half of her estate to her good friend and circle member Mary Meder (1911–1997), as well as "all written, typed or printed matter dealing with Psychic Phenomena,"[62] including books and bookcases. Barber left the other half to Margaret Hamilton Bach "as a contribution towards her wonderful effort in bringing understanding of Psychic Science to our world" (see Figure 4.14).[63] Thanks to Barber's bequest, the Hamilton grants allowed me to reach out to more family members of T.G. Hamilton's research associates during the 1990s, which led to additional collections being directed to UMASC.[64]

Victor Sifton and Sylvia Barber's Experiments with Mary Marshall

After Lillian Hamilton concluded her experiments in 1944, Sylvia Barber conducted séances with Mary Marshall for at least three years beginning in April 1947. Although not involved in the Hamilton research, Barber became friends with Lillian and later Margaret. In her home at 550 Atlantic Avenue, Barber photographed ectoplasmic manifestations with Marshall. Like T.G. Hamilton, she had multiple cameras focused on the medium that she could operate with a remote control apparatus.

On 25 April 1950, Barber photographed with four cameras an ectoplasm on Mary Marshall's face claimed to be the likeness of Walter Stinson (see Figure 4.15). Barber used ordinary roll film and floodlight that she developed in the presence of

Fig. 4.14. Margaret Hamilton Bach displaying William Lyon Mackenzie King memorabilia, January 1979. Photograph by Jeff DeBooy. UMASC, ***Winnipeg Tribune*** fonds, PC 18, Box 1, Folder 20, http://hdl.handle.net/10719/1505414.

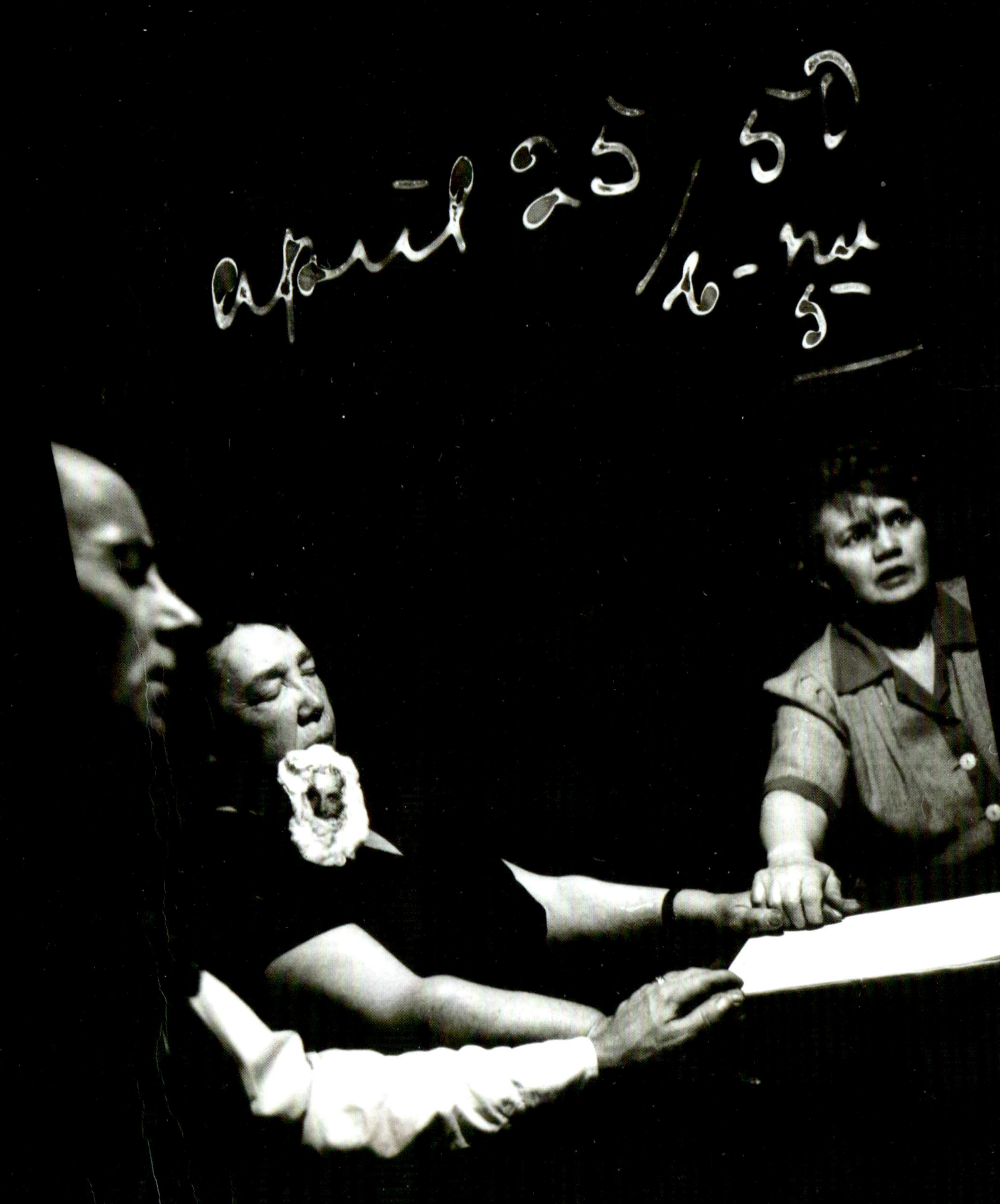

one of the sitters. Victor Sifton, an occasional sitter in the Barber group, might be the man in those images, including one second exposure that shows the ectoplasm retracting into Marshall's mouth. Soon after participating in the séances, Sifton became chancellor of the University of Manitoba (1952–60).

Born in Reykjavik, Iceland, Sylvia came with her family to Winnipeg in 1899. Recorded as Sigurjona Gudmundsson in the 1901 census, she lived with her parents and four siblings on a farm at Selkirk. She was first married to a man with the surname Bryan. Widowed before 1920, Sylvia Bryan married Edmund Cyril Barber (1891–1931), an insurance agent, in All Saints Anglican Church, Winnipeg. For her, there was no doubt about the evidence of survival received through mental and physical mediumship that she documented under the pseudonym Patience Hope in three small books that Victor Sifton likely helped her to publish.[65]

What Does It All Mean?

Although table-tilting seldom provides good evidence of human survival after death, the visual image of the Victorian séance will forever link such phenomena with attempts to communicate with spirits. That is an unfortunate distraction from the importance of T.G. Hamilton's photographs of non-contact table levitations as amazing evidence of telekinesis and the best such collection worldwide. Personal observation in the Victoria Spiritualist study group that met in my home from 1998 to 2010 convinced me that strong psychokinetic table movements can manifest when small groups of like-minded individuals work together.[66] The early 1970s "Philip" experiments conducted by psychical researchers Iris M. Owen (1916–2009) and A.R.G. (George) Owen (1919–2003), with members of the Toronto SPR, demonstrate that macro-PK phenomena can be obtained by a sitter group working to

Fig 4.15. From left, a male sitter holding the right hand of Mary Marshall, whose left hand is controlled by Sylvia Barber. The teleplasm hanging from Marshall's mouth was claimed to be a likeness of Walter Stinson, 25 April 1950. Photograph by Sylvia Barber. UMASC, PC 12, Box 11, Folder 13, http://hdl.handle.net/10719/1524037.

create an imaginary ghost, based upon the Tibetan concept of the Tulpa.[67] In those experiments, a stable group created and empowered a responsive entity, the ghost named Philip. The Owens met Margaret Hamilton Bach about 1977 in Toronto. Reports of the Owens' research are now deposited at UMASC.[68]

After thirty-two years of studying the Hamilton research, I find that the photographs of teleplasm remain a challenge. I find it difficult to believe that the Marshall sisters-in-law tricked the researchers. That the teleplasmic phenomena were genuine was the conclusion of the Hamiltons and their associates as well as most of my Winnipeg informants. Among those close to the mediums, including individuals who disliked the phenomena, none had seen anything to suggest trickery. When Margaret Hamilton's "Is Survival a Fact?" was reprinted in the *Toronto Daily Star* in 1958, Bruce Chown, William Creighton, Isaac Pitblado, and Harry Green allowed their portraits to be included in testimony of phenomena witnessed twenty-five years earlier. The continued association of those professionals with the research attests to the fact that they were unable to discover how the teleplasms might have been produced fraudulently. The case for genuine ectoplasm, among a whole lot of fraud, is supported by the conclusion of my colleague Michel Granger in France, who has spent twenty years investigating 500 historical cases of ectoplasmic phenomena worldwide. When completed, his *La saga de l'ectoplasme* will comprise three volumes.[69]

In the past, I said that I would have preferred to discover fraud during my first visits to Winnipeg. Then I would have walked away from the quiet ridicule that belief in genuine telekinesis and teleplasm attracts.[70] Had I done so, I would have missed out on many wonderful connections established over three decades with descendants of the Hamiltons and their associates and more recently students and artists drawn to study the case. Those friendships have provided amazing opportunities and learning experiences. While I was travelling, sharing my understanding of the Hamilton experiments with other psychical researchers opened doors, facilitated meetings, and introduced T.G. Hamilton through illustrated presentations in Canada, the United States, Britain, the Netherlands, France, Germany, Switzerland, Austria, Australia, and New Zealand. Although Susan MacWilliam and I had then only corresponded, her 2009 Venice Biennale *F-L-A-M-M-A-R-I-O-N* exhibition (see Figure 9.25) provided a good reason to visit Italy while I was in Europe. The following February, Susan was to exhibit in New York City and visit our common friends Eileen and Lisette Coly. We met there for the first time and jointly presented for the Parapsychology Foundation, and Janice Hamilton and her son David came from Montreal for the week. Photographer Shannon Taggart later studied the Hamilton research for her book *Séance* (see Chapter 9). We have met several times, including in Brooklyn when invited to present the Hamiltons as part of her *Morbid Anatomy* series. More recently, Shannon's encouragement prompted my first Hamilton presentation via Zoom to her Lily Dale conference.

After much fence-sitting, I have concluded that the Winnipeg teleplasmic manifestations were genuine, and I am sufficiently convinced to state that, if the Hamilton teleplasms resulted from fraud, then no such thing as genuine ectoplasm exists. Although the strong psychic force demonstrated during T.G. Hamilton's photography of non-contact table levitations does not provide evidence of life after death, the wax moulds of spirit fingertips and the teleplasmic manifestations bearing miniature faces might support the survival hypothesis. The Hamiltons contemplated whether the creative process that produced their photographed teleplasms included an ideoplastic component originating in the minds of the mediums and other sitters. That makes sense based upon the photographic evidence, but it hopelessly muddies the discussion between those who believe it all fraudulent and those convinced that the fact of ectoplasm is somehow evidence of life after death. I am positioned in the middle and believe that the ectoplasm photographed by the Hamiltons was genuine but that only the teleplasms with miniature faces of the deceased suggest evidence of life after death.

Thanks

Thank you to Serena Keshavjee, Shelley Sweeney, and the peer reviewers who read my chapter and suggested ways in which it was improved.

NOTES

1 Figure 2.10 illustrates T.G. Hamilton's study of Elizabeth Poole's trance states.

2 Walter Meyer zu Erpen, "Pursuit of Best Evidence for Survival of Human Consciousness after Permanent Bodily Death," Bigelow Institute for Consciousness Studies essay contest (2021 honourable mention award), https://www.bigelowinstitute.org/wp-content/uploads/2022/10/meyer-zu-erpen-best-evidence-survival.pdf (accessed 23 February 2023).

3 Tom Butler, email communication with the author, 4 November 2022, about his definition, available at https://ethericstudies.org/trans-survival-hypothesis/ (accessed 23 February 2023).

4 James B. Nickels, *The Psychic Research in a Winnipeg Family: The Recollections and Views of Dr. Glen F. Hamilton*, videotape, October 1987.

5 See the SRIC website, survivalresearch.ca (accessed 23 February 2023).

6 T.G. Hamilton delivered the Withers' four children (1914–21). While T.G. was alive, William (Bill) Andrew Wither (1887–1975) and Jeannie (Jean) Taylor (Fardell) Wither (1894–1970) attended the séances only occasionally. In 1931, Bill Wither was elected secretary-treasurer of the Winnipeg SPR. The Withers were more actively involved in the experiments with Lillian Hamilton in 1939–40.

7 Walter Meyer zu Erpen, "Thomas Glendenning Hamilton," 26 January 2022, in *Dictionary of Canadian Biography*, vol. 16, http://www.biographi.ca/en/bio/hamilton_thomas_glendenning_16E.html (accessed 23 February 2023).

8 Janice Hamilton, *Reinventing Themselves: A History of the Hamilton and Forrester Families* (Self-published, 2021).

9 Janice Hamilton, "Bring on Your Ghosts: The Thomas Glendenning Hamilton Family Séances from 1918 to 1944, Winnipeg, Canada," *Paranormal Review—Hamilton Family Fonds Special Issue* 77 (2016): 6–11.

10 Margaret Lillian Hamilton, *Is Survival a Fact? Studies of Deep-Trance Automatic Scripts and the Bearing of Intentional Actions by Trance Personalities on the Question of Human Survival* (London: Psychic Press, 1969).

11 The title of this 1990 *Manitoba Medicine* article mislabelled T.G. Hamilton despite an addendum that Margaret Hamilton Bach had provided shortly before her death stating that her father was "a scientific researcher, not a spiritualist." Alvin E. Rodin, Audrey Kerr, and J.D. Key, "Thomas Glen Hamilton MD FACS Winnipeg Physician Politician and Spiritualist," *Manitoba Medicine* 60, no. 3 (1990): 121–24. Subsequent scholars have cited it without recognizing the error.

12 Walter Meyer zu Erpen, "Afterlife beliefs in the Spiritualist movement," in *The Routledge Companion to Death and Dying*, ed. Christopher M. Moreman (London: Routledge, 2018), 218–219, 228.

13 "New York Correspondence," *Lancaster Examiner and Herald* (Pennsylvania), 26 November 1856, 3.

14 W.T. Allison, "Can Dead Authors Come Back?," *Manitoba Free Press Evening Bulletin*, 7 September 1918, 8, and the four-part series published weekly between 14 September and 5 October.

15 Thomas Glendenning Hamilton, *Intention and Survival: Psychical Research Studies and the Bearing of Intentional Actions by Trance Personalities on the Problem of Human Survival*, ed. Margaret Lillian Hamilton, 2nd ed. (London: Regency Press, 1977), xvii.

16 Lillian Hamilton, "Telepathy Plus Spiritism in the Hamilton Researches in Winnipeg," *Light*, April 1951, 472.

17 The birth registration of Elizabeth Wilson has not been located. She was likely born in 1868–69, not 1870, as previously reported.

18 The middle name MacDonald, inscribed beneath a portrait photograph of Elizabeth Poole, is questionable; it was not recorded on her marriage registration.

19 As they are processed, UMASC Psychical Research and Spiritualism collections are listed at https://libguides.lib.umanitoba.ca/archives/archivalcollections/psychicalspiritualism (accessed 23 February 2023).

20 Thanks to Anton Wagner, who discovered in William Lyon Mackenzie King's diary for 29 September 1933 that John D. MacDonald had visited King at his Ottawa office and mentioned the system of pressurized air.

21 Rae (Bruening) Cannon (1883–1963/64) was the wife of William Martin Cannon (1866–1946), a lawyer, not a judge. In 1947, Rae Cannon was remarried to Chester Michael Grady (1896–1972), a lifetime ASPR member, who died at Hampton, New Hampshire. Locating descendants of Grady's sister Ethel Merrow, who resided in 1972 at Bristol, Connecticut, could lead to Rae Grady's infrared film.

22 Hamilton, *Intention and Survival* (1977), xx.

23 There were also table movements, including full levitations, not photographed successfully.

24 Bruce Chown, "Obituaries," *Canadian Medical Association Journal* 32 (1935): 710–11.

25 Anton Wagner, email communications with the author, February 2022.

26 Through affiliation, the University of Manitoba had responsibility for examinations and the granting of degrees until 1967, when United College became the University of Winnipeg.

27 Lois M. Wilson, letter to the author, 8 July 1992. Wilson was United Church of Canada moderator from 1980 to 1982.

28 E.G.D. Freeman, "One Night a Week in Psychic Research for Two Years, with Dr. T.G. Hamilton," Chapter 30 of "My Life Story," unpublished memoir, 82.

29 UMASC, HFF, MSS 14, Box 9, Folder 14. The Hamilton Family Fonds finding aid is available at https://umlarchives.lib.umanitoba.ca/hamilton-family-fonds (accessed 23 February 2023).

30 Freeman, "One Night," 86.

31 T. Glen Hamilton, *Intention and Survival: Psychical Research Studies and the Bearing of Intentional Actions by Trance Personalities on the Problem of Human Survival*, ed. J.D. Hamilton (Toronto: Macmillan, 1942), 7–8.

32 Walter Meyer zu Erpen, "Of Teleplasms and Wax Fingertips: Dr. William Creighton's Role in Authenticating Physical Phenomena," *Paranormal Review* 77 (2016): 15–16.

33 R.J. Creighton, telephone conversations with the author, 20–21 September 2005 and 6 January 2006.

34 Hamilton, *Intention and Survival* (1977), 214: "A subtle living matter present in the body of a medium, and which is capable of assuming various semi-solid or solid states for a brief time, which can be, and have been felt, and photographed."

35 UMASC, HFF, MSS 14, Box 17, Folder 3, summary.

36 UMASC, HFF, MSS 14, Box 5, Folder 5, manuscript copy of Eva M. Broad's letter made by Lillian Hamilton.

37 Daisy Marshall, telephone conversation with the author, 10 June 1991.

38 UMASC, HFF, MSS 14, Box 15, Folder 10, 6 September 1929 (session 108).

39 UMASC, HFF, MSS 14, Box 5, Folder 4, Mary A. Marshall to Lillian Hamilton, July 1945.

40 Everitt S. McKelvie, telephone conversation with the author, 26 June 1991.

41 George E. Marshall, telephone conversation with the author, 29 December 2006.

42 Daisy Marshall and Cam and Orpha Marshall, telephone conversations with the author, June 1991.

43 For discussion of group mediumship, see Hamilton, *Intention and Survival* (1942), 42–54.

44 Meyer zu Erpen, "Pursuit of Best Evidence," 32–34, regarding secondary personalities.

45 Susan MacWilliam, "Through the Camera: Teleplasmic Appearances in Winnipeg by Flammarion, Stead, Doyle, Lodge and other SPR Members," *Paranormal Review* 77 (2016): 22–23.

46 UMASC, HFF, MSS 14, Box 8, Folder 1, Attendance Register.

47 NBZ (Nathan B. Zimmerman), "Author! Author!!," *The Bill* (Winnipeg Little Theatre) 6, no. 3 (1934): 4.

48 H.A.V. Green, "The Passing World," letter to the editor, *Manitoba Free Press*, 5 December 1928, 15.

49 "H.A.V. Green, QC," *Winnipeg Free Press*, 9 June 1979, 58.

50 David K. Riddle and Donald G. Mitchell, *The Military Cross Awarded to the Canadian Expeditionary Force, 1915–1921, with Full Citations* (Winnipeg: Kirkby-Marlton Press, 1991), 57.

51 Hamilton, *Intention and Survival* (1977), 210.

52 Bruce Chown, "Psychical Research Worthwhile Study," *Winnipeg Free Press*, 18 January 1958, 34.

53 John A. Bovey, interview with the author, 20 March 1991.

54 Allison Chown, telephone conversation with the author, 14 September 1990.

55 Chown, "Obituaries."

56 In some Hamilton photographs, a dark lightbulb is visible near the ceiling; the bulb was red and provided dim light to allow the sitters to enter and leave the room.

57 UMASC, HFF, MSS 14, Box 9, Folders 4–7. All affidavits relate to phenomena photographed in 1928.

58 Hamilton, *Intention and Survival* (1977), 15.

59 UMASC, HFF, MSS 14, Box 16, Folder 2.

60 "Psychical Research Branch Formed Here: Dr. T. Glen Hamilton Elected President of New Winnipeg Society," *Manitoba Free Press*, 12 June 1931, 8.

61 UMASC, HFF, MSS 14, Box 5, Folder 8, letter from Isaac Pitblado to Lillian Hamilton, postmarked 25 November 1950.

62 Currently in the custody of SRIC, the Sylvia Barber–Mary Meder records are intended for deposit at UMASC during 2023.

63 Archives of Manitoba, Sylvia Barber estate file, Q15662, Last Will, 4.

64 Many entries in the UMASC Psychical Research and Spiritualism list (https://libguides.lib.umanitoba.ca/archives/archivalcollections/psychicalspiritualism, accessed 23 February 2023) stem from my early research connections.

65 The three self-published books about Sylvia Barber's research, assembled under her pseudonym Patience Hope, are *Life's Purpose?* (1952), *Life Continuous! Albert Tells His Story* (1957), and *Appeal to Reason: Messages from the Spirit World* (1958).

66 Our group was featured in Donna Zuckerbrot's television documentary *Conjuring Philip*, Reel-Time Images, 2007.

67 The Victoria Spiritualist study group and TSPR Philip experiments are discussed in Walter Meyer zu Erpen, "Canadian Psychical Research Experiments with Table Tilting and Ectoplasm Phenomena in the Séance Room," Chapter 12 in *The Spiritualist Movement: Speaking with the Dead in America and around the World, Vol. 2, Belief, Practice, and Evidence for Life after Death*, ed. Christopher M. Moreman (Santa Barbara, CA: Praeger, 2013), 205–28.

68 See https://survivalresearch.ca/Owen_ARG_and_Iris.pdf (accessed 23 February 2023).

69 Michel Granger, *La Saga de l'ectoplasme*, vol. 1 (Blegny, Belgium: Le Mouvement Spirite Francophone, 2021). Volume 2 will be published during 2023, with volume 3 anticipated during 2024.

70 Discussed in Meyer zu Erpen, "Pursuit of Best Evidence," 42–44 and 55–57, those phenomena are now known as psychokinesis and ectoplasm.

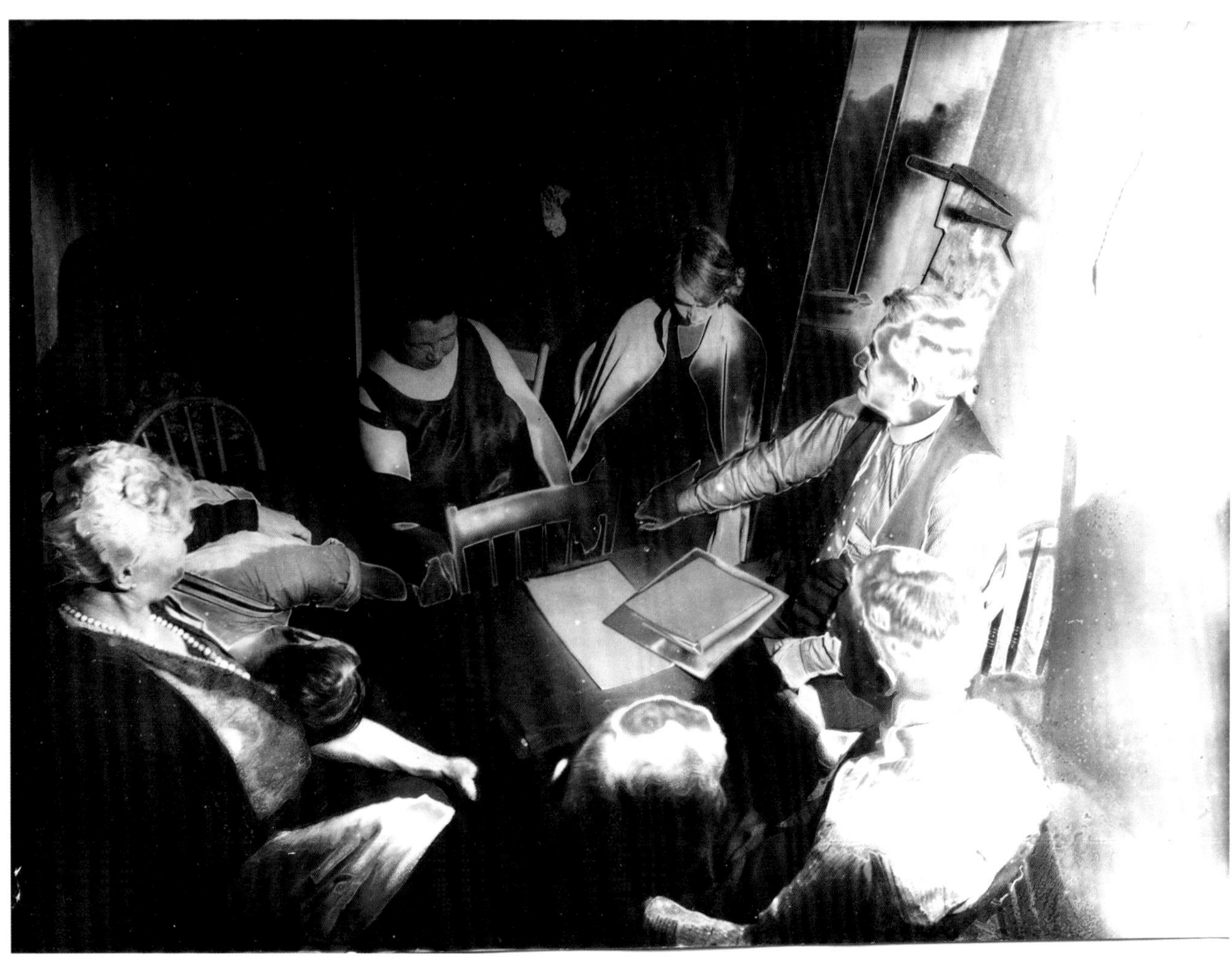

Fig. 5.1. ***Feather Teleplasm***, 22 March 1933. UMASC, PC 12, Box 10, Folder 7, Item 50, http://hdl.handle.net/10719/1410489.

5

Life after Death: New Uses of the Hamilton Family Fonds

Shelley Sweeney

The Hamilton Family Fonds (HFF) is an archival collection inherently rooted in curiosity about psychic phenomena and a possible afterlife as well as in trauma, grieving, and the will to believe. The experiences and emotions captured by the records have inspired use by researchers since the collection was deposited with the University of Manitoba Archives and Special Collections (UMASC) beginning in 1979.[1] The fonds has been the basis for a large number of various uses, making it the most utilized collection of personal records held by UMASC.

The role of archival staff in encouraging those uses through their actions in acquiring, preserving, arranging and describing, providing reference services for, and promoting the materials has been thoroughly studied, but no research has been conducted to date that really gets to the heart of why this collection is so appealing.[2] One can only speculate that the authenticity of the documented experiences, the jaw-dropping photographs, and the poignant personal backstory are what intrigue, move, and engage researchers (see Figure 5.1). The extensive textual and graphic documentation supporting the photos makes the collection even more valuable for subsequent use.

What resulted from the Hamilton séances is an extraordinarily large and detailed archival collection of photographs, albums, glass plate negatives, slides, attendance records, sitting minutes, affidavits, notes, correspondence, speeches, diagrams, newspaper clippings, publications, and audio recordings that documents the psychical investigations, the family's publicizing of the experiments, and their interactions with like-minded people interested in psychic phenomena and life after death (see Figure 5.2). The records cover "rappings, clairvoyance, trance states and trance charts, telekinesis, wax moulds, bell-ringing, trance scripts and visions, as well as teleplasmic manifestations."[3] All of these records have been freely available to researchers since they were processed.

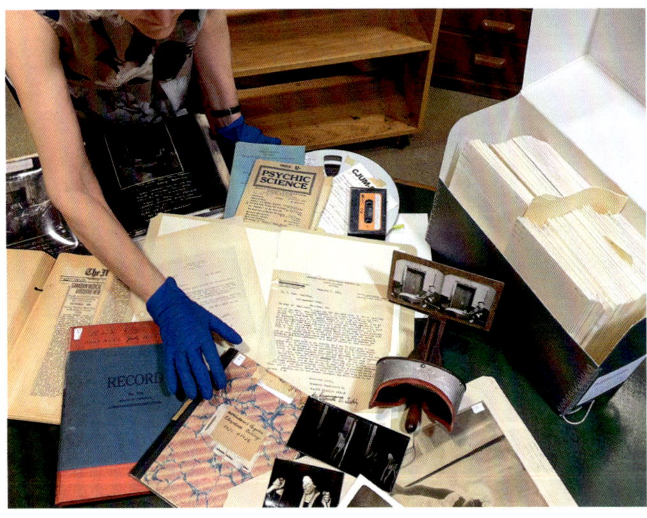

Fig. 5.2. Dr. Sweeney examines some of the records in the Hamilton Family Fonds, 17 February 2022. Photograph by Nicole Aminian. UMASC, HFF, MSS 014. Courtesy of Shelley Sweeney.

Thus, we see that the records have a broad coverage that should have appealed to many researchers. But after the initial flurry and excitement from the records acquisition, interest subsided.[4] This collection could have joined many others sitting on the shelves of the archives waiting for occasional use but for the efforts of three researchers and dedicated archival staff.

One of the first researchers to use and promote the fonds was Walter Meyer zu Erpen, archivist and president of the Survival Research Institute of Canada (see Figure 5.3). He mentioned the Hamilton family in an article entitled "The

Canadian Spiritualist Movement and Sources for Its Study," published in 1990, though he noted that the Hamiltons were conducting scientific experiments and were not Spiritualists.[5] He would go on to write, lecture, promote, and support the Hamilton Family Fonds in Canada and internationally.[6] A major activity that helped to drive interest in the fonds among those focused on the paranormal was Meyer zu Erpen's organizing and editing, along with me, of an issue of the international magazine *Paranormal Review* devoted to the Hamilton Family Fonds.[7] Meyer zu Erpen has been the driving force expanding the collection of Spiritualist and psychical research archives at the University of Manitoba Archives and Special Collections, which in turn has helped to lead other researchers to the university to use the Hamilton fonds.

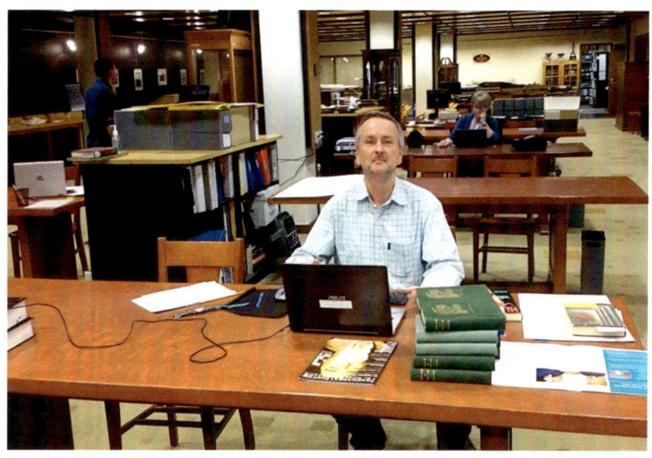

Fig. 5.3. Walter Meyer zu Erpen in the reference room of the University of Manitoba Archives and Special Collections, 11 May 2018. Photograph by and courtesy of Wim Kramer.

The unusual nature of the contents of the fonds meant that it was likely to be covered by the media. It could have been held up to ridicule, but an analysis of the treatment of the fonds shows that it has been widely celebrated instead, particularly by the university and the community.[8] There is a good reason for this. Chris Rutkowski, another early researcher, published the book *Unnatural History: True Manitoba Mysteries* in 1993, which included the Hamilton family.[9] The same year Rutkowski became a media communications officer for the University of Manitoba. His own interest in the Hamilton family as part of a broader interest in paranormal phenomena, in particular UFOs, meant that he was a sympathetic and enthusiastic promoter of the collection when it came time for publicity. With so many news stories at the university vying for attention, Rutkowski ensured that the HFF was promoted to the media. For instance, he chose the fonds for the second of his YouTube series, *Campus Files: The Haunting in Manitoba*, in 2009 to promote the collection.[10] His support was a crucial component of making the collection known to the public in a positive way.

A third important researcher who would play a pivotal role in promoting this collection was Jim Nickels, a professor in the Department of Psychology at the University of Manitoba. Because of his professional interest, Nickels interviewed the oldest Hamilton son, Dr. Glen Forrester Hamilton, and thus provided critical information to the archives that staff could share with researchers. His work led to his article "Psychic Research in a Winnipeg Family: Reminiscences of Dr. Glen F. Hamilton" published in *Manitoba History* in 2007.[11] As a member of the T. Glendenning Hamilton Research Grant Committee and a supporter of the archives, Nickels was an inspiration and a sounding board for ideas to promote the collection.[12]

Several early activities by archival staff made a significant difference in the amount of use of the collection. In 2001, scanning and websites were in their early days, but the archives was able to obtain funds to hire a student to scan selected images from the Hamilton Family Fonds, among others, and to post these images on its website.[13] What happened next showed the reach that such promotional efforts could achieve. Pierre Apraxine, curator of the Gilman Paper Company Collection in New York and noted art historian, was in the final stages of compiling the photographs for a major exhibition in Paris and New York City. His assistant was scouring the internet and discovered the digitized HFF images. After flying to Winnipeg for the weekend, Apraxine viewed the photographs and selected four that appeared in the exhibition entitled *Le Troisième oeil: La photographie et l'occulte* and shown at the Maison européenne de la photographie in Paris from November 2004 to February

Fig. 5.4. This album page was shown in the French exhibit and in both French and English catalogues. The date of the séance was 25 February 1931. UMASC, PC 12, Box 8, Folder 5, Item 34, http://hdl.handle.net/10719/1411758.

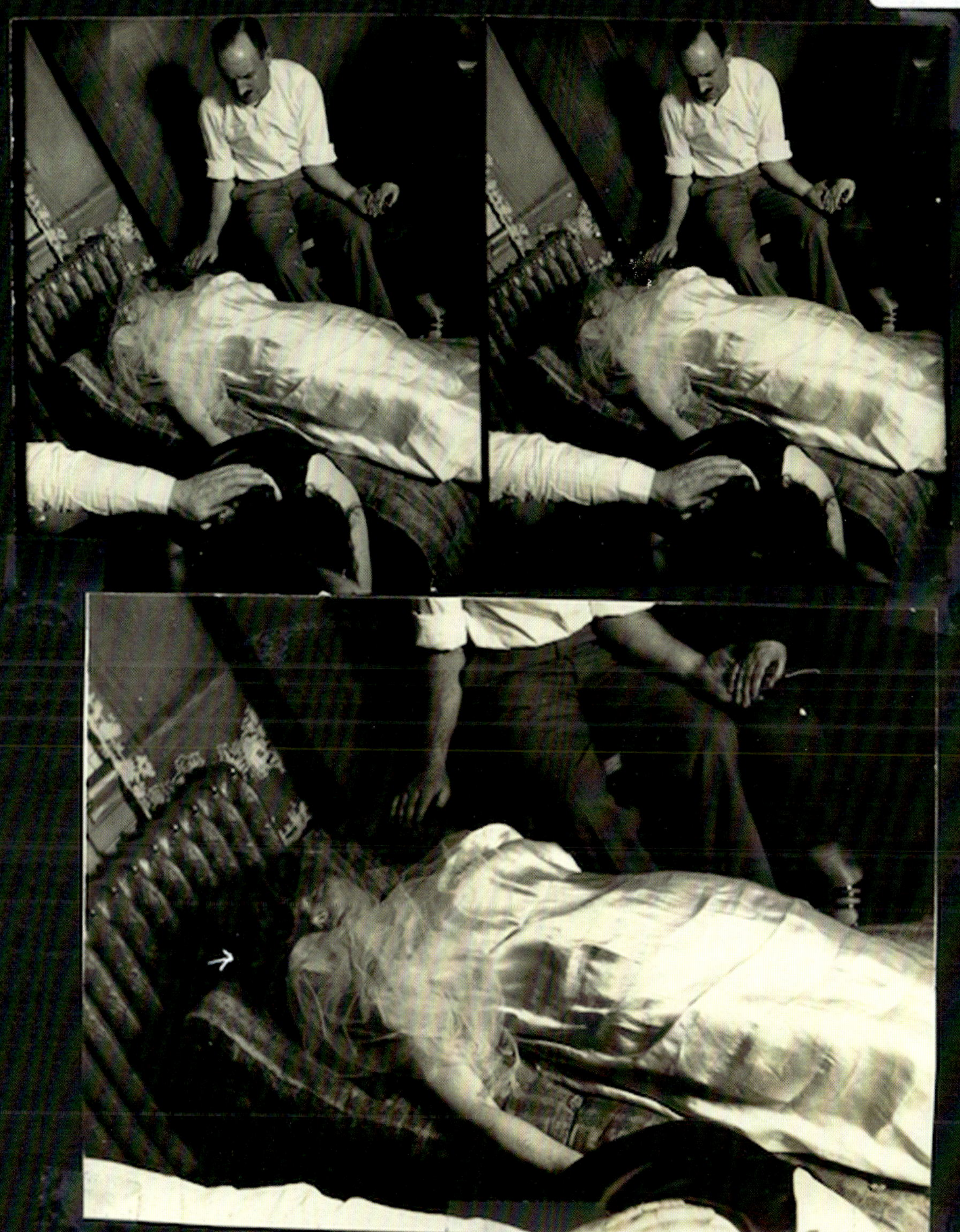

Note the lower and veiled face. Eyes are closed, an inner phenomenon which suggests that the manifesting

2005.[14] Two of those photographs would later appear at the Metropolitan Museum of Art (the Met) in New York when the exhibition moved there (see Figure 5.4).[15] Two separate catalogues, one in French and one in English, were published. The effect of the acknowledgement of the collection by such prestigious institutions and the publicity that resulted from these two international exhibits was immense.[16] This interest in the digitized images led the archives to apply for and receive funds to digitize over 700 photographs in the fonds.[17] Once the images were digitized and posted on the web in 2006, they provided greater opportunities for researchers to find the holdings. Once again the launch of this resource generated an enormous amount of international publicity, including internet stories on sites such as ourstrangeworld.net and print articles such as in the *Psychic News*.[18]

A further project launched from this digitization was the promotional YouTube video entitled *T.G. Hamilton's Photos of Ectoplasm*.[19] At that time, YouTube was relatively young, and archives were just beginning to mount videos featuring their records on the platform.[20] A staff member in the technology support unit suggested that the Hamilton Family Fonds was the most appropriate to use because of its quirky nature.[21] A film studies student, Rob Ross, whom the archives had hired for another project, was asked to create a short video using a selection of HFF photographs. After a couple of attempts, Ross was able to create a video with original music that he wrote and performed that, the archives hoped, would be sufficiently intriguing to capture the attention of casual viewers and make them aware of the collection.

After the video was posted on 27 February 2008, viewings immediately skyrocketed, thanks to a favourable review on an American syndicated late-night radio show called *Coast to Coast AM*. To date, there have been over 364,000 views of, 476 comments on, and 691 likes of the post, remarkable for a video of archival materials. Archival staff reposted the video to the UMASC YouTube channel once it was established, gaining another 23,000 plus views.[22] Again the publicity was astonishing.[23] Many news outlets were looking for videos for their websites, so this foray into a new medium of delivery was timely. The question, of course, is whether individuals were drawn to use the photographs after viewing the video. It is impossible to say for sure, but it seemed that photos from the video showing up in other contexts increased.[24]

Besides the use of actual photos and textual materials as well as reproductions from the Hamilton Family Fonds in a wide variety of art exhibitions all over the world, there have been numerous instances of the fonds being used as inspiration for artistic and cultural projects. Many artists, filmmakers, and writers have based their works upon the fonds in various ways. Both a play and a novel have been based upon the collection, and there have been films, television documentaries, paintings, prints, jewellery, and even reconstructions of the photos by a filmmaker and her friends.

One of the most striking instances of the use of this collection as inspiration was by Northern Irish filmmaker Susan MacWilliam. After she discovered the fonds, she applied to conduct a residency with aceart inc. gallery in Winnipeg and supplemented her residency with grant funds from the archives to spend a month reviewing the materials. The archives provided a special room where she could set up her equipment and leave the materials in place for her to return to every day (see Figure 5.5).

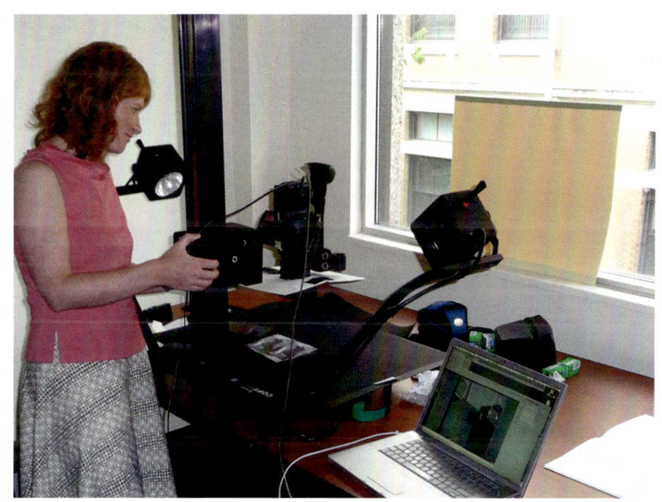

Fig. 5.5. Northern Irish researcher Susan MacWilliam using a copy stand in UMASC, 20 August 2008. Photograph by Shelley Sweeney. UMASC, internal document, 20 August 2008.

The result in 2009 was the seventeen-minute film *F-L-A-M-M-A-R-I-O-N*. Among other photographs from the collection, the film employs an HFF image claimed to be a message from Camille Flammarion (1842–1925), a French psychical researcher, astronomer, and author (see Figure 5.6). *F-L-A-M-M-A-R-I-O-N* was

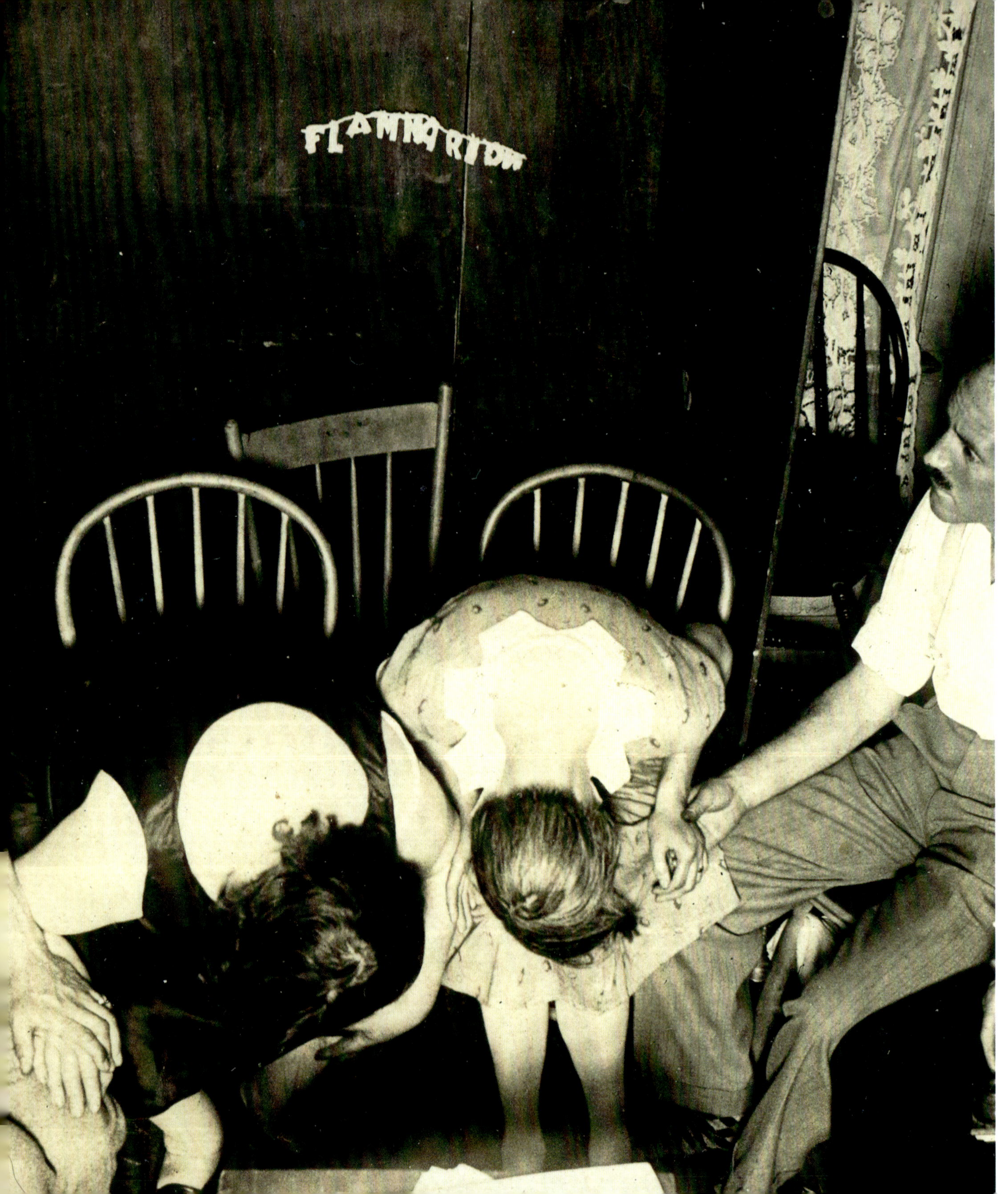
FLAMMARION

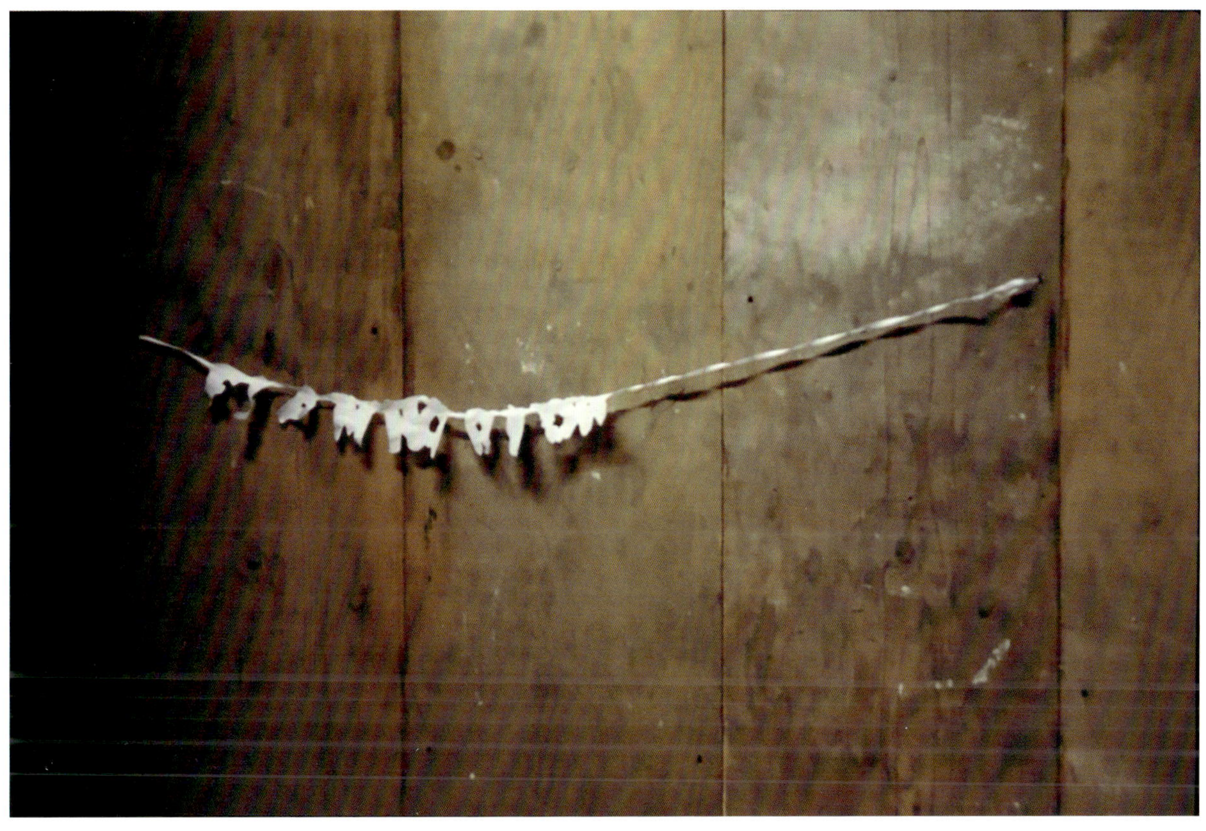

Fig. 5.6. *Left*, ***Printed Teleplasmic Letters, FLAMMARION.*** The séance with the teleplasmic letters spelling the name Flammarion that inspired artist Susan MacWilliam, 10 June 1931. UMASC, PC 12, Box 10, Folder 3, Item 36, http://hdl.handle.net/10719/1411502.

Fig. 5.7. *Above*, Susan MacWilliam, ***Reconstruction of T.G. Hamilton's Séance Cabinet with F-L-A-M-M-A-R-I-O-N 'teleplasm,'*** 2008. © Susan MacWilliam. Courtesy of the artist.

subsequently shown as part of MacWilliam's solo exhibition at the prestigious 53rd Venice Biennale in 2009 and toured around the world in the years after the exhibition ended (see Figures 5.7 and 9.25).[25] The film also featured in the book *Susan MacWilliam: Remote Viewing* by MacWilliam, edited by Karen Downey and published in 2009.[26] Many people have subsequently enjoyed this view of the Hamilton family investigations without ever knowing the original story.[27]

In recent years, there has also been increased use of the Hamilton Family Fonds for academic studies ranging from the role of women as mediums to the connection of the fonds to death, trauma, and grieving.[28] The fonds has been fuelling theses as well. Most recently, Katie Oates defended her doctoral dissertation on women who negotiated social change through the practices of spirit photography and psychical research.[29] Lillian Hamilton was one of the subjects of the study, as was her Winnipeg contemporary Sylvia Barber. Additionally, Oates considered how psychic and spirit photographs and their creators and subjects attracted viewers through affective engagement.

A popular researcher who stands out was a science teacher named Walter David Falk. An archival staff member was concerned that Falk seemed to be photographing every page in the HFF collection. When pressed, he said that T.G. Hamilton had come to him in a dream and told him what he must do. Falk also shared some personal tragedies in his family, making one wonder how much they had contributed to his decision to do this work. Falk spent a further three years transcribing all the handwritten records and studying their contents, followed by years of work creating multiple YouTube videos explaining the Hamiltons' experiments.[30] Then another user in Spain translated the records that Falk had transcribed into Spanish.[31] As with other researchers, Falk's important work has meant that the Hamilton family's experiments have gained new—and different—audiences.

Finally, given the large number of researchers employing the Hamilton Family Fonds and the extraordinary breadth of its use, and the fact that the Canadian Cultural Property Export Review Board certified the fonds as having outstanding cultural and historical value to Canada, University of Manitoba Archives and Special

Collections decided to see whether the fonds could be named to UNESCO's Memory of the World Register, which recognizes the world heritage status of an archive.[32] The archival staff thought that such recognition would further promote the fonds to new audiences at the international level and cement the collection's reputation with the university, the city of Winnipeg, and the province of Manitoba. Over three months, three staff members wrote an extensive and thoroughly documented application that placed the records in the context of international interest in life after death after the First World War and the flu pandemic of 1918–20.[33] It was a struggle to move the application forward. In the end, even with requested rewrites, the Canadian committee could not agree on what to do with the application, but the head of the agency decided to submit it to UNESCO regardless. It was turned down at the next level but once again was sent forward. The application made it all the way to the International Advisory Committee. It was a crushing blow when, after much discussion, the collection ultimately was rejected. Former National Archivist of Canada Ian Wilson, who had done a review of the Memory of the World program, thought that the fonds was just too controversial to ever be accepted even if we applied again with international partners.[34] The final decision was hard to accept, but it reinforced the commitment of the archives to the collection and ultimately enhanced its value for researchers through the extensive process of documentation.

Colleague Brian Hubner, who recently completed a doctoral thesis on the Hamilton Family Fonds, believes that the appeal of the collection is that "you can read into Hamilton almost anything that you want."[35] Although the power of this collection is unusual, it serves as an example of how stories can be rewoven into new narratives well beyond the lifetimes of the original storytellers and how their records can enjoy new life. In this way, the Hamilton Family Fonds has proven that there is life after death after all.

NOTES

1 The word *fonds* refers to a group of records created or collected by a person, family, or organization in the course of daily activity and considered of enduring value. Margaret Hamilton Bach, the oldest child in the Hamilton family, began depositing her family's records in 1979, and the deposit was completed by her estate in 1986. UMASC, HFF, MSS 14, https://umlarchives.lib.umanitoba.ca/hamilton-family-fonds (accessed 3 January 2022).

2 See, for example, Brian Edward Hubner, "'The Ghostly Shadow' in the Archives: An Archival Case Study of the Creation and Recreation of the Hamilton Family Fonds at the University of Manitoba Archives and Special Collections" (PhD diss., University of Amsterdam, 2020).

3 There are 2.5 linear metres of records. UMASC, HFF, MSS 14, https://umlarchives.lib.umanitoba.ca/hamilton-family-fonds (accessed 2 January 2022).

4 Hubner, "'The Ghostly Shadow.'"

5 Joy Lowe and Walter J. Meyer zu Erpen, "The Canadian Spiritualist Movement and Sources for Its Study," *Archivaria* 30 (1990): 71–84.

6 This has included helping to raise funds for the T. Glendenning Hamilton Research Grant, which supports researchers who wish to use the Hamilton Family Fonds, among other collections. See "Research Grants and Endowments: T. Glendenning Hamilton Research Grant," University of Manitoba Libraries, https://libguides.lib.umanitoba.ca/c.php?g=500907&p=3430149 (accessed 27 September 2022).

7 *Paranormal Review: The Magazine of the Society for Psychical Research* 77 (2016).

8 Lawrence Wall of CBC Radio, for example, expressed surprise that the University of Manitoba would acquire papers on this "bizarre subject." Quoted in Hubner, "'The Ghostly Shadow,'" 93.

9 Chris A. Rutkowski, *Unnatural History: True Manitoba Mysteries* (Winnipeg: Chameleon Book Publishers, 1993).

10 *The Campus Files: Ep.2, The Haunting in Manitoba*, 8 June 2009, YouTube, 4:56, https://www.youtube.com/watch?v=7HSS4eXV-fY (accessed 22 September 2022).

11 James B. Nickels, "Psychic Research in a Winnipeg Family: Reminiscences of Dr. Glen F. Hamilton," *Manitoba History* 55 (2007), http://www.mhs.mb.ca/docs/mb_history/55/psychicresearch.shtml (accessed 3 April 2022).

12 All three researchers—Walter Meyer zu Erpen, Chris Rutkowski, and Jim Nickels—eventually donated archival records related to psychical research to UMASC. Additionally, Meyer zu Erpen has arranged to donate in the future the SRIC (Survival Research Institute of Canada) library of paranormal titles to UMASC. Rutkowski donated his records related to the Hamiltons and ghosts in Manitoba as well as his archives related to UFOs and his extensive library on the topic. Nickels donated his research as well as items from the Hamilton Family Fonds that he had recovered.

13 "Thomas Glendenning Hamilton Photograph Gallery," UMASC, https://web.archive.org/web/20011126184948/http://www.umanitoba.ca/libraries/units/archives/collections/spirphoto.htm (accessed 2 February 2022).

14 Clément Chéroux et al., *Le troisième oeil: La photographie et l'occulte*, Maison européenne de la

photographie, Paris, November 2004–February 2005, https://www.mep-fr.org/event/le-troisieme-oeil/ (accessed 5 January 2022).

15 Clément Chéroux et al., *The Perfect Medium: Photography and the Occult*, Metropolitan Museum of Art, New York, September–December 2005, https://www.metmuseum.org/press/exhibitions/2005/the-perfect-medium-photography-and-the-occult (accessed 5 January 2022).

16 See Hubner, "'The Ghostly Shadow,'" for examples.

17 "Hamilton Family Fonds," UMASC, https://digitalcollections.lib.umanitoba.ca/islandora/object/uofm%3Ahamilton_family (accessed 4 February 2022).

18 Hubner, "'The Ghostly Shadow.'"

19 Rob Ross, *T.G. Hamilton's Photos of Ectoplasm*, 27 February 2008, YouTube, 4:06, https://www.youtube.com/watch?v=W0HncGNBCqY&t=146s (accessed 2 January 2022).

20 YouTube was launched on 14 February 2005.

21 Carell Jackimiek had been observing the types of videos that had the most appeal, which led to her suggestion.

22 Ross, *T.G. Hamilton's Photos of Ectoplasm*, 10 December 2008, YouTube, UMASC channel, 4:05, https://www.youtube.com/watch?v=kXXC2RTvF_4 (accessed 2 February 2022). The video was also reposted to at least one other channel with French commentary after it was uploaded. *Ectoplasm Paranormal Fantômes Dr T G Hamilton Winnipeg 1918*, 8 May 2009, YouTube, 2:45, https://www.youtube.com/watch?v=iWZzD-n9u30 (accessed 4 February 2022).

23 Media coverage included local television, the *National Post*, and all local media outlets, which covered the video on their websites. The story was picked up internationally as well, being featured on Spanish and Japanese websites. Hubner, "'The Ghostly Shadow,'" covers a selection of the publicity.

24 Interestingly, the video itself has garnered much attention from archivists and librarians for its success, being featured as a case study in articles, posters, and conference presentations. See, for example, Selene Colburn and Laura Haines, "Measuring Libraries' Use of YouTube as a Promotional Tool: An Exploratory Study and Proposed Best Practices," *Journal of Web Librarianship* 6, no. 1 (2012): 5–31.

25 Susan MacWilliam (representing Northern Ireland), *Remote Viewing*, 53rd Venice Biennale, Venice, 2009.

26 Susan MacWilliam, *Susan MacWilliam: Remote Viewing*, ed. Karen Downey (London: Black Dog Publishing, 2009).

27 MacWilliam also had a profound effect on the collection by suggesting the name change from the T.G. Hamilton Collection to the Hamilton Family Fonds since both Lillian and Margaret played significant roles in the psychical research and its promotion.

28 See, for example, Beth A. Robertson, *Science of the Seance: Transnational Networks and Gendered Bodies in the Study of Psychic Phenomena, 1918–40* (Vancouver: UBC Press, 2017); and Jennifer Douglas, Alexandra Alisauskas, and Devon Mordell, "'Treat Them with the Reverence of Archivists': Records Work, Grief Work, and Relationship Work in the Archives," *Archivaria* 88 (2019): 84–120.

29 Katie Oates, "Women, Spirit Photography and Psychical Research: Negotiating Gender Conventions and Loss" (PhD diss., University of Western Ontario, 2022).

30 See, for example, Walter Falk, *Dr. T. G. Hamilton's Psychic Researches*, YouTube, https://www.youtube.com/user/Falcon1296/videos (accessed 3 January 2022); and Walter Falk, *The T. G. Hamilton Files—Chapter 1–4—Walter D. Falk*, 15 July 2018, YouTube, 1:33:46, https://www.youtube.com/watch?v=iYe2Chu6TAA (accessed 3 January 2022).

31 Francisco Picon translated Falk's transcriptions. See CienciasPsíquicas, "SurvivalafterDeath," 2011–20, http://survivalafterdeath.blogspot.com/ (accessed 2 April 2022).

32 I first ran the idea past a member of the committee that vetted collections for the Memory of the World Register. She thought that it was appropriate to apply. UNESCO, *Memory of the World Register: The Hamilton Family Fonds*, http://www.unesco.org/new/fileadmin/MULTIMEDIA/HQ/CI/CI/pdf/mow/nomination_forms/canada_hamilton_family_fonds.pdf (accessed 2 January 2022).

33 The staff members were me along with Brian Hubner and Mary Horodyski.

34 Personal oral communication with the author, February 2019.

35 Personal email communication with the author, 2 February 2022.

Facing page, Paul Robles, ***Murmurations (Clumps)***, 2022–2023. Origami paper. Courtesy of the artist.

Overleaf, Teresa Burrows, ***Citrinitas 2***, 2020. Digital print. Courtesy of the artist.

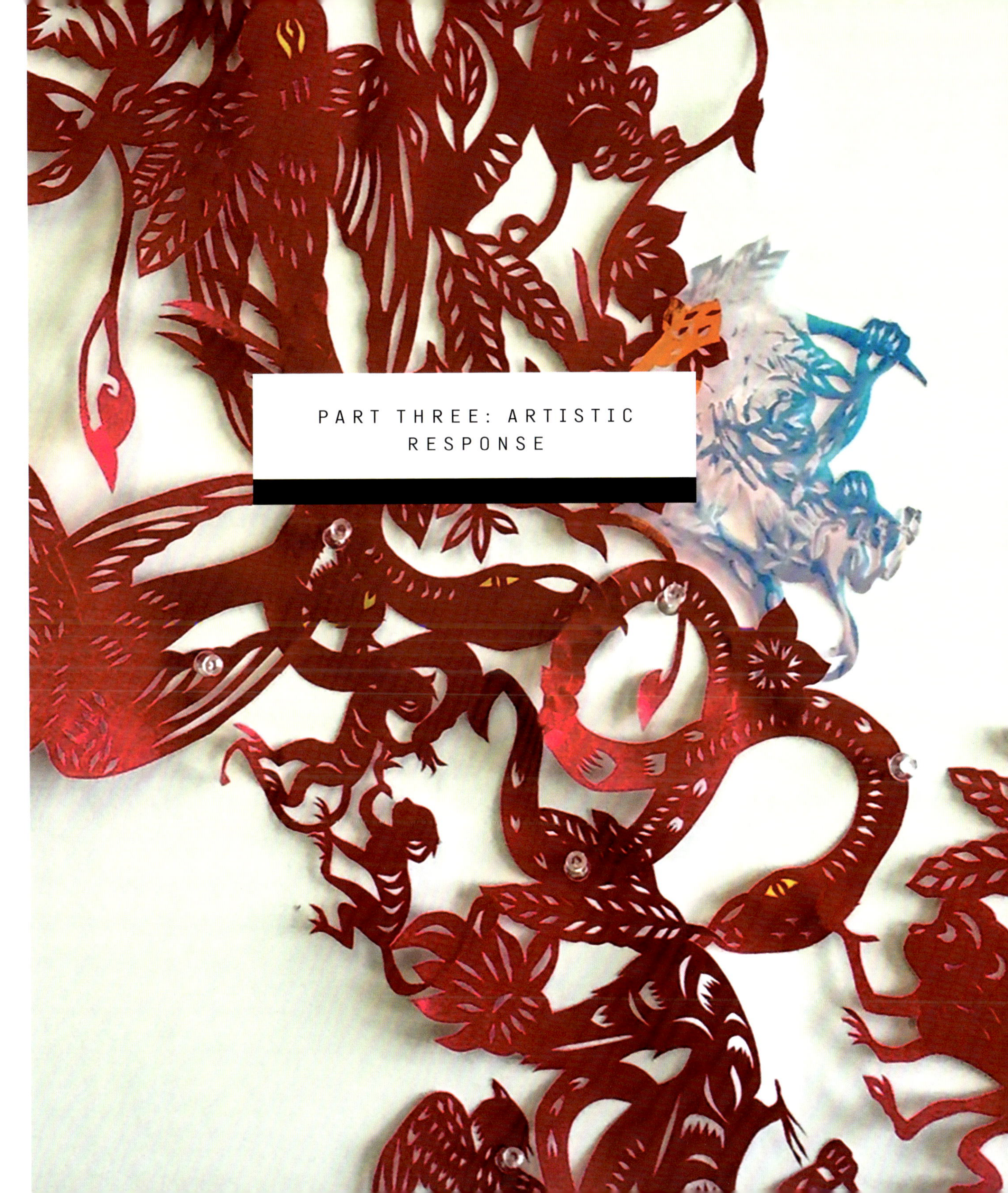

PART THREE: ARTISTIC RESPONSE

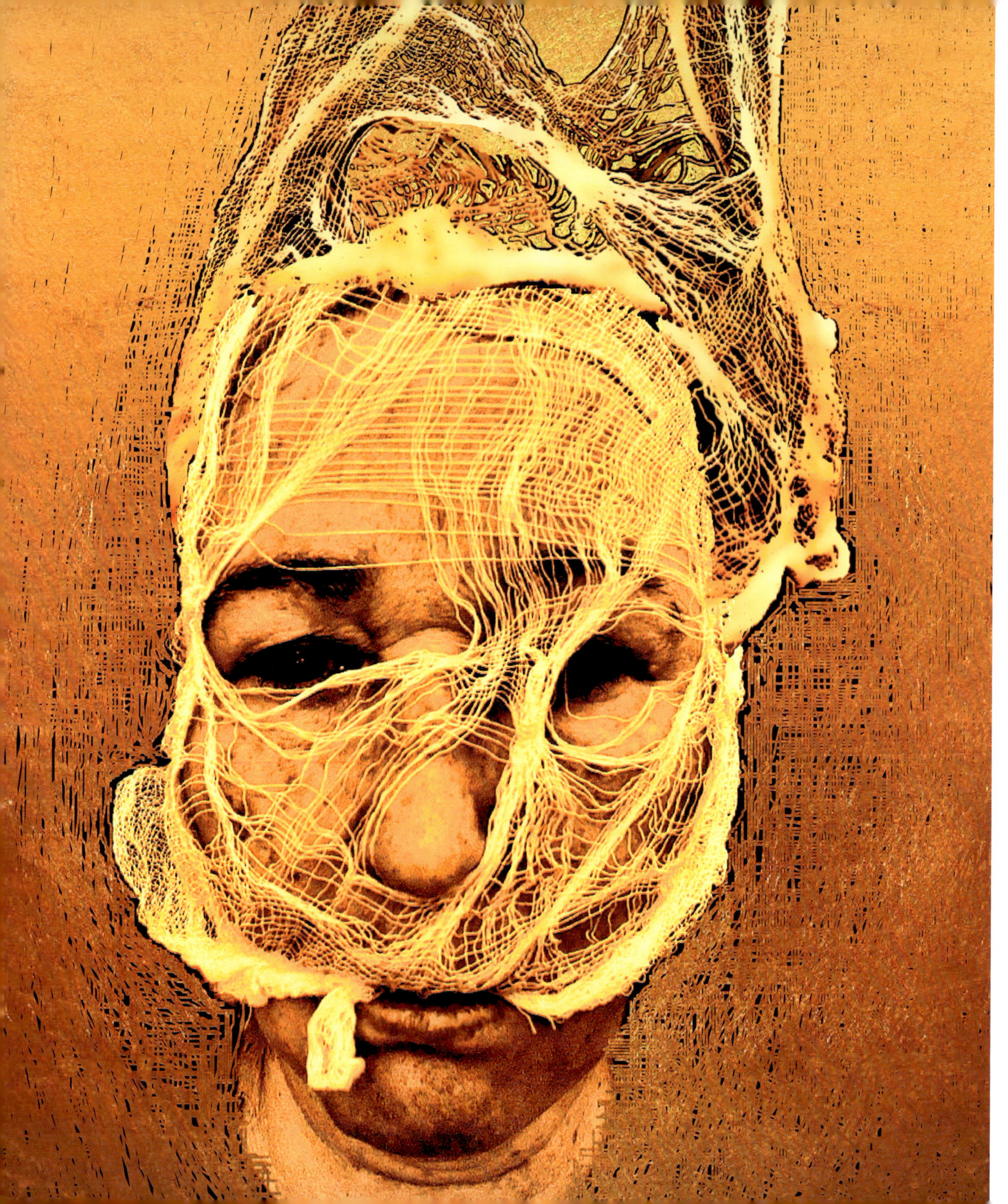

6

"Weird Winnipeg": Or How the Hamilton Family Fonds Helped to Make Winnipeg an Unlikely Centre of the Paranormal

Brian Hubner

The Hamilton Family Fonds (HFF) is Manitoba's most recognized archive, and more than this, it has become part of how Winnipeg is perceived by the outside world.[1] The collection demonstrates how archives can shape a cultural resource of international renown, drawing in researchers and creators from many perspectives and attracting other paranormal collections. Although it was never a major centre of Spiritualism, Winnipeg was the home of some very determined and dedicated psychical researchers. Thanks to them, the city has become a centre for paranormal research and has a reputation for weirdness.

The fonds documents two important investigations of psychic phenomena, psychokinetic (telekinetic) table levitations and ectoplasmic manifestations, many of which contained miniature faces of deceased individuals. The Hamiltons endeavoured to verify séance room phenomena through photography, working

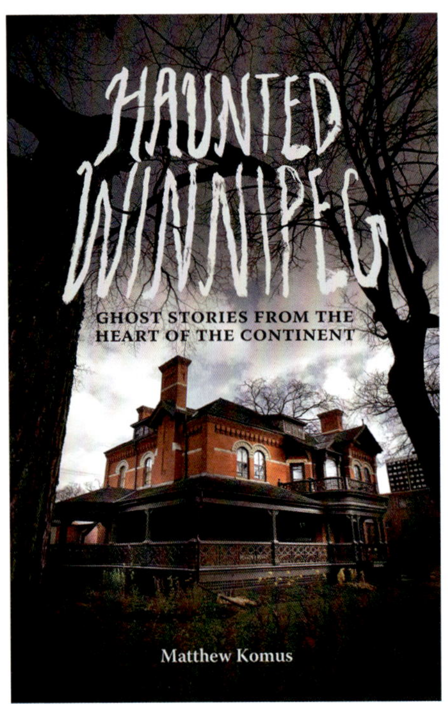

Fig. 6.1. Cover of the book ***Haunted Winnipeg: Ghost Stories from the Heart of the Continent*** (2014), by Matthew Komus. Courtesy of Great Plains Publications.

in specialized rooms in the Hamilton House in Winnipeg's Elmwood neighbourhood. The circulation of these photographs of psychic phenomena beyond the archives has contributed to Winnipeg's identity. For example, Tourism Winnipeg produced a booklet entitled *Factoids: Made in Winnipeg, Canada* (2014) that includes a section on Thomas Glendenning (T.G.) Hamilton and his relationship with Sir Arthur Conan Doyle, who visited Winnipeg in 1923.[2] The provincial report "Imagine. Creative Manitoba!" (2017) highlights the University of Manitoba's archives related to Spiritualism and psychical research. The report concludes that archives "are often the foundation of other cultural activities,"[3] providing inspiration for stories and personal and community histories and source material for TV shows, movies, digital media, songs, books, and magazines. This is exactly what has happened here.

The Hamilton Family Fonds was donated to the University of Manitoba Archives and Special Collections (UMASC) by T.G. and Lillian Hamilton's daughter, Margaret Hamilton Bach, beginning in 1979. When the fonds arrived, the archives had just been established under Dr. Richard Bennett in 1978. He initially believed that the fonds would either be of interest to researchers of Winnipeg's social history or sit on the shelf untouched for years.[4] Despite two high-profile radio interviews, years passed with minimal attention paid to the photographs.

This changed dramatically over time. One of the first local researchers was Chris Rutkowski, a University of Manitoba employee keenly interested in the paranormal. He had been told about the Hamilton Family Fonds by Bennett but also had been in contact with Margaret Hamilton Bach prior to the donation.

What followed was his book *Unnatural History: True Manitoba Mysteries* (1993).[5] Barbara Smith's *Ghost Stories of Manitoba* (1998) also featured the fonds.[6] Mentions of Winnipeg and the Hamiltons also appeared in two books by the prolific Canadian writer John Robert Colombo: *Mysterious Canada: Strange Sights, Extraordinary Events, and Peculiar Places* (1988) and *Personal Accounts of the Paranormal* (1996).[7] Other works by local Winnipeg writers include Cara Hill's *Supernatural Winnipeg: A Guide to a Ghostly Vacation* (2008) and Matthew Komus's *Haunted Winnipeg: Ghost Stories from the Heart of the Continent* (2014) (see Figure 6.1). In the chapter on "Hamilton House," Komus encourages readers to visit the University of Manitoba to assess the validity of the séances for themselves: "The general public is now able to study the work for themselves and draw their own conclusions."[8] A work of juvenile non-fiction, *Haunted Canada 10: More Scary True Stories* (2020), by Joel A. Sutherland, gives young readers a taste of weird séances that the Hamiltons held late at night.[9] The Halloween season regularly sees print and video interviews and presentations on the Hamilton family.[10]

One of the most intriguing publications is Carolin Vesely and Buzz Currie's *The Hermetic Code: Unlocking One of Manitoba's Greatest Secrets* (2007), based upon the research of scholar Frank Albo.[11] Albo traced the origins of the Manitoba Legislative Building, planned by Frank Worthington Simon, who was trained in Paris by members of the Masonic Order and filled the building with Masonic and occult symbols and specifications. Although T.G. Hamilton was a Member of the Legislative Assembly when the building was constructed, research has failed to indicate any connection between him and symbolic meanings of the building. Regardless, *The Hermetic Code* includes a section on "Magical Winnipeg" that outlines Hamilton's paranormal investigations and reproduces several Hamilton photographs. The text repeats Conan Doyle's praise of Winnipeg's magical possibilities, clearly linking them and the photograph to Simon's efforts.[12] This praise came in July 1923 when Conan Doyle passed through Winnipeg. On that visit, he sat in on two séances, including one of Dr. Hamilton's scientific ones, and was so impressed that in a thank-you note of 5 July, from Prince Arthur, Ontario, Conan Doyle

Canadian National Railways

Hotel System.

Prince Arthur Hotel,
Port Arthur, Ont.

July 5 1923.

Dear Mrs Hamilton

I did not thank you sufficiently for the excellent account of the R.L.S. phenomena. I will study it more carefully when I have leisure

Windlesham, Crowboro', Sussex. gets me if ever you have anything to report.

For information about the other circle apply to Colonel Handford, the Solicitor. I think you could each interest the other Winnipeg should be a psychic centre.

With all thanks

A Conan Doyle.

wrote to Lillian proclaiming that "Winnipeg should be a psychic centre" (see Figure 6.2).[13] He made a similar comment in his book *Our Second American Adventure*, published in 1924. Thus, Conan Doyle helped to initiate the idea of Winnipeg as a centre of supernatural activity.[14]

The majority of accounts of the Hamiltons mention the visit of the Doyles, including a substantial article by Laird Rankin in 1982 titled "Ghost Story," based upon an interview with Margaret Hamilton Bach.[15] Jim Nickels, a University of Manitoba psychology professor, was intrigued early on by the papers' potential for research: "Quite frankly, I thought historians, paranormal investigators, photographers, and artistic persons would be highly interested in this material."[16] In 1986, he began to make contact with the Hamilton family in an effort to interview a surviving family member who had been a participant in the Hamilton séances. After Margaret Hamilton Bach died that October, Nickels contacted her brother Glen Forrester Hamilton in 1987 and conducted interviews with him until his death the next year. This research eventually resulted in the article "Psychic Research in a Winnipeg Family: Reminiscences of Dr. Glen F. Hamilton," published in 2007.[17]

This body of research inspired attempts to tell the story of the Hamiltons for a general audience. There were three such examples on Canadian television in the mid-2000s, each enhancing the association of Winnipeg with the paranormal and Spiritualism. First was an episode of *Creepy Canada*, "The Hamilton Archives." It used the docudrama format in which costumed actors acted out aspects of the story and Hamilton photographs were included, with Rutkowski providing expert commentary. The episode's website adds the explanation that "much of his [T.G. Hamilton's] archive still exists and is made available for limited public viewing."[18] A second broadcast was "Chasing Hamilton's Ghost," released as part of CTV's *Manitoba Moments* series in 2005.[19] Its docudrama-style re-enactments of the Hamilton séances were more accurately done, and the show included many

Fig. 6.2. Thank-you note from Arthur Conan Doyle to Lillian Hamilton, 5 July 1923, from Port Arthur, Ontario. Courtesy of Survival Research Institute of Canada.

Hamilton photographs and much text. The experts interviewed included Chris Rutkowski, Serena Keshavjee, Walter Meyer zu Erpen, and Shelley Sweeney. The most elaborate docudrama was the "Spiritualism" episode of the *Northern Mysteries* broadcast in 2006.[20] Its interviews are again with Rutkowski, Sweeney, and Meyer zu Erpen, as well as Stan McMullin, author of *Anatomy of a Seance: A History of Spirit Communication in Central Canada* (2004).[21]

The Haunting in Connecticut (2009), shot in Winnipeg and Teulon, Manitoba, represents a major use of the Hamilton images in a dramatic Hollywood feature film.[22] The Hamilton photographs appear in the film as part of an archive (actually shot in the City of Winnipeg Archives) when the family consults archival records to understand what is occurring in the house. Séance photographs are also seen in the preview and on posters that appear to be recreations based upon Hamilton originals (see Figure 6.3). The film's producers pointed to the UMASC website to convince those who thought that the ectoplasm was just too outlandish to be credible, stating that the substance was not created specifically for the film.[23]

In 2011 came "Raining UFOs/Ectoplasmic Pic," an episode of the series *Fact or Faked: Paranormal Files*.[24] After conducting research in the University of Manitoba Archives and Special Collections, paranormal investigators Ben Hansen and Bill Murphy attempted to recreate the "ectoplasmic pics" of T.G. Hamilton from the séances using any physical means reasonable and available.[25] To their credit, the team journeyed to Winnipeg in the middle of winter, visiting the Hamilton family plots in Elmwood Cemetery and Hamilton House. This American show surely strengthened the reputation of "Weird Winnipeg."

Internationally known avant-garde filmmaker Guy Maddin created *My Winnipeg* (2007), which explicitly shaped the general perception of Winnipeg as a weird place.[26] He constructed Winnipeg as a city of secrets and psychical possibilities. In this fantastical look at his home city, he used a number of Hamilton séance photographs to illustrate several scenes. Maddin's interactive project *Seances* (2016) was also inspired by the Hamiltons (see Figures 7.12 and 7.13).[27] It came out of the earlier project entitled *Hauntings* (2012); collectively, Maddin attempted to recreate

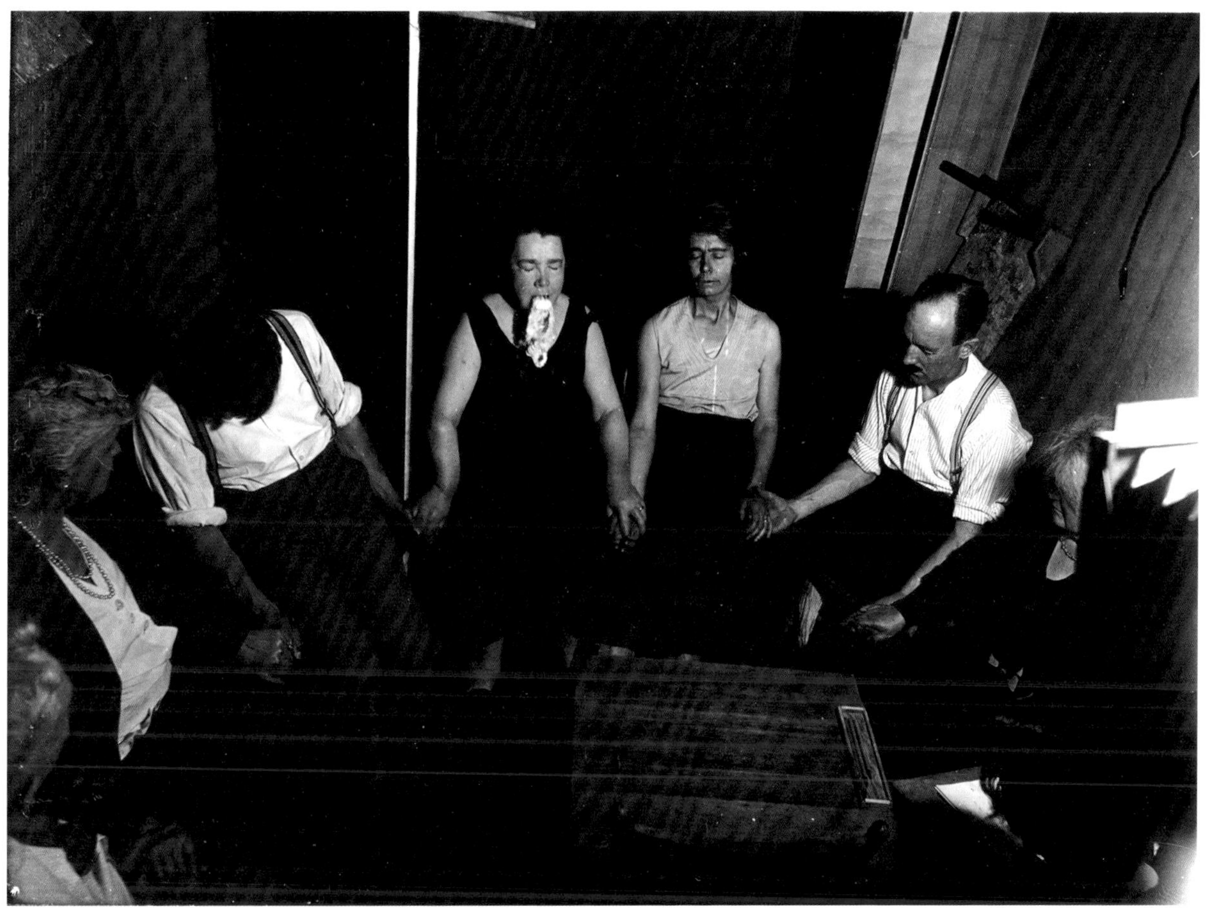

Fig. 6.3. This Hamilton photograph from 22 May 1932 could have been used as a model for ***The Haunting in Connecticut*** poster. UMASC, PC 12, Box 10, Folder 6, Item 47, http://hdl.handle.net/10719/1412613.

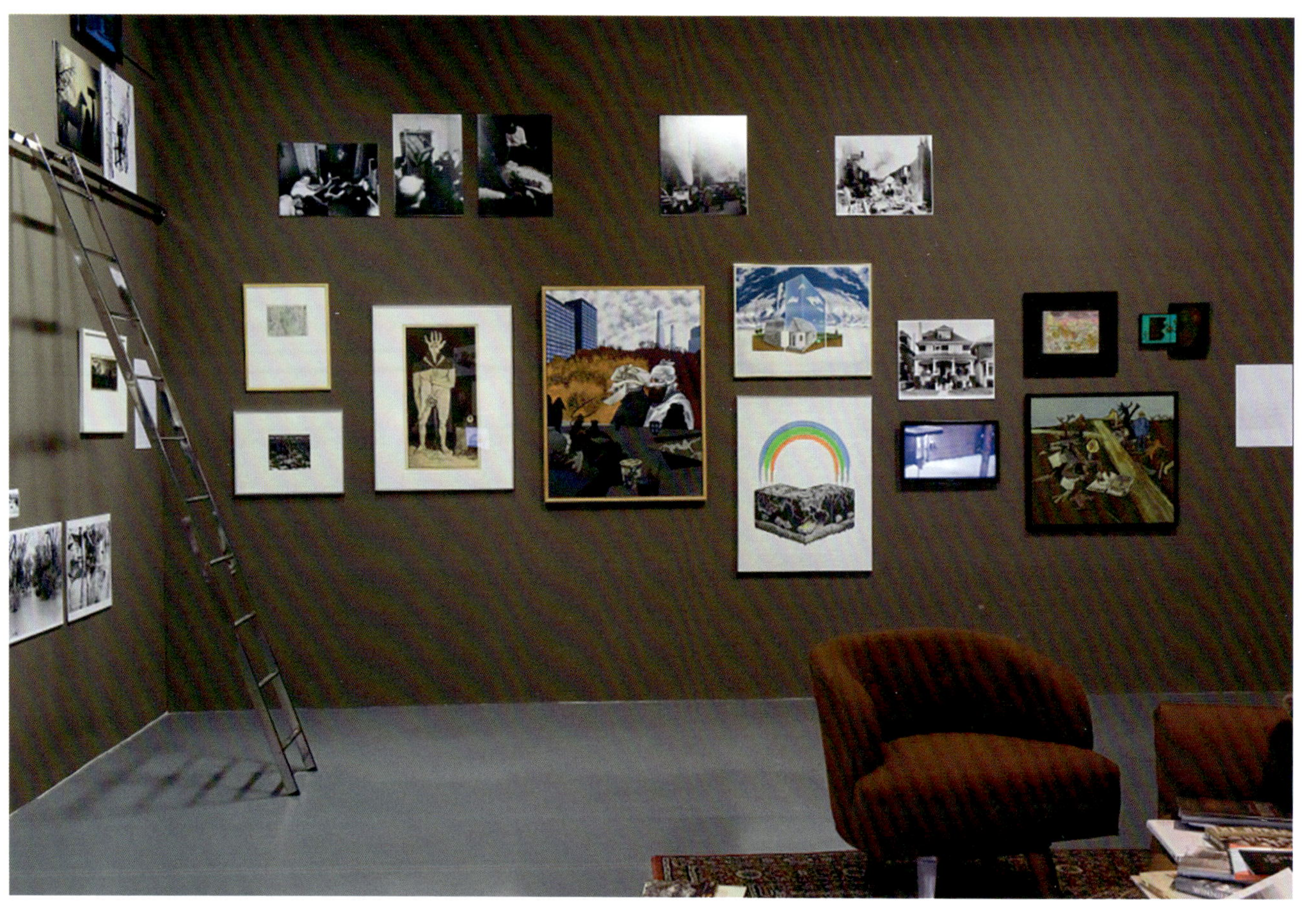

Fig. 6.4. Anthony Kiendl, ***My Winnipeg***, installation view of the exhibition at La Maison rouge, 2011. Courtesy of Plug In ICA.

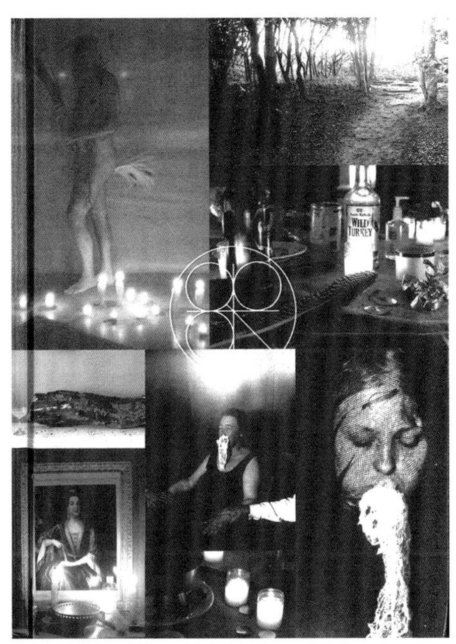

Fig 6.5. Cover of ***Queer Spirits*** (2011), by AA Bronson and Peter Hobbs, published by Winnipeg's Plug In ICA along with Creative Times Books (New York) and JRP Ringier (Zurich). Courtesy of Plug In ICA.

100 lost films in 100 days in various world locations. The films include occult themes featuring shadows, clouds, blurring, and substances that resemble ectoplasm. When Maddin was asked if the Hamilton photographs had influenced him, the answer was yes, but he also indicated that his own life experiences were influential.[28]

A series of exhibits, events, and documentation related to the Hamiltons and the idea of Weird Winnipeg was curated by Sigrid Dahle, the late art collections coordinator at the University of Manitoba. The first was held in 2004 at Gallery One One One (now the School of Art Gallery) at the University of Manitoba and bore the title *Trauerspiel: The Gothic Unconscious.*[29] The exhibit promoted the idea that Winnipeg was on haunted ground through an atmosphere created by the Hamilton photographs. In July 2011, an exhibition of various Manitoban artists called *My Winnipeg* (based upon the title of the Maddin film) was held at La Maison rouge in Paris (and other locales in 2011–12) curated by Dahle and others and included ten Hamilton images (see Figure 6.4).[30] *My Winnipeg* was exhibited in stages at the Plug In Institute of Contemporary Art in Winnipeg in 2012. A companion book, *My Winnipeg (Guide de la scène artistique)*, highlights "Winnipeg, City of Spirits" and includes a description of the Hamilton photographs: "This large and compelling body of photographs are archived at the University of Manitoba." Dahle's essay "There's No Place Like Home: An Incomplete Glossary of Winnipeg" explains that, with "a little cheesecloth and some stellar performances by the mediums," T.G. Hamilton produced the photographs.[31] The drama of these photographs has initiated a DIY ectoplasm industry, as Keshavjee shows in Chapter 9.

The premier exhibit at the new Plug In gallery in 2010, entitled *We Are the Revolution*, also featured séances. They were created by queer artist AA Bronson, who worked with Peter Hobbs from 2006 to 2009 to gather gay men at undisclosed locations in various cities in an "Invocation of Queer Spirits" and photograph the results. Bronson has stated that he was partly inspired by "19th century spiritualist séances" (more likely twentieth-century Hamilton séances)![32] The actual "invocation" was held in the derelict building at the site where the Plug In gallery was eventually built. A follow-up book, *Queer Spirits*, was published in 2011 and showed a number of Hamilton photographs (see Figure 6.5).[33]

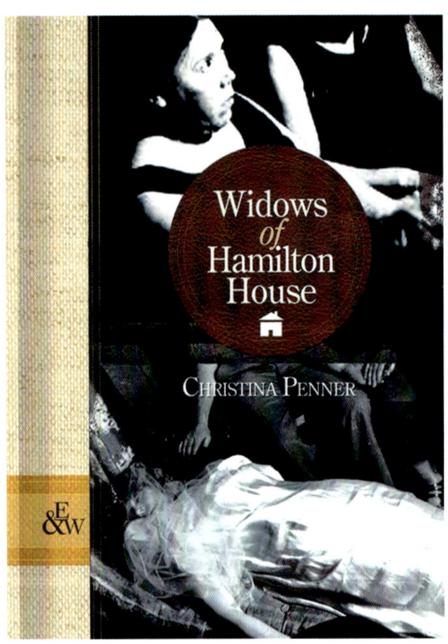

Fig. 6.6. Cover of the novel ***Widows of Hamilton House*** (2008), by Christina Penner. Courtesy of Great Plains Publications.

A notable literary work that built upon the Hamilton family and their home was Christina Penner's *Widows of Hamilton House: A Novel* (2008) (see Figure 6.6).[34] Librarian Ruth Reimer discovers the Hamilton family when the Hamilton book *Intention and Survival* is donated to the library. She learns that she is living in Hamilton House and that the Hamilton papers are at the University of Manitoba Archives and Special Collections. When she researches the history of the Hamilton family, Ruth realizes that just one book cannot tell the whole story, and her investigation of the Hamilton papers forces her to confront what archives conceal as well as reveal.

Carolyn Gray's play *The Elmwood Visitation* (2007) also explored the Hamiltons (see Figure 6.8). Gray had researched the Hamilton family extensively at the archives, and an exhibition of Hamilton family photographs was displayed in the foyer of the playhouse during the play's run.[35] The play is a highly fictionalized version of T.G. Hamilton's research and life, especially as related to Conan Doyle, Dr. L.R.G. Crandon and his wife, the famous medium Mina "Margery" Crandon, and their battle with debunker of Spiritualism Harry Houdini.[36] It shows an affair between T.G. and Margery, an embellishment that upset some surviving Hamilton family members.

The acquisition of the Hamilton Family Fonds and the growth of acquired paranormal collections have led to their use in teaching and instruction at UMASC. Archivists have delivered talks to classes in fields such as art history, religion, and photography; to groups such as Creative Retirement, archivists and librarians, paranormal enthusiasts, and local history buffs; and at academic conferences. Grade school students have also made use of Hamilton documents for their projects, including my son, Cedric, whose film on the Hamilton family featured locations such as Hamilton House, the Hamilton family grave site, and an improvised séance room in our basement.[37] Many of these classes and projects have included a "Weird Winnipeg vibe."[38] The status of "Weird Winnipeg" was cemented when the city hosted the international Preserving the Historical Collections of Parapsychology conference in May 2018 (see Figure 6.7).

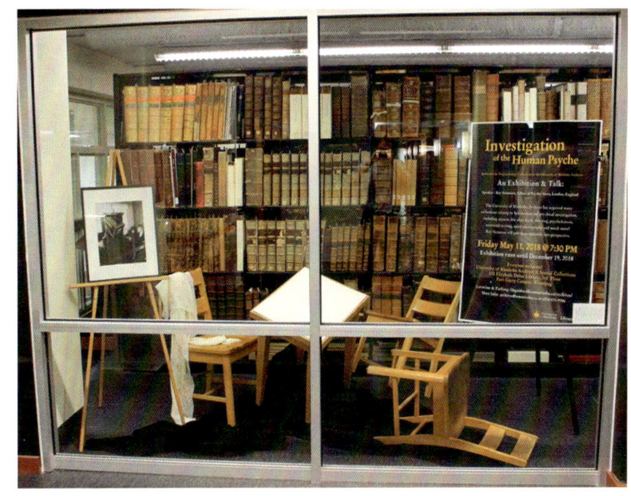

Fig. 6.7. Walter Meyer zu Erpen and Shelley Sweeney curated and mounted an exhibition for the Preserving the Historical Collections of Parapsychology conference in 2018. Photograph by Brian Hubner. Courtesy of UMASC.

After the Hamilton family left the house, it was divided into separate residences, and at one time it included a homeopathic practice. The persistent fear of demolition has been banished for now. In late 2021, the house was purchased by the owner of a Winnipeg retailer, Gags Unlimited, who now has the shop on the main floor and in-person psychic readings on an upper level, thereby offering a

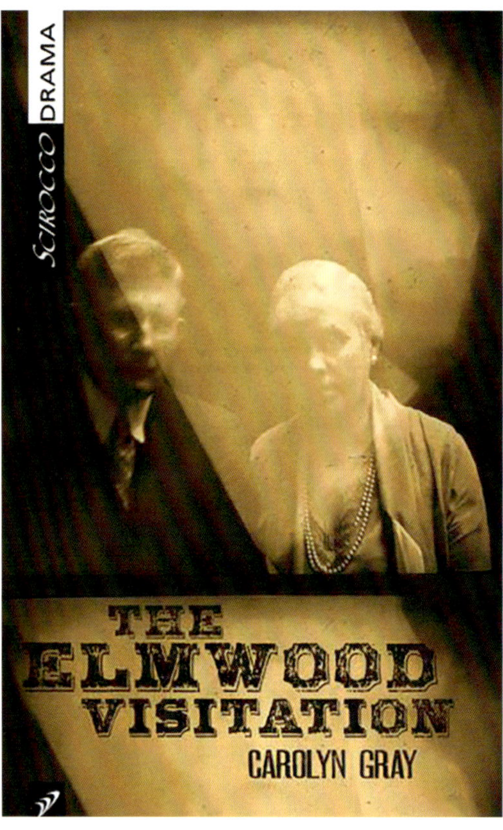

Fig. 6.8. Cover of the play ***The Elmwood Visitation*** (2007), by Carolyn Gray. Courtesy of Scirocco Drama, an imprint of J. Gordon Shillingford Publishing.

unique "Weird Winnipeg" experience—though not, unfortunately, a spooky sleepover as originally planned.[39]

We do not know how many other works used or were inspired by the Hamilton Family Fonds, but we do know that many researchers from highly varied disciplines have come into the archives and used these records for a variety of purposes: education, art, tourism, and more. Together archivists and users of the archives can shape how a city and region are perceived by both locals and outsiders. And here the Hamilton Family Fonds has helped to cement the city's reputation as "Weird Winnipeg."

Thanks

I would first like to acknowledge the invaluable and generous help of Shelley Sweeney in the preparation of this chapter. I would also like to dedicate it to my mother, Freda, and father, Edward, who are not here to see its publication but whose encouragement kept me inspired to complete it and my PhD long after their passing.

NOTES

1 The only possible exception would be the Hudson's Bay Company Archives at the Archives of Manitoba. The word fonds here refers to the archival records of permanent value created or collected by the Hamilton family.

2 "Quirks and Oddities," in *Factoids: Made in Winnipeg*, 6th ed. (Winnipeg: Tourism Winnipeg, c. 2014), 20.

3 Government of Manitoba, Manitoba Culture and Creative Industries Strategy, "Imagine. Creative Manitoba! 2017 Discussion Paper," 5.

4 Richard Bennett, interview with the author, 29 December 2011.

5 Chris Rutkowski, *Unnatural History: True Manitoba Mysteries* (Winnipeg: Chameleon Press, 1993), 100; Chris Rutkowski,email correspondence with the author, 19 and 20 June 2013. Rutkowski is a noted Winnipeg writer, lecturer, and expert on UFOs.

6 Barbara Smith, *Ghost Stories of Manitoba* (Edmonton: Lone Pine Publishing, 1998).

7 John Robert Colombo, *Personal Accounts of the Paranormal* (Toronto: Hounslow Press, 1996); John Robert Colombo, *Mysterious Canada: Strange Sights, Extraordinary Events, and Peculiar Places* (Toronto: Doubleday Canada, 1988).

8 Cara Hill, *Supernatural Winnipeg: A Guide to a Ghostly Vacation* (Winnipeg: Self-published, 2008); Matthew Komus, *Haunted Winnipeg: Ghost Stories from the Heart of the Continent* (Winnipeg: Great Plains Publications, 2014), 62.

9 Joel A. Sutherland, *Haunted Canada 10* (Toronto: Scholastic Canada, 2021), 72–79.

10 See, for example, Kittie Wong, "Stirring the Spirits," *Winnipeg Free Press*, 28 October 2017, D11; see also the interview with Brian Hubner that accompanies the article, by Henrietta Roi, "Otherworldly Archives: University of Manitoba Home to Ghostly Legacy," Canada's History, https://www.canadashistory.ca/explore/museums-galleries-archives/otherworldly-archives (accessed 13 January 2023); and Sabrina Janke and Alex Judge, "The Haunting of Hamilton House," November 2020, in *One Great History*, podcast, 49:21, https://onegreathistory.wordpress.com/2020/11/17/episode-3-the-haunting-of-hamilton-house-2/ (accessed 13 January 2023).

11 Carolin Vesely and Buzz Currie, *The Hermetic Code: Unlocking One of Manitoba's Greatest Secrets* (Winnipeg: Winnipeg Free Press, 2007). See also Terry Melanson, "Book Review: *The Hermetic Code: Unlocking One of Manitoba's Greatest Secrets*," Illuminati: Conspiracy Archive, 15 August 2007, https://www.conspiracyarchive.com/Commentary/Hermetic_Code.htm (accessed 13 January 2023).

12 Vesely and Currie, *The Hermetic Code*, 123–27.

13 Arthur Conan Doyle to Lillian Hamilton, July 5, 1923, from Port Arthur, Ontario. The letter is in the temporary custody of the Survival Research Institute of Canada which intends to deposit it with UMASC.

14 Arthur Conan Doyle, *Our Second American Adventure* (Boston: Little, Brown, 1924).

15 Laird Rankin, "Ghost Story," *Winnipeg Magazine*, May 1982, 24–26, 29, 31.

16 Jim Nickels, email correspondence with the author, 13 December 2013.

17 Jim Nickels, "Psychic Research in a Winnipeg Family: Reminiscences of Dr. Glen F. Hamilton," *Manitoba History* 55 (2007): 51–60; Jim Nickels, *A Video Interview with Dr. Glen F. Hamilton*, 2011, UMASC, DVD.

18 *Creepy Canada*, The Hamilton Archives, Season 2, Episode 6; refer to https://web.archive.org/web/20071223160350/http://www.creepy.tv/season2_e6.html (accessed 13 January 2023).

19 *Chasing Hamilton's Ghost*, dir. Darren Wall, Farpoint Films, 2005 [DVD 2007].

20 *Northern Mysteries*, "Spiritualism," Episodes 5–8, 1 April 2006.

21 Stan McMullin, *Anatomy of a Seance: A History of Spirit Communication in Central Canada* (Montreal and Kingston: McGill-Queen's University Press, 2004).

22 *The Haunting in Connecticut* DVD was released in July 2009; references are to this version.

23 See the IMDb (Internet Movie Database) website for *The Haunting in Connecticut*, http://www.imdb.com/title/tt0492044/ (accessed 13 January 2023).

24 As viewed on YouTube. See also *Fact or Faked: Paranormal Files*, Wikipedia, http://en.wikipedia.org/wiki/Fact_or_Faked:_Paranormal_Files (accessed 26 January 2022).

25 Ben Hansen, interview with the author, 12 September 2014.

26 *My Winnipeg*, dir. Guy Maddin, Buffalo Gal Pictures, 2007.

27 Guy Maddin, Evan Johnson, Galen Johnson, and National Film Board of Canada, *Seances*, http://séances.nfb.ca/ (accessed 13 January 2023).

28 Guy Maddin, "Séances/Spiritismes," talk at the Winnipeg Art Gallery (WAG), 31 October 2012; see also "Winnipeg Now," "Art for Lunch," *My WAG* 100 (2012): 7.

29 Sigrid Dahle, curator, *Trauerspiel: The Gothic Unconscious*, Gallery One One One, Winnipeg, 12–30 January 2004, https://www.umanitoba.ca/schools/art/content/galleryoneoneone/goth26.html (accessed 13 January 2023).

30 University of Manitoba, *Bulletin*, 14 July 2011, 8.

31 Paula Aisemberg et al., *My Winnipeg: Guide de la scène artistique/Guide of the Artistic Scene* (Lyon, France: Fage, 2011), 31; glossary entries, 38–51.

32 See the Plug In ICA website for the exhibit *AA Bronson: We Are the Revolution*, 10 November–19 December 2010, https://plugin.org/exhibitions/a-a-bronson-we-are-the-revolution/ (accessed 13 January 2023).

33 AA Bronson and Peter Hobbs, *Queer Spirits* (Winnipeg: Plug In Editions, 2011); see "Lessons," 22–23, 41, 49–64, and 152–53.

34 UMASC, *Annual Report 2008–2009*, 9.

35 UMASC, *Annual Report 2006–2007*, 5–6; see [Brett Lougheed], "New Digitization Projects at the University of Manitoba Archives and Special Collections," *ACA Bulletin*, January 2007, 6,12. The launch was also mentioned by the president in the *University of Manitoba Senate Report*, 7 February 2007, a very unusual occurrence for the archives. It was also noted in Library and Archives Canada, "Inventory of Canadian Digital Initiatives," Thomas Glendenning Hamilton Photograph Collection, (contributed by Shelley Sweeney), https://web.archive.org/web/20070516234049/http://www.collectionscanada.ca/initiatives-bin/rella?mode=alpha (accessed 13 January 2023). It has been updated as CRKN, "The Canadian National Digital Heritage Index," Hamilton Family Fonds, https://www.cndhi-ipnpc.ca/index.php/en/node/8021 (accessed 18 January 2023).

36 Carolyn Gray, *The Elmwood Visitation—A Play Presented by Manitoba Theatre Projects* (Winnipeg: Scirocco Drama, 2007); UMASC *Annual Report 2006–2007*, 6–8; UMASC Administrative Files, "Outreach 2006–2007".

37 UMASC Administrative Files, "T. G. Hamilton Archives Acquisition File," 2008. Cedric McMaster-Hubner's film was entitled *Les séances de la famille Hamilton à Winnipeg, 1919–1935*.

38 These talks have often been presented by Shelley Sweeney and/or Brian Hubner over approximately the past fifteen years.

39 Katherine Dow, "Winnipeg's Hamilton House, Known for Paranormal Activity, Getting Restored," CTV News Winnipeg, 22 October 2021, https://winnipeg.ctvnews.ca/how-you-can-have-a-spooky-sleepover-at-a-winnipeg-house-known-for-its-paranormal-history-1.5634457 (accessed 13 January 2023); and Cheryl Wiebe, personal conversation with the author, 31 December 2022.

Teleplasm of August 18, 1929

Taken by T. G. H's camera

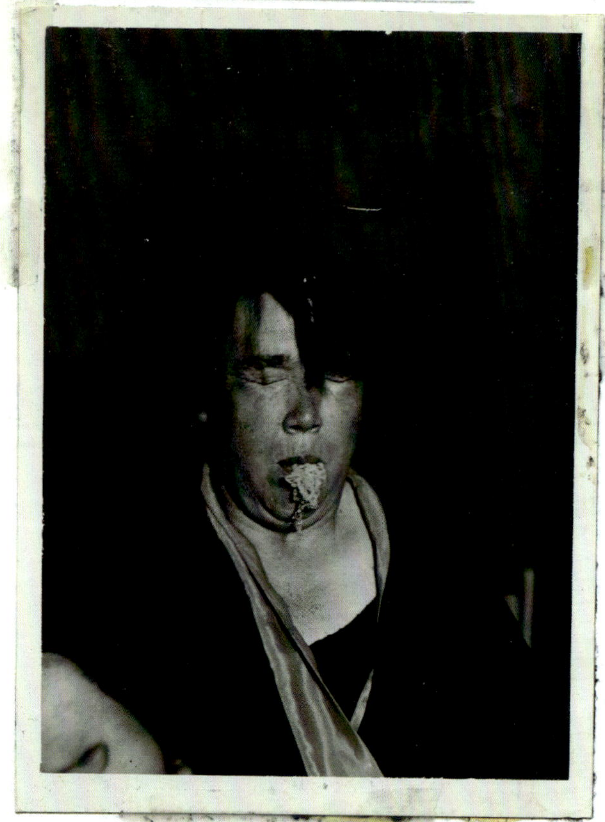

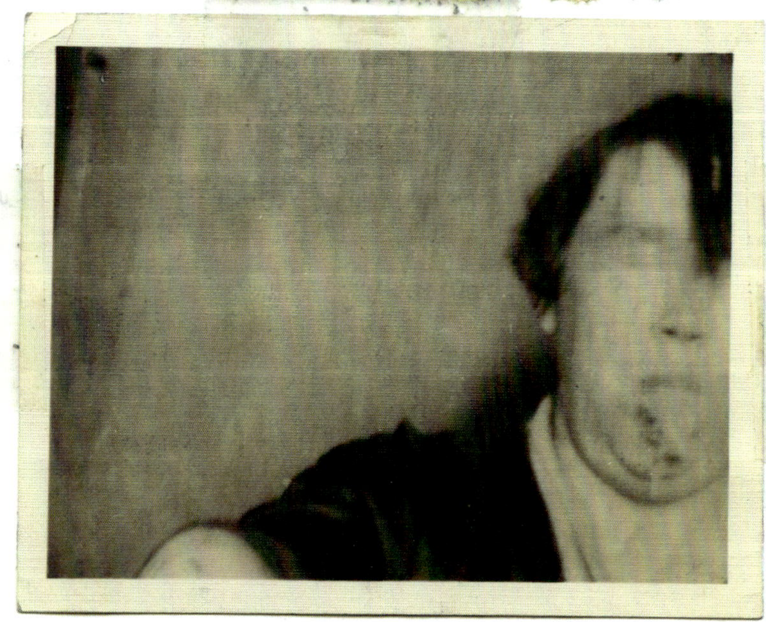

Taken by Mrs. Cannon's movie camera

7

"Mere Symbolic Ectoplasm": The Ectoplasmic Screen

Murray Leeder

Films purporting to document ectoplasmic manifestations present an interesting gap in the Hamilton Family Fonds (HFF) and other records of Spiritualism and psychical research. Séance notes dated 18 August 1929 describe a sitting with Mary Marshall in which Mrs. Rae (Bruening) Cannon of New York, a visitor, held a movie camera on her lap (see Figure 7.1, lower image). A still exists showing Marshall exuding ectoplasm from her mouth, but the film itself sadly has vanished, like a piece of ectoplasm in its own right.

The same can be said of the moving images that Albert von Schrenck-Notzing made of medium Stanisława Tomczyk in 1913; no more than stills survive (see Figure 7.2). In fact, to the best of my knowledge, no authentic moving picture footage of "ectoplasm" from the classic era of psychical research exists anywhere.[1] On a later occasion, Schrenck-Notzing attempted to expand his photographic documentation of the medium Eva C.'s ectoplasmic manifestations. But the movie

Fig. 7.1. ***Group V – Photographs***. Lower image: Rae (Bruening) Cannon, ***Taken by Mrs. Cannon's movie camera***. Still photograph from a spoiled film. UMASC, MSS 14, Box 15, Folder 16, http://hdl.handle.net/10719/1409180.

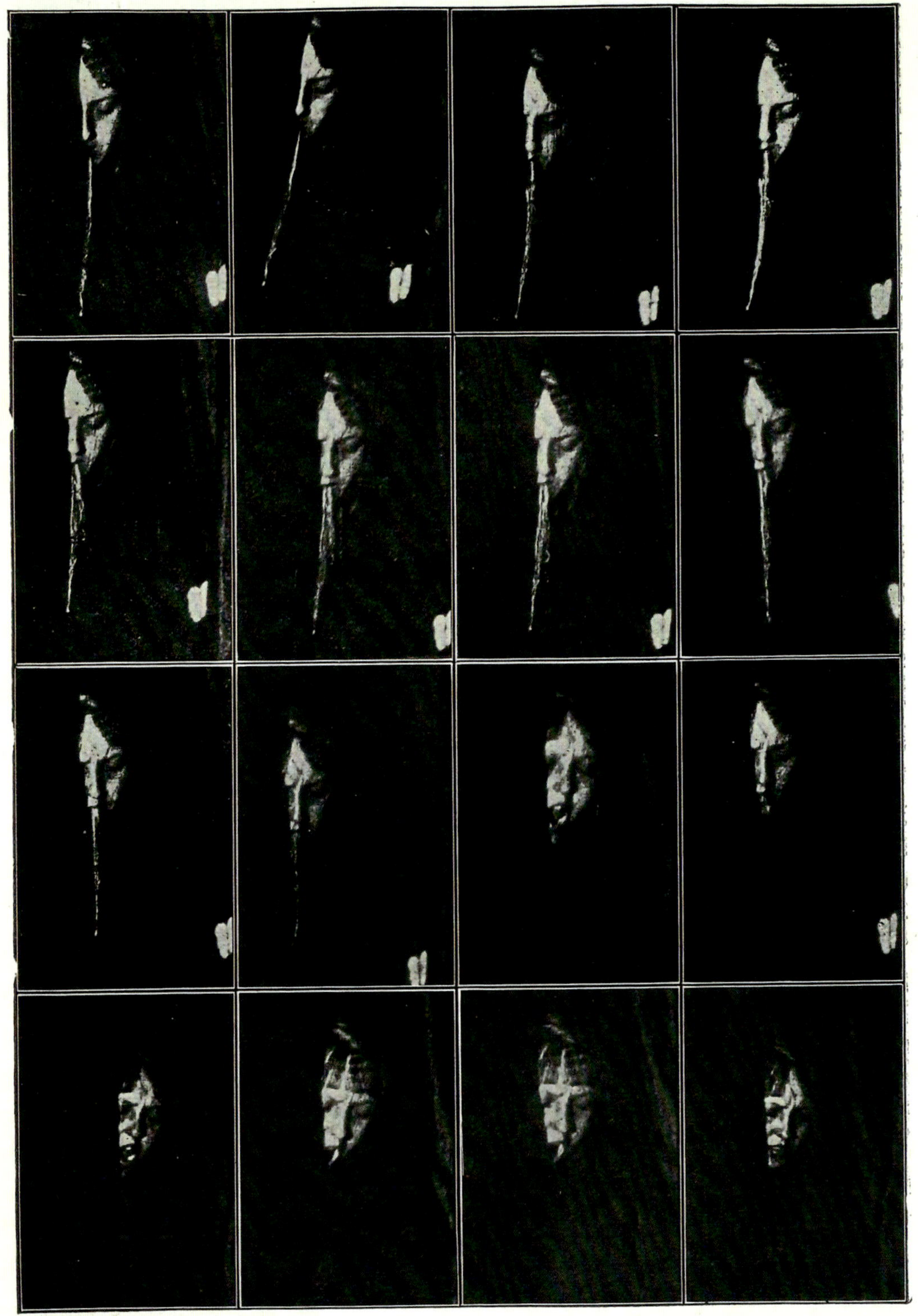

Fig. 180. Selected cinematograph pictures of 13 July, 1913, showing widening and narrowing of the substance, and its recession into the mouth.

camera failed to document what eight still cameras simultaneously caught.[2] Again and again, ectoplasm proves to be both illusive and elusive.

Decades later, in 1969, a documentary with the title *This Psychic World* promised to show "ectoplasm issuing forth from the medium's body—and being used to both lift objects and clothe those who come from the realm of spirit."[3] But no such film was ever released. A few years later the makers of *The Legend of Hell House* (1973) brought professional mediums to the set hoping to produce real ectoplasm, but it was to no avail.[4] Indeed, as far back as 1923, ads for the anti-Spiritualist drama *You Are In Danger* offered $5000 to anyone who could produce ectoplasm photographs that could not be replicated by trick photographer André Barlatier (see Figure 7.3).

In the absence of non-fiction footage of ectoplasm, fiction film has filled that role. If you asked me about ectoplasm when I was eight, I could have told you all about the substance in the *Ghostbusters* (1984–) franchise and maybe pointed to a jar of the stuff (sold as "Ecto-plazm" as a *Ghostbusters* tie-in). The first film contains techno/spiritobabble such as "if the ionization rate is constant for all ectoplasmic entities," and the Ghostbusters drive a repurposed ambulance called Ecto-1 (see Figures 0.5, 7.4, and 7.5). Within the abject, comedic regime of the supernatural in *Ghostbusters*, the term "ectoplasm," itself hovering between science and silliness, serves perfectly, and indeed screenwriter/star Dan Aykroyd was well versed in the history of the paranormal, coming from a Spiritualist family.[5] But *Ghostbusters* scarcely represented the first place ectoplasm was mentioned and represented in fiction film.

So what is this curious substance? It has been described as "a mysterious protoplasmic substance streaming out of the body of mediums. . . . Photographs of ectoplasm often show a gelatinous material oozing from all the natural orifices of the medium's body; from mouth, ears, nose, eyes, and even the lower orifices."[6] This description is read out by the character Wendy (Amanda Crews) in the 2009 film *The Haunting in Connecticut*, and it comes nearly verbatim from Nandor Fodor's *An*

Fig. 7.2. Sequential still images of medium Stanisława Tomczyk, 13 July 1913, from ***Phenomena of Materialisation*** by Schrenck-Notzing (1920). Courtesy of Serena Keshavjee.

September 22, 1923 1399

FOR THE FIRST TIME IN PICTURE HISTORY THE MANY TRICKS OF SPIRITUALISM ARE FULLY EXPOSED, *and in a photo-drama of tremendous action*

"YOU ARE IN DANGER"

IS ONE OF THOSE SURPRISE PICTURES

that seldom appear and never disappoint

"YOU ARE IN DANGER"

IS
a picture that will score and increase your patronage
a picture that will entertain after pulling 'em in
a picture that will make money for you

Dramatists and Critics who have seen this picture pronounce it far superior to anything of its kind heretofore attempted. As a picture attraction it has no equal, and its *exploitation value* is beyond entire description.

Featuring **PAULINE STARKE, MITCHELL LEWIS, CARMEL MYERS,** AND **JAMES MORRISON** ***—all big box office attractions***

ISSUES CHALLENGE TO ALL SPOOK PICTURES

With a certified check for $5,000 as a forfeit and a committee of scientists and photographic experts as the jury, Blair Coan Productions, Inc., producers of "You Are in Danger," challenges all proponents of spiritualism to place their much-discussed ectoplasm photographs alongside of the negative from portions of the movie drama.

If any difference can be detected between the negatives from the film drama and the photographs on which Conan Doyle and other believers in spirit manifestations have based their contentions, the film producers stand ready to give up the forfeit.

Andre Barlatier, master trick photographer, filmed the spirit scenes around which much of the mystery element of "You Are in Danger" is built. Barlatier also took many of the various ectoplasm photographs over which the spiritualists and their opponents are now debating. The producer's forfeit is also offered to anyone who can show an ectoplasm photograph which Barlatier cannot reproduce with every effect of genuineness.

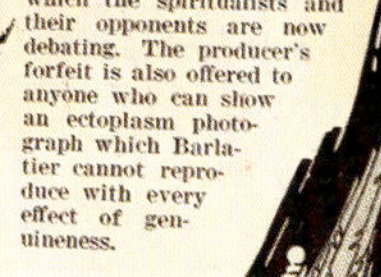

"You Are In Danger"

UNLESS YOU WRITE FOR OUR PRESS SHEET TODAY

Distributed by

PHOTO PRODUCTS EXPORT COMPANY

220 West Forty-second St., New York

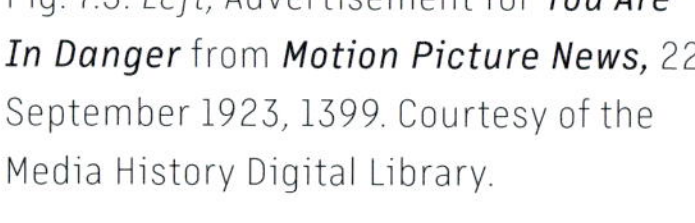

Fig. 7.3. *Left,* Advertisement for ***You Are In Danger*** from ***Motion Picture News,*** 22 September 1923, 1399. Courtesy of the Media History Digital Library.

Fig. 7.4. *Upper Right,* Scene from ***Ghostbusters,*** directed by Ivan Reitman. Still shot, 1984. Courtesy of Moviestore Collection, Alamy Stock Photo.

Fig. 7.5. *Lower Right,* The iconic scene of Peter Venkman being "slimed" with ectoplasm is frequently revisited in ***Ghostbusters*** memorabilia, including this LEGO figure. Courtesy of Alex Miller.

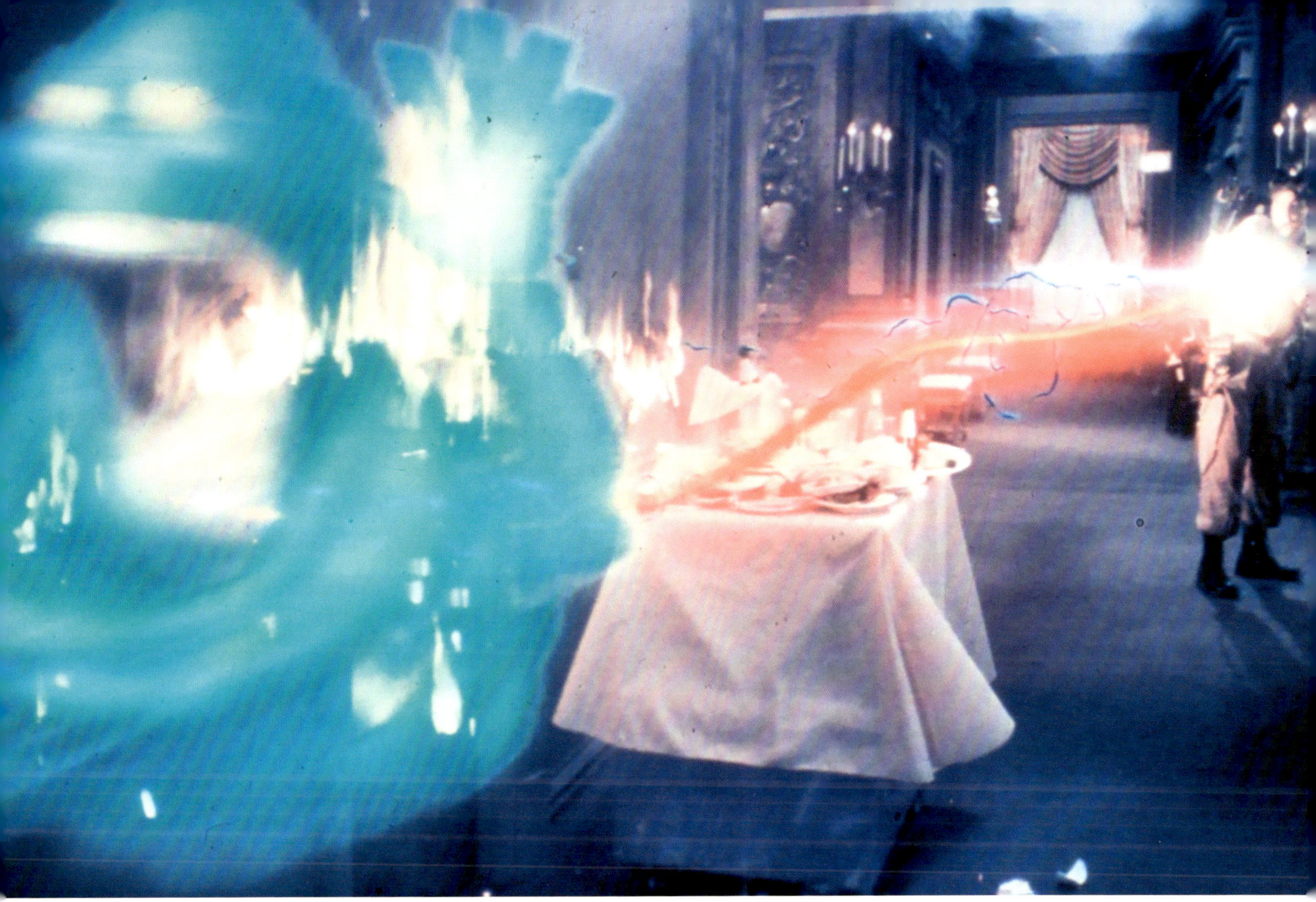

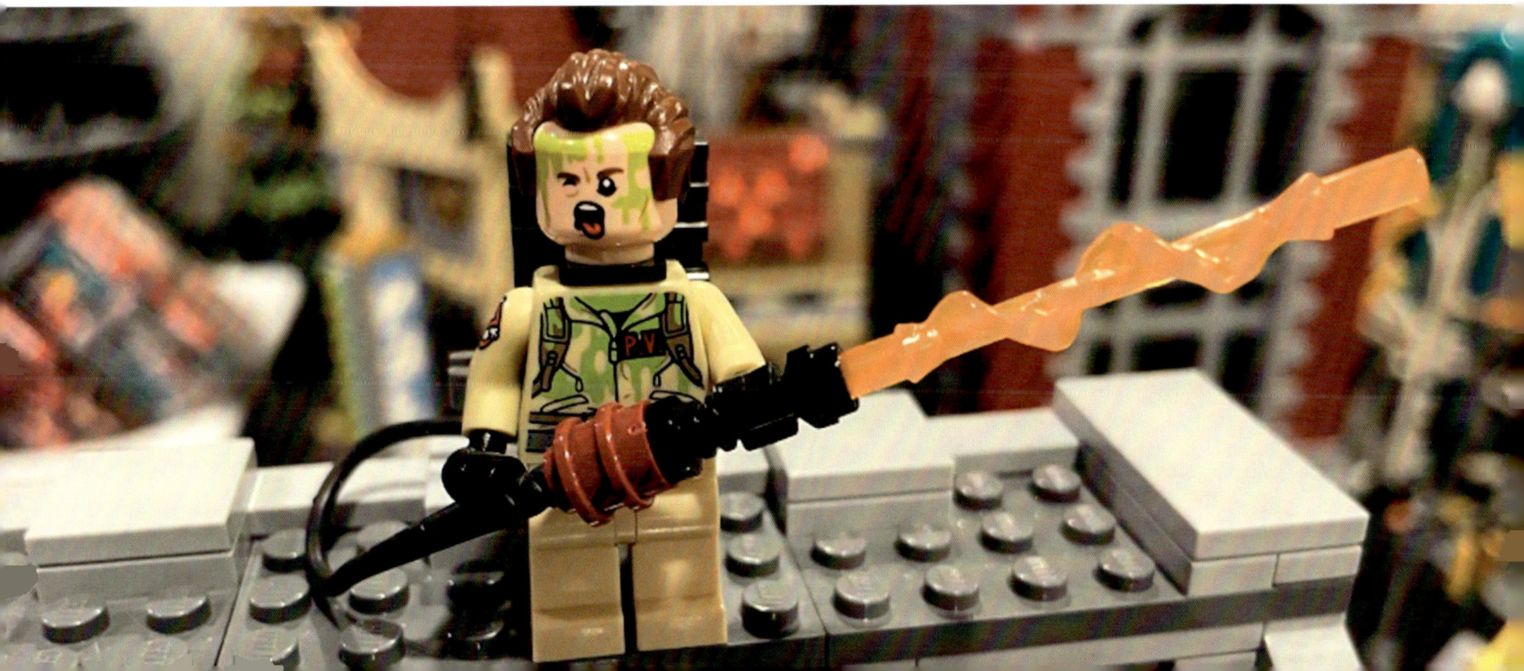

Encyclopaedia of Psychic Science (1963).[7] Other significant properties of ectoplasm include the fact that it is so photosensitive that a camera flash will destroy it, and it is also a means of representation in its own right, frequently transforming into images. When extruding ectoplasm, as Tom Gunning writes, "the medium herself became a sort of camera" or even "an uncanny photomat, dispensing images from her orifices."[8] In ectoplasm, the uncanny subtexts of photography, which makes stillness out of motion and death out of life, are made manifest.

However, as the term circulated in popular culture, "ectoplasm" took on other meanings. It became a shorthand for the intangible, transient, invisible, uncapturable. For example, an article in 1939 described the process of defining a documentary film as being "like trying to grasp an elusive piece of verbal ectoplasm."[9] Early television advertisers, faced with the challenge of marketing women's undergarments without violating standards of taste, recommended "the 'ectoplasm' technique,"[10] which shows the item floating in mid-air without the female body—as if worn by a ghost (see Figure 7.6). Like the censor-friendly nudity in *The Invisible Woman* (1940), it sexualizes the product specifically by not showing a woman's body.

Karen Beckman notes another intriguing dictionary definition of ectoplasm: "*Informal.* An image projected onto a movie screen."[11] Although empirical examples of this usage seem to be scarce, "ectoplasm" at times has served rhetorically to describe cinema in all its paradoxes. A great example appeared in *Theatre Arts* in 1945 in an article by Parker Tyler titled "Supernaturalism in the Movies": "With this power to render the human substance into mere symbolic ectoplasm, the movie camera possesses a perambulation parallel to the movements supposedly initiated in actual Ghost Land."[12] Tyler argues that on some level all cinematic images are ghostly and uses ectoplasm as a master metaphor for the medium. The association of ectoplasm with cinema in the mid-century was strong enough that, in the opening lines of *Invisible Man* (1952), Ralph Ellison stated that "I am not one of your Hollywood-movie ectoplasms."[13] It is no surprise that film and media studies scholars have written extensively on ectoplasm.[14]

FIRST YOU SEE HER, THEN . . .

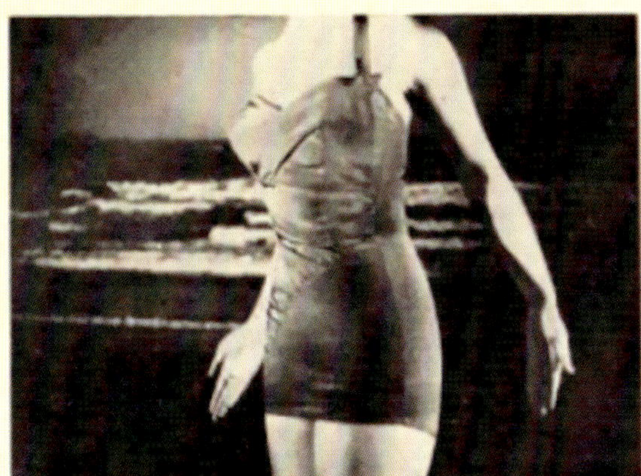

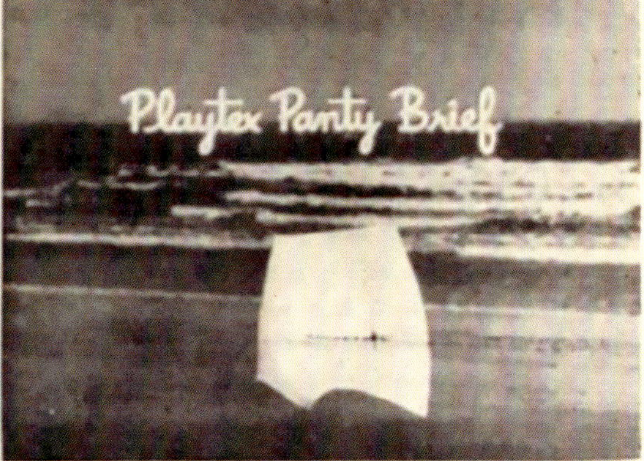

U. S. TELEVIEWERS will be seeing a lot of this and other Playtex commercials if the multimillion dollar films-for-time deal goes through. They feature the so-called "ectoplasm" technique—first the girl is shown on the beach in normal attire, then she vanishes and the girdle carries on alone.

Fig. 7.6. An image from ***Broadcasting Television*** illustrating "the ectoplasm technique," 30 July 1956, 33. Courtesy of the Media History Digital Library.

Actual cinematic representations of ectoplasm would often play on the perhaps silly sound of the term itself. So, though something like ectoplasm appears (if unnamed) in a few mystery dramas such as *Miracles for Sale* (1939), it has a vastly greater presence in supernatural comedies. Well before *Ghostbusters*, the term was associated with another supernatural comedy franchise: the three *Topper* films (1937, 1938, 1941) and later the TV sitcom (1953–55). Advertisements used phrases such as "How's your ectoplasm, Dearie?" and "ECTOPLASM runs riot and blasts trail of hilarity from Fifth Avenue to the French Riviera!" (see Figure 7.7).

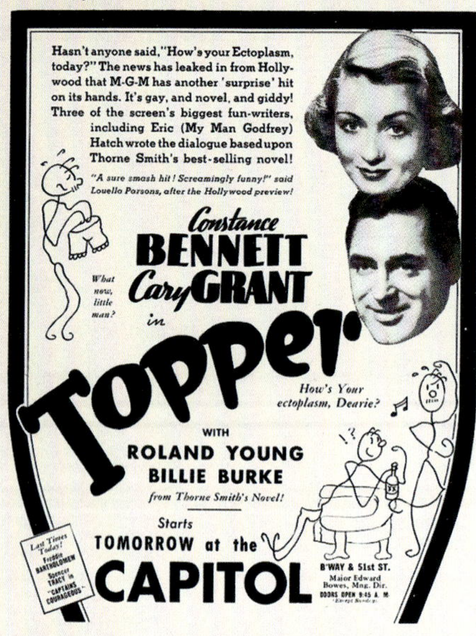

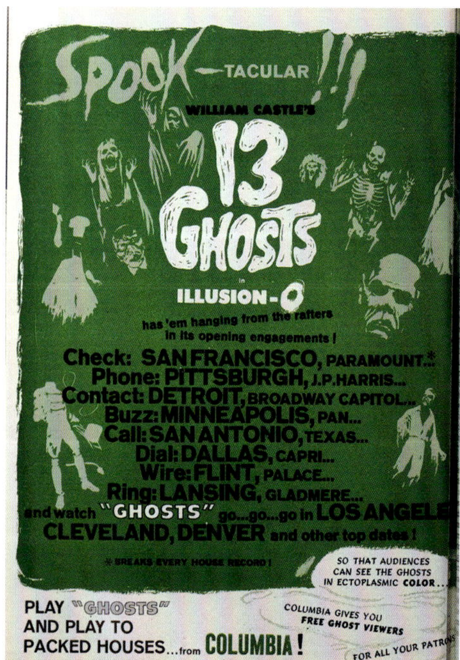

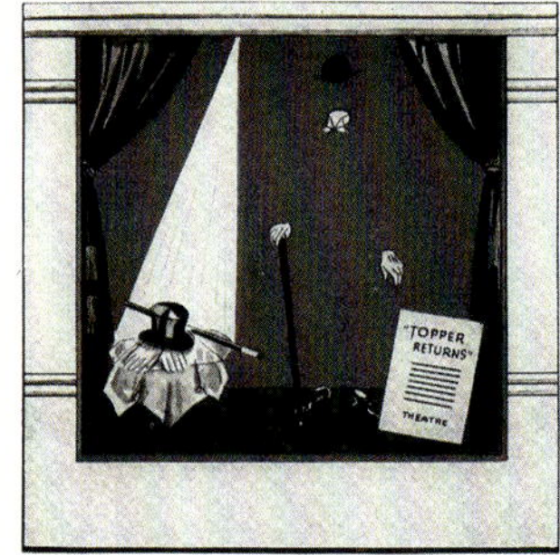

"ECTOPLASMIC" PROMOTION STUNT FOR MEN'S FASHION WINDOWS

There's a neat showmanship angle in "Topper Returns" for a highly important campaign directed toward the windows of leading local department stores. The title of your show fits smoothly into a merchandising campaign which suggests the idea of dressing up for important evening occasions. One way to play this would be to arrange for the spotting of a single prop—a top hat—in the corners of a series of windows based on the "dress-up" idea; plant the tie-in with your show very smoothly with copy along this line — placed adjacent to the top hat: "TOPPER RETURNS" — and now is the time to dress up for those festive spring occasions! See 'TOPPER RETURNS' at the . . . . Theatre."

Equally potent and show-selling would be the novel idea of arranging with the store display manager for clothing promotions which involve goods displayed on an invisible dummy. An ingenious display man could easily contrive to display a complete set of clothes, top hat, suit, shoes, gloves, etc.—on a dummy which does not show a full human figure. This could, of course, be repeated for women's clothes. All in all, the promotion would directly suggest the highly important 'ectoplasmic" angle in your campaign, permitting plenty of room for introduction of a gay comedy note.

Here's a promotion which promises top "Topper" profits and ties in your leading showmanship approach. Give it everything you've got, and let its powerful publicity and interest values do a bang-up job for your show!

Fig. 7.7. *Upper Left*, Advertisement for ***Topper***, twice featuring the word ***ectoplasm***, that appeared in ***Motion Picture Herald***, 28 August 1937, 15. Courtesy of the Media History Digital Library.

Fig. 7.8. *Above*, From the 1941 United Artists pressbook for ***Topper Returns*** (directed by Roy Del Ruth), 7. Courtesy of the Media History Digital Library.

Fig. 7.9. *Lower Left*, An advertisement for ***13 Ghosts*** promises "Ectoplasmic Color" in the ***Independent Exhibitors Film Bulletin***, 25 July 1960, 6. Courtesy of the Media History Digital Library.

Within the *Topper* films, ectoplasm is treated as a kind of ghostly point system. The post-mortem Kirby couple can make themselves visible but often remain unseen to conserve ectoplasm, which is replenished after a period of inactivity. The Danny Kaye vehicle *Wonder Man* (1945) uses the term "ectoplasm" almost identically, as a kind of ghost fuel that can run out.[15]

The pressbook for *Topper Returns* (1941) even recommended an "ecto-plasmic" stunt in fashion windows: a partially dressed mannequin that gave the impression of clothes floating in mid-air (see Figure 7.8). This obviously presaged the aforementioned "ectoplasm method" in its association of clothing and ectoplasm as well as the hint of invisible nudity.

In many other films, the very word *ectoplasm* supplies a laugh. In *Blithe Spirit* (1945), based upon Noël Coward's 1941 play, the daffy medium Madame Arcati (Margaret Rutherford) boasts of having her "first ectoplasmic manifestation when [she] was five and a half."[16] In *Gildersleeve's Ghost* (1944), one ghost tells another to "Be careful. You'll strain your ectoplasm."[17] In *Not Ghoulty* (1959), Casper the Friendly Ghost is expelled from "The Ectoplasm Society" for being too nice.[18] *13 Ghosts* (1960), a horror comedy by "Master of Gimmicks" William Castle, used the playful gimmick of a "ghost viewer" that allowed a viewer to choose whether or not to see the ghosts on screen.[19] Largely promoted as "Illusion-O," some advertisements instead characterized it as "Ectoplasmic Color" (see Figure 7.9).

Later ghost comedies such as *The Frighteners* (1996) and *Extra Ordinary* (2019) draw from *Ghostbusters* and use "ectoplasm" to mean the ghostly body and its residues, as when Frank (Michael J. Fox) in *The Frighteners* complains that his ghost friends get "ectoplasmic muck all over my car seats."[20] The short film *Ectoplasm* (2014) starts seriously but ends with a bawdy joke when it turns out that the title substance is the product of a masturbating male ghost, promoting a persistent subtext to the text.[21]

In numerous non-comedic horror films—such as *The Amityville Horror* (1979), *Poltergeist* (1982), *Prince of Darkness* (1987), and *The Blair Witch Project* (1999)—abject and mysterious supernatural slime is not explicitly called *ectoplasm*, perhaps because the word was largely claimed by comedic films. There are, however, some exceptions. Perhaps the most accurate film about psychical research is *The Legend of Hell House*, adapted by Richard Matheson from his novel *Hell House* (1971).[22] This gem among ghost films concerns an investigation of a dangerous haunted house by a group of scientists and mediums, and though it is a fictional film, it opens with an affidavit by medium Tom Corbett about the accuracy of its depictions of spiritual phenomena. In one of its séance scenes, the young medium Florence Tanner (Pamela Franklin) sits in a trance, under the scrutiny of physicist/parapsychologist Dr. Lionel Barrett (Clive Revill). The scene is lit with red light, and Barrett dictates notes into a recorder throughout. A close-up of Tanner's hand shows white lines developing from her fingers (in the novel, it is described as exuding from her mouth and nose[23]). "Ectoplasm forming," Barrett dictates, and the film shows these stalks of white floating across the room. Lines from each finger merge, and then the two strands join into one. It proceeds through a net and toward a table. Barrett twice says "Leave a sample in the jar, please." But as the ectoplasm begins to encircle the jar, it pops audibly and seems to vanish when Barrett's wife, Ann (Gayle Hunnicut), screams and disrupts Tanner's trance, causing pain to the fragile medium.

Subsequently, the sceptical Barrett insists that ectoplasm proves nothing about life after death and characterizes it as "the organic externalization of thought." The decision to visualize ectoplasm as a glimmering white optical effect makes it seem to be weightless and insubstantial. In the novel, it is clear that the ectoplasm is about to form into a human figure ("a white figure . . . garbed in a shapeless robe, sexless, incomplete, its hands like rudimentary claws"[24]) when it disappears, which the film's special effects, presumably, were unable to depict. Again ectoplasm seems to dance along the edge of the unrepresentable, the uncapturable.

The aforementioned *The Haunting in Connecticut*, directed by Peter Cornwell and written by academic-turned-filmmaker Adam Simon, also names ectoplasm directly and grounds itself in the history of psychical research (see Figure 7.10).[25] Based upon a purportedly true story, it was shot completely in Manitoba and made use of materials from the HFF. It involves a family moving into a house that turns out to have a dark history of necromancy and psychical research in the nineteenth century. Cancer patient

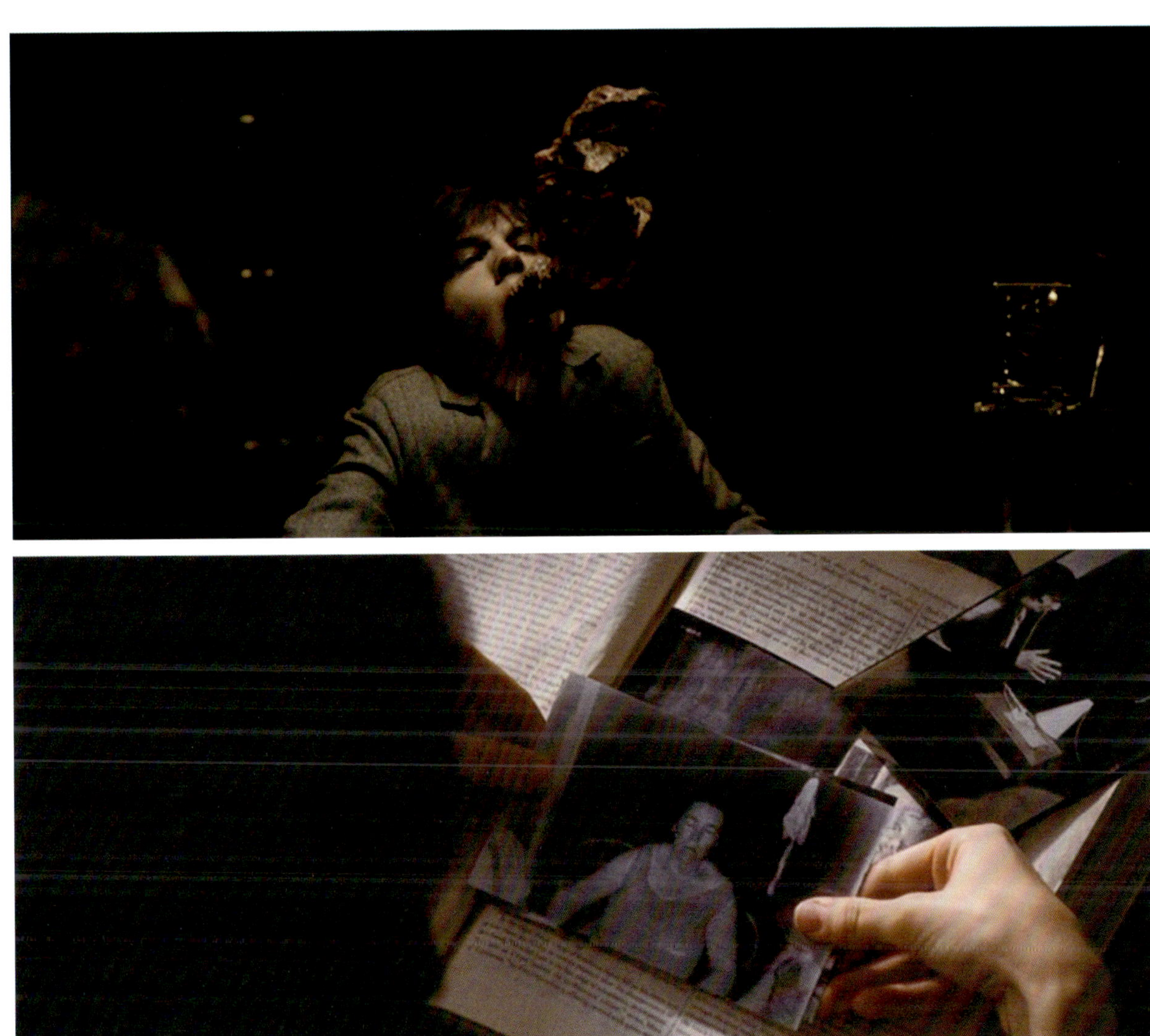

Fig. 7.10. *Upper,* An ectoplasm extrusion recreated with special effects in ***The Haunting in Connecticut,*** directed by Peter Cornwell. Still shot, 2009. Courtesy of Gold Circle Films.

Fig. 7.11. *Lower,* HFF images repurposed in ***The Haunting in Connecticut.*** Still shot, 2009. Courtesy of Gold Circle Films.

Matt (Kyle Gallner) starts to experience visions related to Jonah (Erik Berg), a boy medium used as a tool to bind and control spirits. Matt sees Jonah with black, sludgy ectoplasm extruding from his mouth and hovering in the air. The characters research the history of their house, and we see a montage sequence of them poring over old newspapers and archival documents as well as materials that they have found in the bowels of the house. Genuine ectoplasm photographs from the HFF appear, implicitly "playing" images from the film's backstory, and are placed alongside the film's manufactured historical images (see Figure 7.11). About the film's version of ectoplasm, Simon explains that "I was obsessed with the idea of really creating something that felt like it was neither purely material nor purely spiritual if you know what I mean—everyone from true believers to the great ghost and horror writers seem to get what's so often missed in the movies that this isn't just a matter of light or visual effect but that it had some eerie and I would've thought rather abject body to it."[26]

Ectoplasm is visualized differently in Olivier Assayas' art film/ghost film hybrid *Personal Shopper* (2016). The film focuses on bereaved young American-in-Paris Maureen Cartwright (Kristen Stewart), who attempts to contact her dead twin brother, a spirit medium in life.[27] Early in the film, her search leads her to a hostile spirit who rattles walls, shakes a chandelier, and hovers indistinctly before her. It manifests as a vaguely feminine form that opens its mouth and exudes a mass of golden, shimmering material that hovers in mid-air, lingering for a short time before vanishing. Explaining this encounter later in the film, Maureen describes the ghost as "vomiting ectoplasm." In this scene and elsewhere in *Personal Shopper*, the supernatural is visualized digitally and simultaneously seems to be both of and not of the environments around it. Indeed, ectoplasm has been used as a metaphor for explaining the strangeness, artificiality, and extreme malleability of the digital image.[28]

Fig. 7.12. *Upper Left*, Geraldine Chaplin and Adele Haenel from ***Seances***, directed by Guy Maddin, Evan Johnson, and Galen Johnson. Still shot, 2016. Courtesy of Guy Maddin.

Fig. 7.13. *Lower Left*, Maria de Medeiros from ***Seances***, directed by Guy Maddin, Evan Johnson, and Galen Johnson. Still shot, 2016. Courtesy of Guy Maddin.

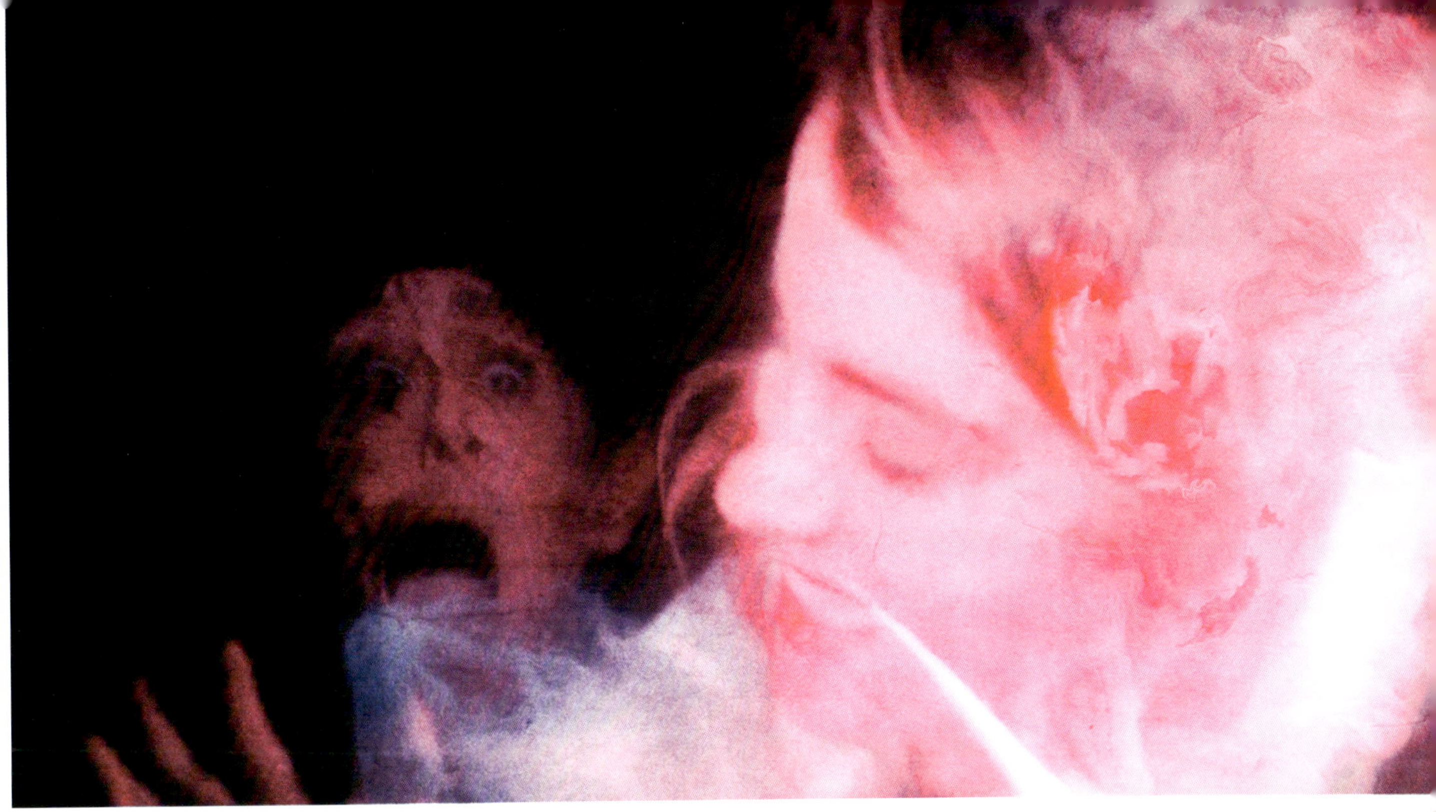

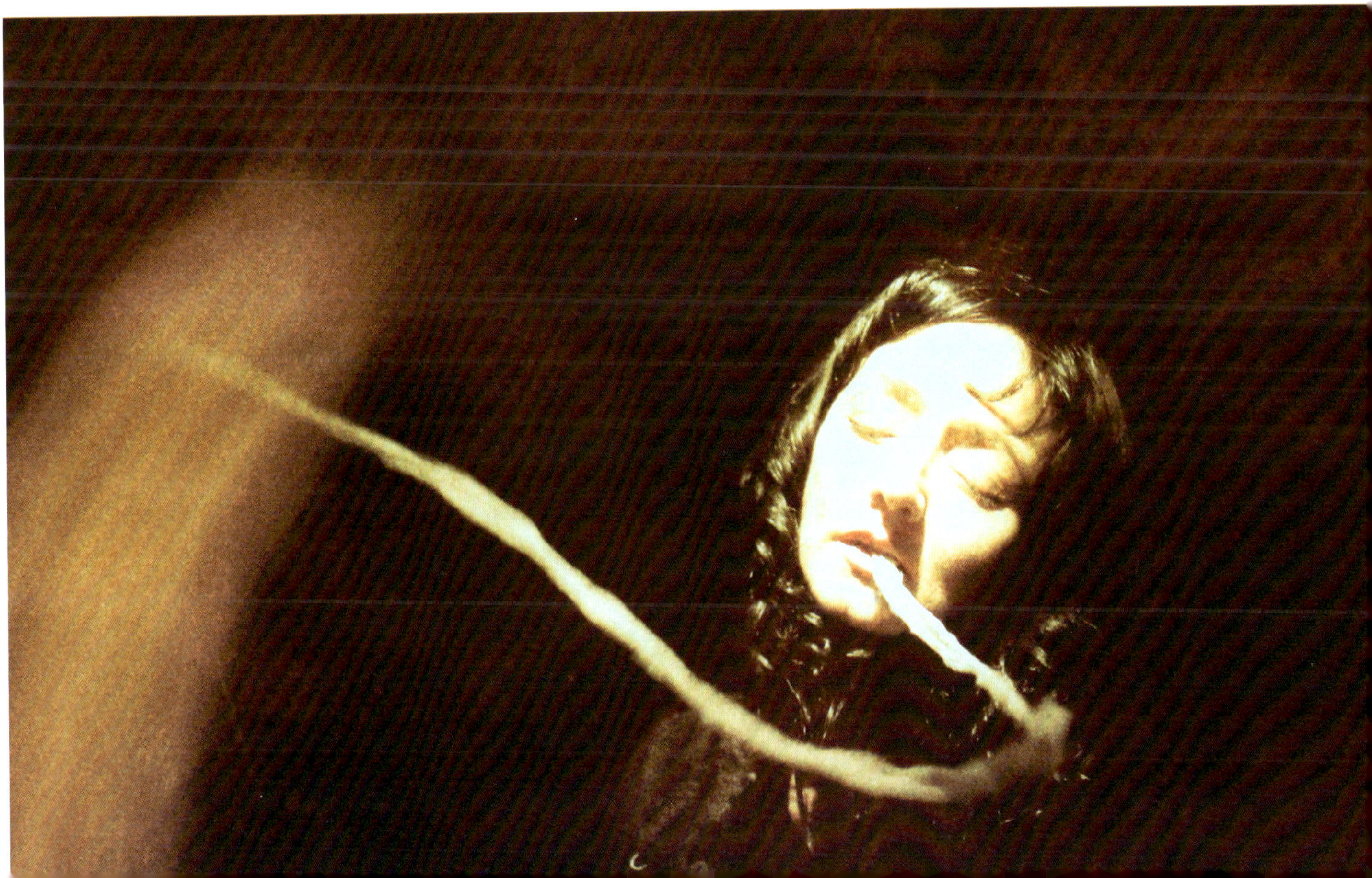

Another digital work fixated on ectoplasm is Guy Maddin's interactive web project *Seances* (2016), made in collaboration with Galen and Evan Johnson.[29] *Seances* generates a unique film for each viewer, both drawing from a selection of filmed segments and further modifying it with audiovisual effects such as datamoshing, sound interruption, sound flowing, rotoscoping, and motion tracking so that literally billions of permutations are possible (see Figures 7.12 and 7.13). The conceit of the project is that each viewing is a séance with a lost film or a film that has never existed. Speaking at the Banff Centre in 2015, Maddin referred to the technique in *Seances* as "ektoplasm-o-vision."[30] With a gauzy, hazy aesthetic, ectoplasm is the master sign under which it operates; each film, each séance that it generates, is a brief presence then lost into the (digital) ether, like ectoplasm's tendency to vanish on being photographed.

Seances was far from Maddin's first foray into the cinematic supernatural, a topic that goes back to his debut short, *The Dead Father* (1985). Perhaps the most famous is *My Winnipeg* (2007), his phantasmatic portrait of his hometown both revealed and transformed through the scrim of memory and the history of cinema. One sequence enacts a séance at the Manitoba Legislative Building with many figures from Winnipeg's past in attendance. Medium and dancer Gweneth Lloyd entrances Viscount Gort with ectoplasm-like tendrils figuring his possession. In a striking image, the legislature itself, with its iconic Golden Boy statue, appears with unfurling ectoplasm superimposed over it (see Figure 7.14). Shortly afterward, Winnipeg itself is described in terms of a giant snow labyrinth in which "mazes of ectoplasm . . . determine our paths through our lives."[31] We also hear that Arthur Conan Doyle spoke of Winnipeg as having the greatest psychical possibility of any city, a claim based upon his visit to Winnipeg in 1923.[32]

Just the year before, Conan Doyle was interviewed for *Movie Weekly* and opined not only that movies of spirits would be made eventually but also that spirits would participate in the film industry more directly: "It must not be forgotten that there are only a very few spirits who know anything about the motion picture business. It is such a new enterprise altogether, and a development of the last quarter of a century, that most of its pioneers are still alive, I suppose. . . . A hundred years from now you would have a greater reservoir to draw from, because more will have died. Thus the motion picture business is like spiritualism in that it is just beginning to find itself."[33] As naive as his utopianism might sound, Conan Doyle expressed something essential in paralleling cinema and Spiritualism as quintessentially modern phenomena. A century later we obviously do not live in the regime of supernatural cinema that he prophesied, but it is equally true that ectoplasm and other facets of Spiritualism and psychical research continued to shape the development of media culture through the twentieth century and into our current digital age.

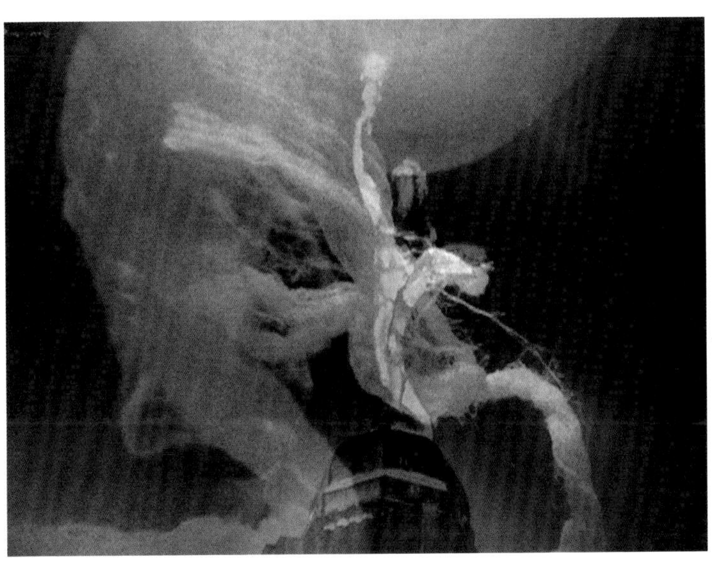

Fig. 7.14. The Manitoba Legislative Building transformed by ectoplasm in ***My Winnipeg***, directed by Guy Maddin. Still shot, 2007. Courtesy of Guy Maddin.

Ectoplasm is mind-boggling because it can be so many things at once. It is a medium of representation that itself tends to escape or exceed representation. It is abject, potentially sexualized, and evanescent. It is serious yet funny. Ectoplasm might seem like an early-twentieth-century curio, but it is as current as the digital image, and in its elusiveness it has attained a curious sort of popular culture ubiquity. And many of its paradoxes are also the paradoxes of the cinematic image itself, which combines properties of presence and absence, permanence and temporariness. In documenting the world, cinema transforms it, to quote Parker Tyler again, into "mere symbolic ectoplasm."

NOTES

1 There is at least one example of contemporary digital footage of ectoplasm, in Shannon Taggart's footage of Kai Muegge. See Chapter 9 of this volume.

2 Samri Frikell, "Sir Arthur Conan Doyle Predicts Spirit Moving Pictures!," *Movie Weekly* 2, no. 22, 12 August 1922, 6.

3 "Successful 'Ghost Film' Promises Understanding," *Business Screen Magazine* 30, no. 6, June 1969, 42.

4 John Hough, audio commentary, *The Legend of Hell House*, Blu-Ray edition, Scream Factory, 2014.

5 Peter H. Aykroyd, *A History of Ghosts: The True Story of Séances, Mediums, Ghosts, and Ghostbusters* (New York: Rodale, 2009).

6 Peter Cornwell, dir., *The Haunting in Connecticut*, Gold Circle Films, 2009.

7 Nandor Fodor, *An Encyclopaedia of Psychic Science* (New Hyde Park, NY: University Books, 1966), 113.

8 Tom Gunning, "Phantom Images and Modern Manifestations," in *Fugitive Images: From Photography to Video*, ed. Patrice Pietro (Bloomington: Indiana University Press, 1995), 36.

9 A.A. Mercey, "New Frontiers for the Documentary Film," *Journal of the Society of Motion Picture Engineers* 33 (1939): 525.

10 See *Broadcasting Television*, 30 July 1956, 33.

11 Karen Beckman, *Vanishing Women: Magic, Film, and Feminism* (Durham, NC: Duke University Press, 2003), 78.

12 Parker Tyler, "Supernaturalism in the Movies," *Theatre Arts* 29 (1945): 363.

13 Ralph Ellison, *Invisible Man* (New York: Vintage Books, 2010), 3.

14 Examples not otherwise cited here include Karl Schoonover, "Ectoplasms, Evanescence, and Photography," *Art Journal* 62, no. 3 (2003): 30–43; Marina Warner, *Phantasmagoria: Spirit Visions, Metaphors and Media into the Twenty-First Century* (Oxford: Oxford University Press, 2006), esp. 290–307; Neil Matheson, "Ectoplasm and Photography: Mediumistic Performances for Camera," in *The Machine and the Ghost: Technology and Spiritualism in Nineteenth to Twenty-First-Century Art and Culture*, ed. Sas Mays and Neil Matheson (Manchester: Manchester University Press, 2016), 78–102; and Leigh Wilson, *Modernism and Magic: Experiments with Spiritualism, Theosophy and the Occult* (Edinburgh: Edinburgh University Press, 2013), esp. 135–67.

15 H. Bruce Humberstone, dir., *Wonder Man*, RKO Radio Pictures, 1945.

16 David Lean, dir., *Blithe Spirit*, General Film Distributors, 1945.

17 Gordon Douglas, dir., *Gildersleeve's Ghost*, RKO Radio Pictures, 1944.

18 Seymour Kneitel, Izzy Sparber, Frank Endres, dirs., *Not Ghoulty*, Famous Studios, 1959.

19 William Castle, dir., *13 Ghosts*, William Castle Productions, 1960.

20 Peter Jackson, dir., *The Frighteners*, WingNut Films, 1996.

21 Similarly, a 2008 episode of *South Park* ("Over Logging") has Randy Marsh blame the predicament of being covered in his own semen on "a ghost!

This is ectoplasm!" See https://www.youtube.com/watch?v=5YxcgK0UArE.

22 John Hough, dir., *The Legend of Hell House*, 20th Century Fox, 1973. I explore other aspects of this film in Murray Leeder, "Victorian Science and Spiritualism in *The Legend of Hell House*," *Horror Studies* 5, no. 1 (2014): 31–46.

23 Richard Matheson, *Hell House* (New York: Tor, 1999), 91.

24 Ibid., 93.

25 Cornwell, *The Haunting in Connecticut*.

26 Adam Simon, personal communication with the author, 16 December 2021.

27 Olivier Assayas, dir., *Personal Shopper*, G.C. Cinéma, 2016.

28 Geoffrey Batchen, "Ectoplasm: Photography in the Digital Age," in *Over Exposed: Essays on Contemporary Photography*, ed. Carol Squiers (New York: New Press, 1999), 9–23.

29 Guy Maddin, Evan Johnson, and Galen Johnson, dirs., *Seances*, National Film Board of Canada, 2016, https://seances.nfb.ca/.

30 Murray Leeder, "Ektoplasm-o-Vision! with Guy Maddin," *Luma—Film and Media Art Quarterly* 1, no. 1 (2015), https://lumaquarterly.com/issues/2015/001-summer-2/ektoplasm-o-vision-with-guy-maddin (accessed 13 December 2022).

31 Guy Maddin, dir., *My Winnipeg*, Buffalo Gal Pictures, 2007.

32 Arthur Conan Doyle, *Our Second American Adventure* (Boston: Little, Brown, 1924), 231.

33 Frikell, "Sir Arthur Conan Doyle," 26.

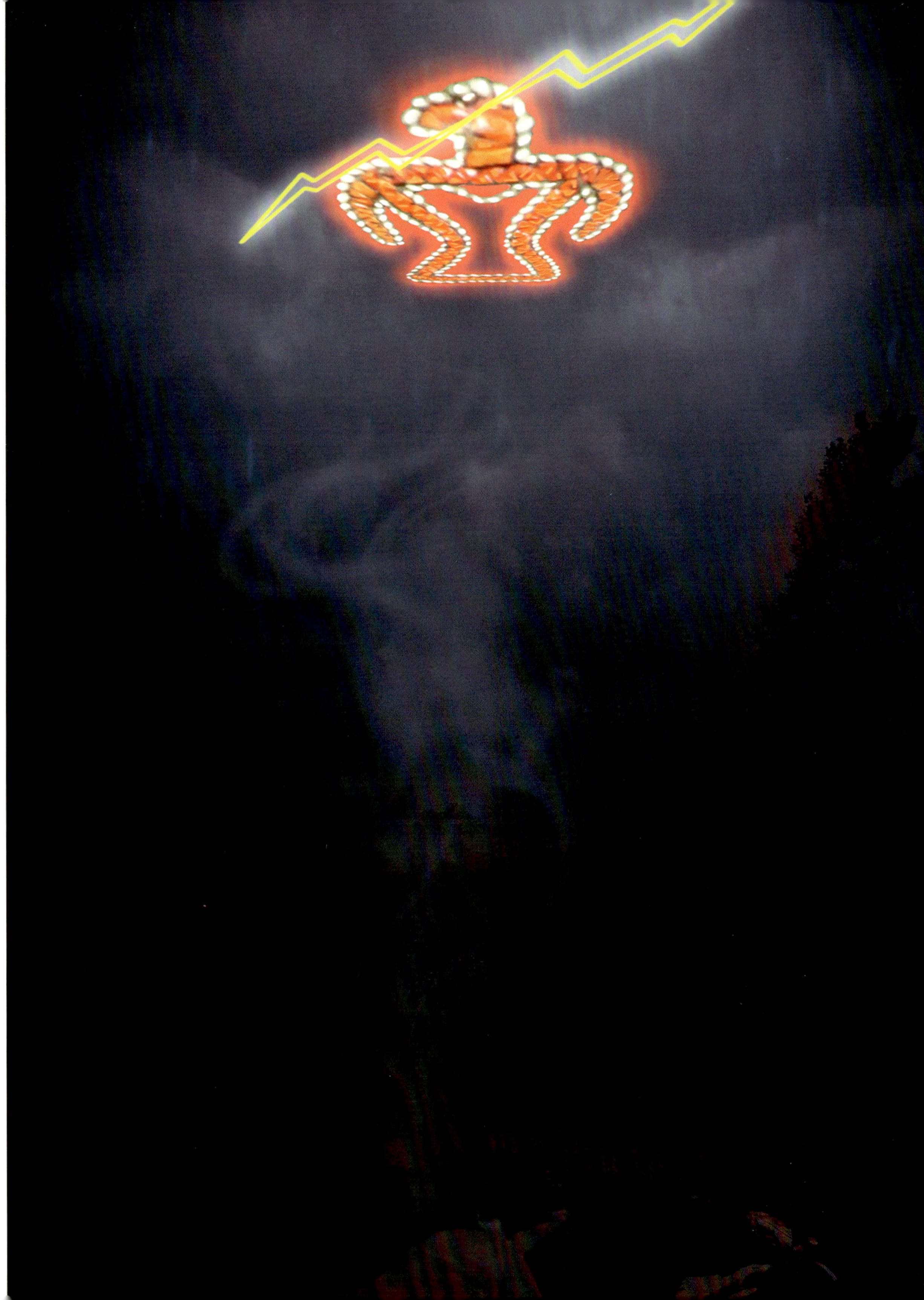

8

Journey to the Spirit Realm

KC Adams

Mino tahkosin! Tansi tooteemac, capipaminat mikisew iskwew nitisinikason. Niimaamaa Judi Adams isi-de-gas-oo ochekiwi sipi neeitooteemack.[1] I see that everyone is having dessert, and I have only just been invited to the table. I can't get comfortable; the table and chair are too stiff. I would prefer to invite everyone to come to my sacred fire and hear my story. So please join me, crawl through the entrance of my dwelling, help yourself to some berries, and lounge on the comfortable furs around the fire while I share with you my relationship with spirit and photography. *Astim, api.*[2]

When I think of photography from its genesis in relation to the original people of Turtle Island, it is from a position of acrimony. Photography is a medium that placed my ancestors in front of the camera instead of the privileged position behind it. And, thanks to a series of oppressive nation-state decisions, we were denied access to this technology. I suppose that we should be grateful for photographers such as Edward S. Curtis and Frank A. Rinehart, compelled to record our "disappearing identity."[3] Yet both used tactics of fashioning props, backgrounds, and

Fig. 8.1. KC Adams, conceptual drawing of forthcoming VR installation, ***kâh kitowak: there is thunder; the thunderbirds are calling***, 2022. Courtesy of KC Adams.

guided poses to achieve their romantic vision of what a "real" Indian should look like. *Hiy! Hiy!* Instead, they should have recorded what was really going on; our traditional territories were disappearing, and our ability to hunt and feed ourselves was compromised because of the fur trade. And, when the Indian Act was introduced, we were placed onto reservations, our movements were controlled by Indian agents, we couldn't speak our languages or practise our ceremonies, and our children were forced into residential schools.[4] So it is no wonder that we were in front of the camera instead of behind it.

Son, go and put another log on the fire.

I can't help but reflect on how much has changed from the origins of photography to today. We are still bound by the Indian Act, but the government made some amendments, such as "allowing" us to vote, speak our languages, and practise our cultural traditions. Did you know that I no longer have to go through forced enfranchisement for being in university?[5] Holeee! But I am not interested in engaging in a conversation about power politics, oppression, or colonization. I am tired of taking on the responsibility of educating others on why my people should be treated with dignity and respect. I digress. I invited you here to fill your tummies and listen to my research on spirit and the tools that I use to manifest its teachings in digital photography, video, and new media.

Let me start by telling you about spirit. I have been taught by Floyd Sutherland from Peguis First Nation that spirit originates from the cosmos, in the direction of the North Star constellations. Our spirit travels along a bright light that descends down to Earth to our mother's womb, and our time on this planet is short compared with our time in the spirit realm.[6] Thunderbirds are spiritual beings that exist within that realm, and according to Elder Sherry Copenace they bring the rain and have the power to give and take life.[7] Once we die, our spirit starts its journey home to be with our ancestors in the cosmos. So our loved ones light a sacred fire for four days and conduct a ceremony to say goodbye and send the spirit home.

Son, open the flap so we can see the stars. Thank you, my boy.

Where was I? Oh, yes, I was talking about spirits or what you would call ghosts. So I thought about representing spirit in photography in a way that honoured my culture and did not cheapen or pan it. It was then that I remembered Métis archaeologist Kevin Brownlee and his navigation with culture in an institution. He helped to excavate an ancient burial of a young nêhiyaw woman near Split Lake, Manitoba, and wasn't satisfied with a stiff archaeological report.[8] Instead, he and Elder William Dumas produced *Pīsim Finds Her Miskanow*, explaining this woman's life utilizing storytelling and knowledge shared by Elders.[9] Thanks to radiocarbon dating and chemical analysis, they surmised that she was a mother, around twenty-five years old at her death, and buried in a fetal position with her tools. She lived on the cusp of the lowland territory of Hudson Bay and the boreal forest around 360 years ago. On her was a simple dress with a belt around her waist, leggings, and pointed moccasins with a seam down the middle.[10] Thanks to Kevin's book, her story came alive to me. I was fascinated by her death; I imagined who buried her and what kind of ceremony her loved ones conducted for her. I even wrote a poem about it; do you want to hear it?

A howl of the wind announces their approach
    i gently lay you down on the cool ground to greet them
They cause the sky to blacken
    your strength is fading
They arrive without ceremony
    your eyes flutter closed
Their wings flap in response
    i can feel your shallow breath
Their eyes start to flash
    your skin is the first to go

They cause the ground to drum
the medicine is leaving your body
Flash
breath
Crack!
breath
Flash
breath
Crack!
your spirit floats up
They let their tears fall to the earth
i whisper "safe travels" as your journey begins

Pretty powerful, hey?

In my mind, I can see her partner lighting a fire to call the thunderbirds to come and clean her, to prepare for her journey home. I can see him carrying her to a patch of land near the water and gently placing her on the ground while the thunderbirds approach. Some of you might be wondering why I chose this woman to be part of my piece. Well, back in 1993, when the burial site was first uncovered, the Elders from the community shared the teaching that "everything happens for a reason." They explained that the appearance of this young mother was so the next generation could learn about the old ways to gain respect for the past.[11] This teaching spoke to me, her story came to me for a reason, and it is my responsibility to share these teachings to the next generation.

There, that is all that I want to share for now. You will have to wait until I finish the work to see how I capture her spirit leaving her body to return home. Thank you for listening, now *awas*![12]

NOTES

1 When you greet others, it is important to introduce and position yourself. Nehiyewmowin for "Good evening! Hello all my relations, my name is Flying Overhead in Circles Eagle Woman. I come from my mother Judi Adams from Fisher River Cree Nation."

2 Nehiyewmowin for "come here, sit."

3 Allison C. Meier, "Native Americans and the Dehumanising Force of the Photograph." *Welcome Collection*, 29 March 2018, https://wellcomecollection.org/articles/WrUTGh8AACAA1FH8 (accessed 14 February 2023).

4 Bob Joseph, "21 Things You May Not Have Known about the Indian Act," *Indigenous Corporate Training Inc.*, 2 June 2015, https://www.ictinc.ca/blog/21-things-you-may-not-have-known-about-the-indian-act (accessed 14 February 2023).

5 Ibid.

6 Ron Cook et al., "pimitisahētān ininīmowin kā kī nakatamākawiyak," ed. Becky Cook, Misipawistik Cree Nation, 2022, https://www.youtube.com/watch?v=sd0qFhV1Tk8.

7 Sherry Copenace, in conversation with the author during the Nibi Gathering, 24 May 2018.

8 Kevin Brownlee and E. Leigh Syms, *Kayasochi kikawenow—Our Mother from Long Ago (An Early Cree Woman and Her Personal Belongings from Nagami Bay, Southern Indian Lake)* (Winnipeg: Museum of Man and Nature, 1999).

9 William Dumas and Leonard Paul, *Pīsim Finds Her Miskanaw*, rev. ed. (Winnipeg: HighWater Press, 2020), 8.

10 Ibid., 6.

11 Brownlee and Syms, *Kayasochi kikawenow*, 1.

12 Nehiyewmowin for "go away."

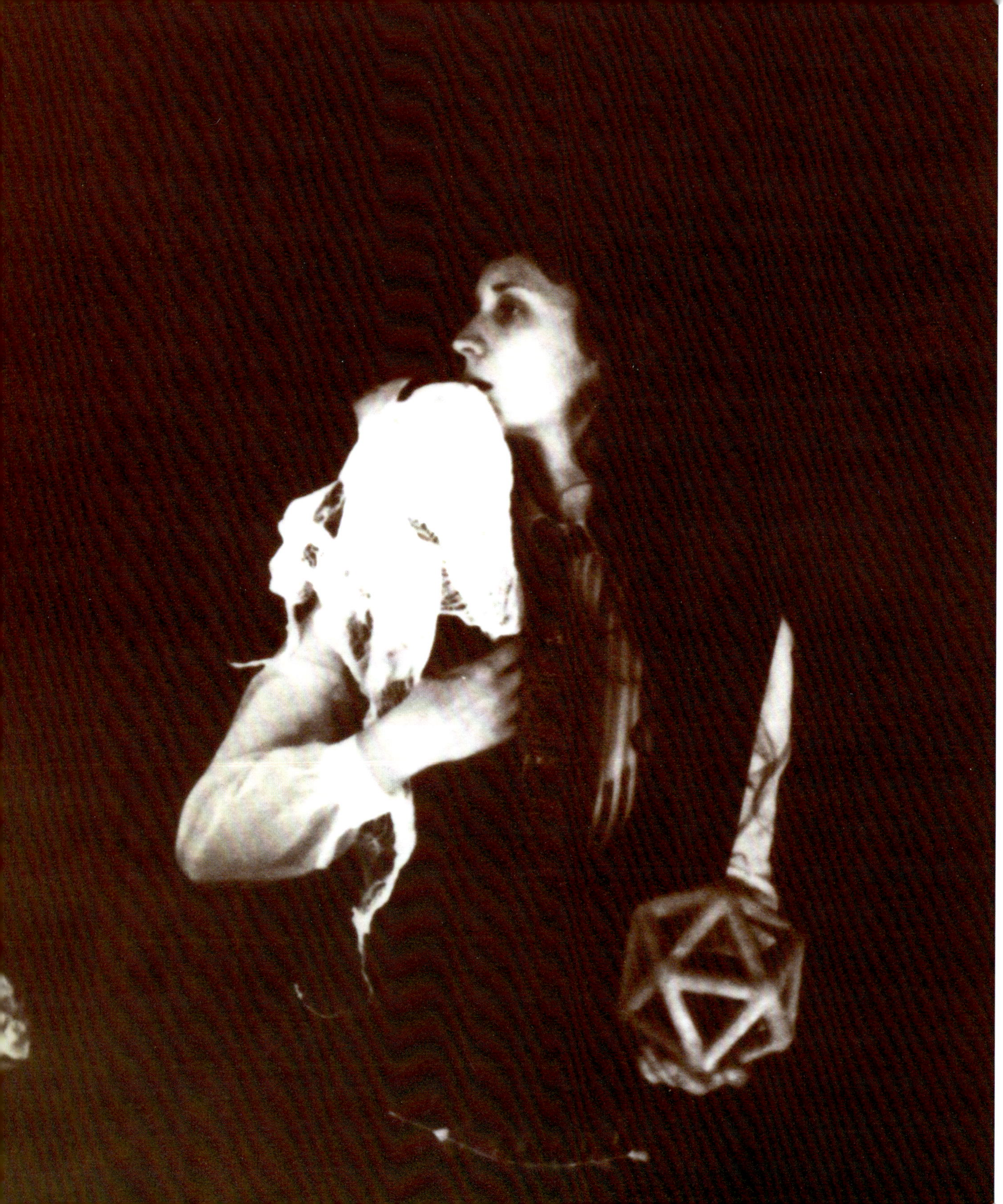

9

Embodying the Dead

Serena Keshavjee

With the 1984 hit movie *Ghostbusters*, a film by Dan Aykroyd, the great-grandson of Spiritualists, the word *ectoplasm* entered into popular culture. Film historian Murray Leeder explains that the term hovers between science and silliness, and has become a joke in Hollywood.[1] Contemporary artists have also poked fun at psychical photographs. Lacey Pripić Hedtke and Maria Molteni, referencing the handcrafted appearance of the substance, published a set of recipes to make ectoplasm in *Ectoplasm Selfies: DIY Ritual in the Age of Social Mediums* (2017) (see Figure 9.1).[2] Jodie Mack nods to the counterfeit look of ectoplasm by substituting mop heads and streamers in her entertaining stop-motion film *ECTO* (2022) (see Figure 9.2). Teresa Burrows recreates the hand-shaped teleplasms with glow-in-the-dark beads (see Figure 9.3), and Erika DeFreitas replaces the white ectoplasm with her grandmother's brightly coloured crocheted doilies (see Figure 9.29).

Even in the height of the serious scientific studies in the twentieth century, ectoplasm elicited jokes (see Figure 9.4). Magician Harry Houdini ridiculed psychical

Fig. 9.1 Lacey Pripić Hedtke with Maria Molteni, ***Maria,*** from the ***Ectoplasm Selfies*** series, 2017. Gold-toned albumen print on watercolor paper from Fuji instant photograph, 21.5 x 28 cm image on 30.5 x 40.6 cm water colour paper. Courtesy of the artist.

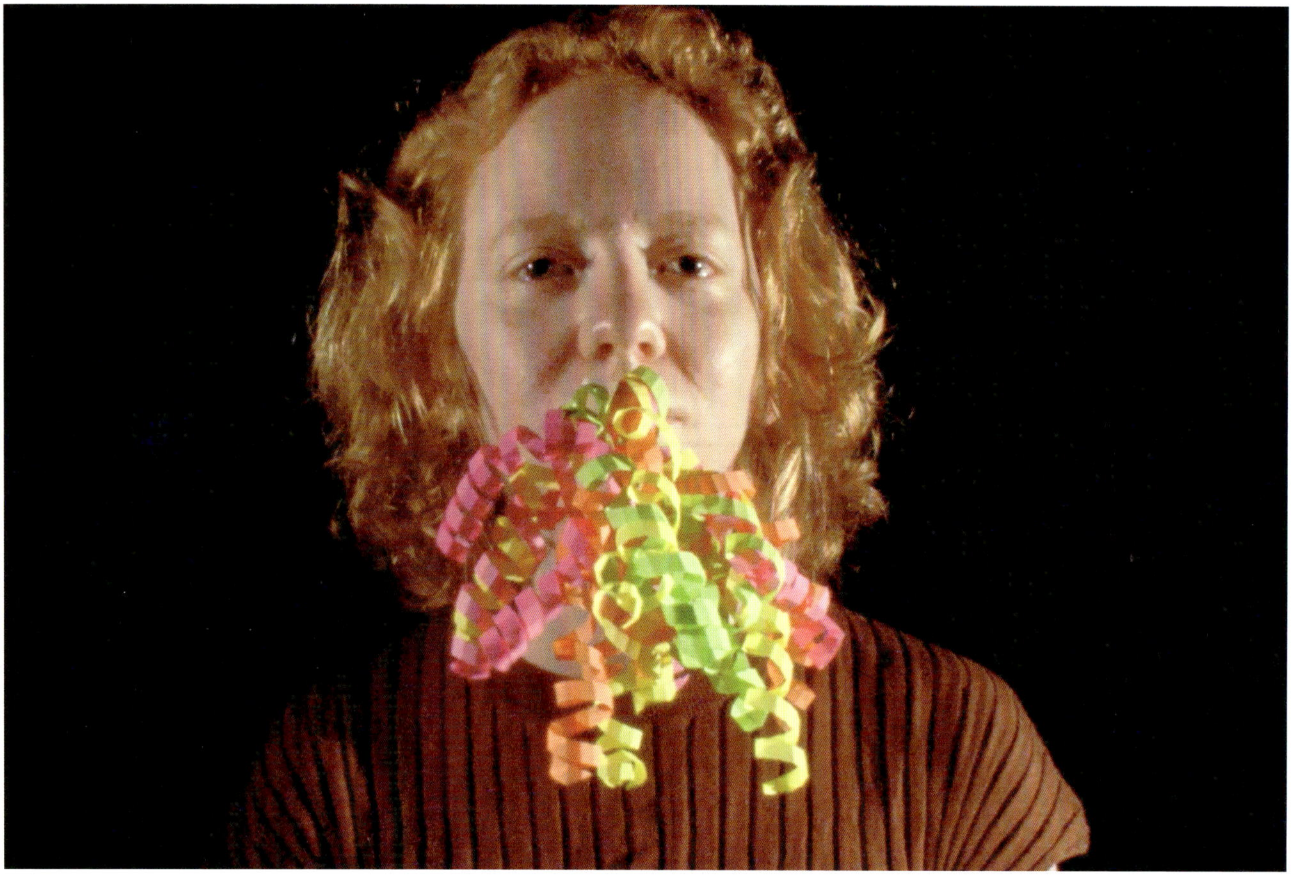

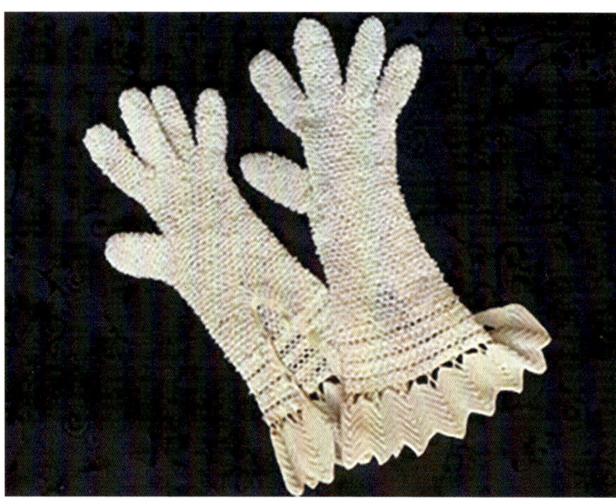

Fig. 9.2. *Above*, Jodie Mack, ***ECTO*** with Kit Duckworth, 2022. Still shot, 16-mm transferred to digital video, colour, no sound, 5m, 19s. Courtesy of the artist.

Fig. 9.3. *Left*, Teresa Burrows, ***Beaded Hand Simulacrum***, 2020. Glow-in-the-dark beads, glow-in-the-dark thread, vintage lace, and crochet, 15.2 x 27.9 cm. Courtesy of the artist.

Fig. 9.4. *Right*, Unknown photographer, ***Spiritualist Image of Houdini Appearing to Houdini***, c.1920. Courtesy of McCord Museum, Montreal, M2014.128.703.29.

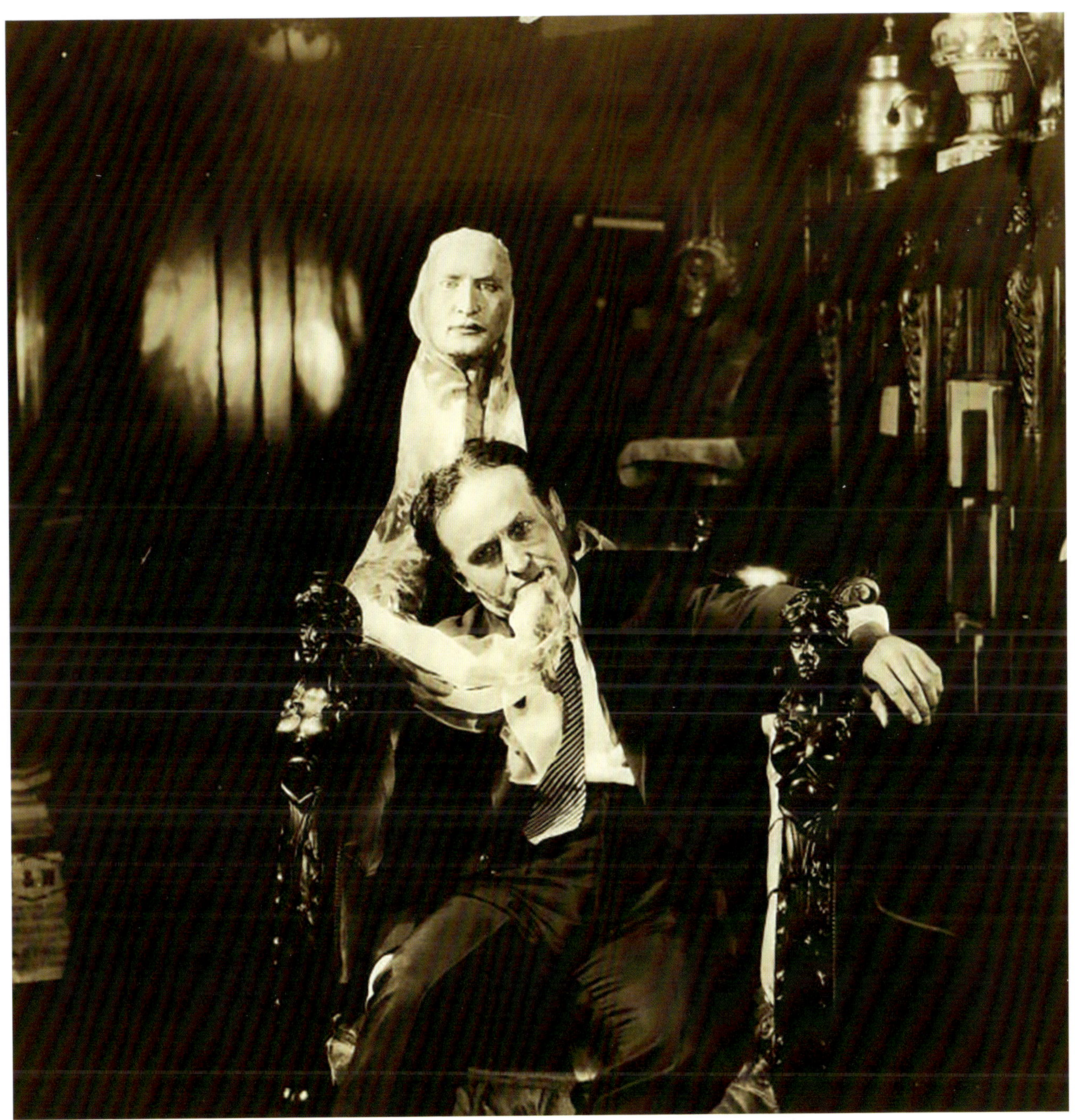

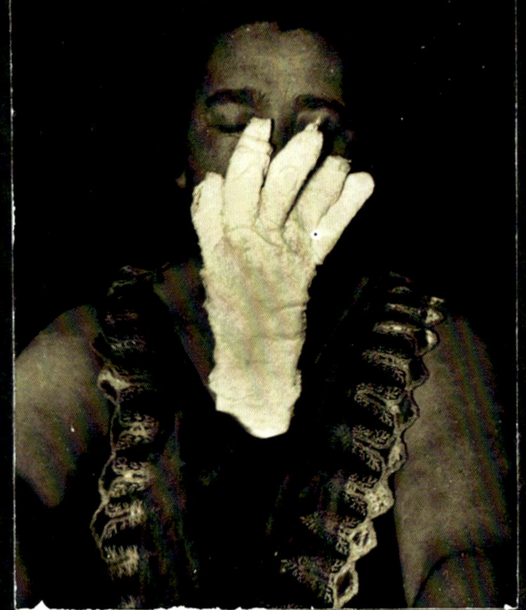

5th January 1930.
One of Walter's Jokes!

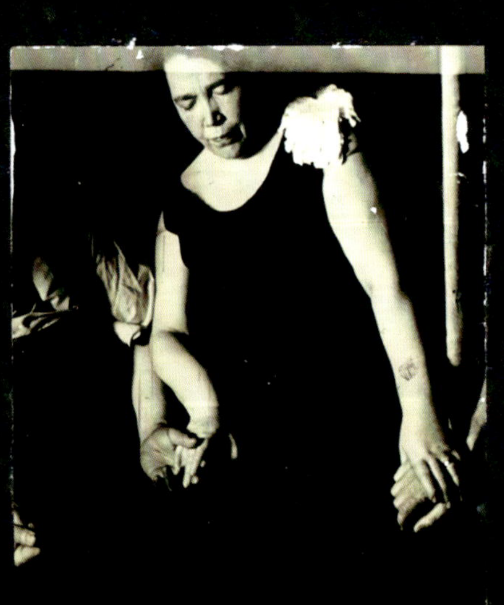

24th May 1931.

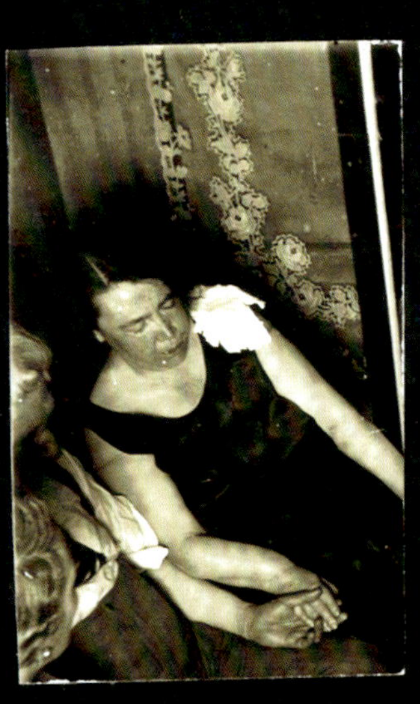

Another variation of the "hand" theme!

Present:- Mary M., H. A. V. Green, Mrs. S. Marshall, W. B. Cooper, Elin. M., Dr. T. G. Hamilton, T. Ginn, Mrs. Herling, H. A. Reed, Mrs. Bruce Chown, W. E. Hobbs, Miss A. Turner, Mrs. F. Campbell, & Dr. J. A. Hamilton. Dr. Bruce Chown, note-taker.

researchers by producing fake photographs of exteriorizations and summed up their research as "flap-doodle stunts" involving "revolting" bodily emanations (see Figure 9.4): "It is my will to believe and if convincing evidence is brought forward I will be the first to acknowledge my mistake, but up to the present day nothing has crossed my path to make me think that the Great Almighty will allow emanations from a human body of such horrible, revolting viscous substance as Baron von Schrenck-Notzing claims, hideous shapes, which like 'genii from the bronze bottle,' ring bells, move handkerchiefs, wobble tables, and do other 'flap-doodle' stunts."[3] "Walter," the "spirit control" who directed the Hamilton family's séance experiments, also kidded around about ectoplasm, when one day, after a boring sitting, he promised "something funny," to keep Thomas Glendenning (T.G.) Hamilton "in good humour," and produced a simulacrum of a hand, resulting in one of the most remarkably shaped ectoplasms in Hamilton's oeuvre.[4] In his photo album Henry Archibald Vaughan Green notes that the hand was "one of Walter's Jokes!", revealing that the members of this scientific circle recognized the strange nature of their photographs (see Figure 9.5).

Dr. Hamilton was among the handful of international researchers who investigated ectoplasm, and he curated a "metapsychic exhibit" of 100 photographs at the Winnipeg Winter Club in 1930 (see Figure 2.2).[5] Hamilton recognized the contradictions in his photographs, defining ectoplasm as "monstrously extraordinary."[6] Margaret Hamilton Bach also tried to rationalize the subject matter of the photographs: "to the uninitiated, such masses are ugly. Just as birth is an ugly thing to witness, just as open heart surgery is ugly to gaze upon . . . on the other hand some of the teleplasmic masses are of very great beauty," implying that this excretion embodies a vitality which makes it universally attractive. Similarly, a reporter from the *Winnipeg Free Press* described the photographs in his exhibition as "ridiculous" yet "beautiful": "The teleplasm as it appears on photographs is not attractive-looking, variously like masses of stiffly beaten whites of egg, of plaster of Paris

Fig. 9.5. T.G. Hamilton, ***Another Variation of the Hand Theme***, 1930–31. UMASC, H.A.V. Green Fonds, MSS 439, Box 1, Folder 2, Item 1.14.

or cotton wool . . . , but while not beautiful on a photograph, it is actually a thing of great beauty."[7] As a bodily excretion, ectoplasm was not attractive in any classical sense, but its grotesque and abject nature aroused curiosity, and its association with scientific theories of evolution and vitalism meant that it held a certain gravitas.[8] On the cover of this book, the coarse, glove-like hand, floating in front of Mary Marshall's face, as if silencing her, accords with the descriptions that Hamilton's teleplasm looks like cheesecloth and plaster of Paris. As introduced in Chapter 2, Hamilton's scientific visualizations seemed to offer evidence of discarnate spirits emanating through the psychic force. Other researchers, including his scientific mentors Drs. Gustave Geley and Charles Richet, linked ectoplasm to foundational processes in nature, such as cellular division, embryology, and chrysalis formation, which offered information on the origins of life and evolution.[9] The representation of ectoplasm as a primal biological material in psychic scientific illustrations closely paralleled developments in biomorphic Modernist art of abstracted organic forms. Ectoplasmic photographs made by scientists in the twentieth century have a Modernist sensibility. In this chapter, I lay out the artistic and scientific principles that shaped the visual culture of ectoplasm from the Victorian era to the emergence of the Modernist style, and into the twenty-first century, when ectoplasm is once again attracting artistic attention.

Picturing Ghosts in the Victorian Era

As Spiritualism developed into a popular religion and more people participated in séances in Britain, France, and North America during the nineteenth century, interest in ghosts flourished. The Ghost Club began in 1862, and the Society for Psychical Research was initiated in 1882, the most prominent members being physicist Oliver Lodge and author Arthur Conan Doyle, both of whom Hamilton knew personally.[10] An art exhibition in London in 1886, *The Phenomena of Materialisation*, explored the formal characteristics of the substance through which ghosts materialized with a display of twenty-eight prints of apparitions, based on real-life observations of séances. Instead of the conventional terms of "ghost," "phantom," or "spirit," this exhibition used the pseudo-scientific term "materialization" in its title indicating the developing scientific interest into ectoplasm.[11]

One of the works in the exhibition, a striking black-and-white mezzotint, was made by the celebrated artist James Jacques Tissot (1836–1902), depicting an infamous séance during which the medium William Eglinton conjured up the ghost of Kathleen Newton and a stereotyped "oriental" ghost, wearing a white turban, named "Ernest" (see Figure 9.6).[12] Alongside Tissot's print was a set of twelve chromolithographs by Johannes Gerrard Keulemans (1842–1912) for John S. Farmer's book *Twixt Two Worlds: A Narrative of the Life and Work of William Eglinton* (1886), of Eglinton extruding "bioplasm"—that is, ectoplasm.[13] In Plate 8 of the book, Keulemans rendered the bioplasm as a luminous radiation emanating from Eglinton's belly button and morphing into a phantom, the same "Ernest" that Tissot had depicted (see Figure 9.7).

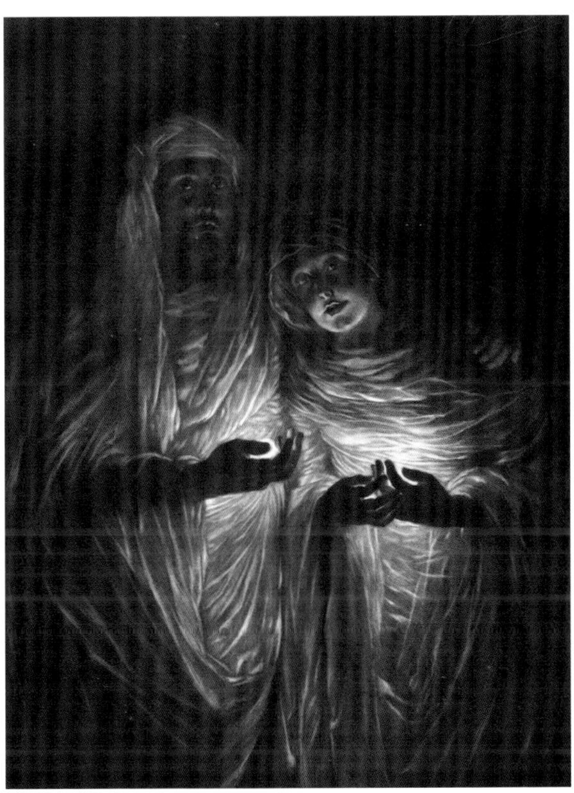

Fig. 9.6. James Tissot, ***Mediumistic Apparition***, 1885. Mezzotint on chine applique on wove paper, 48.9 x 34.2 cm. Gift of Allan and Sondra Gotlieb, 1994. Courtesy of Art Gallery of Ontario.

According to an eyewitness, Eglinton's ghosts materialized through shining orbs of light that powered the spirits, comparable to the brilliant light of a "phosphorescent miner's lamp."[14] Both Keulemans and Tissot included the glowing, hand-held bulbs, possibly referencing the phosphorous lamp invented by the founder of psychical research, the chemist

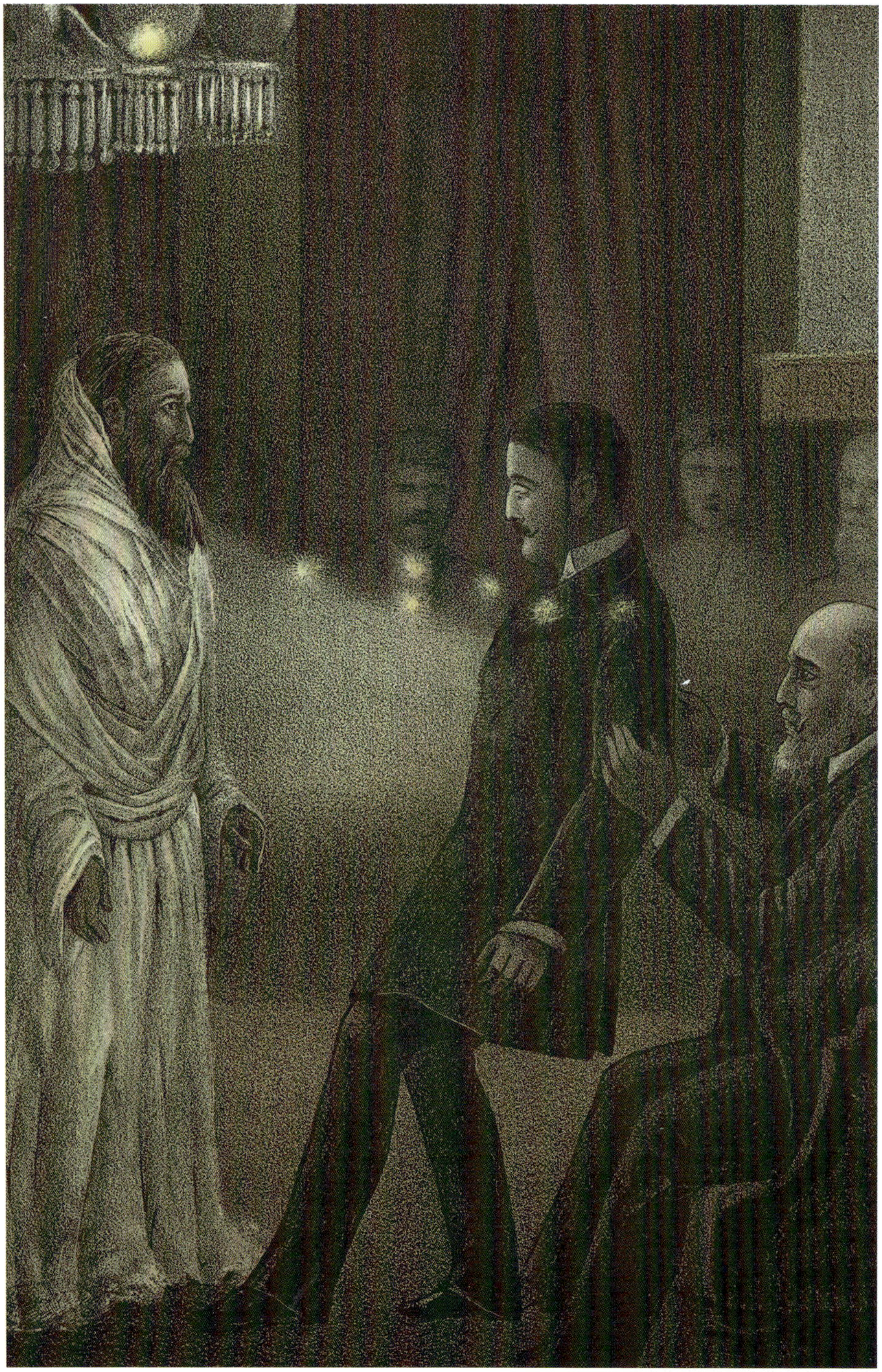

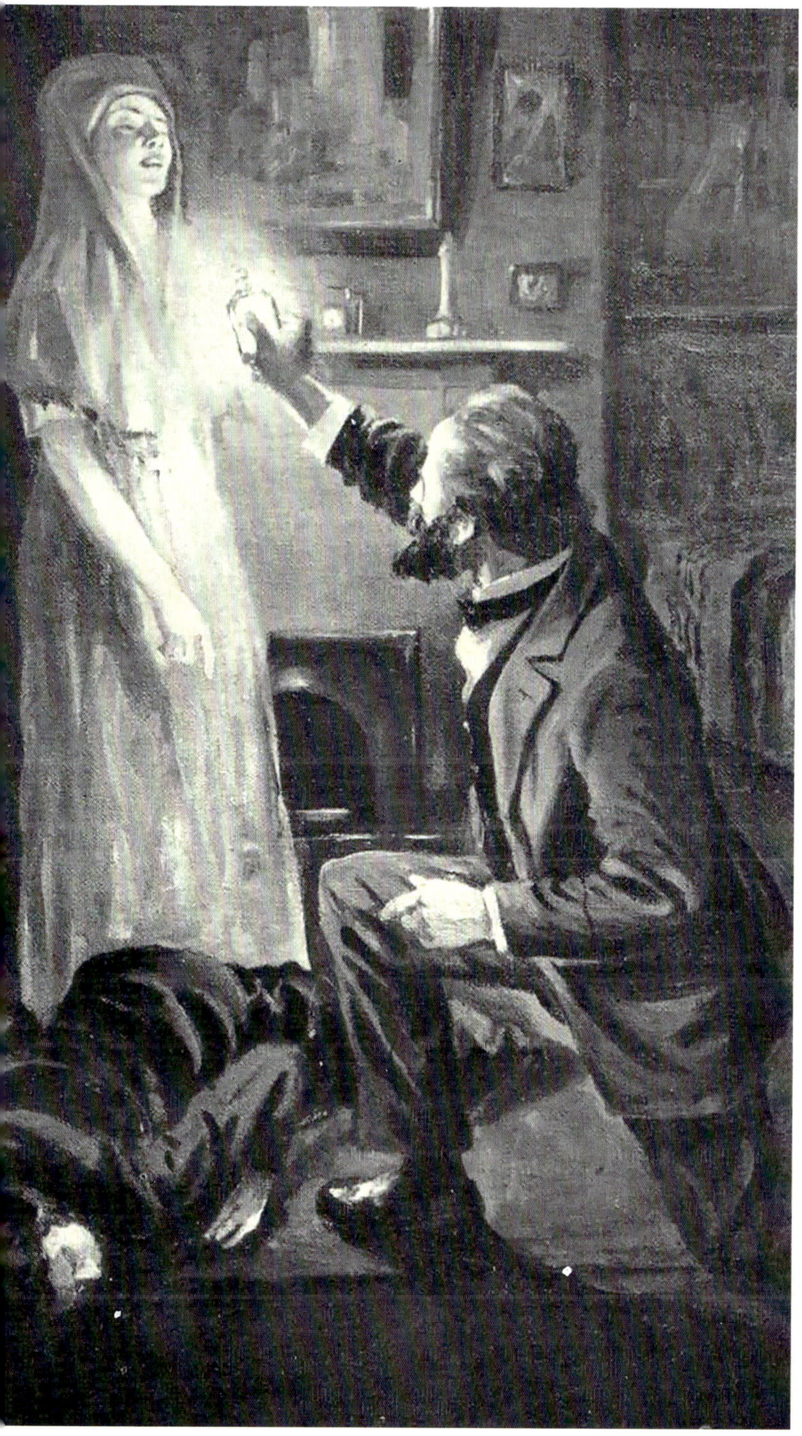

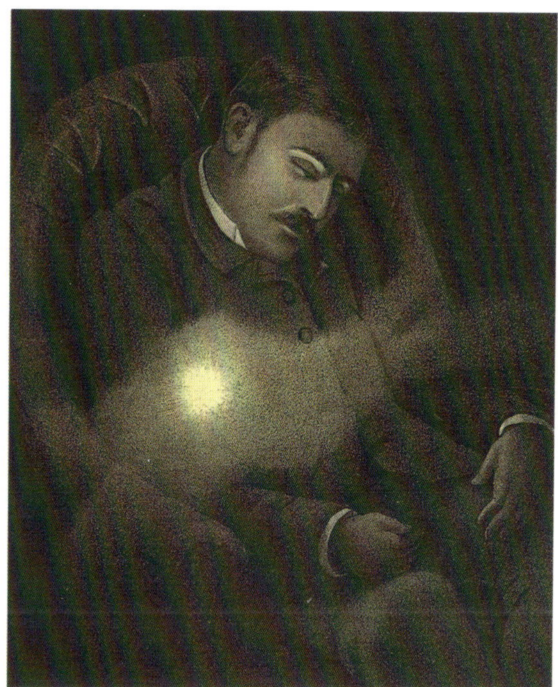

Fig. 9.7. *Far Left*, Johannes Gerrard Keulemans, ***An Apparition Formed in Full View***, 1885, Plate 8, from ***Twixt Two Worlds***, by John S. Farmer (1886). Chromolithograph. UMASC, Rare Book Room.

Fig. 9.8. *Centre*, Albert Besnard, "Nous vîmes la silhouette sombre d'une main," 1887, from ***Force psychique***, by Yveling Rambaud (1889). Courtesy of Serena Keshavjee.

Fig. 9.9. *Left*, Serge Drigin, ***Professor Crookes's Test to Show that the Medium and the Spirit were Separate Entities***, from ***History of Spiritualism,*** by Arthur Conan Doyle (1926). Courtesy of Serena Keshavjee.

Fig. 9.10. *Above*, Johannes Gerrard Keulemans, ***Materialisation 1st Stage***, 1885, Plate 5, from ***Twixt Two Worlds***, by John S. Farmer (1886). Chromolithograph. UMASC, Rare Book Room.

and physicist William Crookes (1883-1919). In 1874, Crookes curtained off a section of his chemistry lab and created a small, hand-held phosphorous lamp in order to better see the ghost of Katie King in the dimly lit space.[15] The story of the lamp was often repeated, and Conan Doyle hired illustrator Serge Drigin to depict the moment for his book *The History of Spiritualism* (see Figure 9.9).[16] The French artist Albert Besnard (1849–1934) also rendered the glowing orb in his drawing for *Force psychique*, a compendium of famous nineteenth-century ghostly materializations, including the séance with Tissot and Eglinton (see Figure 9.8).[17] Like Tissot and Drigin, Besnard turned to Crookes's scientific photographs as models for his drawing of the ghost of Katie King to add realism (see Figures 9.11 and 9.12).

Art historians Sarah Willburn and Martin Kemp point out that both scientific illustrators and artists utilize the same elements of style and pictorial codes, and it is to be expected that they influence each other.[18] Willburn notes that spirit photographers used poses and props typical of Salon painting to give their prints more artistic value, and modeled their style after Salon Impressionism.[19] Similarly, fine artists looked to spirit and psychic photographs to give their art a layer of authenticity. In picking the uncommon print medium of the mezzotint, with its strong tonal contrasts, for *Apparition Mediunimique*, Tissot created an artwork that resembled an evidentiary photograph made by scientists such as Crookes. In turn, Besnard relied on the aura of Crookes's experimental photograph to make his drawing of Katie King's ghost more suitable for the pseudo-scientific treatise *Force psychique*. French Symbolist artists were also fascinated by mediumship and spirit photographs for what they might learn about the unconscious mind, a reserve of great knowledge and unbounded creativity. Elsewhere I have compared Eugène Carrière's lithograph of Auguste Rodin shaping a female figure out of barely visible gaseous masses, to spirit photographs of mediums conjuring ghosts

Fig. 9.11. ***Psychic News***, 8 February 1941, 5, UMASC, http://hdl.handle.net/10719/2946363.

SCIENTIST PHOTOGRAPHED ARM-IN-ARM WITH MATERIALISED SPIRIT

WHEN the Primate of All England's committee of inquiry into Spiritualism reported, its findings were suppressed because they were favourable to Spiritualism. But when one of the world's greatest scientists, Sir William Crookes, made experiments with mediums he freely reported his conclusions and very capably answered the critics who attacked him for nearly everything except his facts.

As Crookes's scientific fame grew and he gathered the honours that belonged to him he never in any way departed from his conclusions. He embodied his facts in books that will always be classic in Spiritualism. He defended his point of view in his Presidential Address to the British Association in 1898. After 30 years he held fast to his views in these words:

"*I have nothing to retract. Indeed, I might add much thereto . . . I think I see a little farther now. I have glimpses of something like coherence among the strange elusive phenomena; of something like continuity between those unexplained forces and laws already known.*"

Crookes was a versatile scientist, as he was driven to explain in self-defence when attacked by an ignoramus "as a specialist of specialists." He was elected a Fellow of the Royal Society at a very early age, was knighted for his discoveries and was honoured among scientists.

It has not yet occurred to materialists and orthodox Churchmen that there must be a reason why leading scientists of the Victorian Age of Materialism—Crookes, Alfred Russel Wallace, Barrett and Lodge—all became convinced of the facts of Spiritualism because of their experiments and experiences with mediums.

No one has yet arisen, in pulpit or in laboratory, to deny or disprove any one of the facts on which these scientists based their belief in Proved Survival.

Crookes feared that unless he and other scientists hastened to test the mediums like D. D. Home, Florrie Cook and Katie Fox, there would come a time when their like would exist no more.

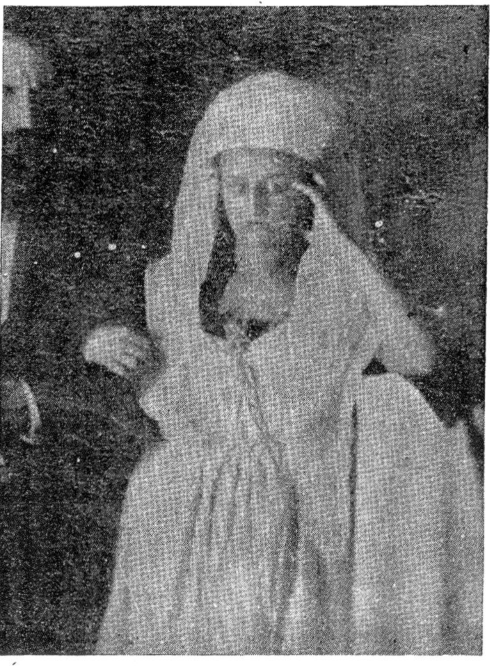

One of Spiritualism's cast-iron proofs—Crookes and a materialisation, photographed together.

The fact is, of course, that there are always new mediums to meet the needs of every generation, and there always will be as long as we continue to serve the real purpose of Spiritualism—to comfort the mourner, heal the sick, and bring the light of spirit truth to those whose minds are darkened by the teachings of orthodox materialism.

"LIVING WOMAN"

Crookes the scientist did almost as he pleased at the test seances with Home and Florrie Cook, especially when he had gained the confidence of Katie King, one of Miss Cook's spirit guides. And what was the reward? Here is an extract from one of his letters to the "Spiritualist":

"I pass on to a seance held last night at Hackney. Katie never appeared to greater perfection, and for nearly two hours she walked about the room conversing familiarly with those present. On several occasions she took my arm when walking, and the impression conveyed to my mind that it was a living woman by my side instead of a visitor from the other world was so strong that the temptation to repeat a recent celebrated experiment became almost irresistible.

"Feeling, however, that if I had not a spirit I had at all events a *lady* close to me, I asked her permission to clasp her in my arms, so as to be able to verify the interesting observations which a bold experimentalist has recently somewhat verbosely recorded.

ADVISED FROM BEYOND

"Permission was graciously given, and I accordingly did—well, as any gentleman would do under the circumstances." So the scientist kissed the

pictures is one in which I am standing by the side of Katie; she has her bare foot upon a particular part of the floor. Afterwards I dressed Miss Cook like Katie, placed her and myself in exactly the same position, and we were photographed by the same cameras, placed exactly as in the other experiment, and illuminated by the same light.

"When these two pictures are placed over each other the two photographs of myself coincide exactly as regards stature, etc., but Katie is half a head taller than Miss Cook, and looks a big woman in comparison with her. In the breadth of her face, in many of the pictures, she differs essentially in size from her medium, and the photographs show several other points of difference."

CROOKES'S TRIBUTE

But in case you imagine that Crookes was only the cold, dry scientist searching in his delicate instruments for evidence of the operation of psychic force, here is another description of Katie King:

"But photography is as inadequate to depict the perfect beauty of Katie's face, as words are powerless to describe her charms of manner.

"Photography may, indeed, give a map of her countenance, but how can it reproduce the brilliant purity of her complexion, or the ever-varying expression of her most mobile features now overshadowed with sadness when relating some of the bitter experiences of her past life, now smiling with all the innocence of happy girlhood when she had collected my children round her, and was amusing them by recounting anecdotes of her adventures in

tific proofs that could be devised.

The great scientist experienced nearly every kind of physical phenomena—levitation of heavy articles and of human beings, direct writing, lights, apports and musical instruments played by other than human hands. He describes some of his experiences in these words:

"A medium, walking into my dining-room, cannot, while seated in one part of the room with a number of persons keenly watching him, by trickery make an accordion play in *my own* hand when I hold it keys downwards, or cause the same accordion to float about the room playing all the time.

"He cannot introduce machinery which will wave window-curtains or pull up Venetian blinds eight feet off, tie a knot in a handkerchief and place it in a far corner of the room, sound notes on a distant piano, cause a card-plate to float about the room, raise a water-bottle and tumbler from the table, make a coral necklace rise on end, cause a fan to move about and fan the company, or set in motion a pendulum when enclosed in a glass case firmly cemented to the wall."

This final triumph of moving the pendulum in the glass case was discussed before it happened as likely to be decisive. But the power that defeats materialism could surely, in the right conditions, be relied on to show the leading scientist of the day that there were more things than his science dreamed of.

The intricacy of the details of Crookes's search are all laid out in his own works, but that is not so impressive to me as his touching human account of the last seance at which Katie King appeared. Another spirit was to take her place. Here are his words:

"When the time came for Katie to take her farewell I asked that she would let me see the last of her. Accordingly, when she had called each of the company up to her and had spoken to them a few words in private, she gave some general directions for the future guidance and protection of Miss Cook.

KATIE KING'S FAREWELL

"From these, which were taken down in shorthand, I quote the following: 'Mr. Crookes has done very well throughout, and I leave Florrie with the greatest confidence in his hands, feeling perfectly sure he will not abuse the trust I place in him. He can act in any emergency better than I can myself, for he has more strength.'

"Having concluded her directions, Katie invited me into the cabinet with her and allowed me to remain there to the end."

The spirit guide's work with that medium was over, and here is the farewell scene between the leading scientist of his day and the materialised spirit:

"*After closing the curtain she conversed with me for some time, and then walked across the room to where Miss Cook was lying senseless on the floor. Stooping over her, Katie touched her, and said, 'Wake up, Florrie, wake up! I must leave you now.' Miss Cook then woke and tearfully entreated Katie to stay a little time longer.*

"'My dear, I can't; my work is done. God bless you,' Katie replied, and then continued speaking to Miss Cook. For several minutes the two were conversing with each other, till at last Miss Cook's tears prevented her speaking.

"Following Katie's instructions, I then came forward to support Miss Cook, who was falling on to the floor, sobbing hysterically. I looked round, but the white-robed Katie had gone."

And so another chapter in the endless encyclopædia of living Spiritualism was closed, but the truth of it marches on in new living pages, imprinted by the work of guides and their mediums as they serve humanity.

PAUL MILLER

PRAYER BY SILVER BIRCH:

OH, Great White Spirit, it is to Thee we turn, to seek Thy light, Thy wisdom, Thy love and Thy understanding, that we may spread these attributes among those who are ready to receive them.

We pay tribute to Thee because Thou art the perfect law in operation, the divine intelligence responsible for the whole of life in all its multitudinous

Our mission is to teach Thy children to find Thee by finding themselves, that they may gain a full and free access to the wonders of Thy heavenly kingdom, which are to be found within their own beings; that they may learn to draw from its infinite resources strength, courage, fortitude and wisdom; so that they may order their lives in the spirit of self-abnegation

(see Figure 9.13).[20] Carrière and Rodin were foundational to the development of Modernist art, especially biomorphic Modernism, a major avant-garde style of the early twentieth century.[21] Carrière used the iconography and composition of spirit photographs to signify that Rodin was accessing the power of his unconscious mind, in the manner of a medium entering a trance state to bring forth spirits. At the turn of the century, both artists and scientists were testing formal elements to try and depict something as nebulous as the unconscious mind.

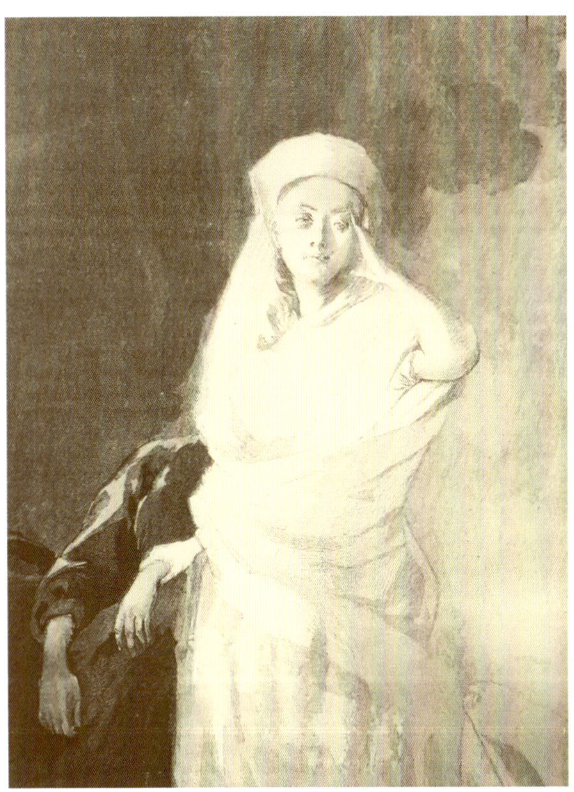

Fig. 9.12. Albert Besnard, ***Katie King et son médium***, 1887, from ***Force psychique***, by Yveling Rambaud (1889). Courtesy of Serena Keshavjee.

Scientist and Nobel Prize winner Charles Richet informs us that by 1900 there were "profound changes" in the understanding of ectoplasm as an organic substance, affecting how it was depicted.[22] Evidence of ectoplasm being accepted as a biological substance can already be discerned in one of the most interesting prints on display at the exhibition *Phenomena of Materialisation* in 1886. In Plate 1, *Spirit Lights* from *Twixt Two Worlds* (see Figure 9.14), Keulemans lays out a series of shaped glowing orbs in a grid, mimicking a scientific chart.[23] The artist uses the term "bioplasm" for the materializing substance, possibly based upon physiologist Lionel S. Beale's *Bioplasm* (1872), reflecting the vital characteristics of protoplasm, a primal and structureless jelly found in elementary animal and vegetal cells, thought to be the building blocks of all lifeforms, and increasingly linked with ectoplasm. In his explanation of this image, Keulemans describes "blood" and "brain matter" inside the glowing orbs: "These two lines are of a pale greyish red, exactly the colour of living brain matter. The red spot is the colour of human blood" (see Figure 9.14).[24] In Britain, Germany, and France, the substance that formed apparitions was described less and less as luminescent radiation and more as a mechanical projection of primal matter, what Geley came to call "supernormal physiology."[25] It was around this time that scientists started to reject hand-drawn illustrations in favour of photographs, a development that contributed to changes in the depiction of ectoplasmic materializations. However elegantly Keulemans, Tissot, and Besnard had rendered glowing radiations in their artistic illustrations, by 1900 the emerging generation of psychical investigators were employing photography as the only evidentiary tool. Victorian prints of apparitions began to seem unreliable and old fashioned to scientists, especially in the tradition of drawing ghosts as full-bodied phantoms.[26] The limitations and benefits of photographic technology, as well as the model of scientific research, changed the aesthetics of ectoplasm from a veiled fully formed phantom to a fragmented, crudely shaped piece of organic material, exemplified in T.G. Hamilton's would-be scientific visualizations.

In the twentieth century, there were two main types of "supernormal photographs": spirit photographs and psychical photographs.[27] Spirit photographs were made to be sold commercially and with the intent of consoling the bereaved. On a trip to London, England, in 1932, the Hamiltons had lunch with Arthur Conan Doyle's widow, Jean (Leckie) Doyle, who most likely arranged for them to meet with the best-known spirit photographers of the time, Ada Deane and William Hope. Handwritten notations on the photographs state that the Hamiltons recognized the spirit extras, one of them being T. G. Hamilton's sister, who had died in 1886 (see Figures 2.16 and 2.17).[28] In his scientific ectoplasmic photographs, Hamilton also documented personalities who had survived death, but from his point of view the photographs were scientific, produced under strict experimental controls and thus more important and reliable than spirit photographs. It might be a moot point to try to differentiate his psychical scientific visualizations from spirit photographs

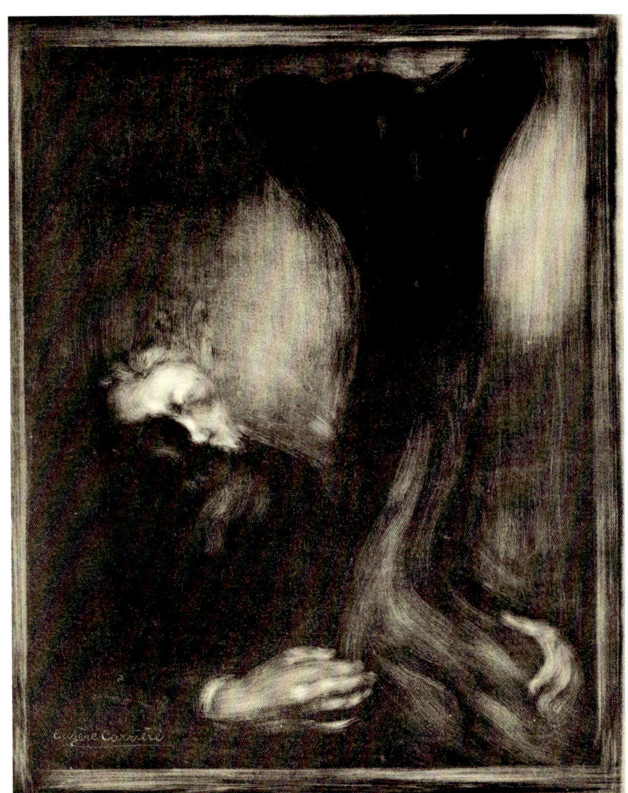

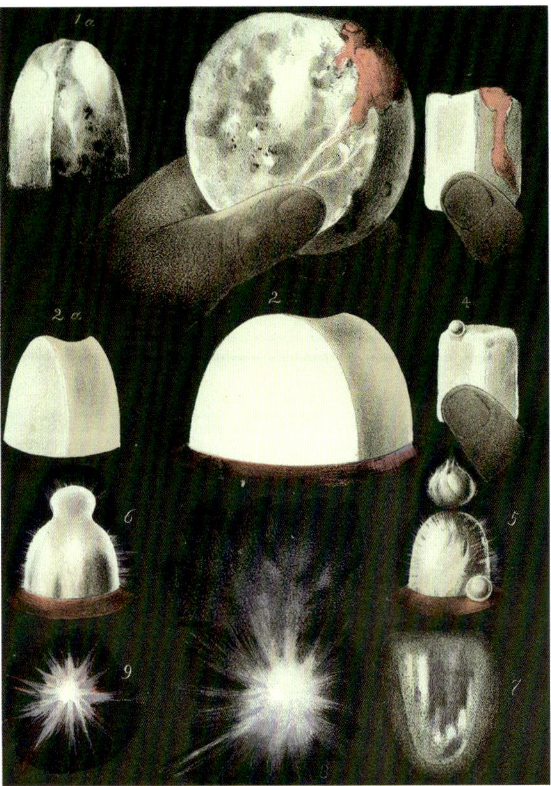

Fig. 9.13. *Left*, Eugène Carrière, ***Rodin Sculpting.*** Lithograph 1, 1900. Courtesy of Iris & B. Gerald Cantor Center for Visual Arts at Stanford University; Mortimer C. Leventritt Fund, 1972.108.

Fig. 9.14. *Right*, Johannes Gerrard Keulemans, ***Spirit Lights***, Plate 1 from ***Twixt Two Worlds***, by John S. Farmer (1886). Chromolithograph. UMASC, Rare Book Room.

given that, by 1924, he accepted that discarnate personalities were communicating with him during séances and that, by 1928, he was taking directions from a "spirit control" named "Walter" (see Figure 4.10). Nonetheless, the difference was important to Hamilton, and his illustrations were neither meant to be sentimental nor sold for profit, nor part of a religious movement, as he saw Spiritualism. His photographs also look very different from conventional spirit photographs. In "Photography of Teleplasm," he laid out the equipment that he had accumulated over the years, including top-of-the-line lenses and cameras, high-speed photographic plates, fast flash powders, and by 1931, flash bulbs and an automatic flash release system, all of which contributed to photographs with sharp contrasts between black and white tones.[29] Because his photographs were scientific illustrations corroborating ectoplasm, Hamilton trained his cameras on the medium's face to capture the substance as it extruded from her mouth and eyes, resulting in close-up, cropped images of Mary Marshall draped in asymmetrical, white protoplasm. Hamilton's photographs reject the Pictorialist Impressionistic style and softer tonality of spirit photographs and exemplify international Modernist art and photography trends of the period.

The Élan Vital: Research Aesthetics of Ectoplasm in the Twentieth Century

In his copy of Gustave Geley's *From the Unconscious to the Conscious*, T.G. Hamilton underlined the term "élan vital," which reflected the "Romantic" strain of biology and evolutionary theory, indicating that the vital force was the directing intelligence behind evolutionary progress, a vitalist theory taken up by psychical researchers.[30] In his widely read book *Creative Evolution* (1907), Henri Bergson, the respected French philosopher and president of the UK-based Society for Psychical Research in 1913, outlined an aesthetically oriented, directed evolutionary impulse—the élan vital (vital force)—responsible for the range of biological forms on the planet. According to historian Sebastien Normandin, by 1900 vitalist biological theories boosted Lamarckian evolutionary theory and dynamic psychology, and I would add psychical research. That a single-celled amoeba could develop into a wondrous array of forms was attributed to the directing and "immaterial force, which has many names—anima, soul, archeus, vital principle, life force, entelechy, élan vital."[31] *Creative Evolution* proposed a dynamic momentum at the core of a unitary universe, countering the conception of the mechanistic universe and attracting artists, philosophers, and scientists, including psychical researchers, as historian Justin Sausman has shown.[32] Bergson utilized vitalism metaphorically as a philosophical challenge to the dominant worldview. However, psychical experimenters, including Richet, Geley, and von Schrenck-Notzing, interpreted this force literally.[33] This group, Hamilton's key scientific sources, accepted that the vital force was aesthetically oriented and teleological in its creation of forms, and similarly they described the amorphous ectoplasmic shapes that they saw on their photographic plates as progressing from simple to complex forms, as directed by "instinct."[34]

In 1923, Hamilton took over his wife's table-turning exercises in the family parlour, moving them to a "laboratory." He already had the beginning of a research library, including Schrenck-Notzing's 1920 book, *The Phenomena of Materialisation*, fully illustrated with black-and-white, Modernist-style photographs focusing on the medium's excrusions. Schrenck-Notzing's book was an expanded English translation of a 1914 publication that the doctor had collaborated on with the French artist Juliette Bisson and the medium Eva Carrière (née Marthe Béraud, 1886–1943).[35] Historian of photography Martyn Jolly states that visualizations of "ghosts" were reformulated by this group in the early twentieth century as "a new form of materialization, not the theatrical unveiling of a full body personality from behind the cabinet curtains but the slow painful extrusion of wet organic matter from the visible body of the medium which gradually formed into an entity."[36] Bisson's and Schrenck-Notzing's photographs reflect emerging vitalistic, protoplasmic concepts that dramatically changed the look of apparitions from electromagnetic luminescent radiations to, quoting Houdini, a "revolting viscous substance."[37] Hamilton used these photographs as his scientific models.

In 1909, Bisson set up a laboratory in a niche of her Paris art studio by curtaining off the space with black cloth. It is rarely noted, but most of the photographs that Schrenck-Notzing published in his 1920 edition were produced in this room, directed by both Bisson and the doctor (see Figure 9.15). Bisson also designed Carrière's séance outfit, combining a set of knitted stockings and bloomers into tights, overlaid with a simple black pinafore into which the medium was sewn (see Figure 9.19).[38] Bisson has been given short shrift in the recent history of psychical science, but not so in the early twentieth century, when she was credited with several innovations.[39] Most importantly, Geley asserted that it was Bisson who proved that the protoplasmic "substance" existed, when in 1909 she captured a grainy photograph of a white streak with a face of sorts using a flash apparatus: "In crediting Mme. Bisson with the discovery of the substance we do no injustice to Dr. von Schrenck Notzing. His collaboration with Mme. Bisson led to great things, and in their extensive publications it is unnecessary to question what originated with one or with the other. There is quite enough glory for both."[40] By covering both the chair and the medium in black cloth, Helen Verrall explains, Bisson made high-quality flash photographs by preventing the light from bouncing off the shiny surface of the wicker chair. These measures were designed to control the séance and highlight the white ectoplasm on the print, but they also contributed to the minimalist aesthetic of the photographs.

Hamilton greatly admired Bisson's and Schrenck-Notzing's photographs, and like Conan Doyle he believed that Bisson was as important as Dr. Marie Curie.[41] Boston-based psychical researcher Dr. Le Roi Crandon paid Hamilton the highest compliment when he stated that the Winnipegger's photographs were even better than those of Schrenck-Notzing: "You have Geley and Schrenck and Walter all knocked out, beaten, left at the post. Nothing like it ever seen."[42] Bisson's and Schrenck-Notzing's visualizations became the standard for psychic photography, as Hamilton expressed in private correspondence.[43] T.G. even pasted one of his own small, close-up photographs of a hand-shaped ectoplasmic extrusion into his copy of Schrenck-Notzing's book, emphasizing the similarities between the two photographs in a notation (see Figure 9.16). Ectoplasmic hands are a consistent motif by artists, as the prints of Tissot, Keulemans, Besnard, and even the beaded gloves of

94 LE MONDE ILLUSTRÉ

LA QUERELLE DES FANTOMES

Nous reprenons encore le titre sous lequel notre confrère *le Matin* a enregistré la récente polémique à laquelle nous faisions allusion dans un précédent numéro (1) concernant la grande querelle qui met aux prises les prestidigitateur et les spirites, pour parler des expériences qui ont pour ainsi dire déchaîné cette polémique.

Ces expériences sont faites avec un médium, Mlle Eva C..., par Mme Juliette Alexandre-Bisson, la veuve du regretté auteur dramatique, qui vient de publier un intéressant volume dans lequel elle relate les curieux résultats qu'elle a obtenus.

Ce livre, copieusement illustré de photographies, a, dès son apparition, été violemment attaqué par certains qui ont cru y découvrir l'indice de supercheries.

Il ne nous appartient pas de nous immiscer dans le débat, mais nous avons cru intéressant de nous renseigner auprès de Mme Bisson elle-même sur les précautions employées pour éviter la fraude et de la prier de bien vouloir nous communiquer le résultat de ses expériences.

Avant tout, notre interlocutrice déclare : « Je n'explique pas, je constate et c'est tout. »

En effet, si extraordinaire que certains résultats puissent sembler, si étrange que paraissent les manifestations, elles sont faites par Mme Bisson, de bonne foi et sans esprit de commerce. C'est là une garantie morale considérable, puisque c'est pour la science qu'elle travaille, que ses expériences loin de lui rapporter de l'argent, lui en coûtent et que seuls des médecins, des savants et quelques intimes sont admis à y assister.

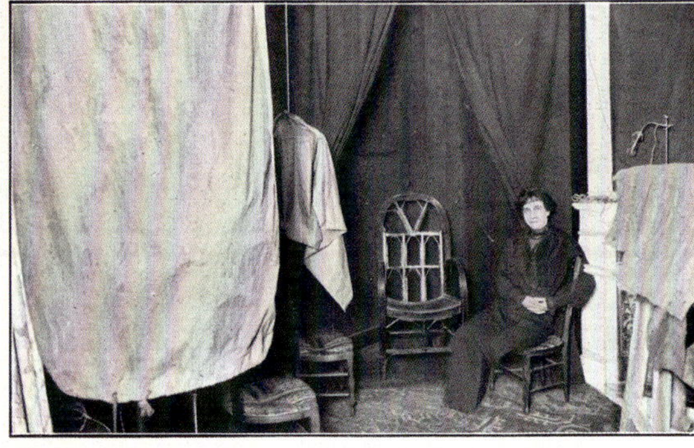

Mme Bisson devant le cabinet du médium.

En ce qui concerne les garanties matérielles dont Mme Bisson s'entoure vis-à-vis de son médium, elles sont des plus minutieuses.

A cet effet une description des lieux est nécessaire.

Les expériences ne se font pas dans le même appartement que celui où elle habite, mais dans un autre donnant sur le même palier. Deux pièces communiquant et dont l'une commande l'autre sont spécialement aménagées. C'est dans la première que le médium est visité ; on pénètre dans la seconde par la baie laissée par une porte à deux battants que l'on a enlevée et c'est dans un des coins qu'a été installé le cabinet du médium. Ce cabinet, que nous avons visité, est formé d'un simple bâti de bois sur lequel est tendu une étoffe noire. Il est fermé par deux rideaux noirs que l'on écarte au moment des expériences.

Devant, sont placés des appareils photographiques et un ballon à magnésium. Une lampe blanche voilée est allumée pendant le sommeil du médium et remplacée par une ampoule rouge au moment de prendre les photographies.

Avant chaque séance, le médium est amené nu dans la première pièce et les médecins procèdent à un examen minutieux qui ne laisse aucune place inexplorée.

Au cours de l'un d'eux on administra même un vomitif au médium afin d'être sur qu'il ne cachait rien dans son estomac, un des assistants ayant émis ce doute.

Le sujet revêt ensuite un maillot noir qui l'emprisonne des pieds jusqu'aux épaules et que l'on coud derrière, pour le fermer, avec du fil blanc.

Par dessus, on lui passe un tablier noir d'écolière.

Il n'a donc ensuite que quelque pas à faire pour se rendre dans le cabinet noir et cela en pleine lumière. Le cabinet est auparavant, bien entendu, minutieusement visité par les assistants ; en outre, des appareils photographiques s'y trouvent placés, intérieurement, et fonctionnent avec l'éclair de ma-

(1) Voir le numéro du *Monde Illustré* du 10 janvier dernier.

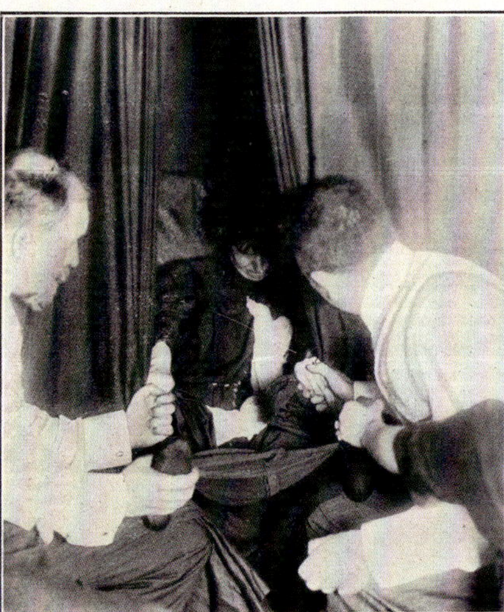

La fameuse « substance » qui apparaît sur le corps du médium (séance du 7 juin 1911).

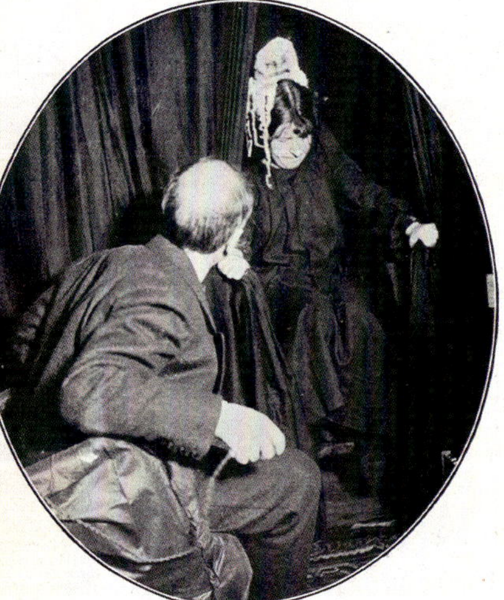

Visage entouré de « substance » apparu dans la séance du 8 avril 1912.

Fig. 9.15. Photographer unknown, ***Juliette Bisson in her studio***, from "La Querelle des fantômes," ***Le Monde illustré***, 7 February 1914, 94. Courtesy of Bibliothèque nationale de France.

Burrows (Figure 9.3), demonstrate. Simulacra of hands also govern psychical photographs seen in the séance laboratories of Geley, Bisson and Schrenck-Notzing. On three occasions between 1930 and 1932 Hamilton photographed hand-shaped teleplasms, thereby aligning his photographs with those of the continental researchers (see Figures 0.1 and 9.5). He also oversaw the production of wax fingers, materialized ectoplasmic hands, which were dipped into molten wax to create a mould, which could be studied more readily than ectoplasm (see Figures 4.7, 4.8, and 9.17). The annotations on the page of Hamilton's copy of Schrenck-Notzing's book acknowledge a very special séance in Bisson's studio, held on 13 March 1911, when thirty ectoplasmic hands, some of which had the ability to flex their fingers, were materialized.[44]

In his 1920 book, Schrenck-Notzing reproduced two images of these spectacular hands: a drawing by the Munich academic artist Karl Gampenrieder (see Figure 9.18) and a photograph that he and Bisson directed (see Figure 9.19). In the drawing, we see a basic forearm configuration stylistically similar to the older leitmotif of radiating light for materializations that Keulemans used (see Figure 9.7).[45] Conversely, in the photograph, flat, white, frozen hands appear on Eva Carrière's shoulder and waist. The difference in representation of the shaped plasm between the drawing and the photograph reflects the fundamental changes in scientific illustrations of the early twentieth century: first, the move from hand drawing to photography; second, the developments in scientific research that transformed the understanding of the vital force from a light radiation to a biologically excreted fragment of a material substance. Geley, Richet, Bisson, and Schrenck-Notzing held that ectoplasm was exteriorized in different states, emerging in gaseous or vaporous form, "instinctually" moving into a liquid or solid state, with the tendency to morph from formlessness to form.[46] The limitations of analogue photography changed early-twentieth-century visualizations of ectoplasm, emphasizing more its solid state. Handmade drawings can depict changes in state, as Gampenrieder's does, but a flash photograph, even with multiple cameras, freezes a moment in time and better depicts a solid material.[47] When Geley praises Carrière's ability to excrete solid ectoplasm, it seems as if he is coming to terms with the limits of photography:

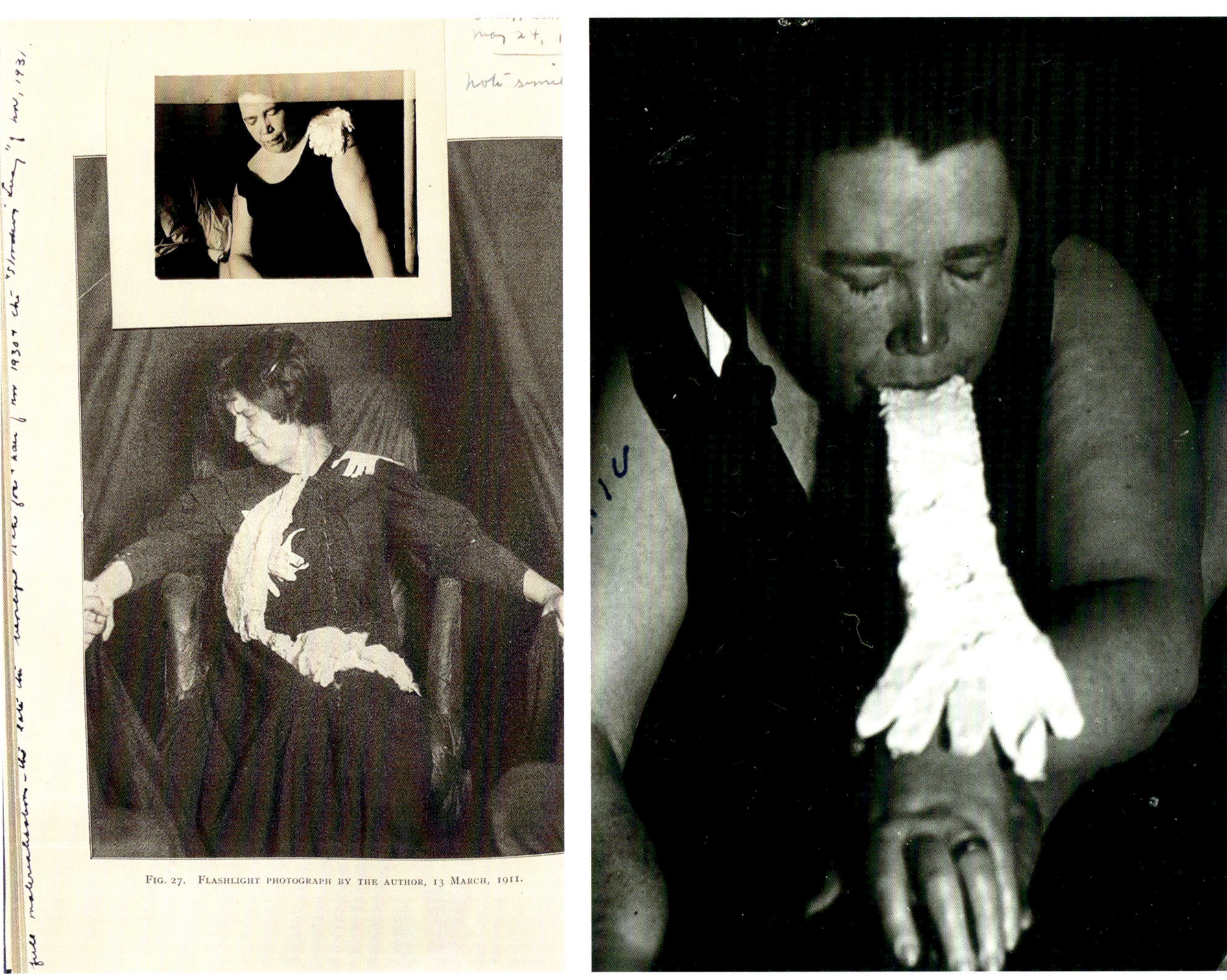

Fig. 9.16. *Left*, T.G. Hamilton's copy of Schrenck-Notzing's ***Phenomena of Materialisation*** (1920), with his own photograph of medium Mary Marshall (Flat Hand, #35), 1931, pasted at the top. UMASC, Rare Book Room.

Fig. 9.17. *Right*, ***Hand Simulacrum, Second Exposure***, 27 April 1932. UMASC, PC 12, Box 10, Folder 5, Item 43b, http://hdl.handle.net/10719/1410287.

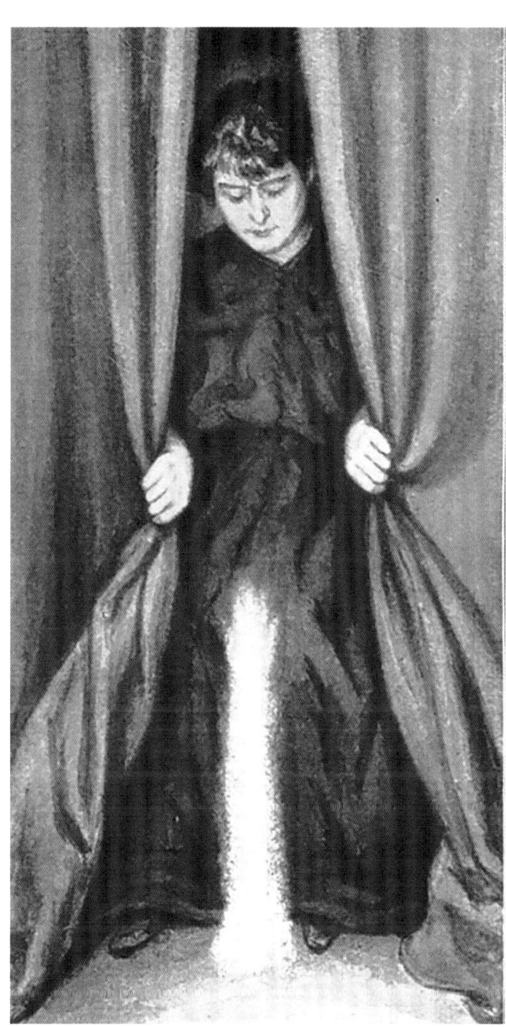

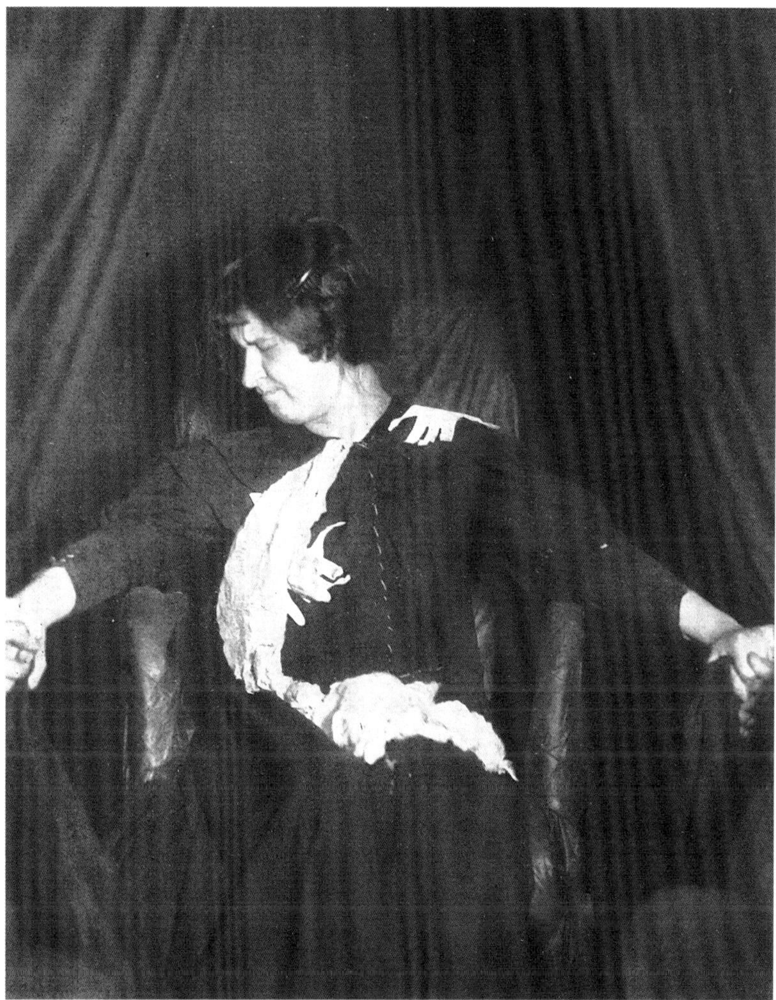

Fig. 9.18. *Left,* Karl Gampenrieder, Drawing after Record of Sitting of 13 March 1911, from ***Phenomena of Materialisation,*** by Schrenck-Notzing (1920). Courtesy of Serena Keshavjee.

Fig. 9.19. *Right,* Albert von Schrenck-Notzing, ***Flashlight Photograph by the Author, 13 March 1911,*** from ***Phenomena of Materialisation,*** by Schrenck-Notzing (1920). Courtesy of Serena Keshavjee.

"The substance of materialization is more amenable to examination under its liquid or solid forms. . . . It has been observed under this form, from several mediums, especially from the famous medium Eglinton. But it is from the medium Eva that this *solid substance is generated with astonishing completeness*."[48] Schrenck-Notzing uses the original meaning of "plastic," mouldable, to describe Carrière's production of "glove-like hands":

> This day's experiments were remarkable for the sculptural character of the teleplastic projections. Some of the head and hand shapes resemble unfinished plastic works of marble, plaster, or clay, on a white background. Perhaps this extraordinary circumstance is explained by the fact that Eva inhabits a room connected with Mme. Bisson's studio. *She is surrounded by sculptures of all sorts, and has, through the artistic activity of her protectress, daily opportunity of observing the various stages of the development of such products.* Without knowing it Mme. Bisson must have played a very important role in the genesis of the psycho-physical images recorded.[49]

Bisson was a marginally successful sculptor, exhibiting at the Salon with the Société des artistes français between 1898 and 1902, achieving an honourable mention in 1901 for a grave monument, *Misère*.[50] As we have seen, she organized the séance laboratory in a niche of her sculpture studio, and a 1914 press photograph shows tarps covering large sculptural pieces, confirming that she was actively producing sculpture while testing Carrière from 1909 onwards (see Figure 9.15). As the quotation above demonstrates, the doctor used Bisson's artistic production to explain the ectoplasmic forms and faces, believing that Carrière was unconsciously ("ideoplastically") influenced by the sculpture.[51] Schrenck-Notzing also assumed that an "anonymous artistic intelligence" shaped the ectoplasm,[52] writing that "the aesthetic impulse towards formation and spatial expression corresponds to the fundamental tendency of nature, which ever produces new forms and shapes, while bearing within itself its own laws and conditions."[53] The reference to the "aesthetic impulse" reflects the popular understanding of Bergson's élan vital and creative evolution as it was being taken up by scientists, artists, and art historians at the *début de siècle*.[54] The German doctor continues with art-oriented metaphors to explain the variety of hands emerging from the thick white plasm: "The whole thing recalled a white block of marble, from which only the profiles of fingers and hand emerged, while the interstices between the fingers were filled with the mass."[55] This passage reminds me of another French sculptor working at the same time, Auguste Rodin, specifically his celebrated *The Hand of God* (1896–1903), a rough-hewn marble base out of which oversized hands mould smooth bodies from the stone, a work significant to emergent Modernism at the time (see Figure 9.20). Art historians refer to the unfinished aesthetic of Rodin's art with the term *non-finito*. In its Modernist sense, *non-finito* reflects the purposely incomplete aesthetic that Rodin cultivated in order to evoke a sense of becoming, the endless possibility of artistic forms.[56] Schrenck-Notzing applied the aesthetic of *non-finito* to rationalize ectoplasm's endless production of forms, the thirty hand shapes, that he was seeing on his photographic prints.

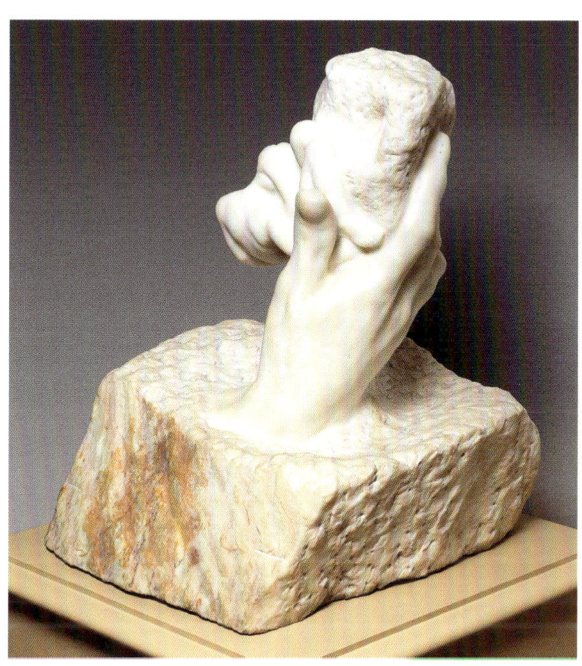

Fig. 9.20. Auguste Rodin, ***The Hand of God***, 1896–1902, c. 1907. Marble, 73.6 x 58.4 x 64.1 cm. Gift of Edward D. Adams, 1908 (08.210). Courtesy of The Metropolitan Museum of Art, New York City and Art Resource, NYC.

Bisson and Schrenck-Notzing lived in the two most important European centres of early twentieth century avant-garde art, Paris and Munich, respectively. It cannot have been a coincidence that both employed artistic metaphors around creation that were emerging in Modernist art. Their scientific photographs were created using similar pictorial codes and at the exact moment that early Modernist artists such as Auguste Rodin and Eugène Carrière, as well as the next generation of biomorphic abstract artists, were experimenting with the aesthetic of incompleteness and fragmentation to signify the unbounded creativity of the unconscious mind. It is especially significant that these cities were the two centres of the emergent style of biomorphic Modernism that featured abstract, organic-shaped forms, as seen in the work of Franz Marc and Wassily Kandinsky in Munich and of František Kupka (who was himself a medium) in Paris, as well as in the work of Hans Arp, who worked and exhibited in both cities.[57] In its shape-shifting quality ectoplasm is characterized as a prima matter with endless creative possibilities, which made it interesting to scientists and artists alike at the turn of the century.

Bisson's and Schrenck-Notzing's dramatic photographs of Eva Carrière and other mediums attracted attention between the two world wars, including that of German writer Thomas Mann, who joined the séances in Munich and wrote about them in his celebrated novel *The Magic Mountain*.[58] But it was attention from the new media pioneer László Moholy-Nagy that contributed to the dissemination of ectoplasmic photographs within Modernist art circles. Moholy-Nagy included thirteen photographs from Schrenck-Notzing's estate in the *Film und Foto* (*FIFO*) exhibition in Stuttgart in 1929.[59] Widely regarded as the first important exhibition of photographic Modernism, and one of the most significant photographic exhibitions of the twentieth century, *FIFO* contributed to the dissemination of Moholy-Nagy's "new vision" for art photography.[60] In Room 1 of *FIFO*, curated by Moholy-Nagy as the introductory exhibition space of this enormous show, Schrenck-Notzing's photographs hung alongside hundreds of applied photographs from the fields of criminology, anthropology, medicine, industry, and journalism as exemplars for fine art photography. In collaboration with Gabriele von Schrenck-Notzing, a respected aviator and the doctor's widow, Moholy-Nagy chose five photographs of medium Willy Schneider (1921–22), and eight photographs of Stanisława Tomczyk (1912–13), rendering ectoplasm as a suspended mass of glowing fibres.[61] Moholy-Nagy encouraged the objective and functional use of the camera, and, by displaying scientific images as models for fine art photography, he contributed to a Modernist aesthetic that dominated the middle decades of the twentieth century.

Art historian Oliver Botar explains that one of Moholy-Nagy's goals was to jettison the blurring and softening effects of the Pictorialist style of art photography, supporting instead the full use of the camera's technical capabilities in the making of photographic art.[62] Schrenck-Notzing's pseudo-scientific photographs realized qualities that the artist advocated, including strong chiaroscuro effects, close-up details, odd angles, and cropped images, echoing some aspects of the many applied photographs on display. Moholy-Nagy might well have known these photographs through popular press reviews, and given his biocentric views it makes sense that he would have been curious about images documenting a vitalistic protoplasm in a style congruent with Modernism.[63] As Bisson and Schrenck-Notzing set up their laboratories and turned to experimental methodologies to test materializations, they updated Victorian science, and like Moholy-Nagy's art photographs they jettisoned Victorian Pictorialist photographic codes common in spirit photographs, for a more objective, straightforward "new vision."

"Sculptural Protoplasm"
—Alfred Barr describing Hans Arp's sculpture, 1936.[64]

Some of the most important abstract artists, Moholy-Nagy, Hans Arp (see Figure 9.21), Wassily Kandinsky, Franz Marc, František Kupka, Barbara Hepworth, and Henry Moore, among many others, have been described as working in a "biomorphic" Modernist style, for which art historians have sketched a complex intellectual milieu that references vitalistic biology, progressive evolutionary theory, and holistic or unitary (monistic) theories of humanity as part of nature.[65] As noted, biomorphic abstract art developed in the early twentieth century between the centres of Paris and Munich, and visually echoed the "forms of cells, organelles and fetuses," figuring conceptions of "life," "origins," and "nature."[66] Typically, these artists used irregular, curvilinear lines to symbolize elements of growth and movement. Biomorphic artists were interested in cell structures, amoebae, and mitosis in line with the rise of biological science and high-quality photomicrographic imagery, available beginning in the mid-nineteenth century but proliferating during the 1920s.[67] As Oliver Botar has noted, biomorphic artists, more often than not, held a "biocentric" worldview, a nature-centric way of regarding the world informed by the relatively new science of biology, and neo-Romantic notions of our place within nature and the evolutionary process.[68] Science historian Robert Brain has also recognized the widespread interest in scientific biomorphic forms reflecting generative forces, and suggests that Schrenck-Notzing's photographs of materializations were of interest to scientists and artists because they offered close-up views of masses of exteriorized vitalistic protoplasm: "Ectoplasm became a special instance of protoplasmic investigation, and therefore of Life in its most fundamental operations, yet within supernormal settings."[69] Dr. Geley, immersed in this environment, also presented his ectoplasmic photographs as informative about the beginning of evolutionary life: "Ectoplasm would thus be able to give us the key to human and animal biology such as the origin of the species. It would really offer in itself the explanation of the mysteries of life."[70] In the period between the two world wars, psychical scientists and biomorphic Modernist artists were interested in revealing the structures of nature in their visualizations, and we can see common biomorphic forms in scientific images and high art.

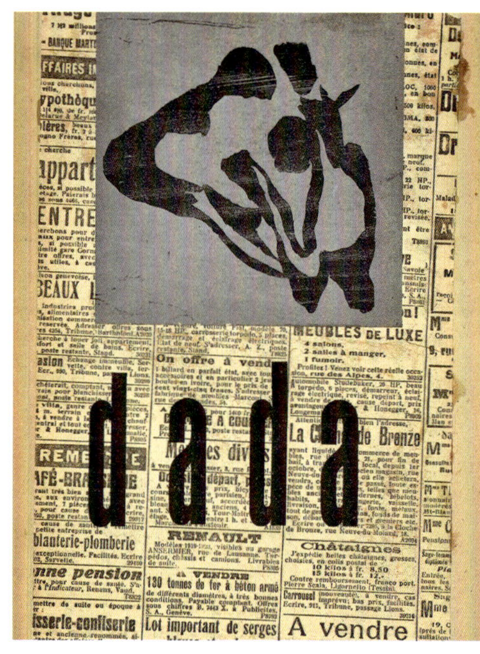

Fig. 9.21. Jean Hans Arp, ***Dada 4–5***. Bois gravé et collage, Zurich, 1919. Bibliothèque des musées de Strasbourg, photograph by Mathieu Bertola. Licensed under the Creative Commons Attribution—Share Alike 4.0 International licence.

In 1936, Museum of Modern Art curator Alfred Barr acknowledged this tendency toward biological forms in high art when he described Hans Arp's *Human*

Concretion as "a kind of sculptural protoplasm, half organic, half the water worn white stone," echoing Schrenck-Notzing's analogy of teleplasm as a marble sculpting material. Barr's choice of cellular terminology, the "silhouette of the amoeba," referencing Arp's biological forms, highlighted the widespread notion at the time that protoplasm was a signifier of generative forces.[71] In his influential catalogue, *Cubism and Abstract Art*, Barr pointed to Munich as one of the important sites of biomorphic abstract art in 1912, referring to the coalescence of the innovative Modernist art group Der Blaue Reiter (The Blue Rider) with two exhibitions, one of which included Arp's graphic art.[72] As we have seen, concomitantly, Munich was both an important site of the new style of visualizing externalized protoplasmic ectoplasm and as Botar explains, the place where the popular scientific writer and central figure of German *Biozentrik*, Raoul Heinrich Francé, established his Munich Biological Institute.[73] Juliette Bisson and Eva Carrière travelled from Paris to Munich in the summer of 1912 to continue their work photographing protoplasmic excretions in Schrenck-Notzing's well-outfitted laboratory. Coinciding with the publication of their books on materializations in 1914, reviewed in popular journals such as *Neues Wiener Tagblatt* (30 December 1913), *Le Matin* (January 1914), and *Le Monde illustré* (February 1914), there was increasing curiosity among the public about protoplasm. This was exemplified by Moholy Nagy including Schrenck Notzing's photographs in the 1929 *FIFO* exhibition of photographic Modernism, and T.G. Hamilton's enthusiasm to display his illustrations in 1930 at the Winnipeg Winter Club, and the press's reception to them.[74]

Artists continue to be interested in scientific theories to illuminate ectoplasmic research. The manner in which Hamilton used physicist Oliver Lodge's etheric universe to explain aspects of the vital force has been taken up by contemporary artists.[75] Chris Dorosz is fascinated with *fin-de-siècle* occult theories that contested the notion that matter is solid. Referencing the "Vibratory Universe," he explains that "science now tells us that reality includes matter we cannot see, but which is critical to how the visible world works. Full reality exists and fluctuates according to unknown, even supernatural rhythms which are always shifting around you."[76]

His conception of a fluctuating universe through which trance personalities might travel recapitulates earlier theories such as Wilhelm Ostwald's energeticism, the notion that matter consists of congealed energy, and Camille Flammarion's dynamic force. In the concept sketch Dorosz uses occult colour theory based on principles of correspondences to communicate the psychic energies he felt when he visited the Hamilton's séance room (see Figure 0.10).

Ectoplasmic Selfies[77]

After the Second World War, while biomorphic Modernism continued as a style of art making, with the ascendancy of physics as the paradigmatic field of science, biocentric and monistic attitudes toward a unitary cosmos fell away. Within parapsychology, from the 1940s, psychical researchers and mediums moved away from scientific testing of ectoplasm in favour of studying extra-sensory perception and psychokinesis.[78] So rare are ectoplasmic materializations today that Shannon Taggart travelled to Basel in 2018 to witness Kai Muegge, one of the few mediums still performing ectoplasmic excretions (see Figure 9.22). Using digital technology, Taggart has made and exhibited one of the only documentary films of an ectoplasmic hand emerging from the mouth of the medium by combining a successive series of still images taken at a séance.[79]

Contemporary artists are drawn to the Hamilton archival photographs for a wide range of reasons, including the high quality aesthetics of the analogue prints, a fascination with alternative science and forgotten history, as well as the performance of twentieth-century gender norms revealed in the staged photographs. Grace A. Williams notes that ectoplasm was mostly carried out by women excreting a substance from bodily orifices, and that few male mediums extruded the substance. In her film *Spiritual Ectoplasm* (2011), Williams animated a 1916–18 still photograph of Eva Carrière, with a ropy, white paste commenting that psychical researchers treated mediums like supernatural photographic printers, especially in the way that miniature faces emerged from the light-sensitive ectoplasm (see Figures 9.23 and 9.24).[80]

Fig. 9.22. Shannon Taggart, ***Medium Kai Muegge Emits an Ectoplasmic Hand***, Basel Switzerland, 2018. Digital still image, 12.7 x 20.3 cm. Courtesy of the artist.

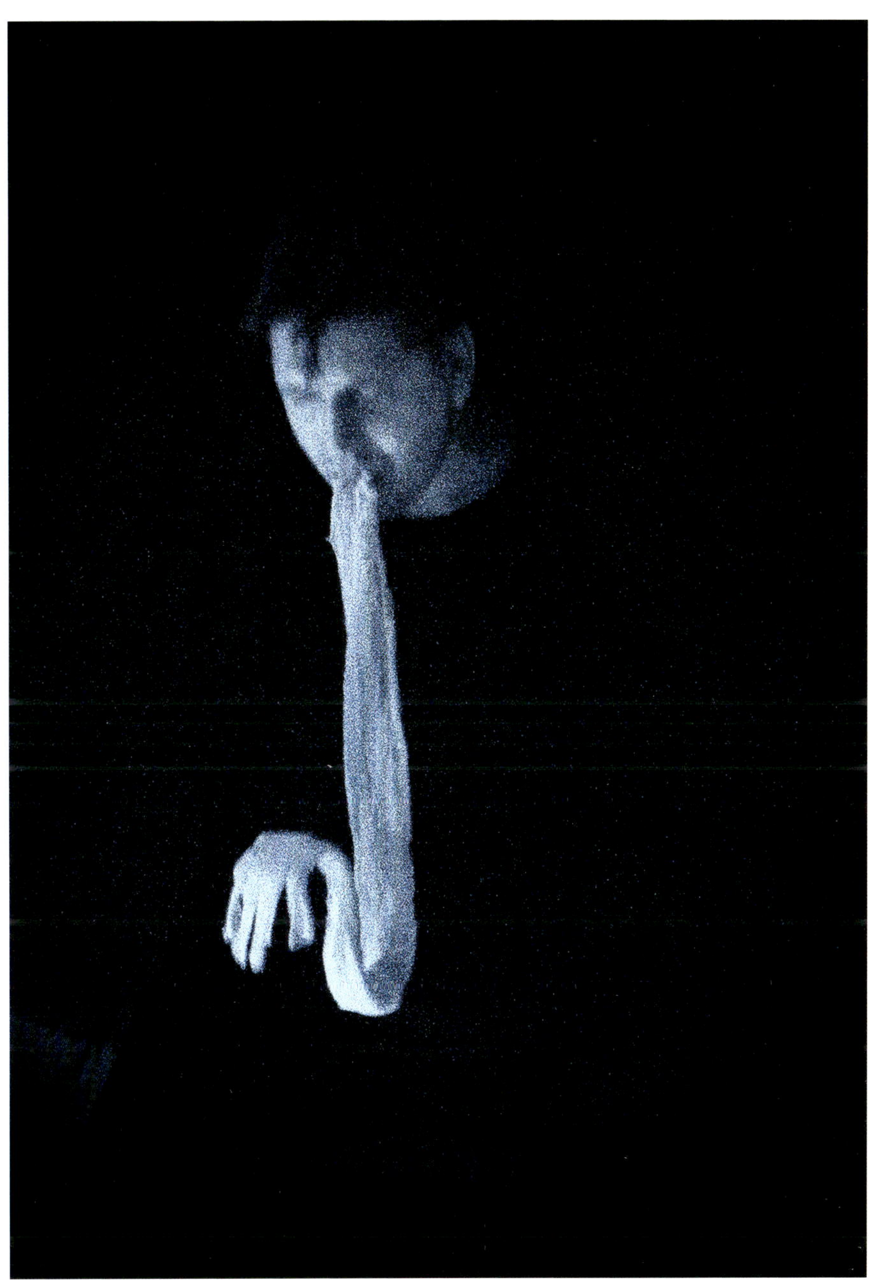

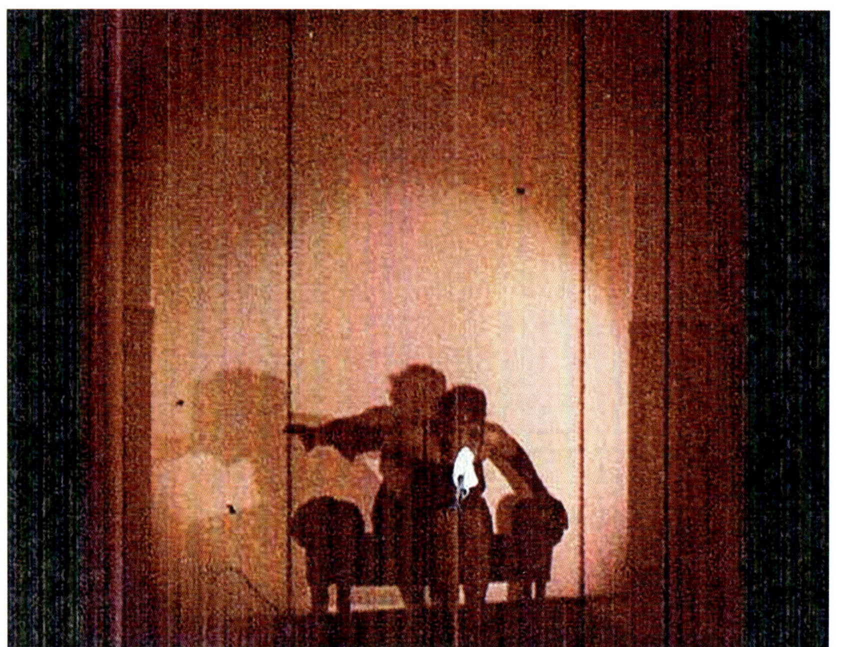

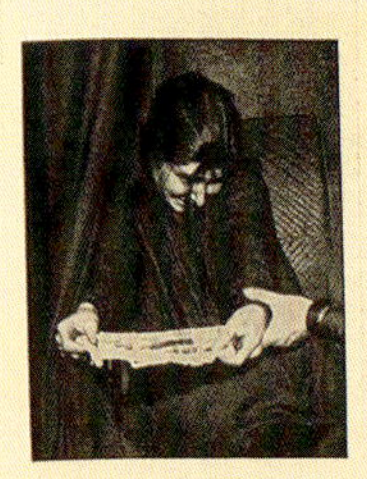

Fig. 201. Teleplasm emerging from the hands.

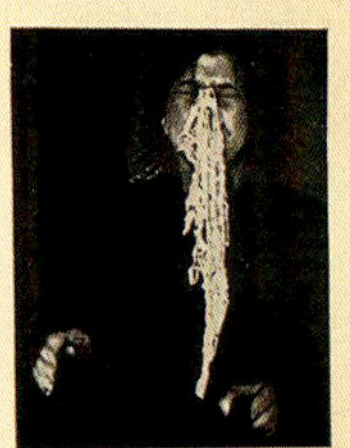

Fig. 202. Emergence of the substance from mouth and nose.

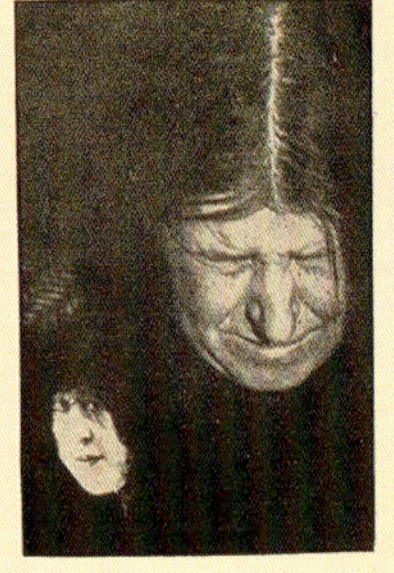

Fig. 203. Face developed from a nebulous mass at the medium's right shoulder. Lips modelled in an otherwise flat face.

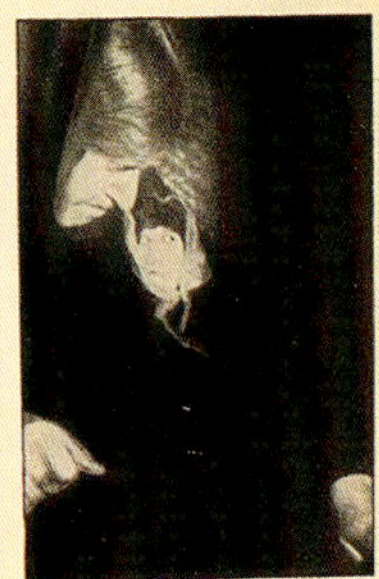

Fig. 204. Face and veil seen to develop from a cloud.

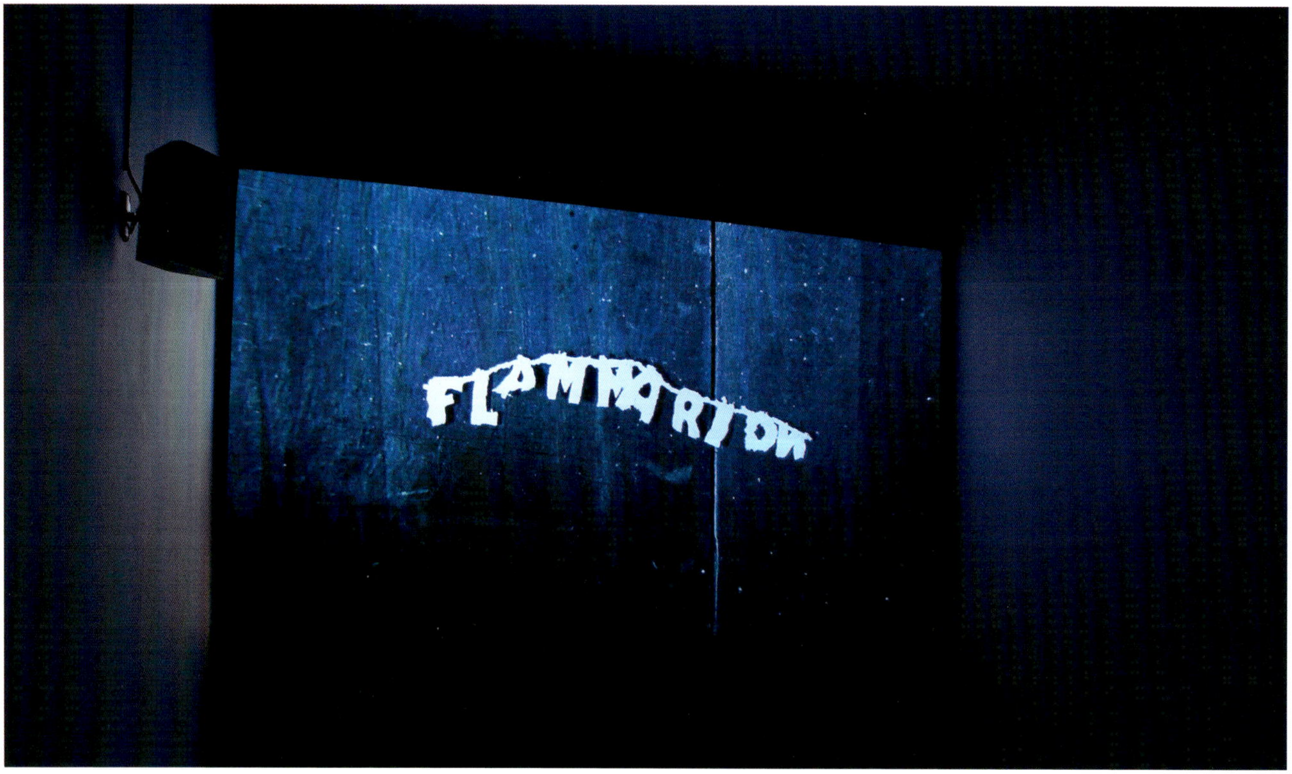

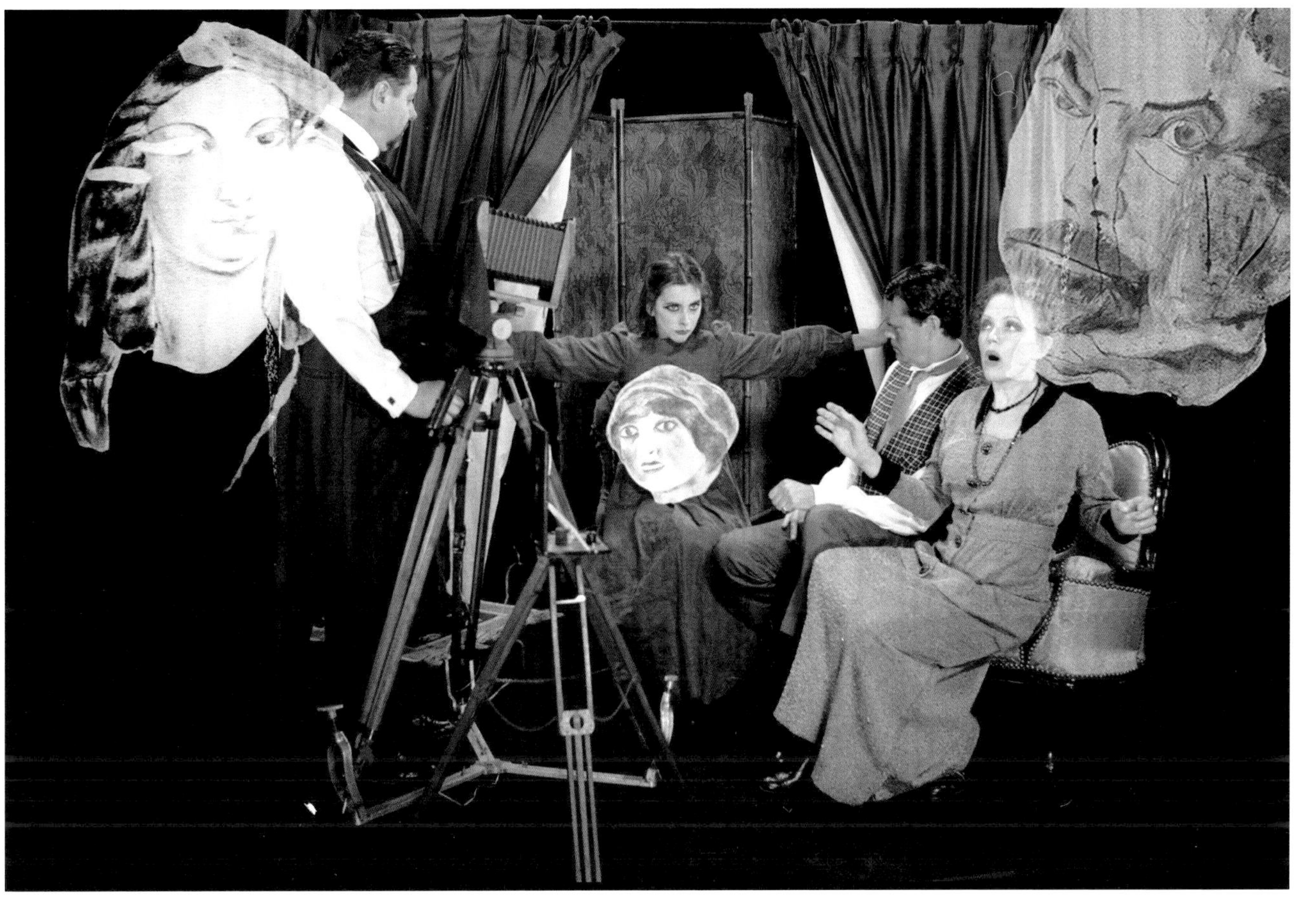

Fig. 9.23. *Left Upper Left*, Grace A. Williams, ***Spiritual Ectoplasm***, 2011. Still shot, hand-tinted film, colour, sound, 1m, 59s. Courtesy of the artist.

Fig. 9.24. *Left Upper Right*, Gustave Geley and Juliette Bisson, ***Eva Carrière***, 1918, from ***Phenomena of Materialisation,*** by Schrenck-Notzing (1920). UMASC, Rare Book Room.

Fig. 9.25. *Left Below*, Susan MacWilliam, installation view of ***F-L-A-M-M-A-R-I-O-N, REMOTE VIEWING.*** Northern Ireland Pavilion at the 53rd Venice Biennale, 2009. Stereo, colour, sound, 17m, 13s. Photograph by Prudence Cuming, © The British Council. Courtesy of the artist.

Fig. 9.26. *Above*, Zoe Beloff, ***The Ideoplastic Materializations of Eva C,*** 2004. Still shot from a Four-Channel Stereoscopic Surround Sound Installation, black and white, sound 2m 41s. Courtesy of the artist.

A flair for exteriorizing "solid" ectoplasm meant that Eva Carrière was one of the most sought-after mediums in the early twentieth century, encouraging scientists to visit Bisson's Paris studio.[81] Zoe Beloff's installation (2004) recreates the cabinet on rue Victor Hugo by projecting life-size materializations into the viewer's space using 3D technology, based on Victorian stereoscopy. Beloff animates the most controversial materializations, the series from 1912 where magazine illustrations appeared in the ectoplasm (see Figure 9.26). When Bisson's and Schrenck-Notzing's books were published, the images were immediately recognized as coming from 1912 copies of the French newspaper *Le Miroir*, leading to widespread ridicule.[82] Schrenck-Notzing did not buckle under these accusations, turning to ideoplastic explanations that the embedded images were memories from reading *Le Miroir* that had transferred to Carrière's ectoplasm.

In *Performing Science and the Virtual*, Sue-Ellen Case notes that Modern theatre and the experimental scientific laboratory developed at the same time, sharing notions of controlled spaces, costumes, and accepted codes of behaviour.[83] Beloff's installation calls attention to the theatre of the séance room by comparing the uncanny visual material that Eva Carrière generated with the equally nonsensical scientific babble by Schrenck-Notzing, neither of which makes sense to the twenty-first-century viewer. Similarly, Susan MacWilliam's staged performance *F-L-A-M-M-A-R-I-O-N* includes the written records from a 1931 séance that T.G. Hamilton conducted in which a new type of shaped ectoplasm was generated, spelling out the name of the famous astronomer and psychical researcher Camille Flammarion (see Figures 9.25, 5.6 and 5.7).[84] Tony Oursler's wondrous film *Imponderable* (2016) artistically recreates important moments in the history of psychical research using scientific "inscriptions," including written records and photographs from the archives, all produced to validate psychical data and all jettisoned by mainstream science after the Second World War. When all these data are represented in these dynamic art installations, it seems clear that both mediums and scientists were "performing" their designated roles in the séance room.[85] Historian Neil Matheson points out that some of the theatrical poses in ectoplasmic photographs were staged especially for the camera and thus went beyond religious or social functions.[86] Margaret Hamilton Bach recalled a particular dramatic séance in Winnipeg: "On two occasions Mrs. Marshall while in the trance state was invaded by what was obviously an evil influence. The entities who were in charge were concerned and said 'Bring Mrs. Marshall out of her trance immediately and leave your room quickly and do not turn on the light yet, just the red light.' Like an insane person who has a bad epileptic seizure she became very violent and physically almost uncontrollable. You could sense the evil. It took three men to subdue her."[87] No doubt the Hamiltons and their friends participated in many extraordinary scenes in the small bedroom on the second floor of their home where the séances took place.

We have seen that the most sought-after mediums in the early twentieth century were women who performed ectoplasmic excretions, and contemporary artists have taken on the role of the medium to point out their objectification and the invasive behaviour that they endured in the name of science.[88] In North America, psychical research was carried out almost exclusively by settlers such as the Hamiltons, and their friends, who had the status and funds to support years of experimentation, often using unpaid mediums. Erika DeFreitas "unsettles these settlers" by posing as the medium, but instead of exteriorizing "white" organic fluff from her mouth, she extrudes colourful, hand-crocheted doilies made by her Guyanese grandmother and mother (see Figure 9.29). DeFreitas was attracted to the Hamilton archive because of the rituals of bereavement evident in the photographs.[89] By trading elaborate hand-crafted doilies for ectoplasm, she also calls attention to the labour involved in producing ectoplasm, whether one believes that it is real or fake, and she notes how the substance, whether ectoplasm or wool doily, silences the sitter. Most séances document that it was painful for mediums to extrude ectoplasm, and there are frequent comparisons to childbirth. The pain and pressure the medium endured is symbolized in Megan Moore's film *Ectoplasms* (2019) through the degenerative properties of the plasm as it is burned with chemicals, melting it before our eyes (see Figure 9.27).[90] Moore's deteriorating ectoplasm is in contrast to the utopian

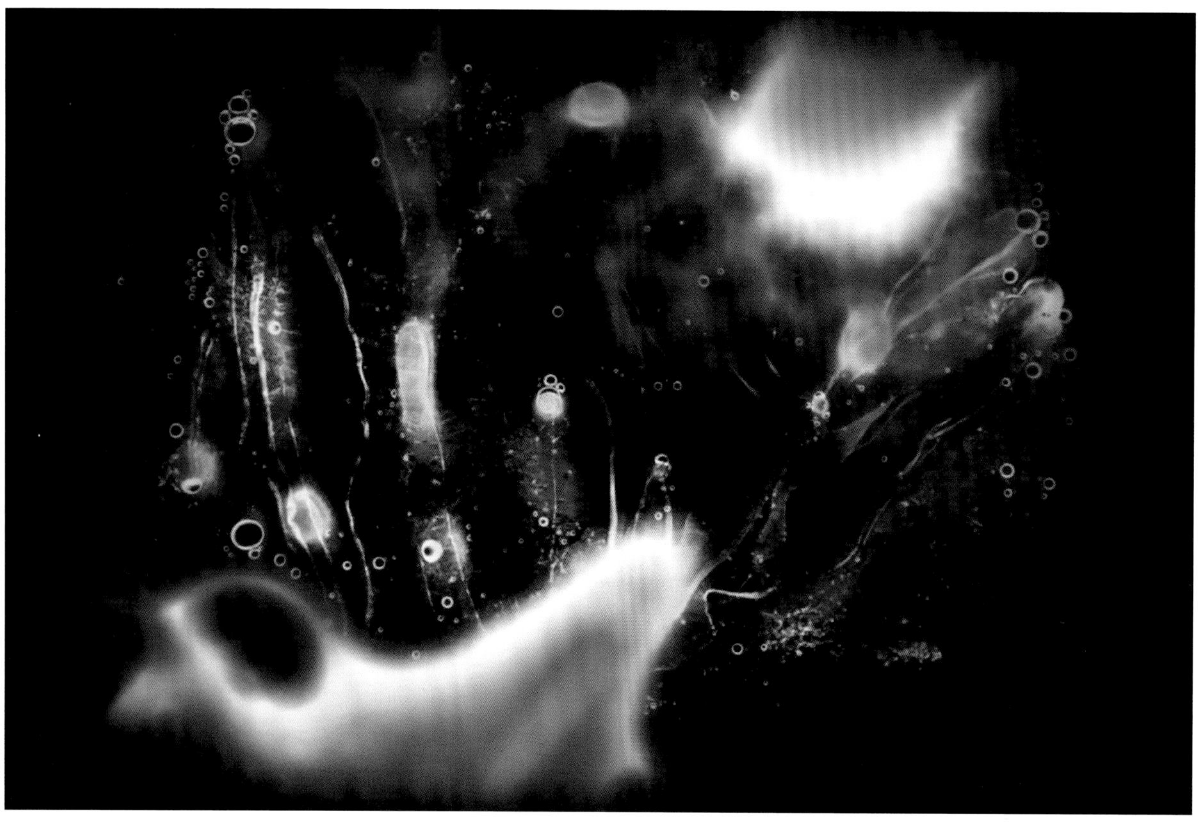

Fig. 9.27. Megan Moore, ***Ectoplasms***, 2019. Still shot, multi-channel video, colour, sound, 20m 57s. Courtesy of the artist.

attitude of Schrenck-Notzing and Geley who presented ectoplasm as reflective of the creative life force.

According to historian Esyllt W. Jones, the pandemic of 1918–19 had been nearly forgotten in the popular imagination prior to the recent pandemic. Like many of us, Teresa Burrows made the connection between the Spanish flu and COVID-19 during the first lockdown of 2020 (see Figure 9.28). Her triptych speaks directly to the surveillance and physical examination that mediums endured in the 1920s.

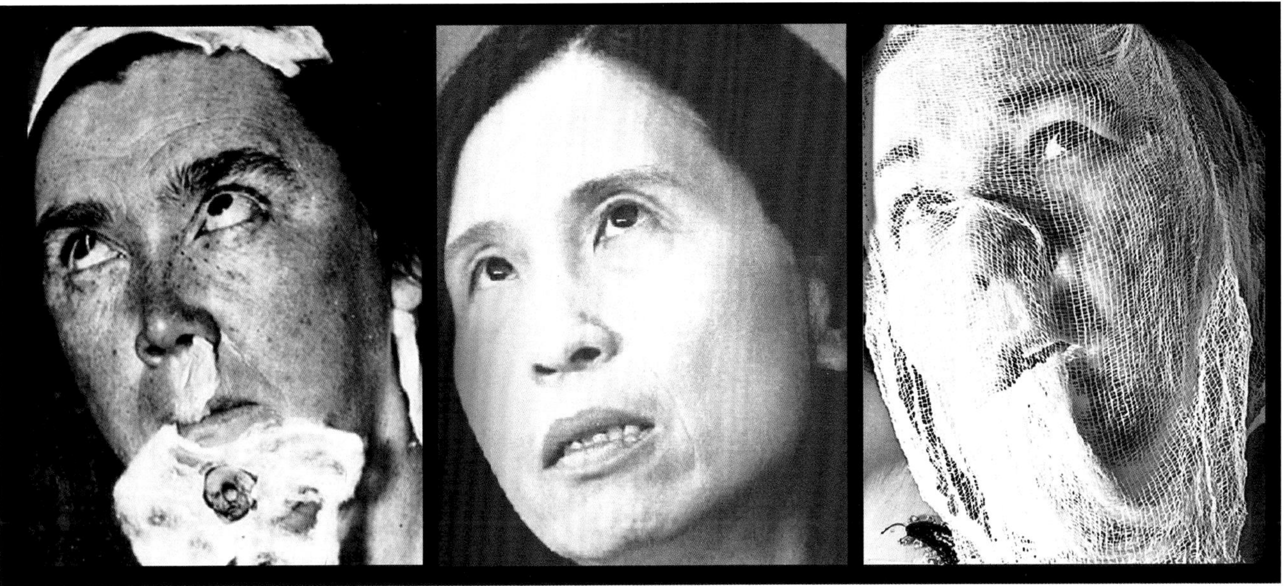

Fig. 9.28. Teresa Burrows, ***Echoes from One Century's Pandemic to Another***, 2020–2023. Digital ink prints, 12.7 x 17.7 cm. Courtesy of the artist.

Burrows also noted that such surveillance continues today, especially through the pressures of social media directed at female figures of authority such as Dr. Theresa Tam, Canada's chief public health officer during the COVID-19 pandemic.[91] In Figure 9.28, we see three grimacing faces, with their eyes rolled up, a traditional way of signifying saints, mediums and hysterics, each scrutinized through technology of the lens; the Hamiltons' medium Mary Marshall, Dr. Tam, and the artist herself.

T.G. Hamilton characterized his ectoplasmic photographs as "monstrously extraordinary," and artists are drawn to the contradiction of ectoplasmic constructions as simultaneously grotesque and wondrous.[92] Estelle Chaigne had dreamed of visiting Winnipeg since 2011 when she walked into the exhibition *My Winnipeg*

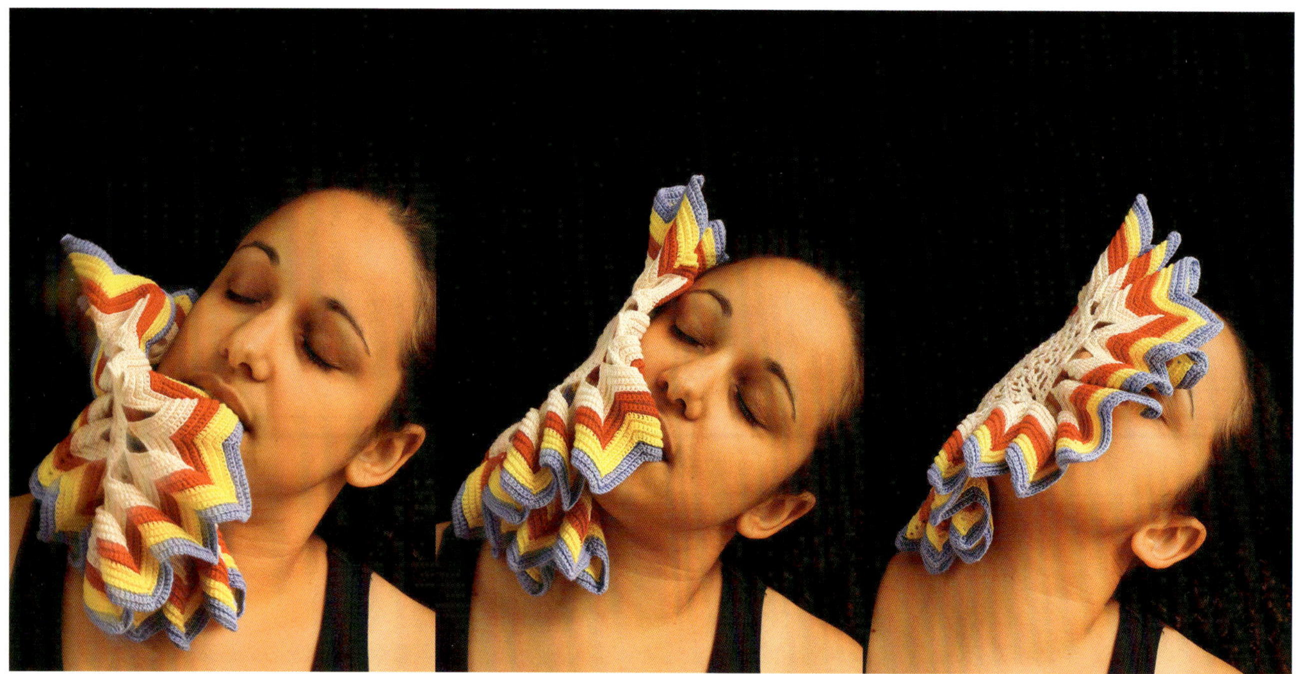

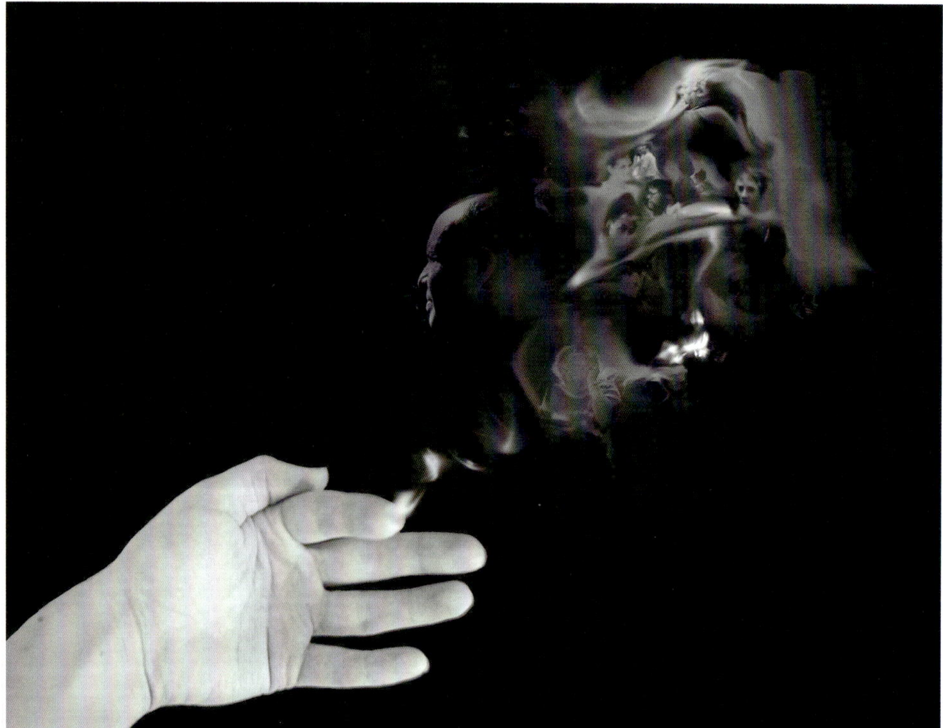

Fig. 9.29. *Above*. Erika DeFreitas, ***A Teleplasmic Study with Doilies (Angie No. 1 a, b, c)***, 2010–2023. Archival inkjet prints, 60.9 x 91.4 cm. Courtesy of the artist.

Fig. 9.30. *Lower Left*, Grace A. Williams, ***Fingertip Forgeries 1***, 2013. Fine art giclée on Hahnemühle photo rag paper, 41.9 x 29.5 cm. Courtesy of the artist.

at La Maison rouge in Paris and saw Guy Maddin's film. In response she designed temporary tattoos of iconic ectoplasmic photographs, including those by Bisson, Schrenck-Notzing, and Hamilton, and applied them to the backs of performers, referencing the episodes of dermographia (automatic skin writing) that appeared on the bodies of "hysterical" women in Dr. Jean-Martin Charcot's laboratory at the Saltpêtrièrie Hospital. Like Moore and Williams, Chaigne calls attention to the fact that mediums and hysterics were similarly pathologized by medical doctors in the late nineteenth century (see Figure 9.32).[93]

Albert von Schrenck-Notzing's and Alfred Barr's analogies of "protoplasmic sculpture," to explore the creative possibilities of protoplasm, continue in contemporary art. Grace A. Williams references ectoplasm as a "form of alternative sculpting" in *Fingertip Forgeries*, at the same time acknowledging the accusations of forgery that plagued psychical research (see Figure 9.30 and 0.7). Paul Robles describes his origami paper cut-out as "dream vomits," ideoplastic embodiments of his unconscious mind. *Murmurations (Clumps)* grew organically on his studio wall over the duration of COVID-19, like a magnificent cluster of colourful amoeba cells (see Figure 9.31). Embedded in the paper cut-outs are figurative motifs significant to Robles, including monkeys, insects, birds, and even hands. Recalling his Catholic grandmother's ghost stories, *Murmurations (Clumps)* reveal messages and stories like the miniature faces that developed inside Hamilton's light-sensitive ectoplasm, as illustrated in the Conan Doyle photograph (see Figure 2.11). In Tony Oursler's *Dust*, eyes, mouths, and hands peek out of a 3D animated cloud-like structure, even emitting a "raspy" voice, combining the atmosphere of a séance and ectoplasmic miniature face forms in one dynamic structure.[94]

Since Bisson mastered the flash and ostensibly took the first photograph of the strange substance in 1909, the question of what ectoplasm consists of dogged scientists, with frequent descriptions of common materials, including cotton wool. Lacey Pripić Hedtke, Maria Molteni, Jodie Mack, and Teresa Burrows have played with the home crafted appearance of ectoplasm in their art, as mentioned above and seen in Figures 9.1, 9.2 and 9.28. Photographer Sarah Hodges-Kolisnyk,

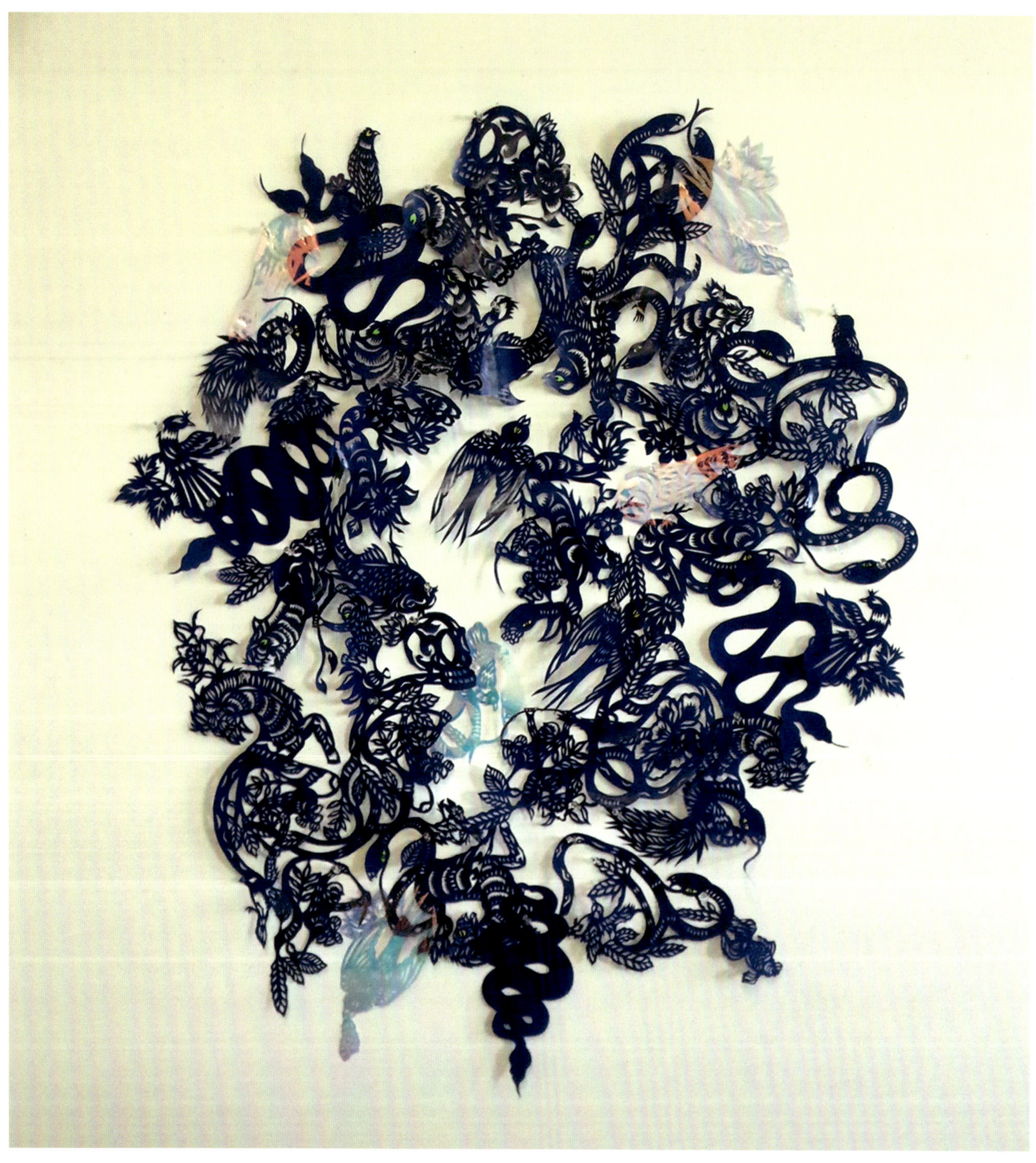

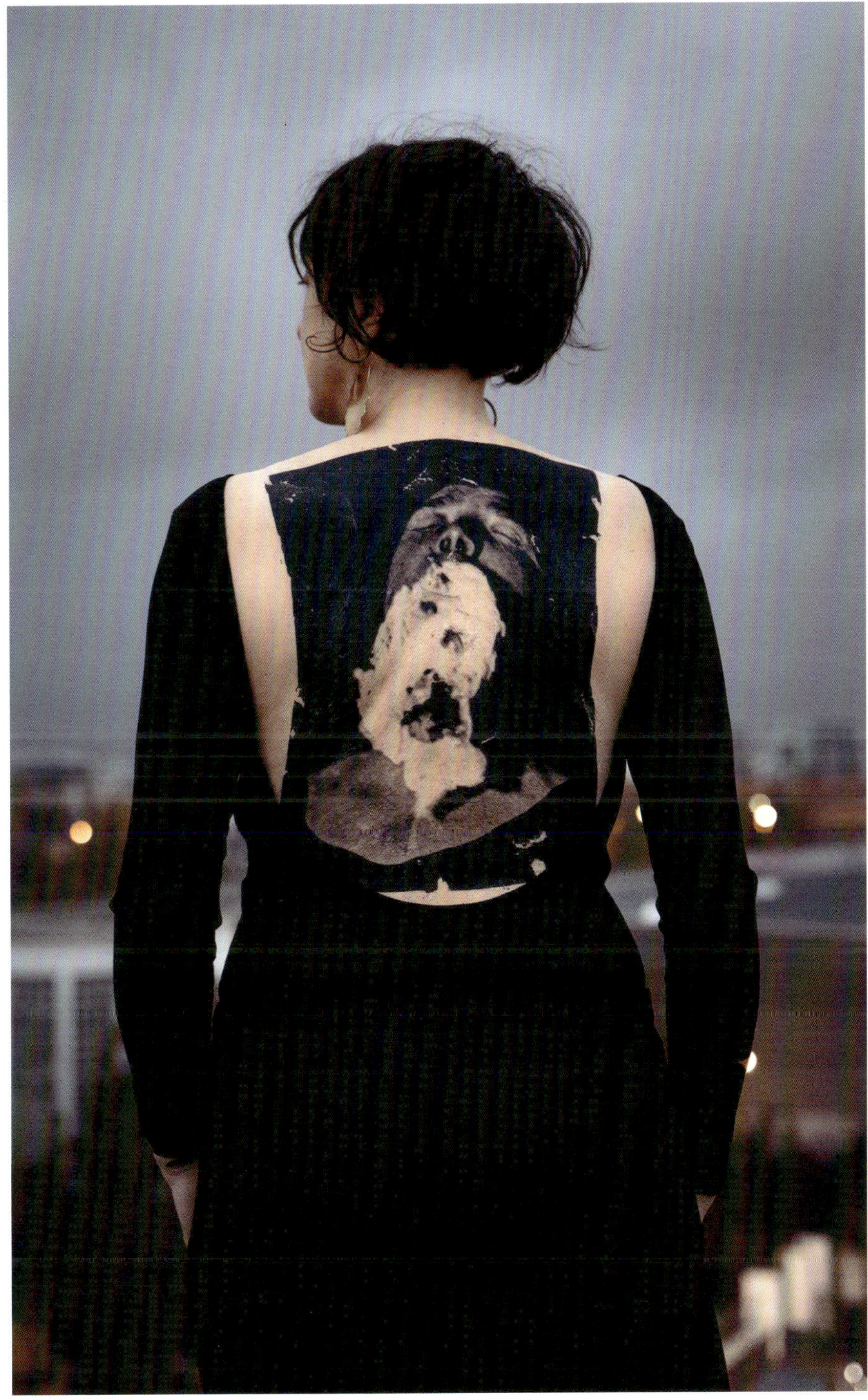

Fig. 9.31. *Left,* Paul Robles, ***Murmurations (Clumps)***, 2022–ongoing. Origami paper. 152.4 x 121.9 cm. Courtesy of the artist.

Fig. 9.32. *Right,* Estelle Chaigne, ***Surfaces Sensibles***, 2022. Transfer print on skin with photographic paper and flash powder. Courtesy of the artist.

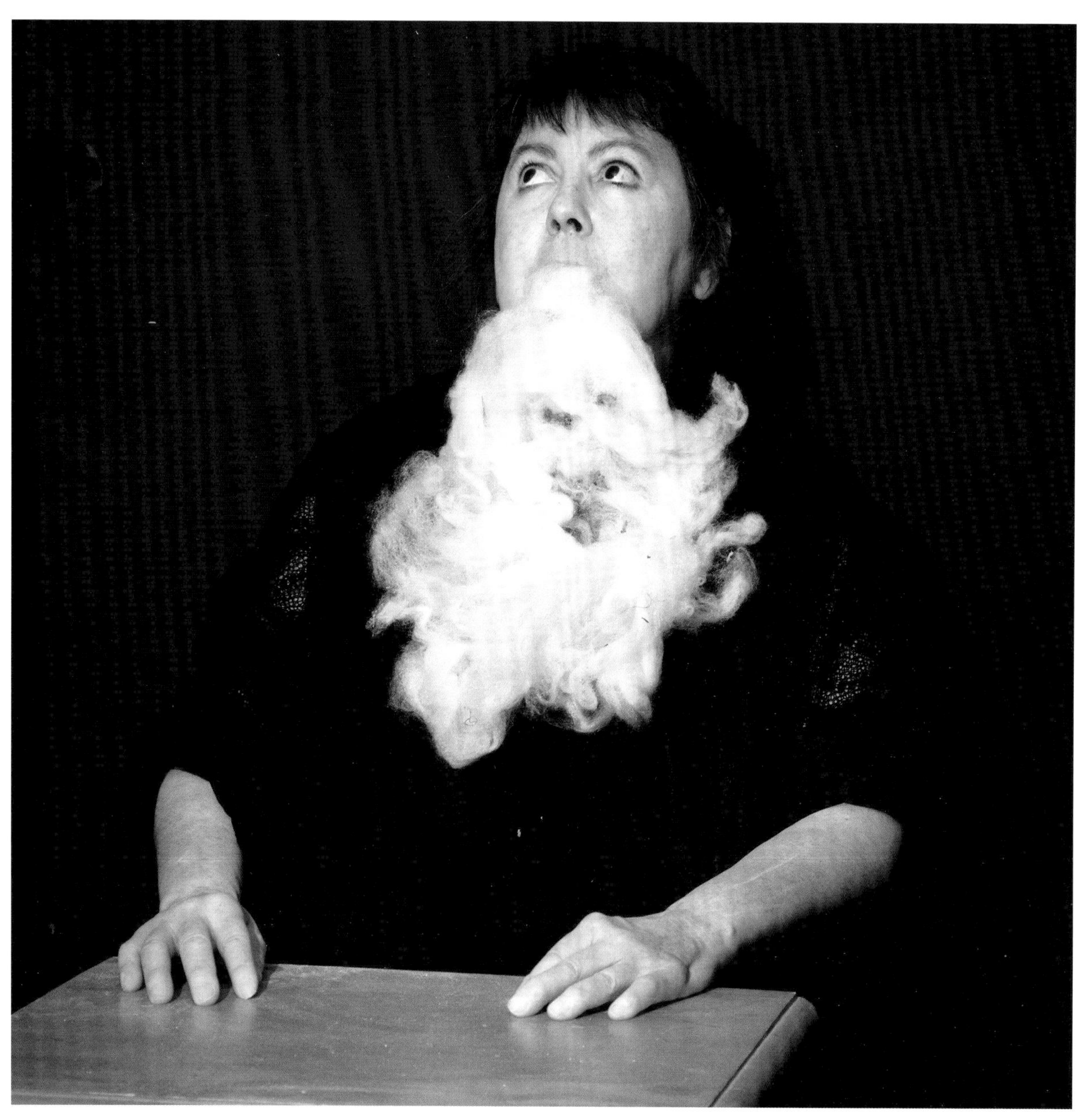

Fig. 9.33. Sarah Hodges-Kolisnyk, ***Ectoplasmic Materialization with Lily Despic***, 2021. Recreation shot with a mid-century large format camera, 20.3 x 25.4 cm. Courtesy of the artist.

investigating analogue photography and acknowledging the early application of new technologies in occulture, created a series of research-oriented photographs made with a 1930 large-plate camera, utilizing cotton batting and plaster of Paris to form the ectoplasm (see Figure 9.33). The resulting prints, made with Modernist principles, come close at least in style to creating the uncanny, dramatic quality of the Hamilton images.

Hamilton's photographs have had two periods when they received international attention: the first, during his lifetime as part of international psychical research, shown in lantern slide lectures around the world, and the second period after the images were digitized and directly inspired artists. These contemporary responses will be brought together for the first time in *The Undead Archive* exhibition in September 2023 in Winnipeg, featuring art based on the Hamilton Family Fonds.[95] Humour, curiosity, the uncanny, and even disgust have attracted us to this rare archive of monstrously extraordinary, pseudo-scientific photographs. In modelling his illustrations on those of Bisson and Schrenck-Notzing, T. G. Hamilton ended up paralleling the "new vision" emerging in Europe and North America in the early twentieth century, a photographic style that continues to resonate with twenty-first-century audiences.

NOTES

1 Peter H. Aykroyd, *A History of Ghosts: The True Story of Séances, Mediums, Ghosts and Ghostbusters* (New York: Rodale Books, 2009). Some of the Aykroyd family papers are housed at UMASC. See Dan Aykroyd's introduction about the family's interest in Spiritualism in Shannon Taggart, *Séance* (Somerset, UK: Fulgur Press, 2019), 9. Also the luminous, vaporous cartoon Casper the Friendly Ghost, created in 1939 by Seymour Reit and Joe Orioloby; see "Obituary: Seymour Reit," *Guardian* [London], 24 December 2001, https://www.theguardian.com/news/2001/dec/24/guardianobituaries.books (accessed 21 August 2020). Marina Warner comments that ectoplasm has ended up as a commodity in joke shops. Marina Warner, "Ethereal Body: The Quest for Ectoplasm: Seeing is believing," *Cabinet Magazine* 12, 2003, dates the term to 1883, n.p. https://www.cabinetmagazine.org/issues/12/warner.php.

2 Lacey Pripić Hedtke and Maria Molteni, *Ectoplasm Selfies: DIY Ritual in the Age of Social Mediums*, 2017, play with the popularity of social media selfies, and the fact that ectoplasm is a bodily excretion and thus expels a DNA portrait.

3 Harry Houdini, *A Magician among the Spirits* (New York: Harper and Brothers, 1924), 179, https://archive.org/details/1924HoudiniAMagicianAmongTheSpirits/page/n195/mode/2up?q=Schrenck. On ectoplasm, see Karen R. Beckman, *Vanishing Women: Magic, Film and Feminism* (Durham, NC: Duke University Press, 2003), 78–92.

4 The ghost of Winnipeg Walter says "I am going to give you something funny. . . . A small picture to keep you in good humour." There is a reference to the appearance of the hand as "a joke" by Walter in a letter to Mrs. W. M. Cannon, 15 Feb, 1930, UMASC, HFF, MSS 14, T.G.H. Correspondence Outgoing 1924-30, Box 4, Folder 5, and it is noted as a 'joke" in the H.A.V. Green photo album, UMASC, MSS 439, A2012-110, no. 14. The reference to "Winnipeg Walter," is to Dr. Crandon, no date, UMASC, HFF, MSS 14, T.G.H. Correspondence Outgoing 1931-34, Box 5, Folder 1. T.G. Hamilton, *Intention and Survival: Psychical Research Studies and the Bearing of Intentional Actions by Trance Personalities on the Problem of Human Survival*, ed. J.D. Hamilton (Toronto: Macmillan, 1942).

5 The term "ectoplasm" was adopted from biology to mean cellular plasm exteriorized from the body, reflecting developments in microbiology and the interest in vitalism. On the exhibition T.G. Hamilton to J.G. Grant, 6 May 1930, UMASC, HFF, MSS 14, T.G.H. Correspondence Outgoing, Box 4, Folder 5. UMASC, HFF, MSS 14, British Medical Association, Winnipeg, Box 1, Folder 12.

6 T.G. Hamilton, "Milestones in Psychical Research," UMASC, HFF, MSS 14, British Medical Association, Winnipeg, Box 1, Folder 12, 8.

7 Richard E. Bennett, "Interview with Margaret Hamilton Bach," 26 November 1980, UMASC, HFF, Box 3, Folder 9, 27, and Margaret Hamilton Bach, "First Archival Symposium," 13 August,1979, Hand simulacrum slides 47-50 in UMASC MSS 14, HFF, M.H. Bach-Lectures, 1965,1979,1981, 1986, Box 1, Folder 15, 16, she describes the "coarse" teleplasm hand. "Pictures of Teleplasm Shown to Delegates," *Winnipeg Free Press*, 28 August 1930. Also see "Psychic Expert Shows Pictures of Experiments," *Winnipeg Tribune*, 28 August 1930. According to this reporter, even Hamilton thought

that the photographs might be "ridiculous": "Dr. Hamilton told of his photographs taken during his experiments. Some of them he indicated might appear ridiculous, but their greatness has been sought in every possible manner." For Hamilton descriptions, see T.G.H. Outgoing Correspondence including letters to Henry Hardwicke, 16 April 1930; and H.A.V. Green's report on the British Medical Association exhibit (1930) describes the exhibition with ten large display boards (22 by 28 inches each) with ten photographs or diagrams each with explanatory notes. UMASC, HFF, MSS 14, British Medical Association, Winnipeg, 1930, Box 1, Folder 12.

8 Leigh Wilson, *Modernism and Magic: Experiments with Spiritualism, Theosophy and the Occult*, Critical Studies in Modernist Culture (Edinburgh: Edinburgh University Press, 2013), Chapter 5, especially 142–44. Marina Warner, "Ethereal Body," dates the use of the term ectoplasm in biology to 1883 (OED), and states that the substance was not a serious scientific topic after 1940. n.p. https://www.cabinetmagazine.org/issues/12/warner.php. Robert Brain, "Materialising the Medium: Ectoplasm and the Quest for Supra-Normal Biology in *Fin-de-Siècle* Science and Art," in *Vibratory Modernism*, ed. Anthony Enns and Shelley Trower (London: Palgrave Macmillan, 2013), 112–41; Justin Sausman, "'It's Organisms that Die, not Life': Henri Bergson, Psychical Research and the Contemporary Uses of Vitalism," in *The Machine and the Ghost: Technology and Spiritualism Nineteenth to Twenty First Century Art and Culture,* ed. Sas Mays and Neil Matheson (Oxford: Manchester University Press, 2016), 16–36. Felicia R. Scatcherd, *Ectoplasm as Associated with Survival* (Manchester: Two Worlds Publishing, 1926).

9 Gustave Geley, *From the Unconscious to the Conscious*, trans. Stanley de Brath (London: William Collins Sons, 1920), Book 1, Part 2, uses these comparisons to explain ectoplasm, including childbirth.

10 Conan Doyle helped set up the Society for the Study of Supernormal Pictures in 1918, which ceased operation in 1923.

11 *The Phenomena of Materialisation* catalogue of drawings and prints see *Light*, 16 January 1886, 34. M.A. Oxon (might be William Stainton Moses?), *Light*, 23 January 1886, 42-43.

12 See Serena Keshavjee, "The 'Scientization' of Spirituality," in *Seductive Surfaces: The Art of Tissot*, ed. Katharine Lochnan (New Haven, CT: Yale University Press, 1999), 213–45; and Melissa Buron and Krystyna Matyjaskiewicz, *James Tissot* (San Francisco: Fine Art Museums of San Francisco, 2020), especially Buron, "The Visions of Tissot," 66–71. Buron, in conversation with me in February 2020, noted that the mezzotint was an unusual medium in the 1880s. See Andreas Fischer, "The Reciprocal Adaptation of Optics and Phenomena: The Photographic Recoding of Materializations," in *The Perfect Medium: Photography and the Occult*, ed. Clément Chéroux et al. (New Haven, CT: Yale University Press, 2005), 172–73; Jennifer Tucker, "The Social Photographic Eye," in *Brought to Light: Photography and the Invisible 1840–1900*, ed. Corey Keller (San Francisco: San Francisco Museum of Modern Art, 2009), 37–50; primary sources in Catalogue of Drawings *Light*, 16 January 1886, 34; and a description of Tissot seeing the ghost of Kathleen Newton in M.A. Oxon (William Stainton Moses?), "Notes by the Way," *Light*, 27 February 1886, 98.

13 John S. Farmer, *Twixt Two Worlds: A Narrative of the Life and Work of William Eglinton* (London: Psychological Press, 1886). Keulemans was a trained scientific illustrator of birds, and a Spiritualist.

14 Baron von Hellenbach noted that it throws "no illumination power beyond its own area." See M.A. Oxon (William Stainton Moses?), "Notes by the Way," *Light*, 27 February 1886, 97–98; William Crookes, "The Last of 'Katie King': The Photographs

of 'Katie King,' by the Aid of the Electric Light," *Spiritualist*, 5 June 1874, 270–71; and "Mr. Crookes on Materializations," *Spiritualist*, 17 July 1874, 29.

15 Fischer, "The Reciprocal Adaptation," 172–73, explains Crookes's cameras and lighting used to take photographs in 1874. See also William Crookes, *Researches into the Phenomena of Modern Spiritualism* (Los Angeles: Austin Publishing Company, 1922), https://www.gole.ca/books/edition/Researches_into_the_Phenomena_of_Modern/PMg0AAAAMAAJ?hl=en&gbpv=1&dq=william+crookes+and+spiritualism&printsec=frontcover. William Crookes and C.G. Helleberg, *Remarkable Spirit Manifestations: Extracts from Researches in the Phenomena of Spirit (1874)*, 1891, 6, 8–9. http://iapsop.com/ssoc/1891__helleberg___remarkable_spirit_manifestations.pdf. Crookes held up his hand-made bright phosphorescent lamp, a "small corked glass bottle" with a little phosphorated oil, to see the ghost better: "Still kneeling, I passed the lamp up and down so as to illuminate Katie's whole figure and satisfy myself thoroughly that I was really looking at the veritable Katie whom I had clasped in my arms a few minutes before and not the phantasm of a disordered brain."

16 See Arthur Conan Doyle, *History of Spiritualism* (1926; reprinted, New York: Arno Press, 1975), 270. A glowing orb is illustrated on the cover of the 1975 reprint. Crookes was the first to use photography for his scientific visualizations, and he conflated the psychic force with the vital force. Both Conan Doyle and Hamilton credited him as the founder of psychical research. Forty-four photographs of the ghost Katie King were published in the *Spiritualist* in 1874.

17 Yveling Rambaud, *Force psychique* (Paris: Baschet, 1889).

18 Martin Kemp, *Visualizations: The Nature Book of Art and Science* (Berkeley: University of California Press, 2001), 4–6.

19 Sarah Willburn, "Viewing History and Fantasy through Victorian Spirit Photography," in *The Ashgate Research Companion to Nineteenth Century Spiritualism and the Occult*, ed. Tatiana Kontou and Sarah Willburn (Farnham, UK: Ashgate, 2012), 359, 363–64. Willburn makes the comparison between pictorialism and impressionism (378 ff.).

20 Serena Keshavjee, "*L'Art inconscient*": Imaging the Unconscious in Symbolist Art for the Théâtre d'art," *RACAR: Revue d'art canadienne/Canadian Art Review* 34, no. 1 (2009): 62–76, https://doi.org/10.7202/1069501ar; Serena Keshavjee, "Carrière, Rodin and the Natural Laws of Making Art," *Cantor Arts Centre Journal* 5 (2006–07): 49–60.

21 Oliver A.I. Botar, "Prolegomena to the Study of the Biomorphic Modernism: Biocentrism, László Moholy-Nagy 'New Vision' and Ernö Kallai's Bioromantik" (PhD diss., University of Toronto, 1998).

22 Richet, *Thirty Years of Psychical Research*, 619.

23 Farmer, *Twixt Two Worlds*, 164. Farmer seems to be quoting or paraphrasing Keulemans in the section explaining the plates (164–66).

24 Ibid.

25 Richet, *Thirty Years of Psychical Research*, 618, describes pseudopodal extensions; Geley, *From the Unconscious to the Conscious*.

26 The full physicality of the ghost of Katie King became suspect especially as the stories of the gullible behaviour of Crookes regarding the ghost came out. Richard Noakes, *Physics and Psychics: The Occult and the Sciences in Modern Britain* (Cambridge, UK: Cambridge University Press, 2019), 203 ff. Richet hints at the issues in *Thirty Years of Psychical Research*, 467. See also Paul Frame, "William Crookes and the Spectral Visitor," Museum of Radiation and Radioactivity, https://

www.orau.org/health-physics-museum/articles/william-crookes-spectral-visitor.html.

27 Cyril Permutt describes "supernormal photographs" during the Victorian era, the early twentieth century, and the 1980s. Cyril Permutt, *Photographing the Spirit World: Images from beyond the Spectrum* (Wellingborough, UK: Aquarian Press, 1988).

28 Thanks to Efram Sera-Shriar for discussing the style of these spirit photographs with me. See Emma Merkling, *The Media of Mediumship*, https://www.sciencemuseumgroup.org.uk/project/media-of-mediumship/ (accessed 20 September 2022). See also Jean Doyle to Lillian Hamilton, Correspondence Outgoing, 1931-56, UMASC, MSS 14, HFF, Box 5, Folder 9. For a survey of commercial studio spirit photographers, see Fred Gettings, *Ghosts in Photographs: The Extraordinary Story of Spirit Photography* (Montreal: Optimum, 1978); Clément Chéroux et al., eds., *The Perfect Medium: Photography and the Occult* (New Haven, CT: Yale University Press, 2005); Arthur Conan Doyle, *The Case for Spirit Photography* (New York: George H. Doran, 1923); Jeremy Stolow, "Mediumnic Lights, X^x Rays, and the Spirit Who Photographed Herself," *Critical Inquiry* vol. 42, no. 4 (July 2016): 923–51, https://doi.org/10.1086/686962. On the Hamiltons and Spiritualism, see Esyllt W. Jones, "Spectral Influenza: Winnipeg's Hamilton Family, Interwar Spiritualism, and Pandemic Disease," in *Epidemic Encounters: Influenza, Society, and Culture in Canada, 1918–20*, ed. Magda Fahrni and Esyllt W. Jones (Vancouver: UBC Press, 2012), 209–10; and Beth A. Robertson, *Science of the Seance: Transnational Networks and Gendered Bodies in the Study of Psychic Phenomena, 1918–40* (Vancouver: UBC Press, 2016).

29 See T.G. Hamilton, "Photography of Teleplasm," UMASC, MSS 14, HFF, Group VI, http://hdl.handle.net/10719/1409843; Kate Flint, "'More Rapid than the Lightning's Flash': Photography, Suddenness, and the Afterlife of Romantic Illumination," *European Romantic Review* 24, no. 3 (2013): 369–83, https://doi.org/10.1080/10509585.2013.787242.

30 Geley, *From the Unconscious to the Conscious*, 163–64. In the translator's note, Stanley de Brath states that Geley was updating Bergson's élan vital with a "concrete energy," defining "energy as an influence forming all the varieties of cellular tissue out of one primordial substance and molding those tissues into organic form under the impulsion of a Directing Idea" (vii). For context, see Robert J. Richards, *The Romantic Conception of Life: Science and Philosophy in the Age of Goethe* (Chicago: University of Chicago Press, 2002). Geley tends to use the terminology of Camille Flammarion's dynamism and directing idea (viii). Schrenck-Notzing, *Phenomena of Materialisation*, 30–31, accepts the vital force and refers to Wilhelm Ostwald's energeticism.

31 Sebastien Normandin, "Visions of Vitalism: Medicine, Philosophy and the Soul in Nineteenth Century France" (PhD diss., McGill University, 2003), 6. See Carlos S. Alvarado, "Human Radiations: Concepts of Force in Mesmerism, Spiritualism and Psychical Research," *Journal of the Society for Psychical Research* 70, no. 884 (2006), 138–62. It was not unusual for the vital force to be conceptualized as the mechanism of the unconscious mind. By the end of the nineteenth century, a range of "new" energies, variously called "animal magnetism, neo-magnetism, nervous force, neuric force, Od, psychic fluid, psychic force, vital energy and vital force," was equated with the discoveries of electricity, light, and heat (138).

32 Sausman states that Bergson's élan vital became a *cause célèbre* for psychical researchers. Sausman, "'It's Organisms that Die, not Life,'" 17, 20, 23–24. On vitalism and art, see Fae Brauer, ed., *Vitalist Modernism: Art, Science, Energy and Creative Evolution* (Oxfordshire, UK: Routledge, 2023).

33 Geley, *From the Unconscious to the Conscious*, 163–64; Richet, *Thirty Years of Psychical Research*, reckoned that the cellular plasm, directed by the vital force, could be projected outside the body like a rod or lever, and he successfully promoted this theory to explain how tables could fly seemingly untouched and how ectoplasmic materializations occurred. "Materializations are ectoplasms: that is, sarcodic extensions emanating from the body of the medium, precisely as a pseudopod is projected from an amoeboid cell" (618).

34 On this topic, German biologist Ernst Haeckel labelled protoplasm *urschleim* (primordial slime), a structureless plasma from which higher lifeforms evolve. Evolutionist Thomas Huxley contributed to debates in 1868 about this ubiquitous, gelatinous medium, describing it as "The Physical Basis of All Life" and comparing it to malleable potter's clay. Thomas Henry Huxley, *On the Physical Basis of Life* (New Haven, CT: College Courant, 1869), 11. See Philip F. Rehbock, "Huxley, Haeckel, and the Oceanographers: The Case of Bathybius haeckelii," *Isis* 66, no. 4 (1975): 504–33; Brain, "Materialising the Medium," 124, 126–128, on protoplasm and the importance of Haeckel. Brain has done the seminal work on sketching out the convergence of ectoplasm and protoplasm, and explains that "protoplasm, central to the most basic levels of animal and vegetal cells, with its characteristics of auto plasticity, comes to signify generative forces in the twentieth century attractive to philosophers, scientists and artists alike" (127). See also Lionel Smith Beale, *Protoplasm: Or, Life, Force, and Matter* (London: J. Churchill, 1870), 277; and Lionel S. Beale, "Bioplasm: An Introduction to the Study of Physiology and Medicine" (London: J. and A. Churchill, 1 January 1872), Internet Archive, https://archive.org/details/b21694370/page/n6/mode/2up, https://www.journals.uchicago.edu/doi/abs/10.1086/351511. See, further, Gerald L. Geison, "The Protoplasmic Theory of Life and the Vitalist-Mechanist Debate," *Isis* 60, no. 3 (1969): 273–92, 275 and 288, http://www.jstor.org/stable/229483; and Andrew Reynolds, "Amoebae as Exemplary Cells: The Protean Nature of an Elementary Organism," *Journal of the History of Biology* 41, no. 2 (2008): 307–37, 317, http://www.jstor.org/stable/29737549.

35 Schrenck-Notzing's and Bisson's photographs were disseminated through their illustrated publications, respectively, Albert von Schrenck-Notzing, *Der Kampf um die Materialisations-Phänomene* (München: Ernest Reinhardt, 1914), and Juliette A. Bisson, *Les phénomènes dits de matérialisation* (Paris: Alcan, 1914). Bisson's hardcover book is well illustrated. Schrenck-Notzing's is a smaller, soft-cover book with few photographs. It was translated as a more substantial book, *Phenomena of Materialisation: A Contribution to the Investigation of Mediumistic Teleplastics*, trans. E.E. Fournier d'Albe (London: Kegan Paul Trench Trubner, 1920), which Hamilton bought in 1922. Bisson also worked with the academic painter Leon Chevreul (1852–1939), the Spiritist Gabriel Delanne (1857–1926), and the professional photographer Guillaume de Fontenay (1861–1914), all of whom had been involved in photographing phantoms. Although Schrenck-Notzing and Bisson list themselves as the creators of the photographs, often they had help setting up, photographing, and even printing the images, as is common for all psychic researchers. See Neil Matheson, "Ectoplasm and Photography: Mediumistic Performances for Camera," in *The Machine and the Ghost: Technology and Spiritualism in Nineteenth-to Twenty-First-Century Art and Culture* eds., Sas Mays and Neil Matheson (Manchester: Manchester University Press, 2013), 78–102, especially 89–90.

36 Martyn Jolly, *Faces of the Living Dead: The Belief in Spirit Photography* (London: British Library, 2006); John Harvey, *Photography and Spirit* (London: Reaktion, 2007) and Warner, "Ethereal Body," n.p.

37 Houdini, *A Magician among the Spirits*, 179.

38 The séance outfit is much commented on in the literature; see Helen de G. Verrall, "The History of Marthe Béraud (Eva C.)," *Proceedings of the Society for Psychical Research* 27 (1914–15): 333–69. See also Schrenck-Notzing, *Phenomena of Materialisation*, 41, on the costume.

39 In 1909, Bisson and her husband, the vaudeville playwright Alexandre Bisson, met the twenty-three-year-old Eva Carrière, who succeeded Eusapia Paladino as the most important subject of the twentieth century. She worked exclusively with Bisson and attracted many psychical scientists to Bisson's laboratory in Paris. Schrenck-Notzing was introduced to Bisson's circle by Gabriel Delanne in 1910. The group was active for three months before Schrenck-Notzing arrived in Paris; see Schrenck-Notzing, *Phenomena of Materialisation*, 37. The photographs published in all editions of their books were mostly produced in Bisson's art studio on rue Victor Hugo between 1909 and 1912. In 1912, after Alexandre Bisson died, Juliette Bisson and Carrière moved to a new flat. The press photo from 7 February 1914 shows tarps covering sculptures, suggesting that Bisson was practising as an artist into 1914. Geley worked with Bisson and Carrière between 1916 and 1918, and the UK SPR brought Bisson and Carrière to London in 1922. See Matheson, "Ectoplasm and Photography," 89–90. See also Andreas Sommer, "Policing Epistemic Deviance: Albert von Schrenck Notzing and Albert Moll," *Medical History* 56, no. 2 (2012): 255–76; Warner, "Ethereal Body," n.p.

40 Gustave Geley, "Ectoplasm," *American Society for Psychical Research*, April 1924, 275, 274. Bisson's contribution was twofold: first, she decided on the term "substance," thus moving away from talk of apparitions or phantoms; second, she was credited with taking an early flash image of the substance. See primary source material on Bisson and Eva Carrière; see, for example, Eric Dingwall, "Report on a Series of Sittings with Eva C.," *Proceedings of the Society for Psychical Research* 32 (1922): 209–343; and Helen Verrall, "The History of Marthe Béraud (Eva C.)," 347.

41 "Madame Bisson, a lady well known in the artistic circles of Paris, in experimenting with the same medium (Eva C) was the first to discover ectoplasm was definitely a substance and it could be photographed by flashlight." T.G. Hamilton, "Milestones in Psychical Research," UMASC, HFF, MSS 14, British Medical Association, Winnipeg, 1930, Box 1, Folder 12. See Conan Doyle, *History of Spiritualism*, 1926, 107, quoting Richet's comparison to Curie: "It is probable that Mme. Bisson will take a place beside her compatriot Mme. Curie in the annals of science."

42 In a letter to Hamilton on 12 November 1930, Dr. Le Roi Crandon compared Hamilton with Schrenck-Notzing, UMSC MSS 14, HFF, T.G.H. Correspondence Incoming, 1929-30, Box 4, Folder 2; Hamilton compared his own photograph with those of Schrenck-Notzing in a letter to J.E. Hett on 22 April 1931; UMASC, HFF, MSS 14, T.G.H. Correspondence Outgoing 1931–34, Box 5, Folder 1. Also see a letter to Crandon, 21 March 1930, PC 12, Annotated Photo Album, Group IV–VIII, Box 8, Folder 4: "The materialized mass very closely resembles some teleplasmic makeup in Schrenck-Notzing and in your own experiences." Lillian worried that Crandon's comments were too strong; Lillian Hamilton to J. Malcom Bird, 14 March 1929, UMASC, MSS 14, Lillian Hamilton, Correspondence Outgoing, 1931-56, Box 5, Folder 9. About the November 1928 ectoplasmic photographs with miniature face forms of Reverend Charles Spurgeon, Crandon responded enthusiastically: "Your last pictures are marvelous beyond words! A critic would say they are either the grossest fraud, or they represent spirit pictures better than any others yet produced." Le Roi Crandon to T.G. Hamilton, 27 December 1928, UMSC MSS 14, HFF, T.G.H. Incoming Correspondence, 1923–1928, Box 4, Folder 1.

43 Neither Hamilton nor Crandon would have known that by the mid-1920s Bisson's, Geley's, and Schrenck-Notzing's photographs were being discredited by the Parisian Institut Métapsychique International. See letters from Bisson to Harry Price in the Harry Price Library of Magical Literature, Senate House Library, University of London, UK, and Rudolf Lambert, "Dr. Geley's Reports on the Medium 'Eva C,'" *Journal of the Society for Psychical Research* 37, 682 (1954). By 1933, Hamilton knew of the controversy surrounding the Schrenck-Notzing and Bisson photographs because he was discussing it with the "ghost" of Geley in the private séances that year. UMASC, HFF, MSS 14, Jay MacDonald, March 1929 to September 1935, Box 14, Folder 17.

44 Schrenck-Notzing, *Phenomena of Materialisation*, 88.

45 Karl Gampenrieder was not working from life, and never went to Paris. Schrenck-Notzing, ibid., describes the moment depicted in the drawing as a "white column of smoke curled upward."

46 Geley, *From the Unconscious to the Conscious*, 52, 33; Geley, "Ectoplasm," 273.

47 Wilson, *Modernism and Magic*, 143–44. On the still flash photograph, see Beckman, *Vanishing Women*, 81–9.

48 Geley, *From the Unconscious to the Conscious*, 52; emphasis added.

49 Schrenck-Notzing, *Phenomena of Materialisation*, 89; emphasis added. He denied that Eva Carrière had any artistic interest or talent, proposing instead that she was influenced by Bisson's art practice (282, 270).

50 Pierre Sanchez, *Les Catalogues des salons 1899–1901* (Dijon: L. Echelle de Jacob, 1901); *Société des artistes français* (Paris: Ludovic Baschet, 1902).

51 Schrenck-Notzing, *Phenomena of Materialisation*, 282, explains that ectoplasm has ideoplastic capacity. He rejects the "spiritistic" view. For the context of ideoplasm and "materialized dream images," see Sommer, "Policing Epistemic Deviance," 259.

52 Schrenck-Notzing, *Phenomena of Materialisation*, 144: "extraordinary artistic achievement." To evaluate the drawings of faces inserted into Eva C.'s ectoplasms, Schrenck-Notzing turned to his friend and academic artist Albert von Keller, who evaluated the ectoplasmic production as evidence of the talent of "great artists" (273.) Also, "the composition and arrangement of this head appear[ed] to be a remarkable artistic performance" (143), and the artistic ability demonstrated an extra-ordinary "artistic arrangement" (114), artistic intelligence (144, 167). Schrenck-Notzing compared the drawings in the ectoplasm of 14 February 1912 to "Leonardo da Vinci Mona Lisa" (145). Schrenck-Notzing and Keller admired the artistic skill of the drawings embedded in the photographs, but not everyone agreed. With the widespread publicity that followed his 1914 book, Schrenck-Notzing's photographs were ridiculed by some colleagues and the press. See Wilson's Marxist analysis of ectoplasm in, *Modernism and Magic*, chapter 5, especially 142–3. See Fischer, "The Reciprocal Adaptation," 181–82, on the aesthetics of these photographs. Also see Flavio A. Geisshuesler, "A Parapsychologist, an Anthropologist, and a Vitalist Walk into a Laboratory: Ernesto De Martino, Mircea Eliade, and a Forgotten Chapter in the Disciplinary History of Religious Studies," *Religions* 10, no. 5 (2019): 304, https://doi.org/10.3390/REL10050304.

53 Schrenck-Notzing, *Phenomena of Materialisation*, 283. He continues that the variety of forms "demonstrate[s] an intention of the creative force." He aligns his interest in the vital force with Camille Flammarion, *Les Forces naturelles inconnues* (Paris: Ernest Flammarion, 1907), and with Wilhelm Ostwald's energeticism (30–31). Geley, *From the Unconscious to the Conscious*, 163–64, states that "this essential factor is a kind of interior impulse, an original and undefined 'vital surge' (*élan vital*).

This vital impulse pertains to an immanent principle which is life, intelligence, and matter. It transcends them all, in the past, present, and the future. It presupposes them, contains them and precreates them. This immanent principle, however, has no final completeness itself; it comes into existence progressively as it creates the evolving universe. It constitutes what M. Bergson calls 'Duration.' This 'Duration' is not very easily understood."

54 In conversation Oliver Botar notes that the reference to the mechanism of evolution suggests familiarity with the popular scientific writings of the Austro-Hungarian biologist Raoul Heinrich Francé, then operating his Munich Biological Institute, which by the early 1920s, would become of great importance to Modernists working in Germany such as László Moholy-Nagy, El Lissitzky and Ludwig Mies van der Rohe. On context of biocentric art, see Botar, "Prolegomena to the Study of Biomorphic Modernism," chapter two, section ii, Biologism.

55 Schrenck-Notzing, *Phenomena of Materialisation*, 87. Also, the flatness of the image is like a "white paper glove" (90).

56 Ruth Butler, *Rodin: The Shape of Genius* (New Haven, CT: Yale University Press, 1993). Serena Keshavjee, "Carrière, Rodin and the Natural Laws of Making Art," 49–60.

57 Oliver A.I. Botar and Isabel Wünsche, *Biocentrism and Modernism* (Surrey, UK: Ashgate, 2011), contextualize biomorphic and biocentric modernism and discuss these artists and more; see the Introduction.

58 High-profile visitors to the Schrenck-Notzing lab in Munich included Thomas Mann, Ludwig Klages, and biologist Hans Driesch, attending séances with a medium named Willi Schneider between 1921 and 1922. Mann's séance scenes in *The Magic Mountain* (1924) are based upon these experiences. Sommer, "Policing Epistemic Deviance," 260–61. See Thomas Mann, *An Experience in the Occult* (New York: Knopf, 1923); and Thomas Mann, *The Magic Mountain*, trans. H.T. Lowe-Porter (London: Penguin, 1983). On Mann and séances, see Wilson, *Modernism and Magic*, 145–48; Germana Pareti, "Hans Driesch's Interest in the Psychical Research: A Historical Study," *Medicina historica* 1, no. 3 (2018): 156–62, https://www.mattioli1885journals.com/index.php/MedHistor/article/view/6749 (accessed 1 November 2022); and Heather Wolffram, "In the Laboratory of the Ghost-Baron: Parapsychology in Germany in the Early 20th Century," *Endeavour* 33, no. 4 (2009): 152–57, https://doi.org/10.1016/j.endeavour.2009.10.001. Fischer, "The Reciprocal Adaptation," notes that Schrenck-Notzing was unhappy with the images of Stanisława Tomczyk because the medium did not produce the "solid forms" of ectoplasm for which Carrière was celebrated, reinforcing my point that the research aesthetics were tied to solid ectoplasm. Leigh Wilson, *Modernism and Magic,* 145–8.

59 Ute Eskildsen and Jan-Christopher Horak, *Film und Foto der zwanziger Jahre* (Stuttgart: Verlag Gerd Hatje, 1979). *Film und Foto* was one of the most important exhibitions to combine art and applied photographs; Oliver A.I. Botar, "László Moholy-Nagy's 'New Vision' and the Aestheticization of Scientific Photography in Weimar Germany," *Science in Context* 17, no. 4: 525–56, 504. Note that Moholy-Nagy included a cropped séance photograph of table turning with twenty-two hands, from the 1922 Fritz Lang film *Dr. Mabus*, in his publication *Malerei, Photographie, Film* (Munich: Albert Langen, 1925). Thanks to Oliver Botar for pointing this out.

60 See Botar, "László Moholy-Nagy's 'New Vision.'" Botar explains that Moholy-Nagy thought that applied photographs, especially scientific photographs, should be models for art photography (528). He integrated applied photographs into his publications and exhibitions that demonstrate their aesthetic possibilities.

61 These photographs were taken right after the series with Eva Carrière but without Bisson. Andreas Fischer, Institut für Grenzgebiete der Psychologie und Psychohygiene, in communication with me, reported that there is no correspondence in the Freiburg archive between Schrenck-Notzing's widow, Gabriele Schrenck-Notzing, and Moholy-Nagy.

62 Botar, "Prolegomena to the Study of Biomorphic Modernism," 533–47, especially 540.

63 With the significance of *Film und Foto* in mind, Hamilton's exhibition in 1930 of his scientific photographs of ectoplasm at the Winnipeg Winter Club might be one of the earliest displays of scientific photographs in Canada.

64 The phrase "sculptural protoplasm" comes from Alfred Barr, *Cubism and Abstract Art* (New York: Museum of Modern Art, 1936), 21.

65 The history of ideas of biomorphic art has been laid out by art historians Oliver Botar and Jennifer Mundy. In particular, see Botar's explanation of biocentrism in "Prolegomena to the Study of Biomorphic Modernism," 47–62, his definition of his term "naturamorphic" analogy in photography, 446, and discussion of the above listed artists. Also Botar, "Defining Biocentrism," in *Biocentrism and Modernism*, ed. Oliver A.I. Botar and Isabel Wünsche, 15–45; Jennifer Mundy, "The Naming of Biomorphism," in *Biocentrism and Modernism*, 61–76. Moholy-Nagy's attraction to microscopic cellular imagery can be situated within the monistic vitalistic context.

66 Oliver A.I. Botar and Isabel Wünsche, "Introduction," in *Biocentrism and Modernism*, 3.

67 I thank Oliver Botar for this information.

68 "Biocentrism" is the best term used to explain the history of ideas underlying this turn to biomorphic forms elucidating the nature-centric views that permeated this aspect of the avant-garde of the time. See Botar, "Defining Biocentrism," especially 16; and Botar, "Prolegomena to the Study of Biomorphic Modernism," 51–58, 497–98. Jennifer Mundy, Oliver Botar, and Edward Juler have outlined that artists using biomorphic forms, especially Hans Arp and Wassily Kandinsky, were interested in protoplasm, cells, and close-up views of amoeba from 1915 to the 1940s. See Mundy, "The Naming of Biomorphism"; and Edward Juler, "Life Forms: Henry Moore, Morphology and Biologism in the Interwar Years," in *Henry Moore: Sculptural Process and Public Identity* (Tate Research Publication, 2015), https://www.tate.org.uk/art/research-publications/henry-moore/edward-juler-life-forms-henry-moore-morphology-and-biologism-in-the-interwar-years-r1151314. Juler aligns this protoplasmic art with Bergson's *Creative Evolution*. Marina Warner and Karen Beckman both describe ectoplasmic photographs as "informe," an art history term typically used to describe the work of biomorphic Modernist artists. See Warner, "Ethereal Body," and Beckman, *Vanishing Women*, 78.

69 Brain, "Materialising the Medium," 127, 116. He continues that "materialisation presented an opportunity to study the workings of protoplasm under special conditions. The mediums' materialisation of limbs, heads and amorphous forms showed distinct similarities to the projection and retraction of pseudopodia from the cells of protozoa and the regeneration of limbs from certain organisms," 126.

70 Geley, "Ectoplasm," 277; Geley, *From the Unconscious to the Conscious*, 163–64.

71 Barr, *Cubism and Abstract Art*, 186, 19.

72 Arp's work was included in the Munich exhibition of graphic works at the Hans Goltz Gallery from February to April 1912. See ibid., 64, 68, on the importance of Munich as a Modernist centre.

73 See Botar, "Prolegomena to the Study of Biomorphic Modernism," chapter two, section ii, Biologism.

74 According to Schrenck-Notzing (292–94), Berthe Barklay began calling out the ectoplasm as fake in December 1913 into January 1914. See Barklay, "Les phénomènes dits de matérialisation ou les joyeusetées psychism," *Psychic Magazine*, 1 January 1914, 1–5. Popular press articles about these ectoplasmic photographs include "La Querelle des fantômes," *Le Monde illustré*, February 1914, 94; *Neues Wiener Tagblatt*, 30 December 1913, and *Le Matin* in December 1913 and into January 1914. I do not have direct evidence that Arp knew of the visualizations of ectoplasmic materializations, but Schrenck-Notzing received so much publicity from 1913 through the 1920s, that, if Arp was interested in protoplasm, as Barr suggests, it would not have been hard to find reproductions of the photographs in the press. Arp's experiments in automatic drawings and even his efforts at creating a sense of flow in his reliefs during the Dada period mimicked the characteristics of vitalistic protoplasm. In general, the emphasis on the asymmetry and incomplete forms in the biomorphic art of Arp, Kandinsky, and Moore parallels the descriptions and images of the extrusions of Eva Carrière and Stanisława Tomczyk.

75 Hamilton sometimes referenced Oliver Lodge's theory of ether to explain teleplasm, which "constitutes an intervening substance by means of which transcendental intelligences are enabled, by ideoplastic or other unknown processes, to transmit their conception of certain energy forms." T.G. Hamilton, UMASC, HFF, MSS 14, Notes 1921–1985, Box 17, Folder 5.

76 Chris Dorosz, *Dark Matter House* (Winnipeg: La Maison des artistes, 2021), 8. These ideas have long been the subject of speculation within the occult sciences over the past 100 years. Schrenck-Notzing, *Phenomena of Materialisation*, 31, references the energy theories of Ostwald and Flammarion. See Enns and Trower, *Vibratory Modernism*.

77 I take the term "ectoplasmic selfies" from Pripić Hedtke and Molteni, *Ectoplasm Selfies*.

78 Lillian Hamilton and Sylvia Barber continued ectoplasmic séances in Winnipeg into the 1940s. See Chapter 4 of this volume where Meyer zu Erpen outlines later ectoplasmic experiments.

79 See details in Taggart, *Séance*, 161–67, 272–75. Muegge has filmed his own ectoplasmic excretions. He also states that he was inspired by the photographs of Bisson and Schrenck-Notzing. Both Hamilton and Schrenck-Notzing had tried to capture the vitality of teleplasm with a film camera, but the low lighting in the séance room undermined their efforts. Hamilton looked into buying a movie camera; see the discussion with Jean Meyer, UMASC, HFF, MSS 14, T.G.H. Outgoing Correspondence, 1931–1934, Box 5, Folder 1. See the note and photograph in UMASC, HFF, MSS 14, Group V Utilitarian Masses, Box 15, Folder 16; Mrs. William Martin Cannon (Rae Bruening Cannon) held a movie camera on her lap on 18 August 1929, but she had obtained only a still photo of the plasm which she sent the Hamiltons. See Letter to Mrs. W. M. Cannon, 5 October 1929, UMASC, HFF, MSS 14, T.G.H. Correspondence Outgoing Box 4, Folder 5. Erika DeFreitas recreates the effect of stop motion animation by posing sequentially with colourful crocheted doilies by Angela DeFreitas, her grandmother, replacing the ectoplasm. Also see DeFreitas related work *The Impossible Speech Act*, 2007 with the equally colorful icing.

80 Grace A. Williams, "The Supernatural Sex: Women, Magick and Mediumship: Assembling a Field of Fascination in Contemporary Art" (PhD diss., Birmingham City University, 2017), https://ethos.bl.uk/OrderDetails.do?did=2&uin=uk.bl.ethos.732983. Williams explains that ectoplasm

with miniature face forms echoes the photographic process (46), referencing Tom Gunning, "Phantom Images and Modern Manifestations," in *Fugitive Images: From Photography to Video*, ed. Patrice Petro (Bloomington: Indiana University Press, 1995), 42–71.

81 Williams, "The Supernatural Sex," 37.

82 Schrenck-Notzing addressed this issue in his book of 1920, but Hamilton fretted about the accusation of fraud, as indicated by his conversations with Geley's ghost in 1933. See UMASC, HFF, MSS 14, Jay MacDonald, March 1929 to September 1935, Box 14, Folder17. I thank Zoe Beloff for explaining her installation and process with me.

83 Sue-Ellen Case, *Performing Science and the Virtual* (Oxfordshire: Routledge, 2006). See Robertson, *Science of the Seance*, 39–40. See also Marina Warner, *Phantasmagoria* (Oxford: Oxford University Press, 2006).

84 In 2009, Susan MacWilliam represented Northern Ireland in the 53rd Venice Biennale, and she brought the Hamilton experiments to the international art world. It is interesting to note that Conan Doyle, Flammarion, and Geley all came as trance personalities to Hamilton. See Matheson, "Ectoplasm and Photography," 78–80.

85 Robertson, *Science of the Seance*, 30, 40, 118, makes this point when she applies Bruno Latour's term scientific "inscriptions" to the records amassed by psychical researchers.

86 Matheson, "Ectoplasm and Photography," 80–81.

87 See Richard E. Bennett, "Interview with Margaret Hamilton Bach," 26 November 1980, UMASC, HFF, Box 3, Folder 9, 16.

88 Williams, "The Supernatural Sex," 37. See Alex Owen, *The Darkened Room: Women, Power and Spiritualism in Late Victorian England* (Philadelphia: University of Pennsylvania Press, 1990). There were other male mediums in the Hamilton group, as Esyllt W. Jones points out in Chapter 1 of this volume.

89 The doilies were hand crocheted by Angela and Cita DeFreitas, Erika's maternal grandmother and mother respectively, during the 1950s to '60s. DeFreitas works intuitively as an artist and interestingly enough she explained to me that she posed with the doilies and produced this body of work before she saw the Hamilton photographs. In a letter from Hamilton to J.E. Hett on 22 April 1931, UMASC, MSS 14, HFF, T.G.H. Outgoing Correspondence, 1931–34, Box 5, Folder 1, T.G. emphasized the whiteness of the ectoplasm, which can be associated with the aesthetics of white stone and marble in biomorphic Modernist sculptures, including those by Rodin, Arp, and Moore.

90 Megan Moore is well aware of the invasive gynecological exams and strip searches that mediums had to endure, all in the guise of preventing fraud under laboratory conditions. Marshall was bathed, and parts of her body were checked.

91 Teresa Burrows, "Swallowed a Spirit: Manifestations in Beadwork of Mary Marshall and Ectoplasm," unpublished notes sent to the author in 2022. Burrows has made connections between the green tints of the microscopic representations of the COVID-19 virus on the news, green glass beads in her collection, and ectoplasmic protoplasm.

92 Hamilton, "Milestones in Psychical Research," 8. UMASC, HFF, MSS 14, British Medical Association, Winnipeg, 1930, Box 1, Folder 12, 8.

93 See Janet Beizer's influential book *Ventriloquized Bodies: Narratives of Hysteria in Nineteenth-Century France* (Ithaca, NY: Cornell University Press, 1994). Serena Keshavjee "L'Art inconscient" and "L'Esthétique des esprits": Science, Spiritualism and the Imaging of the Unconscious in French

Symbolist Art" (PhD dissertation, University of Toronto, 2002).

94 The iconography of the symbols in the second Conan Doyle ectoplasm is that "there is no death." The skull represents death, the profile of the young woman humanity gazing fearfully at death, the youth in the centre is humanity realizing there is no death, and the joy from the proof of immortality is evident in Doyle's smile. See Margaret Hamilton Bach, First Annual Archives Symposium, 23 November 1979, slide 65. UMASC, MSS 14, HFF, Margaret Hamilton Bach—Lectures, Box 1, Folder 15. Paul Robles, in conversation with the author, 2021–22. Tony Oursler references theosophy and thought forms in this work, but I see the ectoplasmic form in *Dust*. See the Broad Museum for an illustration, https://www.thebroad.org/art/tony-oursler/dust (accessed 27 January 2023).

95 I thank Blair Fornwald for this phrase and for the title of the exhibition *The Undead Archive*. I think that the Hamilton photographs are well received because of their high quality and Modernist aesthetic, and the fact that they are accessible online. It is instructive to compare Hamilton's work with that of the Crandons, tightly composed with distracting backgrounds and bulky costumes that compete with the main image of the medium. The Crandons' ectoplasm was so visceral that it went past the uncanny into the unappealing. Hamilton met the Crandons in person in both Winnipeg (1926) and Boston (1925 and 1928).

ACKNOWLEDGEMENTS

Archival research can uncover lost or forgotten histories, but it is also a slow process. To carry out this research I received financial support from the Social Sciences and Humanities Research Council of Canada, the University of Winnipeg, the Survival Research Institute of Canada (SRIC), and a Fellowship from the Harry Ransom Center at the University of Texas, Austin. These funds enabled me to travel to the major psychical archives in Europe and North America. I conducted research at the Sir Arthur Conan Doyle Collection, located in the Harry Ransom Center at the University of Texas, Austin; the Society for Psychical Research, housed at Cambridge University Library, UK; the Harry Price Library of Magical Literature in Senate House Library at the University of London; the American Society for Psychical Research located in New York City; the Institut Métapsychique International in Paris; and the Thomas Fisher Rare Book Library at the University of Toronto. At each of these institutions I relied on knowledgeable archivists, and I want to thank Sian Collins at the Cambridge University Library and Jocelyne Boban at L'Institut Métapsychique International in particular.

In Winnipeg I worked very closely, and throughout the pandemic, with the team at the University of Manitoba Archives and Special Collections, and I thank Heather Bidzinski, Brian Hubner, Nicole Aminian, Linda Eddy, and Shelley Sweeney. Dr. Sweeney introduced me to archivist Walter Meyer zu Erpen, who has researched the Hamilton Family Fonds for thirty years, and who spent many hours fact checking and finding new sources for my research. Meyer zu Erpen facilitated with SRIC to fund the colour photographs in this publication, and to help the

University of Manitoba Archives and Special Collections acquire pertinent research materials, publications, and photographs, in particular the H.A.V. Green album.

The authors who have contributed to this volume have interpreted the fonds from different academic points of view, including the history of technology, art, religion, science, and disease. I thank KC Adams, Brian Hubner, Esyllt W. Jones, Murray Leeder, Walter Meyer zu Erpen, Katie Oates, and Shelley Sweeney for their chapters. I thank Oliver Botar, Dallas Harrison, Walter Meyer zu Erpen, Tim Pearson, and Shelley Sweeney for reading chapters of the book, and the peer reviewers for their insightful comments.

The University of Manitoba Press provided lots of support. Thank you to Glenn Bergen, Barbara Romanik, Jess Koroscil, Jill McConkey, and the production, design, and marketing teams.

A range of grants including a SSHRC Insight grant, a University of Winnipeg Graduate Student Scholarship, the Indigenous Summer School Program, and The Space Between Us, supported emerging scholars as research assistants. Between 2021 to 2023, I worked most regularly with Emma Dux and Christina Thomson on the editorial production of the book. Dux and Thomson compiled the bibliography, biographies, helped organize the illustrations, and contributed to curatorial research. During 2020 and 2021, Sierra Hill researched the contemporary artists included in this book and in the accompanying exhibition *The Undead Archive*. Sarah Hodges-Kolisnyk created a set of analogue research photographs published here. The Hamilton Family Fonds is a massive archive: Catherine van Reenen, Laura Bergen and Sabrina Sethi did bibliographical and archival research, while Shaneela Boodoo, Stephen Rose, and Alireza Bayat also helped. I thank all the funding bodies for this support to train students.

Many of the ideas in this book were developed in academic conferences, and I thank my colleagues for organizing academic panels I participated in, where I had the chance to test my ideas: Fae Brauer, Melissa Buron, Christine Ferguson, Linda Henderson, Julie Nagam, Efram Sera-Shriar, and Shannon Taggart.

Family sustained me during this long COVID-era project. I thank Oliver, Nadir and Devin Botar, Fatehalli, Lucy, Devin, David, and Myles Keshavjee, and Miriam Gaum.

APPENDIX

Hamilton Family Publications Psychical Research Experiments and Family History

Compiled by Walter Meyer zu Erpen

Part 1: Hamilton Family Fonds: Where to Start? A Proposed Reading List

The volume of photographic images and textual records in the Hamilton Family Fonds (HFF) and other related fonds is significant. Likewise, the material published about the T.G. Hamilton family and their psychical research experiments is voluminous and continues to grow.

A comprehensive bibliography of the psychical research experiments is available through the University of Manitoba Archives and Special Collections webpage for the HFF (https://libguides.lib.umanitoba.ca/c.php?g=703103). This proposed reading list is intended to help orient those new to the psychical research experiments conducted in Winnipeg during the 1920s and 1930s and/or to the HFF. University of Manitoba psychology professor James B. Nickels (1931–2021) was one of the first independent Winnipeg academics to investigate the Hamilton family's experiments:

> Nickels, James B. "Psychic Research in a Winnipeg Family: Reminiscences of Dr. Glen F. Hamilton." *Manitoba History* 55 (2007): 51–60. http://www.mhs.mb.ca/docs/mb_history/55/psychicresearch.shtml.

In 2016, *Paranormal Review*, the magazine of the Society for Psychical Research (SPR), featured the HFF in a special issue (77). Archivists Walter Meyer zu Erpen and Shelley Sweeney were guest editors of that issue, which comprised eight articles, illustrated with thirty Hamilton photographs, spanning twenty-six pages of carefully coordinated Hamilton content. Author and family historian Janice Hamilton, one of the Hamiltons' granddaughters, was invited to write the lead article:

> Hamilton, Janice. "Bring on Your Ghosts: The Thomas Glendenning Hamilton Family Séances from 1918 to 1944, Winnipeg, Canada." *Hamilton Family Fonds,* special issue of *Paranormal Review* 77 (2016): 6–11. The special issue is available for purchase from the SPR (https://www.spr.ac.uk/).

Based upon correspondence received from Mrs. T.G. Hamilton, "Records of a Canadian Circle: A Study of Psychic Messages and Physical Phenomena," *Light*, 10 June 1922, 362–63, is the earliest published record of the Hamilton research.

For an overview of the Hamilton research published within Manitoba during T.G. Hamilton's lifetime, this article was published two months after the founding of the Winnipeg Society for Psychical Research:

> Garden, Leslie. "Seeing the Unseen: Remarkable Evidence of Mysterious Phenomena Caught by Cameras of Psychical Research Society." *Western Home Monthly*, August 1931, 18–19, 54. https://libguides.lib.umanitoba.ca/ld.php?content_id=36482474.

The two books published by the Hamilton family are essential reading for serious students of the Hamilton psychical research experiments. Thanks to permission from the copyright holders, with the costs of digitization borne by the Survival Research Institute of Canada, both are available for free download through the University of Manitoba Libraries website.

The first was published in T.G. Hamilton's name, edited by his son James Drummond Hamilton (1915–1980) with assistance from the widowed Lillian May Hamilton:

> Hamilton, T.G. *Intention and Survival: Psychical Research Studies and the Bearing of Intentional Actions by Trance Personalities on the Problem of Human Survival*. Edited by James D. Hamilton. 1st ed. Toronto: Macmillan Company of Canada, 1942. https://archives.lib.umanitoba.ca/media/Hamilton_Intention_and_Survival.pdf.

The second was published over a quarter century later by the Hamiltons' daughter, Margaret Lillian Hamilton Bach (1909–1986), based upon a manuscript that her mother had been working on during the 1950s:

> Hamilton, Margaret Lillian. *Is Survival a Fact? Studies of Deep-Trance Automatic Scripts and the Bearing of Intentional Actions by Trance Personalities on the Question of Human Survival*. London: Psychic Press, 1969. https://archives.lib.umanitoba.ca/media/Hamilton_Is_Survival_A_Fact.pdf.

In 1977, Margaret Lillian Hamilton published a revised, second edition of *Intention and Survival*. That edition is not available in digital format:

> Hamilton, T.G. *Intention and Survival: Psychical Research Studies and the Bearing of Intentional Actions by Trance Personalities on the Problem of Human Survival*. Edited by Margaret Lillian Hamilton. 2nd ed. London: Regency Press, 1977.

In 2021, based upon research over a dozen years, Janice Hamilton (the daughter of James D. Hamilton) published her family's history, the last chapters of which cover T.G. and Lillian Hamilton's family and their psychical research experiments:

> Hamilton, Janice. *Reinventing Themselves: A History of the Hamilton and Forrester Families*. Montreal: Self-published, 2021.

The *Dictionary of Canadian Biography* entry for T.G. Hamilton provides a succinct overview of his life, career, and interests. The draft sketch was submitted in 2006 and finally published in January 2022:

> Meyer zu Erpen, Walter. "Thomas Glendenning Hamilton." In *Dictionary of Canadian Biography*, vol. 16, 26 January 2022. http://www.biographi.ca/en/bio/hamilton_thomas_glendenning_16E.html.

Part 2: Articles by T.G. Hamilton (1873–1935) Published in Psychical Research Journals, Listed Chronologically (1929–35)

1929	"A Summary of Ten Years of Psychical Research." *Light*, 9 March 1929, 110–11.
1929	"Teleplasmic Phenomena in Winnipeg." *Quarterly Transactions of the British College of Psychic Science* (*BCPS*) 8, no. 3 (1929): 179–208, plus eleven unnumbered pages containing plates 1–15.
1930	"Teleplasmic Phenomena in Winnipeg; Article 2: Amorphous Teleplasms." *BCPS* 8, no. 4 (1930): 247–52, plus seven unnumbered pages containing plates 1–7.
1930	"Teleplasmic Phenomena in Winnipeg; Article 3: Mary M. Teleplasms, Including Another Miniature Face." *BCPS* 9, no. 2 (1930): 88–93, plus six unnumbered pages containing plates 1–6.
1931	"Some New Facts Regarding Teleplasms: An Address Delivered by Dr. T. Glen Hamilton to Members and Friends of the British Medical Association on August 27th, 1930, at Winnipeg, Manitoba, Canada." *BCPS* 9, no. 4 (1931): 262–70.
1931	"The Teleplasms of Mary M. in the Winnipeg Phenomena." *Journal of the American Society for Psychical Research* (*JASPR*) 25 (1931): 5–9.

1931 "Some Physical Phenomena Observed with the Medium Elizabeth M. during the First Period of Her Development." *JASPR* 25, no. 9 (1931): 378–86.

1931 "Mediumship of Elizabeth M.: Scale Equipment for Testing Telekinetic Force." *JASPR* 25, no. 10 (1931): 413.

1932 "The Mary M. Teleplasm of Oct. 27, 1929." *BCPS* 10, no. 4 (1932): 244–57, plus fourteen unnumbered pages containing plates 1–9. This article was also separately "Reprinted from 'Psychic Science' January 1932," with different pagination; a copy of that reprint is included at page 65 in the Hamilton family scrapbook, "Book One."

1933 "Chapter XLVIII: Margery in Winnipeg, Three Seances of December 1926." In "The Margery Mediumship [II]," edited by E.E. Dudley, *Proceedings of the American Society for Psychical Research* 21 (1933, dated 1926–27): 556–67.

1933 "'Katie King' Manifestations in the Mary M. Experiments." *BCPS* 11, no. 4 (1933): 254–78.

1933 "Dr. Glen Hamilton on His Experiments." *Light*, 21 July 1933, 453. Reprinted from the *Winnipeg Free Press* (*WFP*).

1933 "Dr. Glen Hamilton on Trance Personality." *Light*, 28 July 1933, 469. This article is based upon the fourth of a series of articles in the *WFP*, published on 23 February 1933.

1933 "Dr. Glen Hamilton's Psychic Studies: Human Faces in Teleplasm." *Light*, 29 September 1933, 613. Excerpted from an article that T.G. Hamilton contributed to the *WFP*.

1933 "The C.H. Spurgeon Case: Evidence Pointing to Survival and Continued Activity." *Light*, 6 October 1933, 628–29.

1933 "Has C.H. Spurgeon Returned? What the Cameras Revealed and the 'Voices' Described." *Light*, 13 October 1933, 645–47.

1933 "Has C.H. Spurgeon Returned? Efforts to 'Put Through' Religious Teachings from the 'Other Side.'" *Light*, 27 October 1933, 679.

1933 "The C.H. Spurgeon Case: 'Stupendous Re-Statement of the Central Claims of Christianity.'" *Light*, 3 November 1933, 695.

1934 "Some Further 'Katie King' Phenomena." *BCPS* 12, no. 4 (1934): 244–62, plus six unnumbered pages containing plates 1–6.

1934 "A Study of the Winnipeg Group Mediumship in Its Relation to the Dawn Teleplasms." *JASPR* 28 (1934): 117–30.

1935 "Reality of Psychic Force: Winnipeg Investigator's Clear Lead to Science." *Light*, 10 January 1935, 17–18.

Part 3: Articles by Lillian May Hamilton (1880–1956) Published in Psychical Research Journals, Listed Chronologically (1934–54)

1934	"Children Who See 'Angels': Interesting New Canadian Cases Provide Strong Evidence of Survival." *Light*, 13 July 1934, 409–10.
1935	"Two Strange Dog Stories." *Light*, 15 April 1935, 259.
1936	"'Elizabeth M.': The Wonderful Story of Dr. Glen Hamilton's First Medium." *Light*, 18 June 1936, 385–87.
1937	"The Death of Kitty A.: A Case of Supernormal Cognition." *BCPS* 16, no. 1 (1937): 8–15, plus one unnumbered page containing a photograph of Lillian May Hamilton.
1941	"Robert Louis Stevenson Calling! Communications Received by the Glen Hamilton Circle in Winnipeg, Canada." *Light*, 8 May 1941, 145–47.
1944	"A Remarkable War Prophecy by a Trance Communicator Claiming to be Raymond Lodge." *Psychic Science: The Journal of the International Institute for Psychic Investigation* 23, no. 2 (1944): 51–55.
1950	"Supernormal Drawing Obtained in Complete Darkness: Canadian Researches into Physical Phenomena." *Two Worlds: The Leading Spiritualist Weekly*, 2 September 1950, 897.
1951	"Telepathy Plus Spiritism in the Hamilton Researches in Winnipeg." *Light*, April 1951, 472–74.
1954	"The Houghtaling Case in Winnipeg: Strong Evidence for Individual Survival." *Light*, July 1954, 173–77.

Part 4: Articles by Margaret Hamilton Bach (1909–1986) Published in Newspapers (1958) and a Conference Proceeding (1979)

During 1957 Margaret Hamilton Bach, BA, ARCT, wrote a series of articles about her parents' psychical research experiments. Victor Sifton (1897–1961), LLD (Hon.), editor and publisher of the *Winnipeg Free Press*, read some of those articles and asked Margaret to prepare a series for the Winnipeg newspaper. She agreed to do so without a fee but requested that Sifton write the editorial lead, entitled "Is Survival a Fact? Remarkable Experiments Conducted in Winnipeg."

At the time, Sifton was chancellor of the University of Manitoba (1952–59). Not surprisingly, the lead article does not bear his name. Dr. Bruce Chown (1893–1986) wrote an article entitled "Psychical Research Worthwhile Study" that appeared alongside Margaret Hamilton's prefatory remarks. Sifton also had the series reprinted as the booklet *Is Survival a Fact?* that Margaret distributed to public libraries across Canada.

In her 1958 and 1969 publications and the second edition of *Intention and Survival* that she edited in 1977, Margaret Hamilton Bach used her maiden name, Margaret Lillian Hamilton.

1958 "Is Survival a Fact?" was first published in a series of thirteen articles in the *Winnipeg Free Press (WFP)* in January and February 1958:

Article 1	*WFP*, 18 January 1958, 34.
Article 2	*WFP*, 20 January 1958, 14.
Article 3	*WFP*, 21 January 1958, 5.
Article 4	*WFP*, 22 January 1958, 7.
Article 5	*WFP*, 23 January 1958, 4.
Article 6	*WFP*, 24 January 1958, 14.
Article 7	*WFP*, 25 January 1958, 2.
Article 8	*WFP*, 27 January 1958, 2.
Article 9	*WFP*, 28 January 1958, 10.
Article 10	*WFP*, 29 January 1958, 6.
Article 11	*WFP*, 30 January 1958, 6.
Article 12	*WFP*, 31 January 1958, 6.
Article 13	*WFP*, 1 February 1958, 46.

1958 When the series was offered to other Canadian dailies, the *Toronto Daily Star* accepted it promptly. It published the series beginning on 21 April 1958 and included portraits of T.G. Hamilton, his widow, Lillian May Hamilton, and four of the well-known professional men who had participated in the experiments: medical doctors William Creighton (1885–1972) and Bruce Chown (1893–1986) and lawyers Isaac Pitblado (1867–1964) and H.A.V. (Harry) Green (1888–1979).

1979 Margaret Hamilton Bach. "Life and Interests of Dr. T. Glendenning Hamilton." In *Proceedings of the First Annual Archives Symposium*, edited by Richard Bennett, 88–96. Winnipeg: University of Manitoba Department of Archives and Special Collections, 1979.

BIBLIOGRAPHY

Compiled by Emma Dux

Archival Collections

University of Manitoba Archives and Special Collections, Winnipeg.

Elizabeth (Poole) Shand fonds. A2016-024.

Hamilton Family fonds. MSS 14 and PC 12.

Henry Archibald Vaughan (Harry) Green (HAVG) fonds. MSS 439.

Janice Hamilton fonds. MSS 323.

Harry Ransom Center, University of Texas, Austin.

Sir Arthur Conan Doyle Collection. MS-1207.

Works Cited

Ahmed, Sarah. *The Cultural Politics of Emotion.* Edinburgh: Edinburgh University Press, 2004.

Aisemberg, Paula, Sigrid Dahle, Hervé di Rosa, Noam Gonick, and Anthony Kiendl, curators. *My Winnipeg*. Co-presented by La Maison rouge, Paris; du Musée International des Arts Modestes, Sete; Plug In ICA, Winnipeg, 2011–2012.

———. *My Winnipeg: guide de la scène artistique/guide of the artistic scene*. Lyon, France: Fage, 2011.

Allison, W.T. "Can Dead Authors Come Back?" *Manitoba Free Press Evening Bulletin*, 7 September 1918.

Alvarado, Carlos S. "Human Radiations: Concepts of Force in Mesmerism, Spiritualism and Psychical Research." *Journal of the Society for Psychical Research* 70.3, no. 884 (2006): 138–62.

Apraxine, Pierre, and Sophie Schmit, curators. *The Perfect Medium: Photography and the Occult*. Metropolitan Museum of Modern Art, New York, 2005.

Asprem, Egil. *The Problem of Disenchantment: Scientific Naturalism and Esoteric Discourse, 1900–1939*. Albany: State University of New York Press, 2018.

Assayas, Olivier, dir. *Personal Shopper*. Paris: G.C. Cinéma, 2016.

Aykroyd, Peter H. *A History of Ghosts: The True Story of Séances, Mediums, Ghosts, and Ghostbusters.* Emmaus, PE: Rodale, 2009.

Barklay, Berthe. "Les Phénoménes dits de matérialisations ou les joyeusetées psychism." *Psychic Magazine*, 1 January 1914.

Barr, Alfred H., Jr. *Cubism and Abstract Art*. New York: The Museum of Modern Art, 1936.

Batchen, Geoffrey. "Ectoplasm: Photography in the Digital Age." In *Over Exposed: Essays on Contemporary Photography,* edited by Carol Squiers, 9–23. New York: The New Press, 1999.

Baudouin, Philippe. *Surnaturelles: Une histoire visuelle des femmes mediums*. Paris: Éditions Pyramyd, 2021.

Beale, Lionel S. *Bioplasm: An Introduction to the Study of Physiology & Medicine*. London: J. and A. Churchill, 1872. https://archive.org/details/b21694370/page/n6/mode/2up.

———. *Protoplasm: Or Life, Force, and Matter*. London: J. Churchill, 1870.

Beckman, Karen. *Vanishing Women: Magic, Film, and Feminism*. Durham, NC: Duke University Press, 2003.

Beizer, Janet. *Ventriloquized Bodies: Narratives of Hysteria in Nineteenth-Century France.* Ithaca, NY: Cornell University Press, 1994.

Bergson, Henri. *Creative Evolution.* Paris: Felix Alcan, 1907.

Bisson, Juliette. *Les Phénomènes de Matérialisation*. Paris: Felix Alcan, 1914.

Botar, Oliver A.I. "Defining Biocentrism." In *Biocentrism and Modernism*, edited by Oliver A.I. Botar and Isabel Wünsche, 15–45. Farnham, Surrey: Ashgate, 2011.

———. "László Moholy-Nagy's 'New Vision' and the Aestheticization of Scientific Photography in Weimar Germany." *Science in Context* 17, no. 4 (2004): 525–56. https://doi.org/10.1017/S0269889704000250.

———. "Prolegomena to the Study of Biomorphic Modernism: Biocentrism, László Moholy-Nagy's 'New Vision' and Ernö Kallai's Bioromantik." PhD diss., University of Toronto, 1998.

Bowler, Peter J. *Reconciling Science and Religion: The Debate in Early-Twentieth-Century Britain*. Chicago: University of Chicago Press, 2001.

Bowler, Peter J. *The Non-Darwinian Revolution: Reinterpreting a Historical Myth*. Baltimore: Johns Hopkins University Press, 1988.

Brain, Robert. "Materialising the Medium: Ectoplasm and the Quest for Supra-Normal Biology in *Fin-De-Siècle* Science and Art." In *Vibratory Modernism*, edited by Anthony Enns and Shelley Trower, 112–41. London: Palgrave Macmillan, 2013.

Brandon, Ruth. *The Spiritualists: The Passion for the Occult in the Nineteenth and Twentieth Centuries*. New York: Alfred A. Knopf, 1983.

Brauer, Fae, ed. *Vitalist Modernism: Art, Science, Energy and Creative Evolution.* Abingdon, Oxfordshire: Routledge, 2023.

Bristow, Nancy. "The Practices of Social Forgetting: Rewriting, Obscuring and Silencing the 1918 Influenza Pandemic in the United States." In *Pandemic Re-Awakenings: The Forgotten and Unforgotten "Spanish" Flu of 1918–1919,* edited by Guy Beiner, 332–45. Oxford: Oxford University Press, 2022.

Bronson, AA, and Peter Hobbs. *Queer Spirits*. Winnipeg: Plug In Editions with Creative Time, 2011.

Brower, Brady. *Unruly Spirits: The Science of Psychic Phenomena in Modern France*. Urbana: University of Illinois Press, 2010.

Brownlee, Kevin, and E. Leigh Syms. *Kayasochi Kikawenow = Our Mother from Long Ago: An Early Cree Woman and Her Personal Belongings from Nagami Bay, Southern Indian Lake*. Aboriginal Archeology Internship Report. Winnipeg: The Manitoba Museum of Man and Nature, 1999.

Buron, Melissa E. *James Tissot*. San Francisco: de Young Fine Arts Museums of San Francisco, 2019.

Butler, Ruth. *Rodin: The Shape of Genius*. New Haven: Yale University Press, 1993.

"A Case of Heresy." *Winnipeg Free Press Home Journal*, 25 May 1899.

Case, Sue-Ellen. *Performing Science and the Virtual*. London: Routledge, 2006.

Castle, William, dir. *13 Ghosts*. Los Angeles: William Castle Productions, 1960.

"Catalogue of Drawings." *Light* 6, no. 263 (16 January 1886): 34. http://iapsop.com/archive/materials/light/light_v6_n263_jan_16_1886.pdf.

Chéroux, Clément. *The Perfect Medium: Photography and the Occult*. New Haven: Yale University Press, 2005.

Chéroux, Clément, and Andreas Fischer. "Le troisième oeil: La photographie et l'occulte." Maison européenne de la Photographie, November 2004 to February 2005, Paris. https://www.mep-fr.org/event/le-troisieme-oeil/.

Chown, Bruce. "Obituaries." *Canadian Medical Association Journal* 32 (1935): 710–11.

———. "Psychical Research Worthwhile Study." *Winnipeg Free Press*, 18 January 1958.

"City Mourns as Pioneer Doctor Is Laid to Rest." *Winnipeg Tribune*, 9 April 1935.

"Clubdom." *Manitoba Free Press*, 12 April 1927.

"Clubs." *Winnipeg Evening Tribune*, 12 April 1927.

Colburn, Selene, and Laura Haines. "Measuring Libraries' Use of YouTube as a Promotional Tool: An Exploratory Study and Proposed Best Practices." *Journal of Web Librarianship* 6, no. 1 (2012): 5–31.

Colombo, John Robert. *Mysterious Canada: Strange Sights, Extraordinary Events, and Peculiar Places*. Toronto: Doubleday Canada, 1988.

———. *Personal Accounts of the Paranormal*. Toronto: Hounslow Press, 1996.

"Conan Doyle Lectures on Spirit Phenomena." *Winnipeg Evening Tribune*, 4 July 1923.

Comer, Stuart, curator. *Tony Oursler: Imponderable*. Museum of Modern Art, New York, 2017.

Cook, Ron, et al. "Pimitisahētān Ininīmowin Kā Kī Nakatamākawiyak." Edited by Becky Cook, Misipawistik Cree Nation, YouTube, 23 February 2022. https://www.youtube.com/watch?v=sd0qFhV1Tk8.

Cornwell, Peter, dir. *The Haunting in Connecticut*. Santa Monica: Gold Circle Films, 2009.

Creepy Canada, Season 2, Episode 6. https://web.archive.org/web/20071223160350/http:/www.creepy.tv/season2_e6.html.

Crookes, William. "The Last of 'Katie King.' The Photographs of 'Katie King' by the Aid of the Electric Light." *The Spiritualist*, no. 93 (5 June 1874): 270–71.

———. "Mr. Crookes on Materialisations." *The Spiritualist*, no. 99 (17 July 1874): 29.

———. *Remarkable Spirit Manifestations*. Cincinnati: C.G. Helleberg, 1891. http://iapsop.com/

ssoc/1891__helleberg___remarkable_spirit_manifestations.pdf.

———. *Researches into the Phenomena of Modern Spiritualism* (1904). Los Angeles: Austin Publishing, 2007.

Dahle, Sigrid, curator. "Trauerspiel: The Gothic Unconscious." Gallery One One One, Winnipeg, 12–30 January 2004. https://www.umanitoba.ca/schools/art/content/galleryoneoneone/goth26.html.

"Death of T. Glen Hamilton ends life of marked achievement." *Elmwood Herald*, 11 April 1935.

Delgado, Anne. "Bawdy Technologies and the Birth of Ectoplasm." *Genders 1998–2013: College of Arts and Sciences,* University of Colorado Boulder, 1 September 2011. https://www.colorado.edu/gendersarchive1998-2013/2011/09/01/bawdy-technologies-and-birth-ectoplasm.

Di Bello, Patrizia. *Women's Albums and Photography in Victorian England: Ladies, Mothers and Flirts*. London: Ashgate, 2007.

Dingwall, Eric J. "Report on a Series of Sittings with Eva." *Proceedings of the Society for Psychical Research* 32 (1922): 209–343.

Dorosz, Chris. *Dark Matter House*. Winnipeg: La Maison des artistes visuels francophones, 2021.

Douglas, Gordon, dir. *Gildersleeve's Ghost*. New York: RKO Radio Pictures, 1941.

Douglas, Jennifer, Alexandra Alisauskas, and Devon Mordell. "'Treat Them with the Reverence of Archivists': Records Work, Grief Work, and Relationship Work in the Archives." *Archivaria* 88 (Fall 2019): 84–120.

Dow, Katherine. "Winnipeg's Hamilton House, Known for Paranormal Activity, Getting Restored." CTV News Winnipeg, 22 October 2021. https://winnipeg.ctvnews.ca/winnipeg-s-hamilton-house-known-for-paranormal-activity-getting-restored-1.5634457.

Doyle, Arthur Conan. *The History of Spiritualism, Vol. 1 and 2.* London: Cassell, 1926. https://www.arthur-conan-doyle.com/index.php/The_History_of_Spiritualism.

———. "Lectures at the International Spiritualist Congress of Paris 1925." *The Arthur Conan Doyle Encyclopedia.* https://www.arthur-conandoyle.com/index.php/Lectures_at_the_International_Spiritualist_Congress_of_Paris_1925.

———. *Our American Adventure.* London: Hodder and Stoughton, 1923.

———. *Our Second American Adventure*. London: Hodder and Stoughton, 1924.

Dumas, William, and Leonard Paul. *Pīsim Finds Her Miskanaw.* Rev. ed. Winnipeg: HighWater Press, 2020.

"Ectoplasm Paranormal Fantômes: Dr. T.G. Hamilton Winnipeg, 1918." YouTube, 8 May 2009. https://www.youtube.com/watch?v=iWZzD-n9u30.

Ellenberger, Henri F. *The Discovery of the Unconscious: The History and Evolution of Dynamic Psychiatry*. New York: Basic Books, 1970.

Ellison, Ralph. *Invisible Man*. New York: Vintage Books, 2010.

Endres, Frank, Seymour Kneitel, and Izzy Sparber, dirs. *Not Ghoulty.* New York: Famous Studios, 1959.

Eskildsen, Ute, and Jan-Christopher Horak. *Film und Foto der Zwanziger Jahre*. Stuttgart: Gerd Hatje, 1979.

Falcon, Kyle. "The Ghost Story of the Great War: Spiritualism, Psychical Research and the British War Experience, 1914–1939." PhD diss., Wilfrid Laurier University, 2019. https://scholars.wlu.ca/etd/2125.

Falk, Walter. "Dr. T.G. Hamilton's psychic researches." Part 1–8, YouTube, 21 February 2011. https://www.youtube.com/user/Falcon1296.

———. "The T. G. Hamilton FilesChapter 1–4—Walter D Falk." YouTube, 15 July 2018. https://www.youtube.com/watch?v=iYe2Chu6TAA.

Farmer, John S. *'Twixt Two Worlds: A Narrative of the Life and Work of William Eglinton*. London: The Psychological Press, 1886.

Ferguson, Christine. "Review of *The New Prometheans: Faith, Science, and the Supernatural Mind*, by Courtenay Raia." *Victorian Studies* 63, no. 4 (2021): 580–82. https://muse.jhu.edu/article/842988.

Finkel, Irving L. *First Ghosts Most Ancient of Legacies*. London: Hodder and Stoughton, 2021.

Fischer, Andreas. "The Reciprocal Adaptation of Optics and Phenomena: The Photographic Recording of Materializations." In *The Perfect Medium: Photography and the Occult*, edited by Chéroux Clément and Andreas Fischer, 171–216. New Haven: Yale University Press, 2005.

Fisher, Jane. *Envisioning Disease, Gender, and War: Women's Narratives of the 1918 Influenza Pandemic*. New York: Palgrave Macmillan, 2012.

Flint, Kate. "'More Rapid than the Lightning's Flash': Photography, Suddenness, and the Afterlife of Romantic Illumination." *European Romantic Review* 24, no. 3 (June 2013): 369–83. https://doi.org/10.1080/10509585.2013.787242.

Fodor, Nandor. *Encyclopaedia of Psychic Science*. New Hyde Park, NY: University Books, 1966.

Frame, Paul. "William Crookes and the Spectral Visitor." Oak Ridge Associated Universities, Museum of Radiation and Radioactivity. Accessed 28 January 2023. https://www.orau.org/health-physics-museum/articles/william-crookes-spectral-visitor.html.

Freeman, E.G.D. *My Life Story*. Unpublished memoir, n.d.

Frikell, Samri. "Sir Arthur Conan Doyle Predicts Spirit Moving Pictures!" *Movie Weekly* 2, no 22 (12 August 1922): 6–7, 26.

Geison, Gerald L. "The Protoplasmic Theory of Life and the Vitalist-Mechanist Debate." *Isis* 60, no. 3 (October 1969): 273–92. https://doi.org/10.1086/350498.

Geisshuesler, Flavio A. "A Parapsychologist, an Anthropologist, and a Vitalist Walk into a Laboratory: Ernesto de Martino, Mircea Eliade, and a Forgotten Chapter in the Disciplinary History of Religious Studies." *Religions* 10, no. 5, 304. (1 May 2019). https://doi.org/10.3390/rel10050304.

Geley, Gustave. "Ectoplasm." Translated by Helen C. Lambert, *American Society for Psychical Research* 18 (April 1924): 272–79.

———. *From the Unconscious to the Conscious*. Translated by Stanley de Brath. London: William Collins Sons, 1920.

Gettings, Fred. *Ghosts in Photographs: The Extraordinary Story of Spirit Photography*. Montreal: Optimum, 1978.

Gordon, Beth Rae. *Darwin's Dancers: On the Construction of Hysteria and the Influence on the Arts*. Vermont: Ashgate Publishing, 2009.

Grainge, Christopher. "Breath of Life: The Evolution of Oxygen Therapy." *Journal of the Royal Society of Medicine* 97, no. 10 (2004): 489–93.

Granger, Michel. "D'où vient le mot 'ectoplasme' dans son acception spirite et métapsychique?" *Revue spirit* 157, no. 2 (2014): 15–17.

———. *La Saga de l'ectoplasme: Enquête critique et objective sur le phénomène des matérialsations médiumniques d'hier et d'aujourd' hui, Tome 1.* Blegny, Belgium: Le Mouvement spirite francophone, 2021.

Gray, Carolyn. *The Elmwood Visitation—A Play Presented by Manitoba Theatre Projects.* Winnipeg: Scirocco Drama, 2007.

Green, Henry Archibald Vaughan. "The Passing World." Letter to the editor, *Manitoba Free Press*, 5 December 1928, 15.

Gunning, Tom. "Phantom Images and Modern Manifestations." In *Fugitive Images: From Photography to Video*, edited by Patrice Pietro, 42–71. Bloomington: Indiana University Press, 1995.

———. "Phantom Images and Modern Manifestations: Spirit Photography, Magic Theatre, Trick Films, and Photography's Uncanny." In *Cinematic Ghosts: Haunting and Spectrality from Silent Cinema to the Digital Era,* edited by Murray Leeder, 17–38. New York: Bloomsbury Academic, 2015.

Hamilton, Janice. "Bring on Your Ghosts: The Thomas Glendenning Hamilton Family Séances from 1918 to 1944, Winnipeg, Canada." *Paranormal Review—Hamilton Family Fonds Special Issue* 77 (Winter 2016): 6–11.

———. *Reinventing Themselves: A History of the Hamilton and Forrester Families.* Montreal: Self-published, 2021.

Hamilton, Lillian. "'Elizabeth M': The Wonderful Story of Dr. Glen Hamilton's First Medium." *Light* 56 (18 June 1936): 385–87.

———. "Telepathy Plus Spiritism in the Hamilton Researches in Winnipeg." *Light* 71 (April 1951): 472–74.

Hamilton, Margaret Lillian. *Is Survival a Fact? Studies of Deep-trance Automatic Scripts and the Bearing of Intentional Actions by the Trance Personalities on the Question of Human Survival.* London: Psychic Press, 1969.

Hamilton, Thomas Glendenning. *Intention and Survival: Psychical Research Studies and the Bearing of Intentional Actions by Trance Personalities on the Problem of Human Survival.* Edited by James D. Hamilton, 1st ed. Toronto: The Macmillan Company of Canada, 1942.

———. *Intention and Survival: Psychical Research Studies and the Bearing of Intentional Actions by Trance Personalities on the Problem of Human Survival.* Edited by Margaret Lillian Hamilton, 2nd ed. London: Regency Press, 1977.

———. "Teleplasmic Phenomenon in Winnipeg." *Psychic Science: Quarterly Transactions of the British College* 8, no. 3 (1929): 179–208.

Harvey, John. *Photography and Spirit.* London: Reaktion Books, 2007.

Hazelgrove, Jenny. *Spiritualism and British Society Between the Wars.* Manchester: Manchester University Press, 2000.

Henriquez, Phillipe. "La Querelle des Fantomes." *Le Monde illustré*, February 1914.

"The Heresy Sermon." *Winnipeg Free Press Home Journal,* 1 June 1899.

Hill, Cara. *Supernatural Winnipeg: A Guide to a Ghostly Vacation.* Self-published, 2008.

Hirsch, Marianne. *Family Frames: Photography, Narrative, and Postmemory.* Cambridge, MA: Harvard University Press, 1997.

Hirsch, Marianne, and Leo Spitzer. "School Photos and Their Afterlives." In *Feeling Photography,* edited by Elspeth H. Brown and Thy Phu, 252–72. Durham, NC: Duke University Press, 2014.

Holland, Patricia. "'Sweet it is to Scan . . .': Personal Photographs and Popular Photography." In *Photography: A Critical Introduction*, edited by Liz Wells, 5th ed., 133–88. London and New York: Routledge, 2015.

Holland, Steve. "Obituary: Seymour Reit." *The Guardian*, 24 December 2001.

Homer, Michael W. "Arthur Conan Doyle's Adventures in Winnipeg." *Manitoba History*, no. 25 (4 July 1993). http://www.mhs.mb.ca/docs/mb_history/25/doyleinwinnipeg.shtml.

———. "Sir Arthur Conan Doyle: Spiritualism and 'New Religions.'" *Dialogue: A Journal of Mormon Thought* 23, no. 4 (1990): 97–121. http://www.jstor.org/stable/45225937.

Houdini, Harry. *A Magician Among the Spirits*. New York: Harper Brothers, 1924. https://archive.org/details/1924HoudiniAMagicianAmongTheSpirits/page/n195/mode/2up?q=Schrenk.

Hough, John, dir. *The Legend of Hell House.* Los Angeles: 20th Century Fox, 1973.

———. *The Legend of Hell House* (1973). Audio commentary, Shout! Factory, 2014. Blu-Ray Disc.

Hubner, Brian Edward. "'The Ghostly Shadow' in the Archives: An Archival Case Study of the Creation and Recreation of the Hamilton Family Fonds at the University of Manitoba Archives and Special Collections." PhD diss., University of Amsterdam, 2020.

Humberstone, H. Bruce, dir. *Wonder Man.* Los Angeles: RKO Radio Pictures, 1945.

Huxley, Thomas Henry. *On the Physical Basis of Life*. New Haven: The College Courant, 1869.

Jackson, Peter, dir. *The Frighteners*. Wellington, NZ: WIngNut Films, 1996.

Jaggar, Allison M. "Love and Knowledge: Emotion in Feminist Epistemology." In *Women, Knowledge, and Reality: Explorations in Feminist Philosophy,* edited by Ann Garry and Marilyn Pearsall, 151–76. New York: Routledge, 1996.

Jaher, David. *The Witch of Lime Street: Séance, Seduction, and Houdini in the Spirit World*. New York: Crown, 2015.

Janke, Sabrina, and Alex Judge. "The Haunting of Hamilton House." *One Great History*, November 2020. Podcast. https://onegreathistory.wordpress.com/episodes/.

Jolly, Martyn. *Faces of the Living Dead: The Belief in Spirit Photography*. London: British Library, 2006.

Jones, Esyllt W. "Open Secrets: Silence, Suppression and Memory in the History of Canada's 1918–1920 Influenza Pandemic." *Canadian Journal of Health History* 39, no.1 (2022): 99–124.

———. "Spectral Influenza: Winnipeg's Hamilton Family, Interwar Spiritualism, and Pandemic Disease." In *Epidemic Encounters: Influenza, Society, and Culture in Canada, 1918–20*, edited by Magda Fahrni and Esyllt W. Jones, 193–221. Vancouver: University of British Columbia Press, 2013.

Joseph, Bob. "21 Things You May Not Have Known about the Indian Act." *Indigenous Corporate Training Inc.*, 2 June 2015. https://www.ictinc.ca/blog/21-things-you-may-not-have-known-about-the-indian-act-.

Juler, Edward. "Life Forms: Henry Moore, Morphology and Biologism in the

Interwar Years." In *Henry Moore: Sculptural Process and Public Identity*. Tate Research Publication, 2015. https://www.tate.org.uk/art/research-publications/henry-moore/edward-juler-life-forms-henry-moore-morphology-and-biologism-in-the-interwar-years-r1151314.

Julin, Richard, curator. *Spiritus.* Magasin III Museum for Contemporary Art, Stockholm, 2003. https://magasin3.com/en/exhibition/spiritus-2/.

Keller, Evelyn Fox. *Reflections on Gender and Science*. New Haven: Yale University Press, 1985.

Kemp, Martin. *Visualizations: The Nature Book of Art and Science*. Berkeley and Los Angeles: University of California Press, 2000.

Keshavjee, Serena. "Carrière, Rodin and the Natural Laws of Making Art." *Cantor Arts Centre Journal* 5 (2006–2007): 49–60.

———. "'L'Art inconscient' and 'L'Esthétique des esprits': Science, Spiritualism, and the Imaging of the Unconscious in French Symbolist Art." PhD diss., University of Toronto, 2002. https://hdl.handle.net/1807/120985.

———. "Science and the Visual Culture of Spiritualism: Camille Flammarion and the Symbolists in *fin-de-siècle* France." *Aries* 13, no. 1 (2013): 37–69. https://doi.org/10.1163/15700593-01301004.

———. "The 'Scientization' of Spirituality." In *Seductive Surfaces: The Art of Tissot*, edited by Katharine Lochnan, Studies in British Art, Vol. 6: 213–45. New Haven: Yale University Press, 1999.

———. "Visualizations of the Vital-Psychic Force." In *Vitalist Modernism: Art, Science, Energy and Creative Evolution*, edited by Fae Brauer, 81–104. Oxfordshire: Routledge, 2023.

Keshavjee, Serena, ed. "The Visual Culture of Science and Art in Fin-De-Siècle France." Special issue, *RACAR*: no. 1 (2009): 5-104. https://doi.org/10.7202/1069501ar.

Klassen, Linda. "Glen Hamilton, Family Doctor." In *Reinventing Themselves: A History of the Hamilton and Forrester Families*, by Janice Hamilton. Montreal: Self-published, 2021.

Komus, Matthew. *Haunted Winnipeg: Ghost Stories from the Heart of the Continent*. Winnipeg: Great Plains Publications, 2014.

Kuhn, Annette. *Family Secrets: Acts of Memory and Imagination*. London: Verso, 2002.

Lachapelle, Sofie. *Investigating the Supernatural: From Spiritism and Occultism to Psychical Research and Metapsychics in France, 1853–1931*. Baltimore: Johns Hopkins University Press, 2011.

Lambert, Rudolf. "Dr. Geley's Reports on the Medium 'Eva C.'" *Journal of the Society for Psychical Research* 37, no. 682 (1954): 380–86.

Leaf, Horace. "Obituary." *Light* 55, no. 2840 (13 June 1935): 373. http://iapsop.com/archive/materials/light/light_v55_n2840_jun_13_1935.pdf.

Lean, David, dir. *Blithe Spirit.* London: General Film Distributors, 1945.

Leeder, Murray. "Ektoplasm-o-vision! with Guy Maddin." *Luma—Film & Media Art Quarterly* 1 (2015). https://lumaquarterly.com/issues/2015/001-summer-2/ektoplasm-o-vision-with-guy-maddin/.

———. "Victorian Science and Spiritualism in *The Legend of Hell House.*" *Horror Studies* 5, no. 1 (2014): 31–46.

Lowe, Joy, and Walter J. Meyer zu Erpen. "The Canadian Spiritualist Movement and Sources for Its Study." *Archivaria* 30 (Summer 1990): 71–84.

MacWilliam, Susan. *F-L-A-M-M-A-R-I-O-N, Remote Viewing*. 53rd Venice Biennale, 2009.

———. *Susan MacWilliam: Remote Viewing*. Edited by Karen Downey. London: Black Dog Publishing, 2009.

———. "Through the Camera: Teleplasmic Appearances in Winnipeg by Flammarion, Stead, Doyle, Lodge and other SPR Members." *Paranormal Review—Hamilton Family Fonds Special Issue* 77 (Winter 2016): 22–23.

Maddin, Guy, dir. *My Winnipeg*. Winnipeg: Buffalo Gal Pictures, 2007.

Maddin, Guy, Evan Johnson, and Galen Johnson, dirs. *Seances*. National Film Board of Canada, 2016. https://seances.nfb.ca/.

Maddin, Guy, Evan Johnson, Galen Johnson, and the National Film Board of Canada. "Séances/ Spiritismes." Talk at the Winnipeg Art Gallery (WAG), 31 October 2012.

Manitoba Department of Sport, Culture, and Heritage. "Imagine. Creative Manitoba! 2017 Discussion Paper." Manitoba Culture and Creative Industries Strategy, Government of Manitoba, 2017. https://www.gov.mb.ca/asset_library/en/imaginecreative/discussion-paper.pdf.

Mann, Thomas. "An Experience in the Occult." In *Three Essays* (1923). Translated by H.T. Lowe-Porter. New York: Knopf, 1983.

———. *The Magic Mountain* (1929). Translated by H.T. Lowe-Porter. Reprint, London: Penguin, 1990.

Marryat, Florence. *There Is No Death*. New York: National Book Company, 1891.

Massicotte, Claudie. "Talking Nonsense: Spiritual Mediums and Female Subjectivity in Victorian and Edwardian Canada." PhD diss., University of Western Ontario, 2013. https://ir.lib.uwo.ca/etd/1656.

———. *Trance Speakers: Femininity and Authorship in Spiritual Séances, 1850–1930*. Montreal: McGill-Queen's University Press, 2017.

Matheson, Neil. "Ectoplasm and Photography: Mediumistic Performances for Camera." In *The Machine and the Ghost: Technology and Spiritualism in Nineteenth to Twenty-First-Century Art and Culture*, edited by Neil Matheson and Sas Mays, 78–102. Manchester: Manchester University Press, 2013.

Matheson, Richard. *Hell House*. New York: Tor, 1999.

McGarry, Molly. *Ghosts of Futures Past: Spiritualism and the Cultural Politics of Nineteenth-Century America*. Berkeley: University of California Press, 2008.

McMullin, Stan. *Anatomy of a Seance: A History of Spirit Communication in Central Canada*. Montreal: McGill-Queen's University Press, 2004.

Meier, Allison C. "Native Americans and the Dehumanising Force of the Photograph." *Wellcome Collection*, 29 March 2018. https://wellcomecollection.org/articles/WrUTGh8AACAA1FH8.

Melanson, Terry. "Book Review: The Hermetic Code: Unlocking One of Manitoba's Greatest Secrets." Illuminati: Conspiracy Archive, 15 August 2007. https://www.conspiracyarchive.com/Commentary/Hermetic_Code.htm.

Mercey, A.A. "New Frontiers for the Documentary Film." *Journal of the Society of Motion Picture Engineers* 33 (November 1939): 525–32.

Merkling, Emma. "Using Science to Investigate the Paranormal." *The Media of Mediumship*, Science and Media Museum, 2022. https://www.scienceand-mediamuseum.org.uk/objects-and-stories/science-investigating-paranormal.

Meyer zu Erpen, Walter. "Afterlife Beliefs in the Spiritualist Movement." In *The Routledge Companion to Death and Dying*, edited by Christopher M. Moreman, 218–29. London: Routledge, 2018.

———. "Canadian Psychical Research Experiments with Table Tilting and Ectoplasm Phenomena in the Séance Room." In *The Spiritualist Movement: Speaking with the Dead in America and Around the World, Vol. 2, Belief, Practice, and Evidence for Life after Death,* edited by Christopher M. Moreman, 205–28. Santa Barbara: Praeger, 2013.

———. "Of Teleplasms and Wax Fingertips: Dr. William Creighton's Role in Authenticating Physical Phenomena." *Paranormal Review—Hamilton Family Fonds Special Issue* 77 (Winter 2016): 15–16.

———. "The Quest for Immortality: Psychical Research in Winnipeg and the Role of Medical Doctors, Lawyers, Clergymen, and Other Community Leaders between 1918 and 1935." Compiled 1992–2018. https://survivalresearch.ca/Quest_for_Immortality_19922018_compilation.pdf.

———. "Sir Arthur Conan Doyle." Unpublished biography, 1998.

———."Thomas Glendenning Hamilton." *Dictionary of Canadian Biography*, vol. 16, 2022. http://www.biographi.ca/en/bio/hamilton_thomas_glendenning_16E.html.

Milne, Ida. "Through the Eyes of a Child: 'Spanish' Influenza Remembered by Survivors." In *Growing Pains: Childhood Illness in Ireland, 1750–1950,* edited by Anne MacLellan and Alice Mauger, 159–74. Newbridge, Ireland: Irish Academic Press, 2013.

Moholy-Nagy, László. *Malerei, Photographie, Film.* München: Langen, 1925.

Monroe, John. *Laboratories of Faith: Mesmerism, Spiritism, and Occultism in Modern France.* Ithaca, NY: Cornell University Press, 2008.

Moore, Megan. *Anti-Heroines and Ectoplasm.* Unpublished, 2018.

Mundy, Jennifer. "The Naming of Biomorphic." In *Biocentrism and Modernism*, edited by Oliver A.I. Botar and Isabel Wünsche, 61–76. Farnham, Surrey: Ashgate, 2011.

Natale, Simone. "The Medium on the Stage: Trance and Performance in Nineteenth-Century Spiritualism." *Early Popular Visual Culture* 9, no. 3 (2011): 239–55. https://doi.org/10.1080/17460654.2011.601166.

Nickles, James B. "A Video Interview with Dr. Glen F. Hamilton." The University of Manitoba Archives and Special Collections, DVD, 2011.

———. "Psychic Research in a Winnipeg Family: Reminiscences of Dr. Glen F. Hamilton." *Manitoba History* 55 (June 2007): 51–60. http://www.mhs.mb.ca/docs/mb_history/55/psychicresearch.shtml.

Noakes, Richard. *Physics and Psychics: The Occult and the Sciences in Modern Britain.* Cambridge: Cambridge University Press, 2019.

Normandin, Sebastien. "Visions of Vitalism: Medicine, Philosophy and the Soul in Nineteenth Century France." PhD diss., McGill University, 2005. https://escholarship.mcgill.ca/concern/theses/n583z027g.

Oates, Katie. Review of *Oscar G. Rejlander: Artist and Photographer*, edited by Lori Pauli.

RACAR: Revue d'art canadienne/Canadian Art Review 46, no. 1 (2021): 121–23. https://www.racar-racar.com/uploads/5/7/7/4/57749791/racar_46_1_zz_oates.pdf.

———. "'Tool of Enlightenment': The Dreamachine's Effects for Individual Autonomy." *Refract: An Open Access Visual Studies Journal* 1, no. 1 (2018): 87–102. https://doi.org/10.5070/R71141450.

———. "Women's Spirit Photography: Negotiating Gender Conventions & Loss." PhD diss., University of Western Ontario, 2022. https://ir.lib.uwo.ca/etd/8405/.

Outka, Elizabeth. *Viral Modernism: The Influenza Pandemic and Interwar Literature*. New York: Columbia University Press, 2020.

———. "'Wood for the Coffins Ran Out': Modernism and the Shadowed Afterlife of the Influenza Pandemic." *Modernism/modernity* 21, no. 4 (2014): 937–60.

Owen, Alex. *The Darkened Room: Women, Power, and Spiritualism in Late Victorian England.* London: Virago, 1989.

Owens, Susan. *The Ghost: A Cultural History*. London: Tate Publishing, 2017.

Oxon, M.A. "Notes by the Way." *Light* 6, no. 269 (27 February 1886): 97–98. http://www.iapsop.com/archive/materials/light/light_v6_n269_feb_27_1886.pdf.

———. "'Twixt Two Worlds': A Narrative of the Life and Work of William Eglinton." *Light* 6, no. 264 (23 January 1886): 42–43. http://www.iapsop.com/archive/materials/light/light_v6_n264_jan_23_1886.pdf.

Pareti, Germana. "Hans Driesch's Interest in the Psychical Research. A Historical Study." *Medicina Historica* 1, no. 3 (2017): 156–62. https://www.mattioli1885journals.com/index.php/MedHistor/article/view/6749.

Parker, Trey. "Over Logging." Episode. *South Park*, Season 12, Episode 6. Comedy Central, 16 April 2008.

Permutt, Cyril. *Photographing the Spirit World: Images from Beyond the Spectrum*. Wellingborough, Northamptonshire, England: Aquarian Press, 1988.

"Pictures of Teleplasm Shown to Delegates." *Winnipeg Free Press*, 28 August 1930.

"Play on Spiritualism in 1920s Winnipeg." *Manitoba History*, 2 January 2007. http://www.mhs.mb.ca/news/spiritualismplay.shtml.

Prince, Walter Franklin. *Noted Witnesses for Psychic Occurrences* (1928). New Hyde Park, NY: University Books, 1963.

"Psychic Expert Shows Pictures of Experiments." *Winnipeg Tribune*, 28 August 1930.

"Psychical Research Branch Formed Here: Dr. T. Glen Hamilton Elected President of New Winnipeg Society." *Manitoba Free Press*, 12 June 1931.

"Quirks and Oddities." In *Factoids: Made in Winnipeg*, 6th ed. Winnipeg: Tourism Winnipeg, c. 2014.

Raia, Courtenay. *The New Prometheans: Faith, Science, and the Supernatural Mind in the Victorian Fin de Siècle*. Chicago: University of Chicago Press, 2019.

Rambaud, Yveling. *Force Psychique*. Paris: Ludovic Baschet, 1889.

Rankin, Laird. "Ghost Story." *Winnipeg Magazine*, May 1982.

Rehbock, Philip F. "Huxley, Haeckel, and the Oceanographers: The Case *of Bathybius haeckelii*." *Isis* 66, no. 4 (December 1975): 504–33. https://doi.org/10.1086/351511.

Reynolds, Andrew. "Amoebae as Exemplary Cells: The Protean Nature of an Elementary

Organism." *Journal of the History of Biology* 41, no. 2 (18 September 2007): 307–37. https://doi.org/10.1007/s10739-007-9142-8.

Richards, Robert J. *The Romantic Conception of Life: Science and Philosophy in the Age of Goethe.* Chicago: University of Chicago Press, 2002.

Richet, Charles. "Concerning the Phenomenon Called Materialisation." *Annals of Psychical Science* 2 (1905): 207–89.

———. *Thirty Years of Psychical Research: Being a Treatise on Metapsychics.* Translated by Stanley De Brath. London: William Collins Sons and New York: MacMillan, 1923.

Riddle, David K., and Donald G. Mitchell. *The Military Cross Awarded to the Canadian Expeditionary Force, 1915–1921, with Full Citations.* Winnipeg: Kirkby-Marlton Press, 1991.

Robertson, Beth A. *Science of the Seance: Transnational Networks and Gendered Bodies in the Study of Psychic Phenomena, 1918–40.* Vancouver: UBC Press, 2016.

Rodin, Alvin E., Audrey M. Kerr, and Jack D. Key. "Kindred Souls: The Meeting of Drs. Arthur Conan Doyle and Thomas Hamilton." *Canadian Medical Association Journal* 135 (1986): 1216–17.

———. "Thomas Glen Hamilton MD FACS—Winnipeg Physician Politician and Spiritualist." *Manitoba Medicine* 60, no. 3 (1990): 121–24.

Roi, Henrietta. "Otherwordly Archives: University of Manitoba Home to Ghostly Legacy." *Canada's History*, 9 September 2019. https://www.canadashistory.ca/explore/museums-galleries-archives/otherworldly-archives.

Ross, Rob. "T.G. Hamilton's Photos of Ectoplasm." YouTube, 27 February 2008. https://www.youtube.com/watch?v=W0HncGNBCqY&t=146s.

Rutkowski, Chris A. *Unnatural History: True Manitoba Mysteries.* Winnipeg: Chameleon Book Publishers, 1993.

Salvesen, Britt, curator. *3-D: Double Vision.* Los Angeles County Museum, Los Angeles, 2018.

Sanchez, Pierre. *Les Catalogues des salons, Vol. 19: 1899–1901.* Dijon: Echelle De Jacob Editions, 2010.

Sausman, Justin. "'It's Organisms That Die, Not Life': Henri Bergson, Psychic Research, and the Contemporary Uses of Vitalism." In *The Machine and the Ghost: Technology and Spiritualism in Nineteenth- to Twenty-First-Century Art and Culture*, edited by Neil Matheson and Sas May, 16–36. Manchester: Manchester University Press, 2013.

Scatcherd, Felicia Rudolphina. *Ectoplasm as Associated with Survival.* London: The Two Worlds Publishing, 1926.

Schiebinger, Londa L. *The Mind Has No Sex? Women in the Origins of Modern Science.* Cambridge, MA: Harvard University Press, 1989.

Schoonover, Karl. "Ectoplasms, Evanescence, and Photography." *Art Journal* 62, no. 3 (Autumn 2003): 30–43.

Schrenck-Notzing, Albert von. *Phenomenon of Materialization.* Translated by E.E. Fournier d'Albe. London: Kegan Paul, Trench, Trubner and New York: E.P. Dutton, 1923.

Sera-Shriar, Efram. "Photographic Plates and Spirit Fakes: Remembering Harry Price's Investigation of William Hope's Spirit Photography at its Centenary." *Science Museum Group Journal* 17 (2 February 2022): https://doi.org/10.15180/221707.

———. *Psychic Investigators: Anthropology, Modern Spiritualism, and Credible Witnessing in the Late Victorian Age*. Pittsburgh: University of Pittsburgh Press, 2022.

Sharman, Lindsay, curator. *Conjured Images: Spirit Photography from the Turn of the 20th Century*. Art Gallery of Alberta, Edmonton, 2022.

Sharp, Lynn L. *Secular Spirituality: Reincarnation and Spiritism in Nineteenth-Century France*. Lanham, MD: Lexington Books, 2006.

Smith, Barbara. *Ghost Stories of Manitoba*. Edmonton: Lone Pine Publishing, 1998.

Société des artistes français. *Catalogue illustré du salon de 1902*. Paris: Ludovic Baschet, 1902.

Sommer, Andreas. "Policing Epistemic Deviance: Albert von Schrenck-Notzing and Albert Moll." *Medical History* 56, no. 2 (April 2012): 255–76. https://doi.org/10.1017/mdh.2011.36.

Spelman, E.V. "Anger and Insubordination." In *Women, Knowledge, and Reality: Explorations in Feminist Philosophy,* edited by Ann Garry and Marilyn Pearsall, 73–95. Boston: Unwin Hyman, 1989.

Spence, Jo, and Patricia Holland. *Family Snaps: The Meaning of Domestic Photography*. London: Virago, 1991.

Starr, Isaac. "Influenza in 1918: Recollections of the Epidemic in Philadelphia." *Annals of Internal Medicine* 145, no. 2 (2006): 138–40.

Stolow, Jeremy. "Mediumnic Lights, Xx Rays, and the Spirit Who Photographed Herself." *Critical Inquiry* 42, no. 4 (2016): 923–51. https://doi.org/10.1086/686962.

Straughan, Roger. "Sir Arthur Conan Doyle: 'The St. Paul of Spiritualism.'" In *The Spiritualist Movement: Speaking with the Dead in America and Around the World*, edited by Christopher M. Moreman, Vol.1, 115–28. Santa Barbara: Praeger, 2013.

Student of Psychic Phenomena. "Psychic Science." *The Kingston Whig-Standard*, 20 November 1928.

"Successful 'Ghost Film' Promises Understanding." *Business Screen* 30, no. 6 (June 1969): 42. https://digital.hagley.org/BusinessScreen_1969_V30_N06#page/42/mode/2up.

Sutherland, Joel A. *Haunted Canada 10*. Toronto: Scholastic Canada, 2021.

Sweeney, Shelley. "New Digitization Project at the University of Manitoba Archives and Special Collections." *ACA Bulletin* (January 2007).

Taggart, Shannon. *Séance*. Somerset, UK: Fulgur Press, 2019.

Tietze, Thomas. *Margery: An Entertaining and Intriguing Story of One of the Most Controversial Psychics of the Century*. New York: Harper and Row, 1973.

Tompkins, Matthew L. *The Spectacle of Illusion: Magic, the Paranormal and the Complicity of the Mind*. London: Wellcome Collection, 2019.

Tucker, Jennifer. "The Social Photographic Eye." In *Brought to Light: Photography and the Invisible, 1840–1900*, edited by Corey Keller, 37–50. San Francisco: San Francisco Museum of Modern Art, in association with Yale University Press, New Haven and London, 2008.

Tyler, Parker. "Supernatural in the Movies." *Theatre Arts* 29 (June 1945): 362–69.

UNESCO. "Memory of the World Register: the Hamilton Family fonds." *UNESCO Memory of the World.*

University of Manitoba Archives and Special Collections. *Annual Report,* 2006–2007, and 2008–2009.

———. "Psychical Research and Spiritualism Collections." University of Manitoba Libraries. Accessed 23 February 2023. https://libguides.lib.umanitoba.ca/archives/archivalcollections/psychicalspiritualism.

———. "Research Grants and Endowments: T. Glendenning Hamilton Research Grant." University of Manitoba Libraries. Accessed 7 September 2022. https://libguides.lib.umanitoba.ca/c.php?g=500907&p=3430149.

———. "T.G. Hamilton Archives Acquisition File." University of Manitoba Libraries, 2008.

———. "T.G. Hamilton's Photos of Ectoplasm." YouTube, 10 December 2008. https://www.youtube.com/watch?v=kXXC2RTvF_4.

———. "Thomas Glendenning Hamilton Photograph Gallery." University of Manitoba Libraries. Accessed 2 February 2022. https://web.archive.org/web/20011126184948/http://www.umanitoba.ca/libraries/units/archives/collections/spirphoto.htm.

University of Manitoba. "The Campus Files: Ep.2, The Haunting in Manitoba." YouTube, 8 June 2009. https://www.youtube.com/watch?v=7HSS4eXV-fY.

Verrall, Helen de G. "The History of Marthe Beraud (Eva C.)." *Proceedings of the Society for Psychical Research* 27 (1914–15): 333–69.

Vesely, Carolin, and Buzz Currie. *The Hermetic Code: Unlocking One of Manitoba's Greatest Secrets*. Winnipeg: Winnipeg Free Press, 2007.

Warner, Marina. "Ethereal Body: The Quest for Ectoplasm." *Cabinet Magazine* 12 (Fall/Winter 2003). https://www.cabinetmagazine.org/issues/12/warner.php.

———. *Phantasmagoria: Spirit Visions, Metaphors and Media into the Twenty-first Century.* Oxford: Oxford University Press, 2006.

Wehr, Anne, ed. *Imponderable*. New York: Museum of Modern Art, 2017.

Willburn, Sarah. "Viewing History and Fantasy Through Victorian Spirit Photography." In *The Ashgate Research Companion to Nineteenth Century Spiritualism and the Occult*, edited by Tatiana Kontou and Sarah Willburn, 318–38. Farnham: Ashgate, 2012.

Williams, Grace A. "The Supernatural Sex: Women, Magick and Mediumship: Assembling a Field of Fascination in Contemporary Art." PhD diss., Birmingham City University, 2017. https://ethos.bl.uk/OrderDetails.do?did=2&uin=uk.bl.ethos.732983.

Wilson, Leigh. *Modernism and Magic: Experiments with Spiritualism, Theosophy and the Occult.* Edinburgh: Edinburgh University Press, 2013.

Winter, Jay. "History, Memory and the Flu." In *Pandemic Re-Awakenings: the Forgotten and Unforgotten "Spanish" Flu of 1918–1919,* edited by Guy Beiner, xxv–xxviii. Oxford: Oxford University Press, 2022.

Wolffram, Heather. "In the Laboratory of the Ghost-Baron: Parapsychology in Germany in the Early 20th Century." *Endeavour* 33, no. 4 (December 2009): 152–57. https://doiorg/10.1016/j.endeavour.2009.10.001.

Wong, Kittie. "Stirring the Spirits." *Winnipeg Free Press*, 28 October 2017.

Zimmerman, Nathan B. "Author! Author!!" *The Bill* 6, no. 3 (1934): 4.

Zuckerbrot, Donna, dir. *Conjuring Philip*. Reel-Time Images, 2007.

CONTRIBUTORS

Compiled by Christina Thomson

KC Adams (flying overhead in circles eagle woman) is Anishinaabe, Ininew, and British, living in Winnipeg. She is an award-winning relational maker, a creator whose work connects to Indigenous epistemology. Recognizing her role as an educator, activist, community member, and mentor, Adams creates work exploring technology and its relationship to her identity and knowledge systems. Her process is to start with an idea and use a medium that embodies her conceptual intent, resulting in a practice spanning adornment, clay, drawing, installation, painting, photography, printmaking, public art, video, and welding. Adams holds a BFA from Concordia University and an MA in Cultural Studies with a focus on Curatorial Practices from the University of Winnipeg where she received the graduate student of highest achievement award.

Brian Hubner is an archivist at the University of Manitoba Archives and Special Collections. He received his PhD from the University of Amsterdam in 2020 and holds an MA in Archival Studies from the University of Manitoba and in History from the University of Saskatchewan. In March 2022, he discussed the Hamilton Family Fonds as part of a panel on "Archiving the Impossible" at Rice University in Houston. His PhD dissertation was titled "'The Ghostly Shadow' in the Archives: An

Archival Case Study of the Creation and Recreation of the Hamilton Family Fonds at the University of Manitoba Archives and Special Collections," and his conference papers include "The Hamilton Family Fonds and Community Engagement" (2018).

Esyllt W. Jones is a professor of History and Community Health Sciences at the University of Manitoba. She is a historian of infectious diseases and socialized medicine. Her publications on the social and cultural impacts of pandemic influenza include "Open Secrets: Silence, Suppression, and Memory in the History of Canada's 1918–20 Influenza Pandemic," in *Canadian Journal of Health History* (2022); "Spectral Influenza: Winnipeg's Hamilton Family, Interwar Spiritualism, and Pandemic Disease," in *Epidemic Encounters: Influenza, Society, and Culture in Canada, 1918–1920* (2012), co-edited with Madga Fahrni; and *Influenza 1918: Disease, Death and Struggle in Winnipeg* (2007). Other projects include *Medicare's Histories: Origins, Opportunities, and Omissions in Canada* (2022), co-edited with James Hanley and Delia Gavrus; and *Radical Medicine: The International Origins of Socialized Health Care in Canada* (2019).

Serena Keshavjee is a professor of Art and Architectural History at the University of Winnipeg, where she coordinates the Curatorial Practices stream of the master's program in Cultural Studies. Keshavjee's publications focus on the intersection of art and science in visual culture of the *fin de siècle*. Her publications include "Visualizing the Vital Force," in *Vitalist Modernism: Art, Science, Energy and Creative Evolution*, ed. Fae Brauer (2023); *Picturing Evolution and Extinction: Regeneration and Degeneration in Modern Visual Culture*, co-edited with Fae Brauer (2015); and "Science and the Visual Culture of Spiritualism: Camille Flammarion and the Symbolists in Fin-de-Siècle France" (*Aries,* 2013). In 2009, Keshavjee edited a special issue of *Canadian Art Review* (*RACAR)* entitled *The Visual Culture of Science and Art in* Fin-De-Siècle *France.*

Murray Leeder is an adjunct professor in the Department of English, Film, Theatre and Media at the University of Manitoba. He is the author of *Horror Film: A Critical Introduction* (2018), *The Modern Supernatural and the Beginnings of Cinema* (2017), and *Halloween* (2014), and he is the editor of *Cinematic Ghosts: Haunting and Spectrality from Silent Cinema to the Digital Era* (2015) and *ReFocus: The Films of William Castle* (2018). He has published articles in journals such as *Horror Studies*, *Canadian Journal of Film Studies*, *Journal of Popular Culture*, and *Journal of Popular Film and Television*.

Walter Meyer zu Erpen is an archives consultant with a Master of Archival Studies degree (UBC). In 1991, he co-founded the Survival Research Institute of Canada and has lectured widely about the Hamiltons' psychical research experiments, based upon his detailed case study. Meyer zu Erpen's publications include *Study of the Archival Record and Its Context: Meaning and Historical Understanding* (1985), "The Canadian Spiritualist Movement and Sources for Its Study" in *Archivaria: The Journal of the Association of Canadian Archivists* (1990), "Canadian Psychical Research Experiments with Table Tilting and Ectoplasm Phenomena in the Séance Room" in *The Spiritualist Movement: Speaking with the Dead in America and around the World*, ed. Christopher Moreman, 2013), and "Afterlife Beliefs in the Spiritualist Movement" in *The Routledge Companion to Death and Dying*, ed. Christopher Moreman (2018). With Shelley Sweeney, he co-edited the Hamilton Family Fonds special issue of *Paranormal Review* (2016).

Katie Oates is a Research Associate at the University of Western Ontario in the Department of Visual Arts, where she completed her Postdoctoral Fellowship, PhD in Art and Visual Culture and MA in Art History. She earned her Honours BA in Art History and English from Carleton University. She also works as a Community Engaged Learning Coordinator and has held numerous research and writing positions at Western University. Oates's dissertation, "Women's Spirit Photography: Negotiating Gender Conventions & Loss" (2022) is available through

Scholarship@Western. Her writing has been published in *RACAR* (2021), "Lori Pauli, ed., *Oscar G. Rejlander: Artist Photographer,*" and in *Refract: An Open Access Visual Studies Journal* (2018) "'Tool of Enlightenment': The Dreamachine's Effects for Individual Autonomy."

Shelley Sweeney, MAS, PhD, CA, is archivist emerita and retired head of the University of Manitoba Archives and Special Collections. She has a keen interest in the Hamilton Family Fonds and has promoted the collection locally, nationally, and internationally at every opportunity. Sweeney has written on archival practices and the Hamilton Family Fonds, such as her chapter "Moved by the Spirit: Opportunistic Promotion of the Hamilton Family Séance Collection," in *Outreach: Innovative Practices for Archives and Special Collections* (2014). In 2016, Sweeney co-edited an issue of *Paranormal Review* with Walter Meyer zu Erpen dedicated to the Hamilton Family Fonds.

INDEX

Page numbers in italics indicate figures on corresponding page.

C

D

F

G

H

N

O

S

T

U

V

W

Y